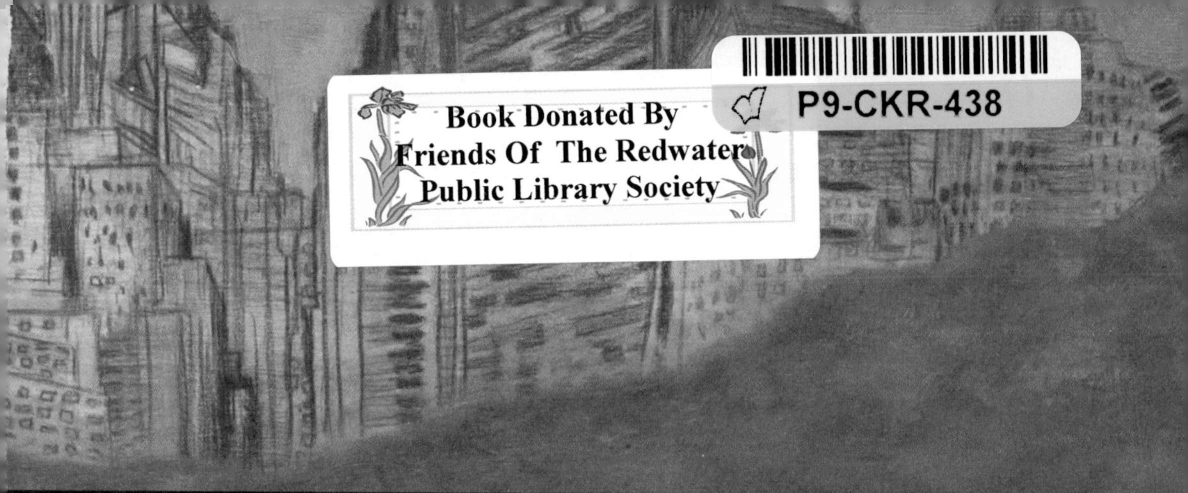

FABLES: LEGENDS IN EXILE

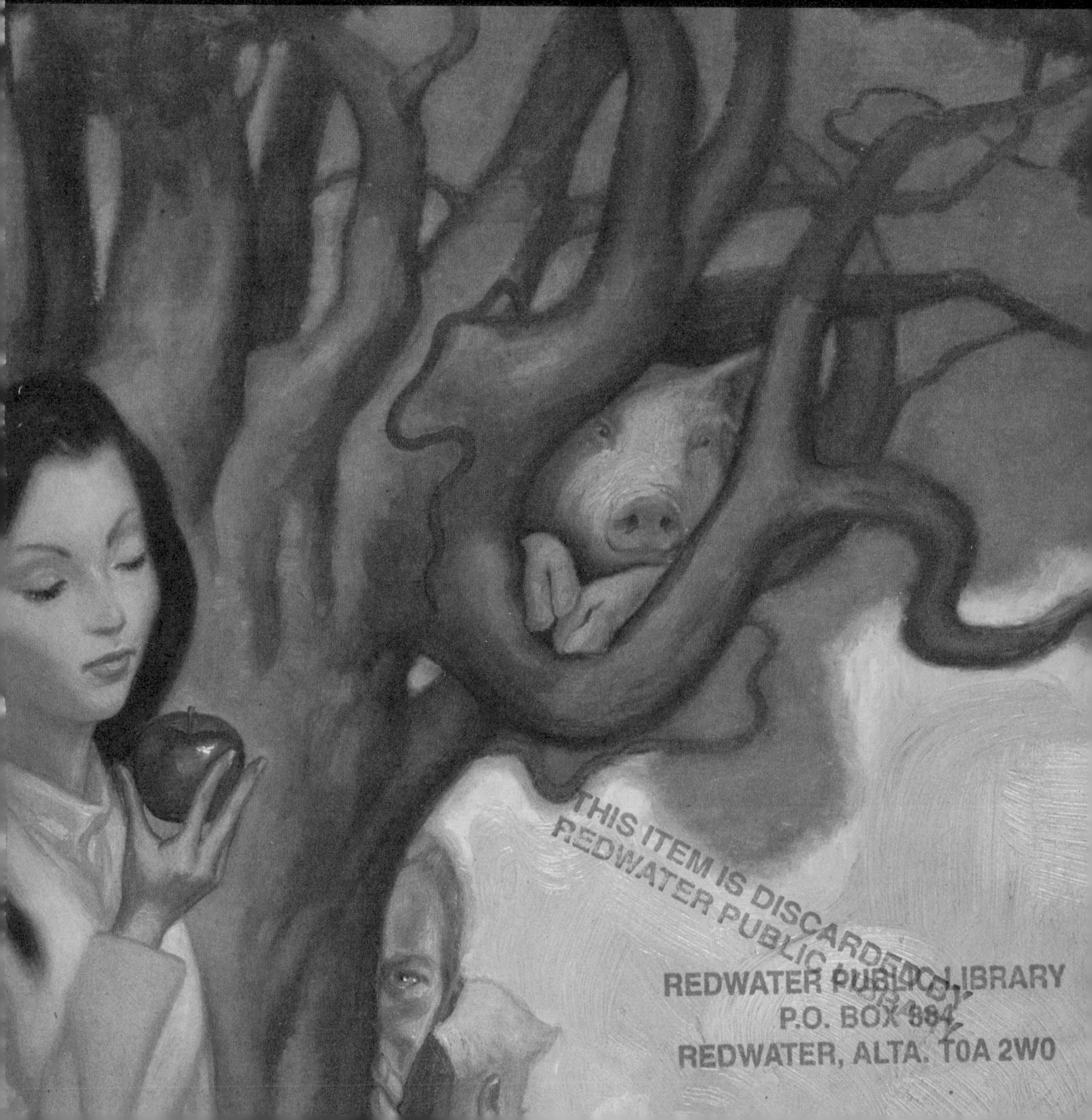

FABLES: LEGENDS IN EXILE

FABLES CREATED BY BILL WILLINGHAM

Bill Willingham
Writer

Lan Medina
Penciller

Steve Leialoha
Craig Hamilton
Inkers

Sherilyn van Valkenburgh
Colorist

Todd Klein
Letterer

Mark Buckingham
Cover Art

James Jean
Alex Maleev
Original Series Covers

SHELLY BOND
Executive Editor – Vertigo &
Editor – Original Series

MARIAH HUEHNER
Assistant Editor – Original Series

SCOTT NYBAKKEN
Editor

ROBBIN BROSTERMAN
Design Director – Books

HANK KANALZ
Senior VP – Vertigo & Integrated Publishing

DIANE NELSON
President

DAN DIDIO and **JIM LEE**
Co-Publishers

GEOFF JOHNS
Chief Creative Officer

JOHN ROOD
Executive VP – Sales, Marketing & Business
Development

AMY GENKINS
Senior VP – Business & Legal Affairs

NAIRI GARDINER
Senior VP – Finance

JEFF BOISON
VP – Publishing Planning

MARK CHIARELLO
VP – Art Direction & Design

JOHN CUNNINGHAM
VP – Marketing

TERRI CUNNINGHAM
VP – Editorial Administration

ALISON GILL
Senior VP – Manufacturing & Operations

JAY KOGAN
VP – Business & Legal Affairs, Publishing

JACK MAHAN
VP – Business Affairs, Talent

NICK NAPOLITANO
VP – Manufacturing Administration

SUE POHJA
VP – Book Sales

COURTNEY SIMMONS
Senior VP – Publicity

BOB WAYNE
Senior VP – Sales

To Shelly Bond
Intrepid Vertigo editor, who insisted on
taking FABLES when I was trying to sell
her another idea entirely.
— Bill Willingham

FABLES: LEGENDS IN EXILE

DC Comics, 1700 Broadway, New York, NY 10019
A Warner Bros. Entertainment Company.
Printed in the USA. Second Printing.
ISBN: 978-1-4012-3755-4

SUSTAINABLE
FORESTRY
INITIATIVE

Certified Chain of Custody
Promoting Sustainable Forestry
www.sfiprogram.org
SFI-01042
APPLIES TO TEXT STOCK ONLY

Library of Congress Cataloging-in-Publication Data

Willingham, Bill.
  Fables vol. 1 : legends in exile (new edition) / Bill Willingham,
Lan Medina, Steve Leialoha. — New ed.
    p. cm.
  "Originally published in single magazine form as Fables 1-5"—T.p.
verso.
  ISBN 978-1-4012-3755-4 (alk. paper)
  1. Legends—Adaptations—Comic books, strips, etc. 2. Graphic novels.
I. Medina, Lan. II. Leialoha, Steve. III. Title. IV. Title: Legends in
exile.
  PN6727.W52F38 2012
  741.5'973—dc22
                              2012002612

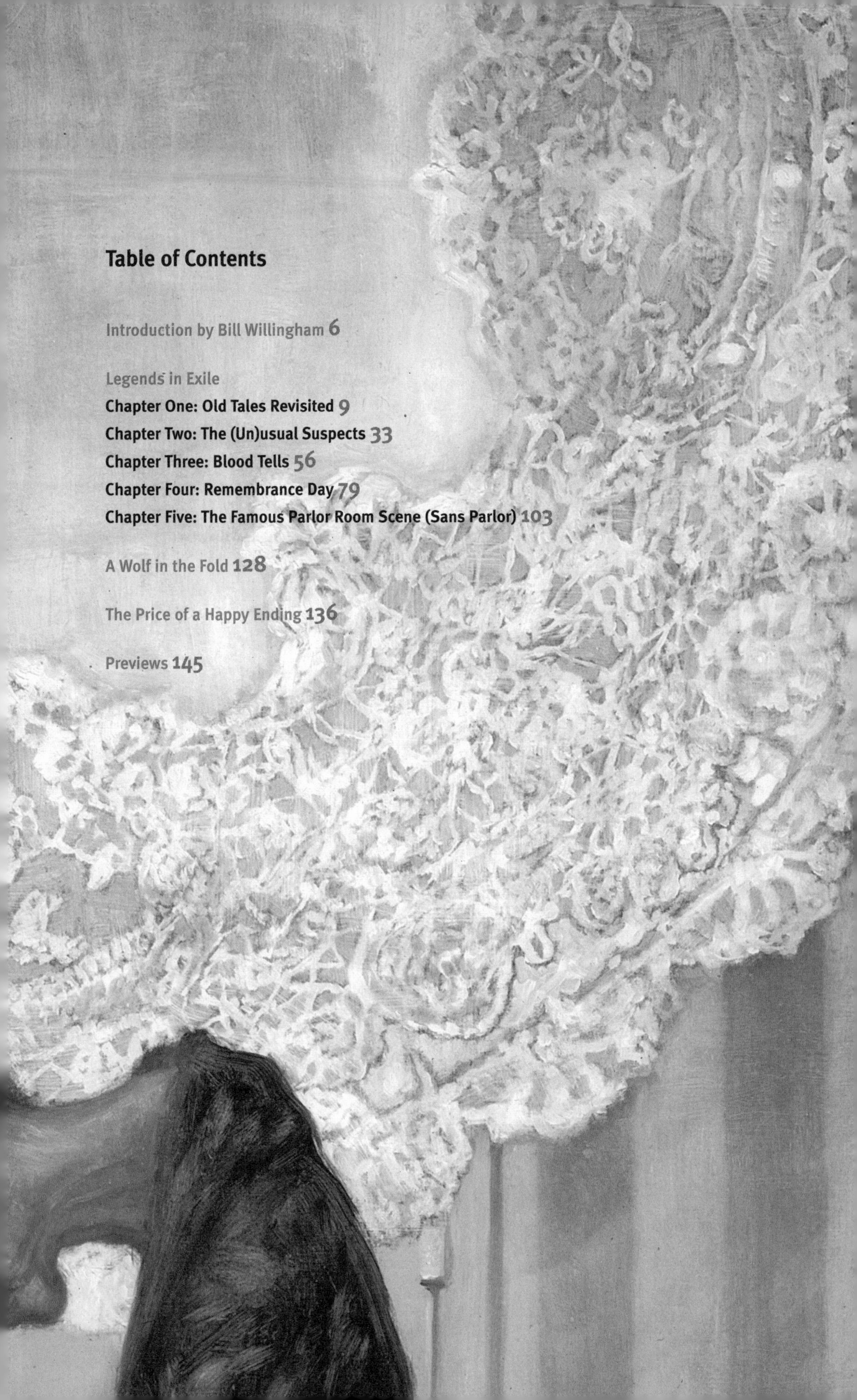

Table of Contents

DOWN IN THE DEEP GRAND GREEN

BY BILL WILLINGHAM

Thank you for picking up this first volume of the collected FABLES comic book series.
This edition reprints the first five monthly issues of FABLES in their entirety, with a few extra
tidbits thrown in. At this point, there are sixteen or so trade paperback volumes collecting the
sweeping FABLES saga, with no end in sight, because the sweeping FABLES saga is still ongoing
at the rate of one new issue each month. And that's a good thing. I'm not in a hurry to see these
stories come to an end. I hope you feel the same.

Just prior to writing this introduction, I completed the following line of dialogue for the 88th issue
of the monthly FABLES series: "I'm here because all fairy tales take place in the woods, King Cole,
even those that don't." Never mind who said those words, or why they were spoken to Old King
Cole — yes, that fellow of the merry old soul. It doesn't matter. What does matter here is that this
turns out to be an apt line with which to begin your introduction to the FABLES series.

Welcome to the woods, where all fairy tales take place — even those that don't.

Fables are fairy tales, folktales, whispered legends and ribald ballads, sung too loud and off-key,
but with vigor and purpose. They're mysteries about things unknown, and perhaps unknowable,
but desired, or feared, or both. The woods are and always have been a place of the deepest
mysteries, the heart of the unknown. FABLES takes place in the woods.

Sure, you'll find out in the very first panel of the very first page that I've just told a whopper. I'm
the worst sort of liar, I admit it. I've lied, boldly and bald faced, because anyone can see with a
glance that these stories take place in New York City, where our hapless characters are living in
secret as refugees. Ah, but the woods are here, dear reader. Since we traffic in fairy tales, we have
magic among our bag of tricks. And using such powers we've taken those enchanted glades with
us, those ancient and venerable stands of oak and ash, yew and hawthorn, bright linden and

cursed juniper. We've taken them and tarted them up in urban drag — the gaudy dress of stone, steel, plaster and glass. From the very first page, FABLES begins in a building called The Woodland, and its hallways are the dark and twisted trails of the deep forest. Its rooms, even the very big ones (and you'll quickly see that there are impossibly big ones), are close and brooding, with dense green canopies overhead that filter, edit, and rephrase what natural light gets through, until it is very unnatural indeed. The Woodland is a place where you only get to know what we tell you, and you should never trust a fraction of it. It's a place beyond the fields that you know, where the forgotten old monsters still lurk and wait and husband their years until they can venture out again, stalking their new young prey that probably should have listened to the dotty old-timers and heeded their dire warnings. It's a place where you can spread all the breadcrumbs behind you that you like; you're still going to get lost.

Lost, but not alone. You're about to meet some old friends that you haven't seen in a while. You already know their first stories — their adventurous tales from long ago. Now you get to find out what they've been up to lately. Some you can trust. Others you should never turn your back on. But isn't that always the way of things?

Welcome to the woods.

And now it's time for our stories to begin.

— **Bill Willingham**
Written in the Woods

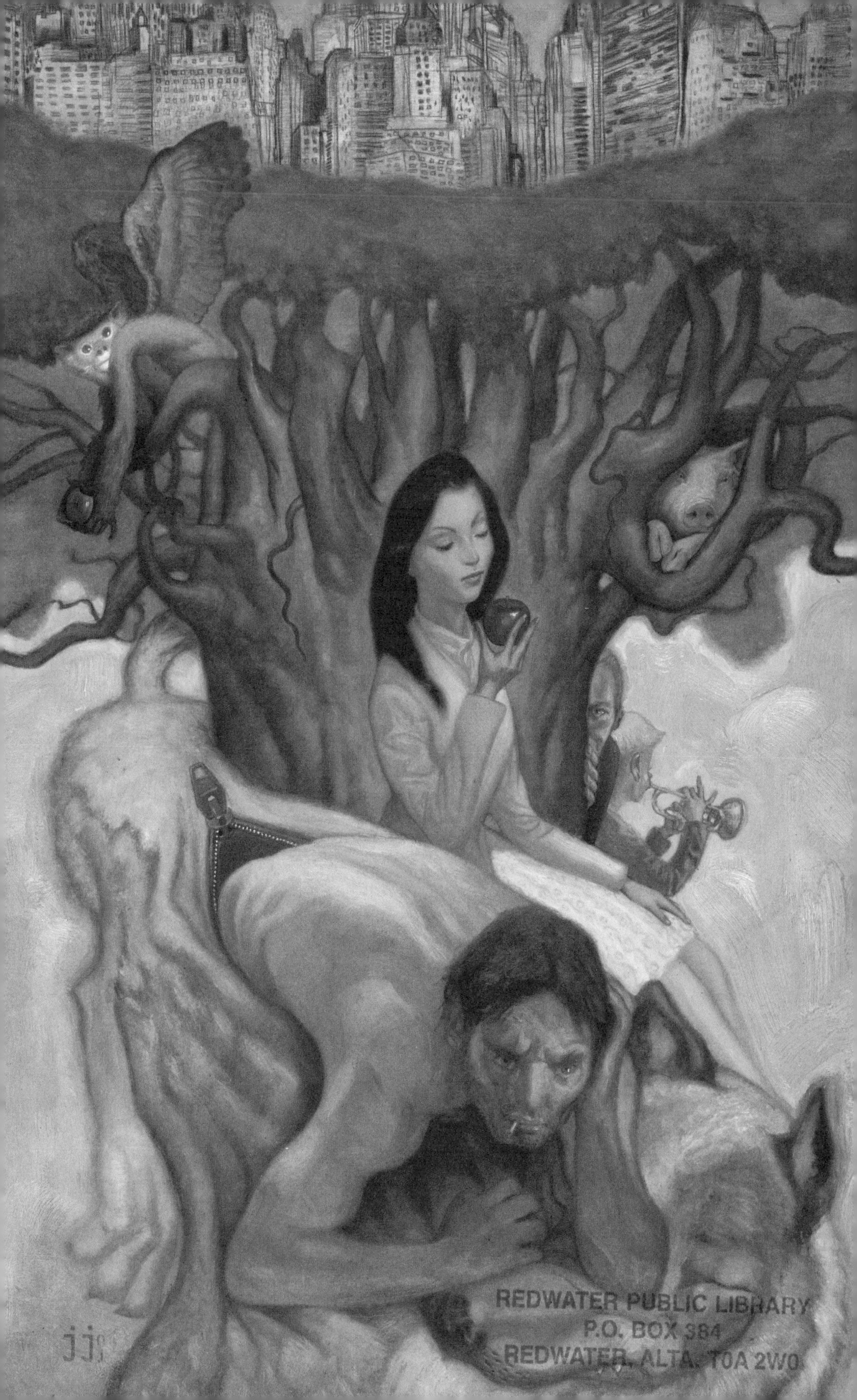
JJ

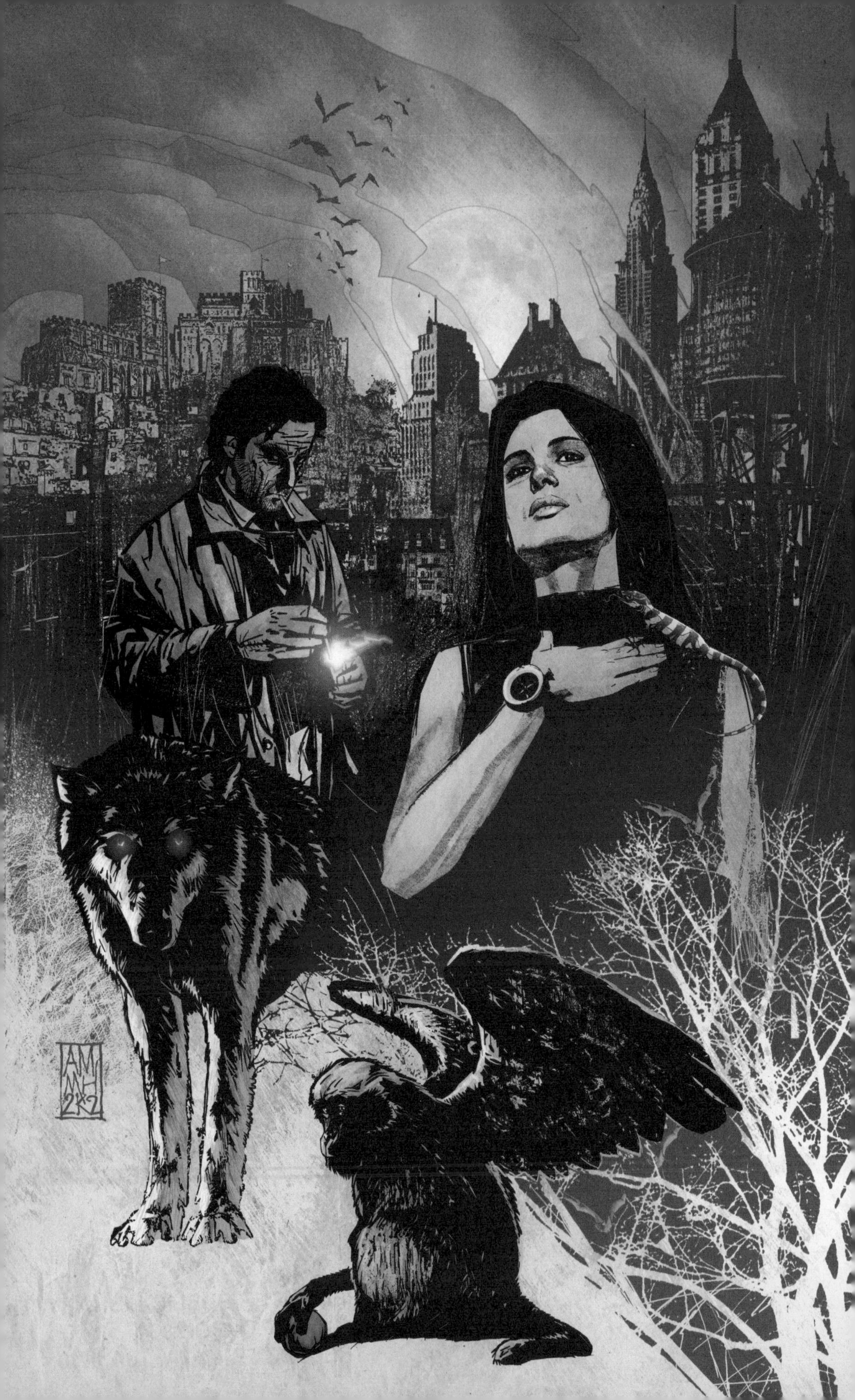

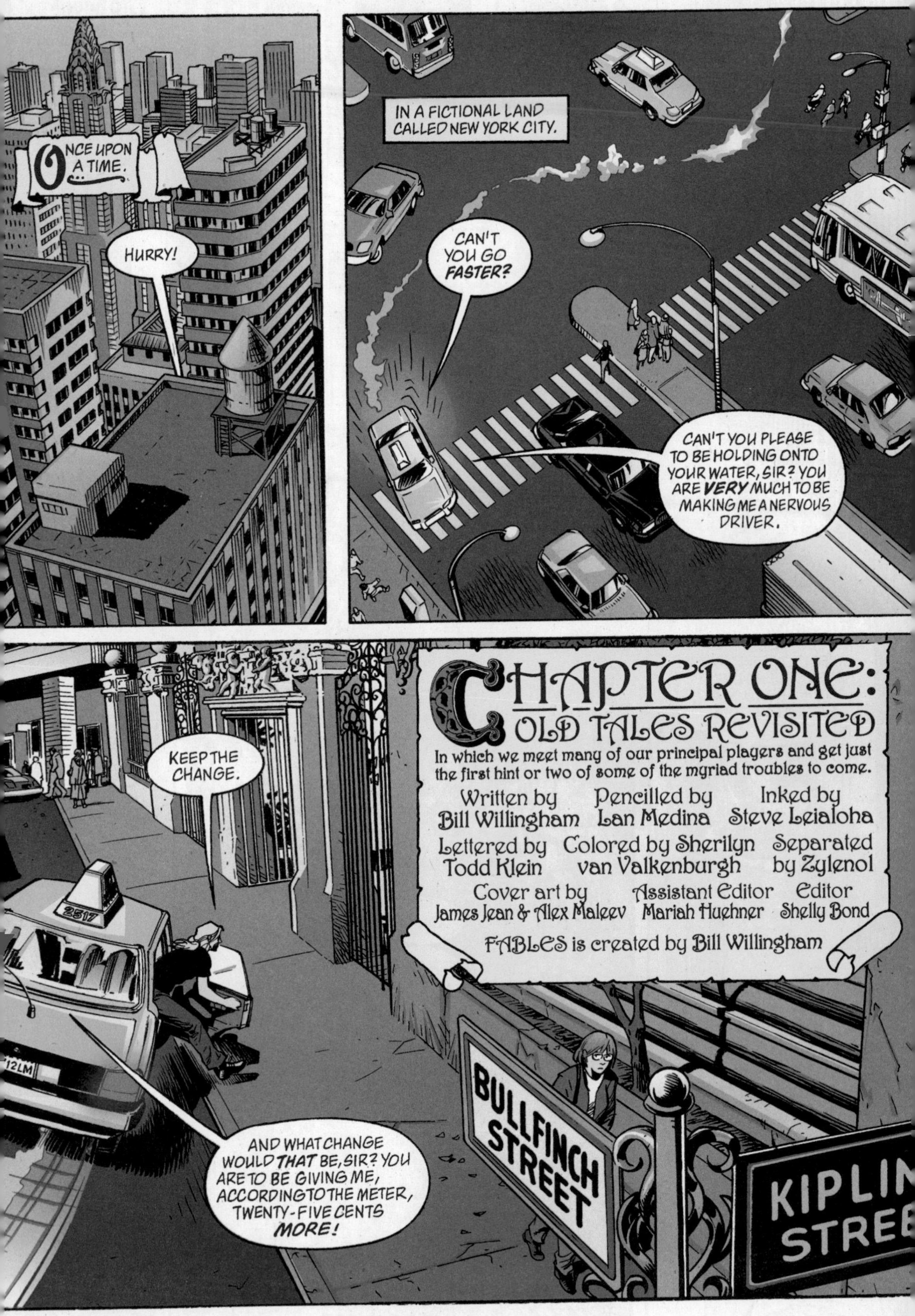
ONCE UPON A TIME...
HURRY!
IN A FICTIONAL LAND CALLED NEW YORK CITY.
CAN'T YOU GO FASTER?
CAN'T YOU PLEASE TO BE HOLDING ONTO YOUR WATER, SIR? YOU ARE VERY MUCH TO BE MAKING ME A NERVOUS DRIVER.
CHAPTER ONE: OLD TALES REVISITED
In which we meet many of our principal players and get just the first hint or two of some of the myriad troubles to come.
Written by Bill Willingham
Pencilled by Lan Medina
Inked by Steve Leialoha
Lettered by Todd Klein
Colored by Sherilyn van Valkenburgh
Separated by Zylenol
Cover art by James Jean & Alex Maleev
Assistant Editor Mariah Huehner
Editor Shelly Bond
FABLES is created by Bill Willingham
KEEP THE CHANGE.
AND WHAT CHANGE WOULD THAT BE, SIR? YOU ARE TO BE GIVING ME, ACCORDING TO THE METER, TWENTY-FIVE CENTS MORE!
2517
BULLFINCH STREET

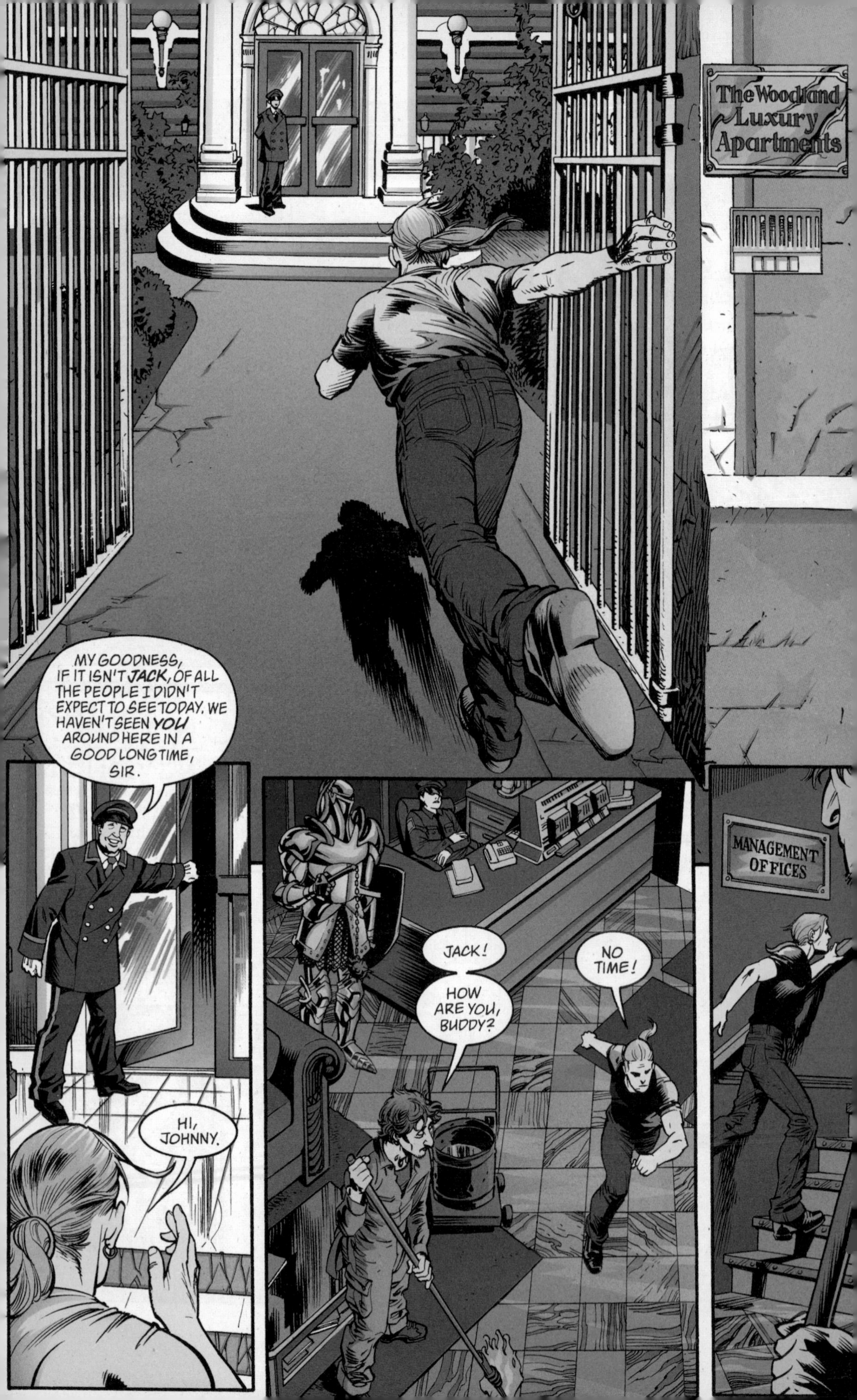
The Woodland Luxury Apartments
MY GOODNESS, IF IT ISN'T JACK, OF ALL THE PEOPLE I DIDN'T EXPECT TO SEE TODAY. WE HAVEN'T SEEN YOU AROUND HERE IN A GOOD LONG TIME, SIR.
HI, JOHNNY.
JACK!
HOW ARE YOU, BUDDY?
NO TIME!
MANAGEMENT OFFICES

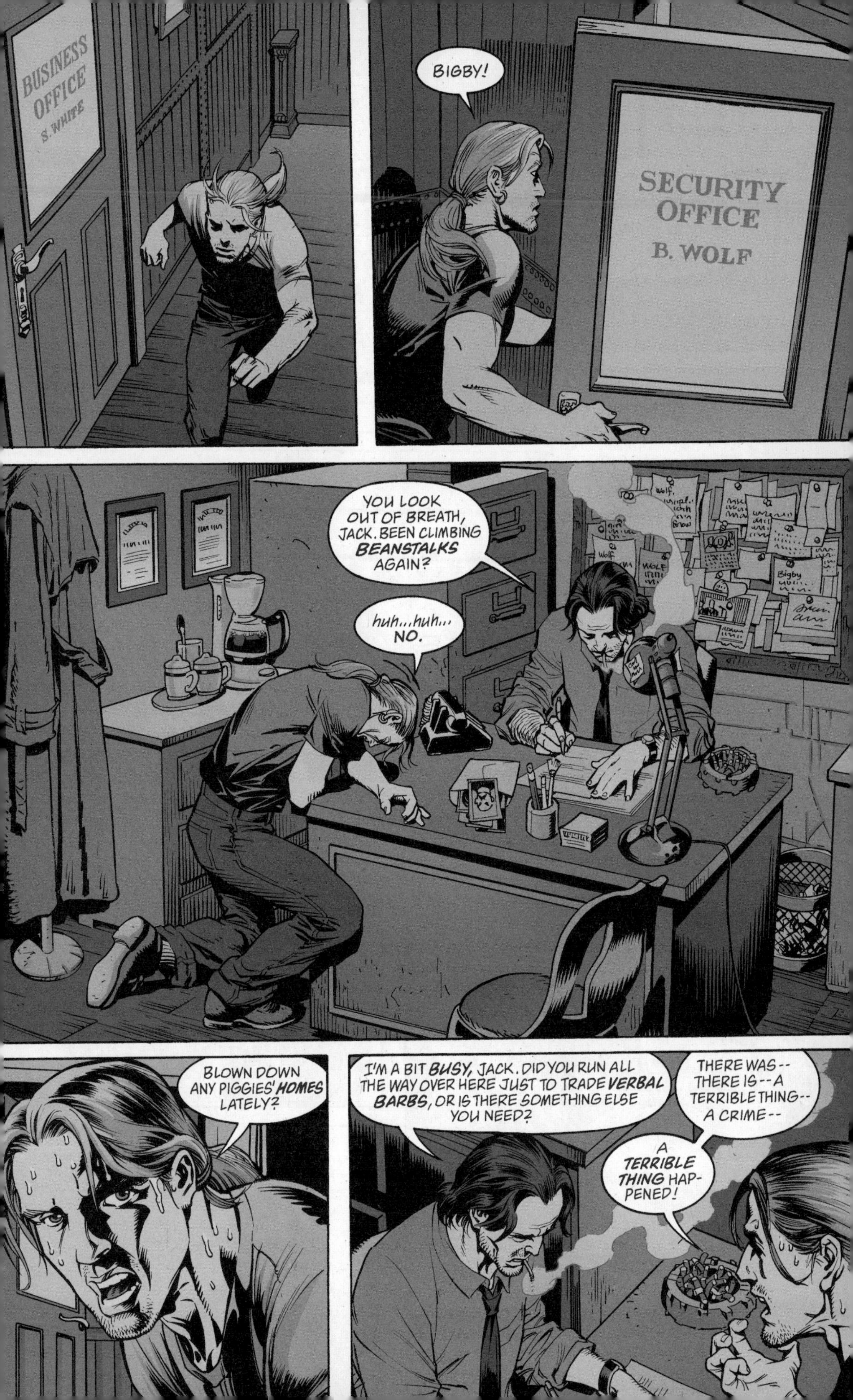
BUSINESS OFFICE S. WHITE
BIGBY!
SECURITY OFFICE B. WOLF
YOU LOOK OUT OF BREATH, JACK. BEEN CLIMBING **BEANSTALKS** AGAIN?
huh...huh... **NO.**
BLOWN DOWN ANY PIGGIES' ***HOMES*** LATELY?
I'M A BIT ***BUSY,*** JACK. DID YOU RUN ALL THE WAY OVER HERE JUST TO TRADE ***VERBAL BARBS,*** OR IS THERE SOMETHING ELSE YOU NEED?
THERE WAS-- THERE IS--A TERRIBLE THING-- A CRIME--
A ***TERRIBLE THING*** HAPPENED!

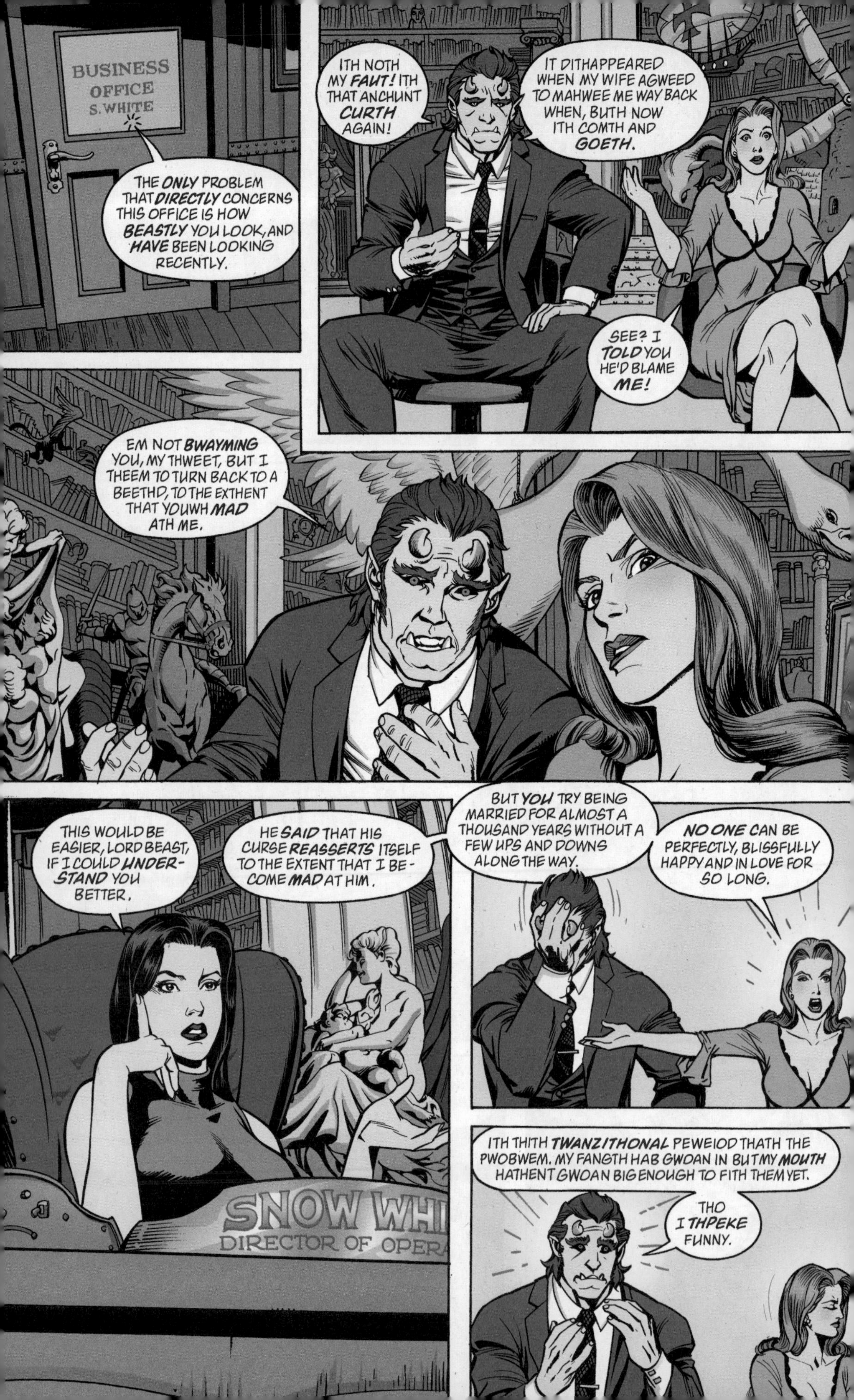
BUSINESS OFFICE S. WHITE
THE ONLY PROBLEM THAT DIRECTLY CONCERNS THIS OFFICE IS HOW BEASTLY YOU LOOK, AND HAVE BEEN LOOKING RECENTLY.
ITH NOTH MY FAUT! ITH THAT ANCHUNT CURTH AGAIN!
IT DITHAPPEARED WHEN MY WIFE AGWEED TO MAHWEE ME WAY BACK WHEN, BUTH NOW ITH COMTH AND GOETH.
SEE? I TOLD YOU HE'D BLAME ME!
EM NOT BWAYMING YOU, MY THWEET, BUT I THEEM TO TURN BACK TO A BEETHD, TO THE EXTHENT THAT YOUWH MAD ATH ME.
THIS WOULD BE EASIER, LORD BEAST, IF I COULD UNDER-STAND YOU BETTER.
HE SAID THAT HIS CURSE REASSERTS ITSELF TO THE EXTENT THAT I BE-COME MAD AT HIM.
SNOW WHI
DIRECTOR OF OPERA
BUT YOU TRY BEING MARRIED FOR ALMOST A THOUSAND YEARS WITHOUT A FEW UPS AND DOWNS ALONG THE WAY.
NO ONE CAN BE PERFECTLY, BLISSFULLY HAPPY AND IN LOVE FOR SO LONG.
ITH THITH TWANZITHONAL PEWEIOD THATH THE PWOBWEM. MY FANGTH HAB GWOAN IN BUT MY MOUTH HATHENT GWOAN BIG ENOUGH TO FITH THEM YET.
THO I THPEKE FUNNY.

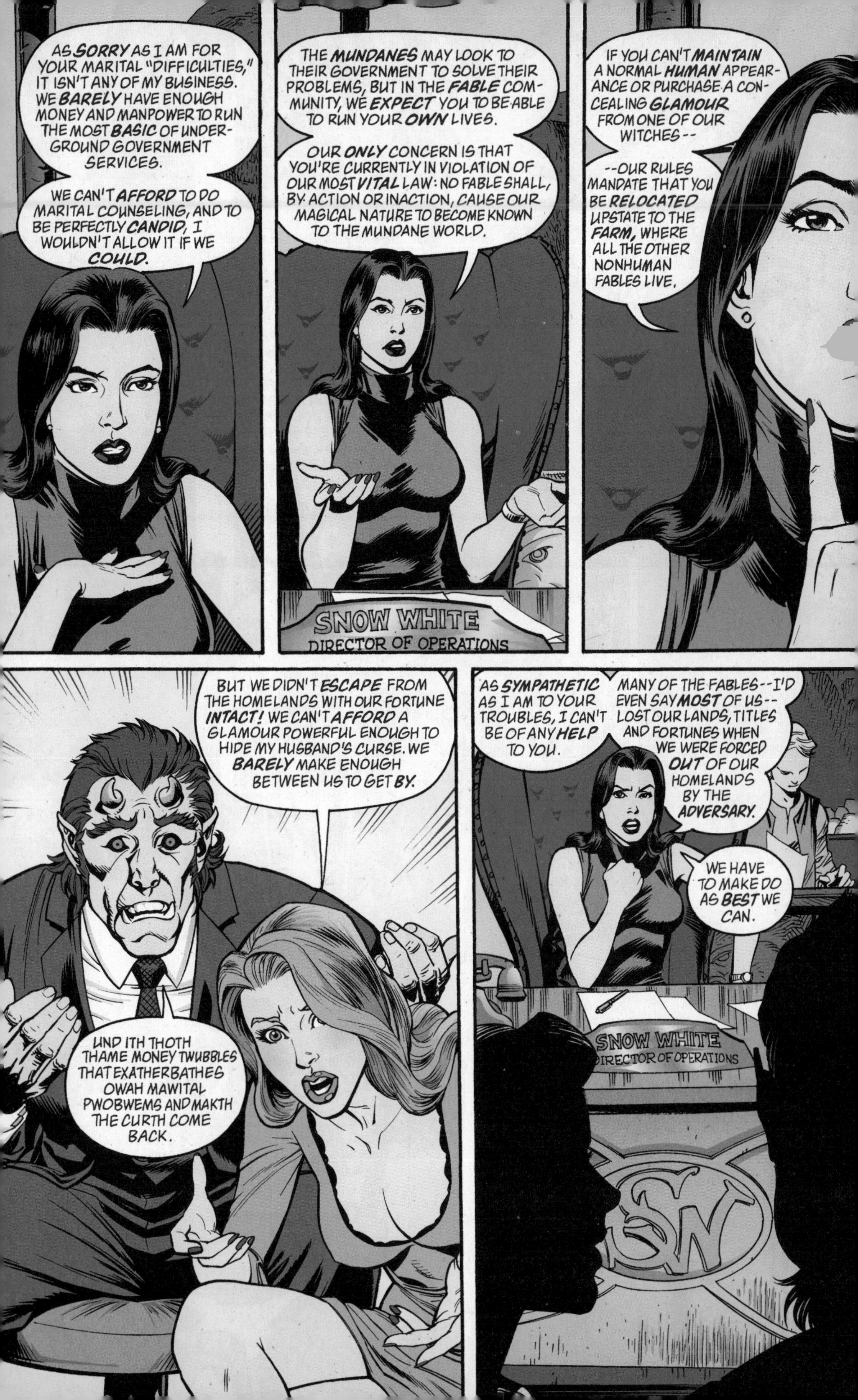
AS SORRY AS I AM FOR YOUR MARITAL "DIFFICULTIES," IT ISN'T ANY OF MY BUSINESS. WE BARELY HAVE ENOUGH MONEY AND MANPOWER TO RUN THE MOST BASIC OF UNDERGROUND GOVERNMENT SERVICES.
WE CAN'T AFFORD TO DO MARITAL COUNSELING, AND TO BE PERFECTLY CANDID, I WOULDN'T ALLOW IT IF WE COULD.
THE MUNDANES MAY LOOK TO THEIR GOVERNMENT TO SOLVE THEIR PROBLEMS, BUT IN THE FABLE COMMUNITY, WE EXPECT YOU TO BE ABLE TO RUN YOUR OWN LIVES.
OUR ONLY CONCERN IS THAT YOU'RE CURRENTLY IN VIOLATION OF OUR MOST VITAL LAW: NO FABLE SHALL, BY ACTION OR INACTION, CAUSE OUR MAGICAL NATURE TO BECOME KNOWN TO THE MUNDANE WORLD.
SNOW WHITE
DIRECTOR OF OPERATIONS
IF YOU CAN'T MAINTAIN A NORMAL HUMAN APPEARANCE OR PURCHASE A CONCEALING GLAMOUR FROM ONE OF OUR WITCHES--
--OUR RULES MANDATE THAT YOU BE RELOCATED UPSTATE TO THE FARM, WHERE ALL THE OTHER NONHUMAN FABLES LIVE.
BUT WE DIDN'T ESCAPE FROM THE HOMELANDS WITH OUR FORTUNE INTACT! WE CAN'T AFFORD A GLAMOUR POWERFUL ENOUGH TO HIDE MY HUSBAND'S CURSE. WE BARELY MAKE ENOUGH BETWEEN US TO GET BY.
UND ITH THOTH THAME MONEY TWUBBLES THAT EXATHERBATHES OWAH MAWITAL PWOBWEMS AND MAKTH THE CURTH COME BACK.
AS SYMPATHETIC AS I AM TO YOUR TROUBLES, I CAN'T BE OF ANY HELP TO YOU.
MANY OF THE FABLES--I'D EVEN SAY MOST OF US--LOST OUR LANDS, TITLES AND FORTUNES WHEN WE WERE FORCED OUT OF OUR HOMELANDS BY THE ADVERSARY.
WE HAVE TO MAKE DO AS BEST WE CAN.
SNOW WHITE
DIRECTOR OF OPERATIONS
SW

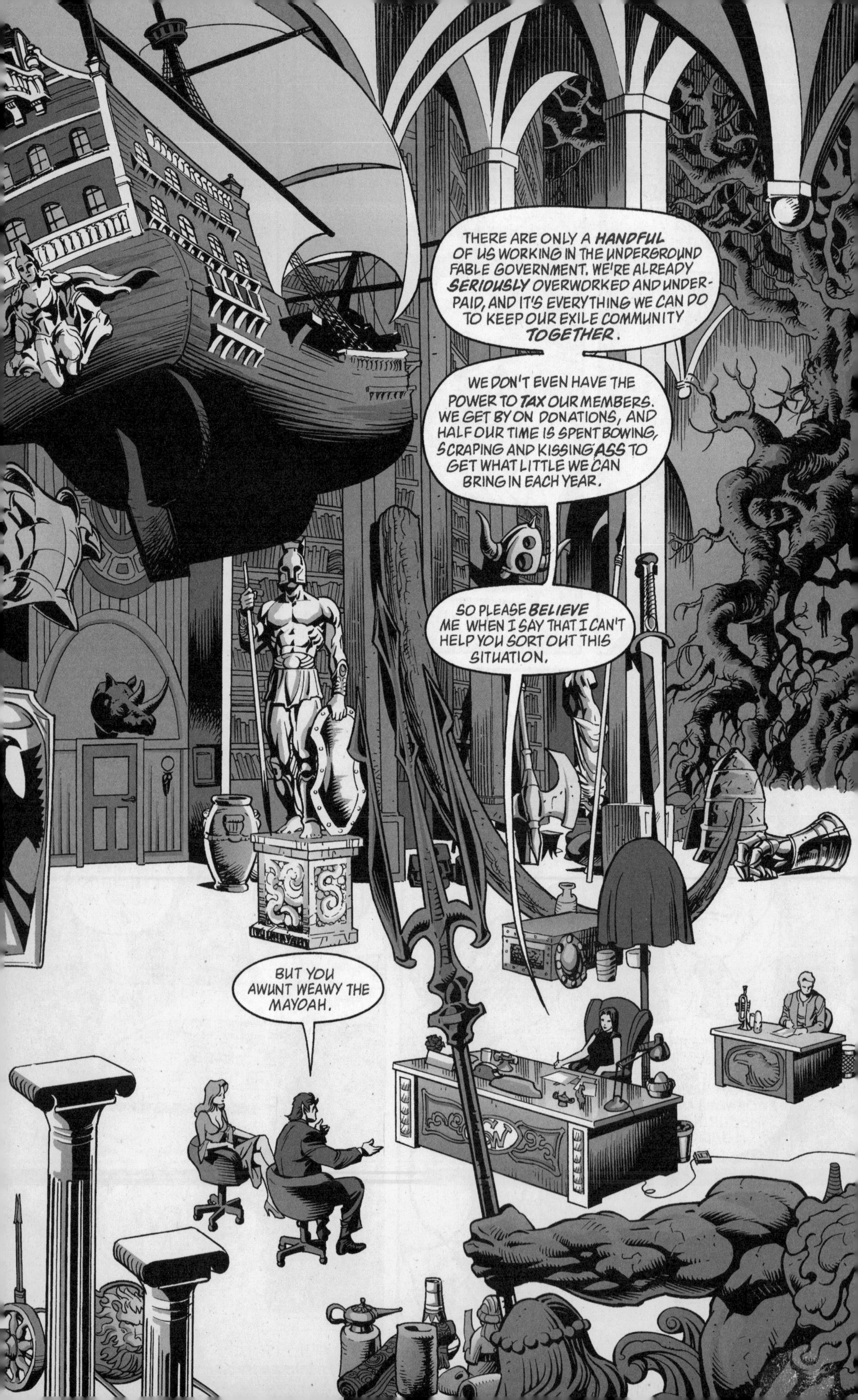
THERE ARE ONLY A HANDFUL OF US WORKING IN THE UNDERGROUND FABLE GOVERNMENT. WE'RE ALREADY SERIOUSLY OVERWORKED AND UNDER-PAID, AND IT'S EVERYTHING WE CAN DO TO KEEP OUR EXILE COMMUNITY TOGETHER.
WE DON'T EVEN HAVE THE POWER TO TAX OUR MEMBERS. WE GET BY ON DONATIONS, AND HALF OUR TIME IS SPENT BOWING, SCRAPING AND KISSING ASS TO GET WHAT LITTLE WE CAN BRING IN EACH YEAR.
SO PLEASE BELIEVE ME WHEN I SAY THAT I CAN'T HELP YOU SORT OUT THIS SITUATION.
BUT YOU AWUNT WEAWY THE MAYOAH.

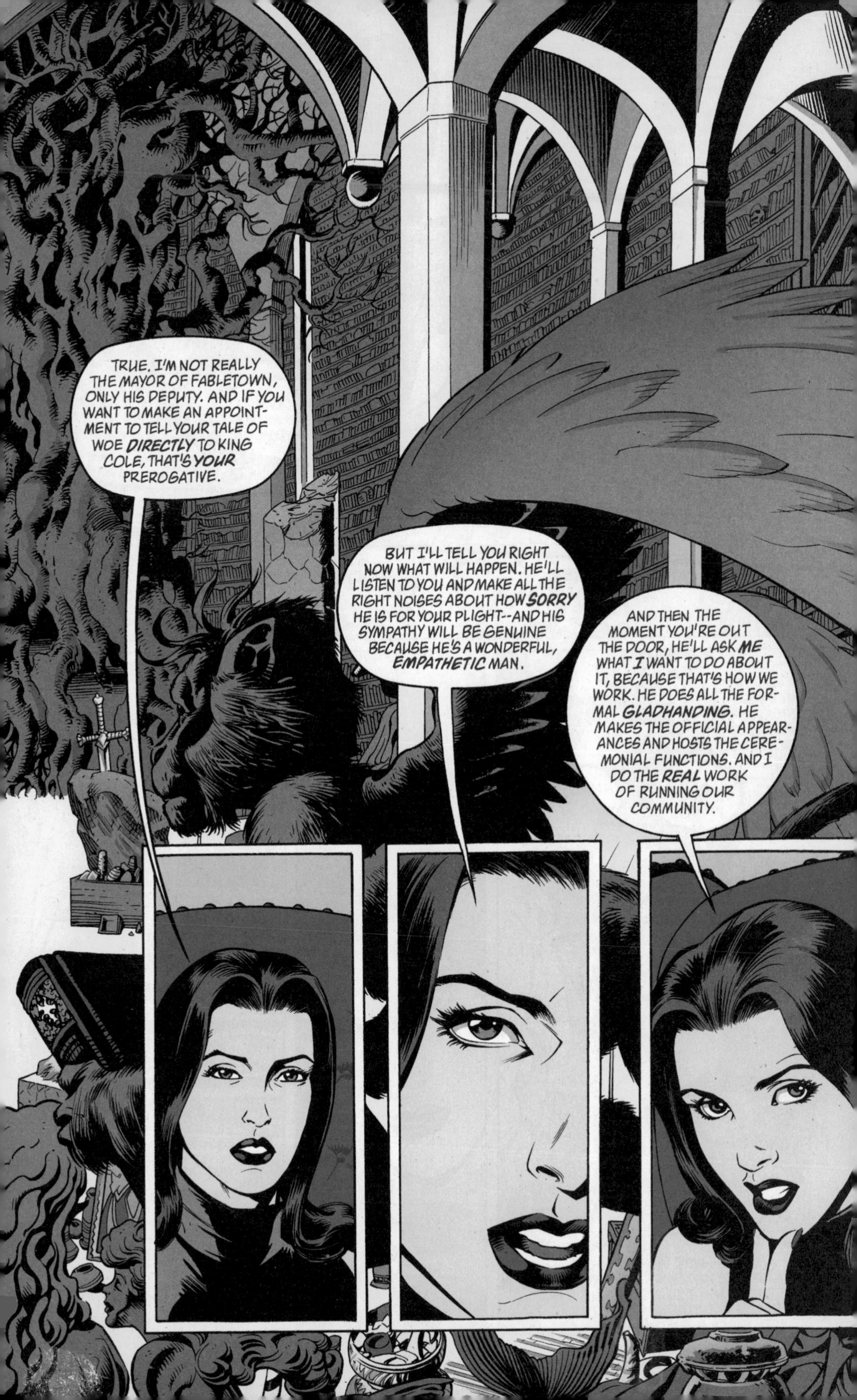
TRUE, I'M NOT REALLY THE MAYOR OF FABLETOWN, ONLY HIS DEPUTY. AND IF YOU WANT TO MAKE AN APPOINTMENT TO TELL YOUR TALE OF WOE DIRECTLY TO KING COLE, THAT'S YOUR PREROGATIVE.
BUT I'LL TELL YOU RIGHT NOW WHAT WILL HAPPEN. HE'LL LISTEN TO YOU AND MAKE ALL THE RIGHT NOISES ABOUT HOW SORRY HE IS FOR YOUR PLIGHT--AND HIS SYMPATHY WILL BE GENUINE BECAUSE HE'S A WONDERFUL, EMPATHETIC MAN.
AND THEN THE MOMENT YOU'RE OUT THE DOOR, HE'LL ASK ME WHAT I WANT TO DO ABOUT IT, BECAUSE THAT'S HOW WE WORK. HE DOES ALL THE FORMAL GLADHANDING. HE MAKES THE OFFICIAL APPEARANCES AND HOSTS THE CEREMONIAL FUNCTIONS. AND I DO THE REAL WORK OF RUNNING OUR COMMUNITY.

FOR BETTER OR *WORSE*, YOU'VE JUST HAD YOUR *APPEAL* TO CITY HALL.

YOU DIVORCED *YOUR* PRINCE *CENTURIES* AGO. YOU HAVE *NO IDEA* HOW HARD IT IS TO KEEP A MARRIAGE GOING SO LONG.

SNOW WHITE
DIRECTOR OF OPERATIONS

NOWAH, DEAH. THEWES NO WEASON TO GET *PERSONOAH.*

DON'T GET *PERSONAL?* AFTER SHE OPENLY *CRITICIZED* OUR MARRIED LIFE?

I DID *NO SUCH THING.*

AND JUST WHO IS *SHE* TO CRITICIZE *ANYONE'S* PERSONAL LIFE, AFTER WHAT *I* HEARD ABOUT HER TAWDRY LITTLE ADVENTURE WITH THOSE SEVEN DWARVES?

OKAY, FOLKS, BUSINESS IS PILING *UP* AND WE NEED TO MOVE THINGS ALONG TO MISS WHITE'S *NEXT* APPOINT- MENT.

SNOW WHITE
DIRECTOR OF OPERATIONS

BUT--?

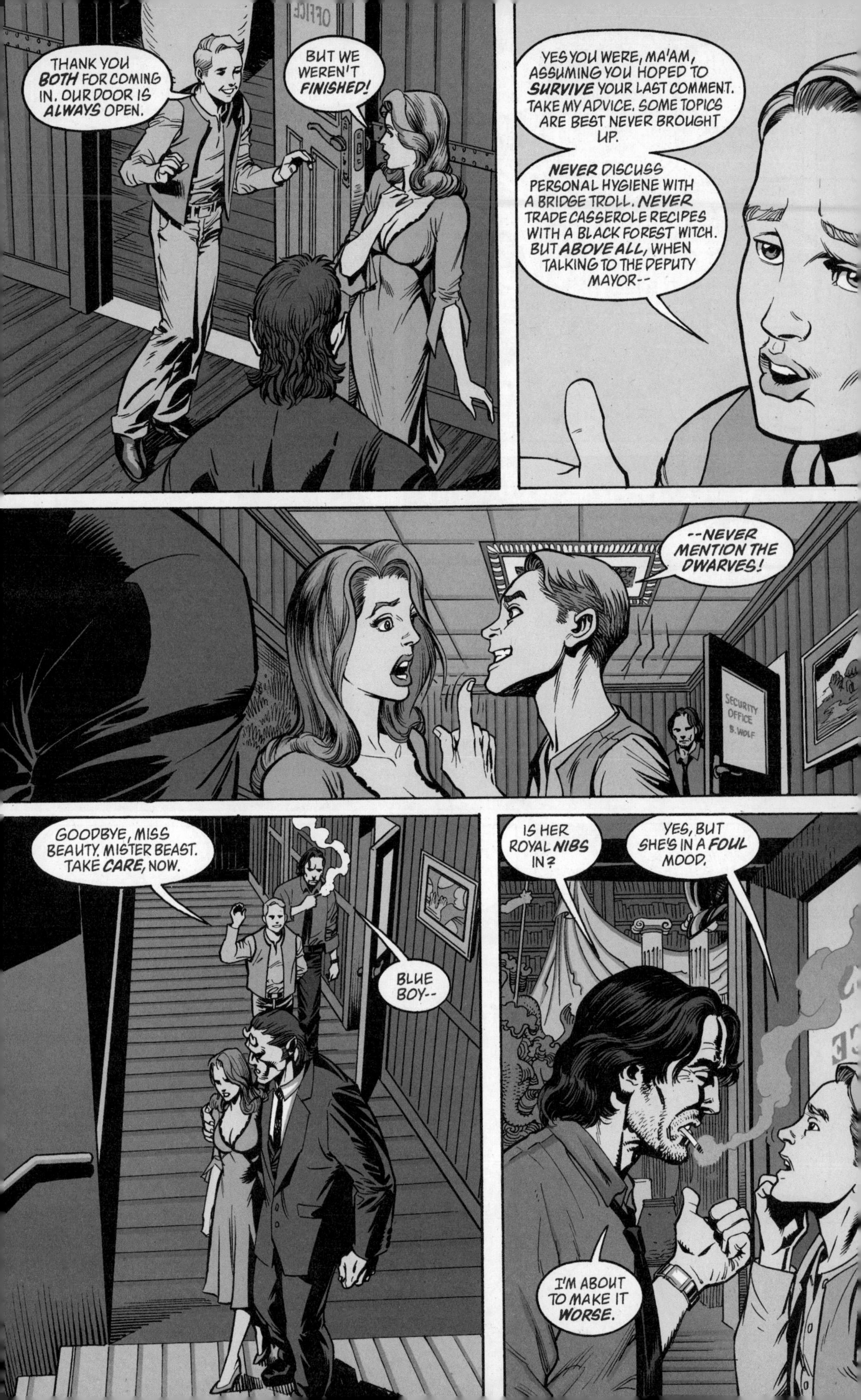
OFFICE
THANK YOU BOTH FOR COMING IN. OUR DOOR IS ALWAYS OPEN.
BUT WE WEREN'T FINISHED!
YES YOU WERE, MA'AM, ASSUMING YOU HOPED TO SURVIVE YOUR LAST COMMENT. TAKE MY ADVICE. SOME TOPICS ARE BEST NEVER BROUGHT UP.
NEVER DISCUSS PERSONAL HYGIENE WITH A BRIDGE TROLL. NEVER TRADE CASSEROLE RECIPES WITH A BLACK FOREST WITCH. BUT ABOVE ALL, WHEN TALKING TO THE DEPUTY MAYOR--
--NEVER MENTION THE DWARVES!
SECURITY OFFICE B. WOLF
GOODBYE, MISS BEAUTY. MISTER BEAST. TAKE CARE, NOW.
BLUE BOY--
IS HER ROYAL NIBS IN?
YES, BUT SHE'S IN A FOUL MOOD.
I'M ABOUT TO MAKE IT WORSE.

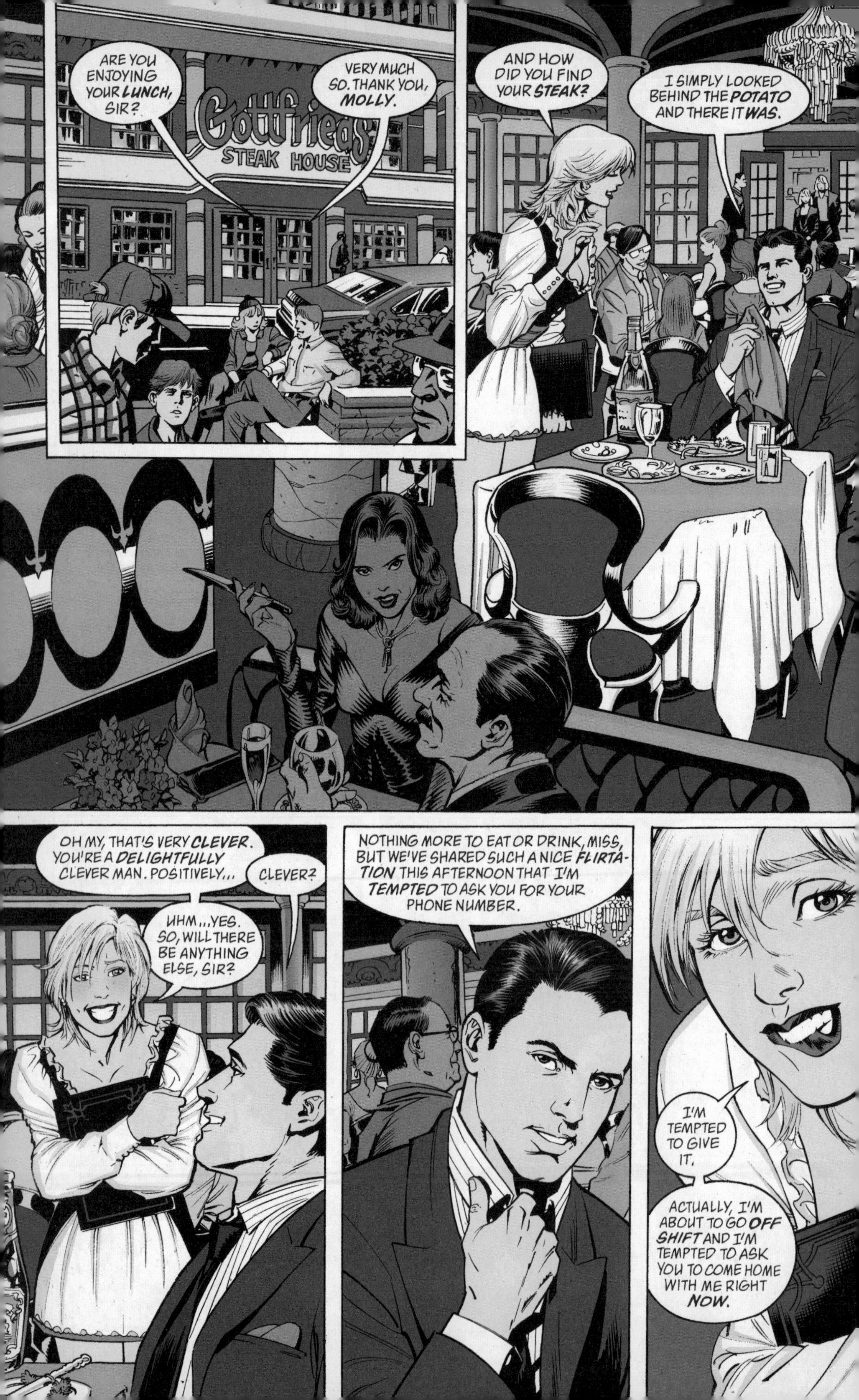

ARE YOU ENJOYING YOUR LUNCH, SIR?
VERY MUCH SO. THANK YOU, MOLLY.
Gottfried's STEAK HOUSE
AND HOW DID YOU FIND YOUR STEAK?
I SIMPLY LOOKED BEHIND THE POTATO AND THERE IT WAS.
OH MY, THAT'S VERY CLEVER. YOU'RE A DELIGHTFULLY CLEVER MAN. POSITIVELY...
CLEVER?
UHM...YES. SO, WILL THERE BE ANYTHING ELSE, SIR?
NOTHING MORE TO EAT OR DRINK, MISS, BUT WE'VE SHARED SUCH A NICE FLIRTATION THIS AFTERNOON THAT I'M TEMPTED TO ASK YOU FOR YOUR PHONE NUMBER.
I'M TEMPTED TO GIVE IT.
ACTUALLY, I'M ABOUT TO GO OFF SHIFT AND I'M TEMPTED TO ASK YOU TO COME HOME WITH ME RIGHT NOW.

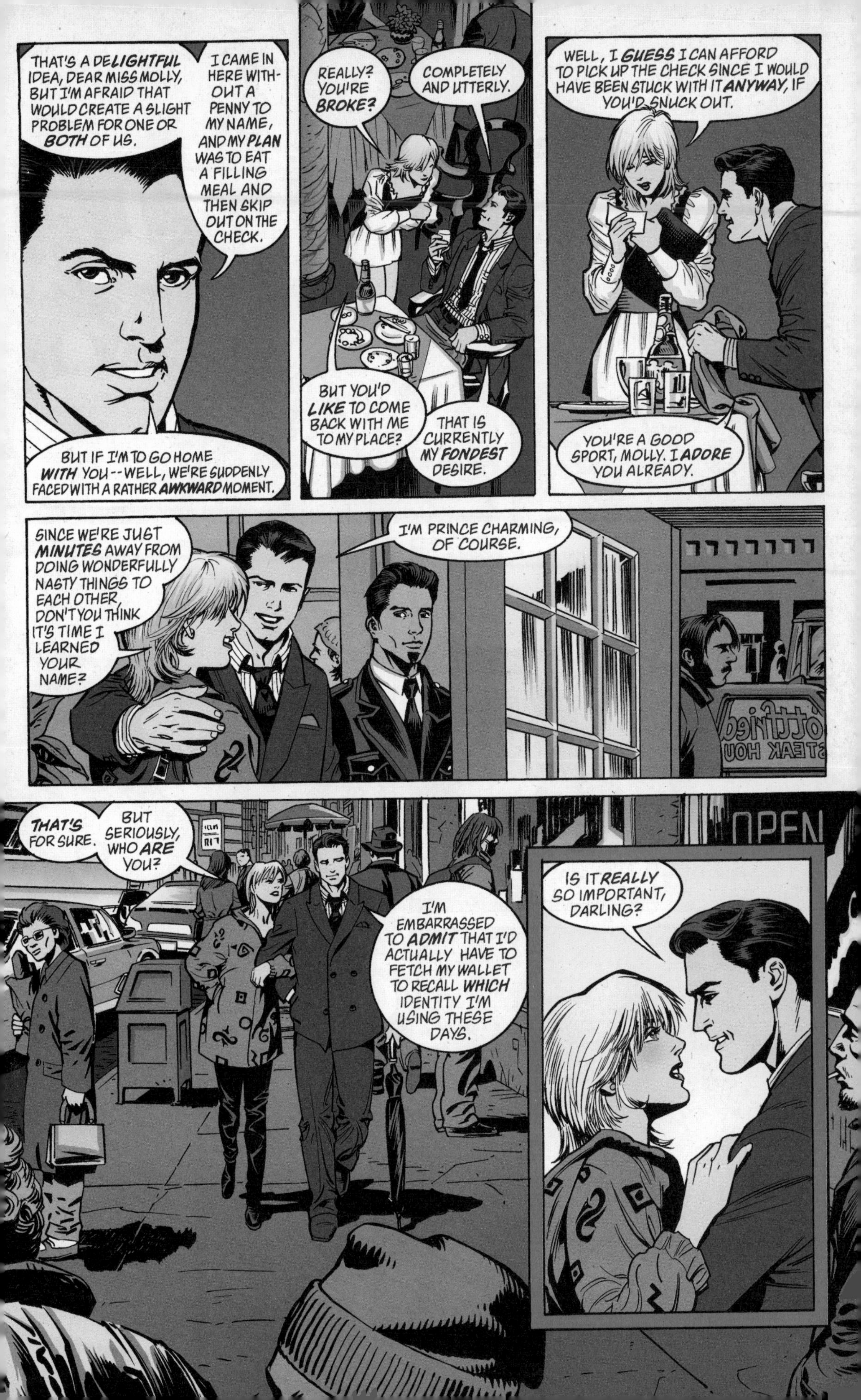
THAT'S A DELIGHTFUL IDEA, DEAR MISS MOLLY, BUT I'M AFRAID THAT WOULD CREATE A SLIGHT PROBLEM FOR ONE OR BOTH OF US.
I CAME IN HERE WITHOUT A PENNY TO MY NAME, AND MY PLAN WAS TO EAT A FILLING MEAL AND THEN SKIP OUT ON THE CHECK.
BUT IF I'M TO GO HOME WITH YOU--WELL, WE'RE SUDDENLY FACED WITH A RATHER AWKWARD MOMENT.
REALLY? YOU'RE BROKE?
COMPLETELY AND UTTERLY.
BUT YOU'D LIKE TO COME BACK WITH ME TO MY PLACE?
THAT IS CURRENTLY MY FONDEST DESIRE.
WELL, I GUESS I CAN AFFORD TO PICK UP THE CHECK SINCE I WOULD HAVE BEEN STUCK WITH IT ANYWAY, IF YOU'D SNUCK OUT.
YOU'RE A GOOD SPORT, MOLLY. I ADORE YOU ALREADY.
SINCE WE'RE JUST MINUTES AWAY FROM DOING WONDERFULLY NASTY THINGS TO EACH OTHER, DON'T YOU THINK IT'S TIME I LEARNED YOUR NAME?
I'M PRINCE CHARMING, OF COURSE.
THAT'S FOR SURE.
BUT SERIOUSLY, WHO ARE YOU?
I'M EMBARRASSED TO ADMIT THAT I'D ACTUALLY HAVE TO FETCH MY WALLET TO RECALL WHICH IDENTITY I'M USING THESE DAYS.
OPEN
IS IT REALLY SO IMPORTANT, DARLING?

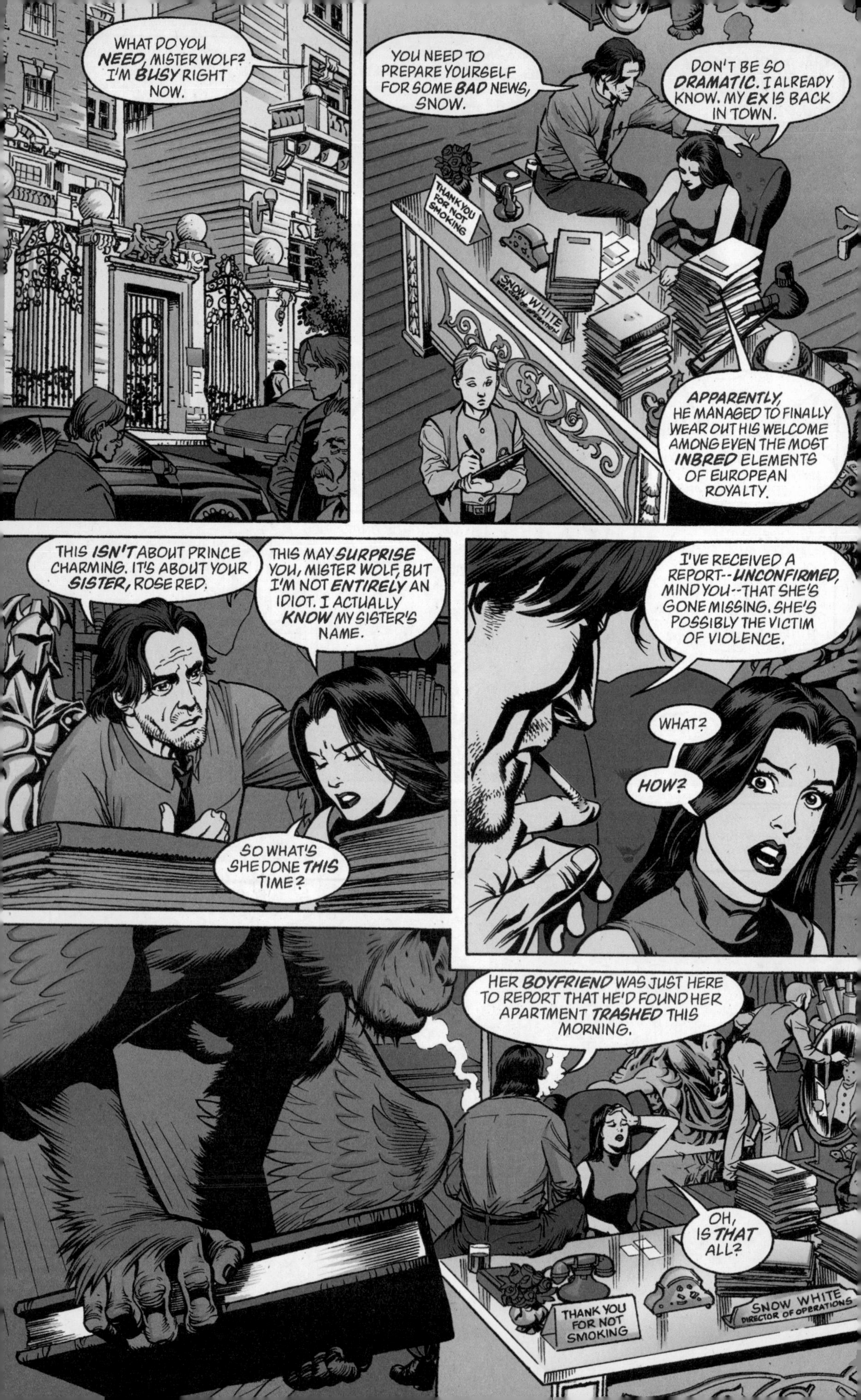
WHAT DO YOU NEED, MISTER WOLF? I'M BUSY RIGHT NOW.
YOU NEED TO PREPARE YOURSELF FOR SOME BAD NEWS, SNOW.
DON'T BE SO DRAMATIC. I ALREADY KNOW. MY EX IS BACK IN TOWN.
THANK YOU FOR NOT SMOKING
SNOW WHITE
APPARENTLY, HE MANAGED TO FINALLY WEAR OUT HIS WELCOME AMONG EVEN THE MOST INBRED ELEMENTS OF EUROPEAN ROYALTY.
THIS ISN'T ABOUT PRINCE CHARMING. IT'S ABOUT YOUR SISTER, ROSE RED.
THIS MAY SURPRISE YOU, MISTER WOLF, BUT I'M NOT ENTIRELY AN IDIOT. I ACTUALLY KNOW MY SISTER'S NAME.
SO WHAT'S SHE DONE THIS TIME?
I'VE RECEIVED A REPORT--UNCONFIRMED, MIND YOU--THAT SHE'S GONE MISSING. SHE'S POSSIBLY THE VICTIM OF VIOLENCE.
WHAT?
HOW?
HER BOYFRIEND WAS JUST HERE TO REPORT THAT HE'D FOUND HER APARTMENT TRASHED THIS MORNING.
OH, IS THAT ALL?
THANK YOU FOR NOT SMOKING
SNOW WHITE DIRECTOR OF OPERATIONS

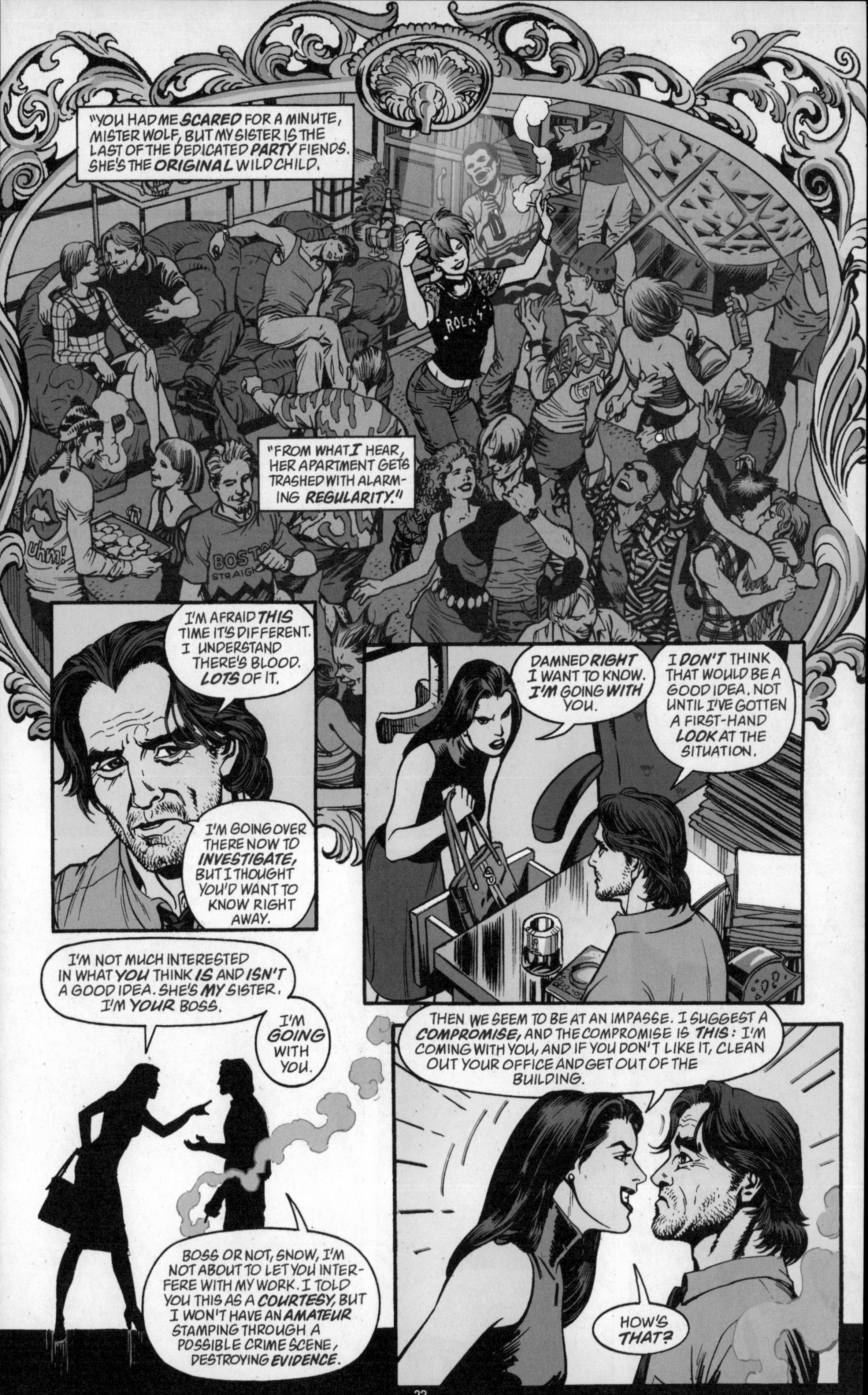
"YOU HAD ME SCARED FOR A MINUTE, MISTER WOLF, BUT MY SISTER IS THE LAST OF THE DEDICATED PARTY FIENDS. SHE'S THE ORIGINAL WILD CHILD.
"FROM WHAT I HEAR, HER APARTMENT GETS TRASHED WITH ALARMING REGULARITY."
I'M AFRAID THIS TIME IT'S DIFFERENT. I UNDERSTAND THERE'S BLOOD. LOTS OF IT.
I'M GOING OVER THERE NOW TO INVESTIGATE, BUT I THOUGHT YOU'D WANT TO KNOW RIGHT AWAY.
DAMNED RIGHT I WANT TO KNOW. I'M GOING WITH YOU.
I DON'T THINK THAT WOULD BE A GOOD IDEA. NOT UNTIL I'VE GOTTEN A FIRST-HAND LOOK AT THE SITUATION.
I'M NOT MUCH INTERESTED IN WHAT YOU THINK IS AND ISN'T A GOOD IDEA. SHE'S MY SISTER. I'M YOUR BOSS.
I'M GOING WITH YOU.
BOSS OR NOT, SNOW, I'M NOT ABOUT TO LET YOU INTERFERE WITH MY WORK. I TOLD YOU THIS AS A COURTESY, BUT I WON'T HAVE AN AMATEUR STAMPING THROUGH A POSSIBLE CRIME SCENE, DESTROYING EVIDENCE.
THEN WE SEEM TO BE AT AN IMPASSE. I SUGGEST A COMPROMISE, AND THE COMPROMISE IS THIS: I'M COMING WITH YOU, AND IF YOU DON'T LIKE IT, CLEAN OUT YOUR OFFICE AND GET OUT OF THE BUILDING.
HOW'S THAT?

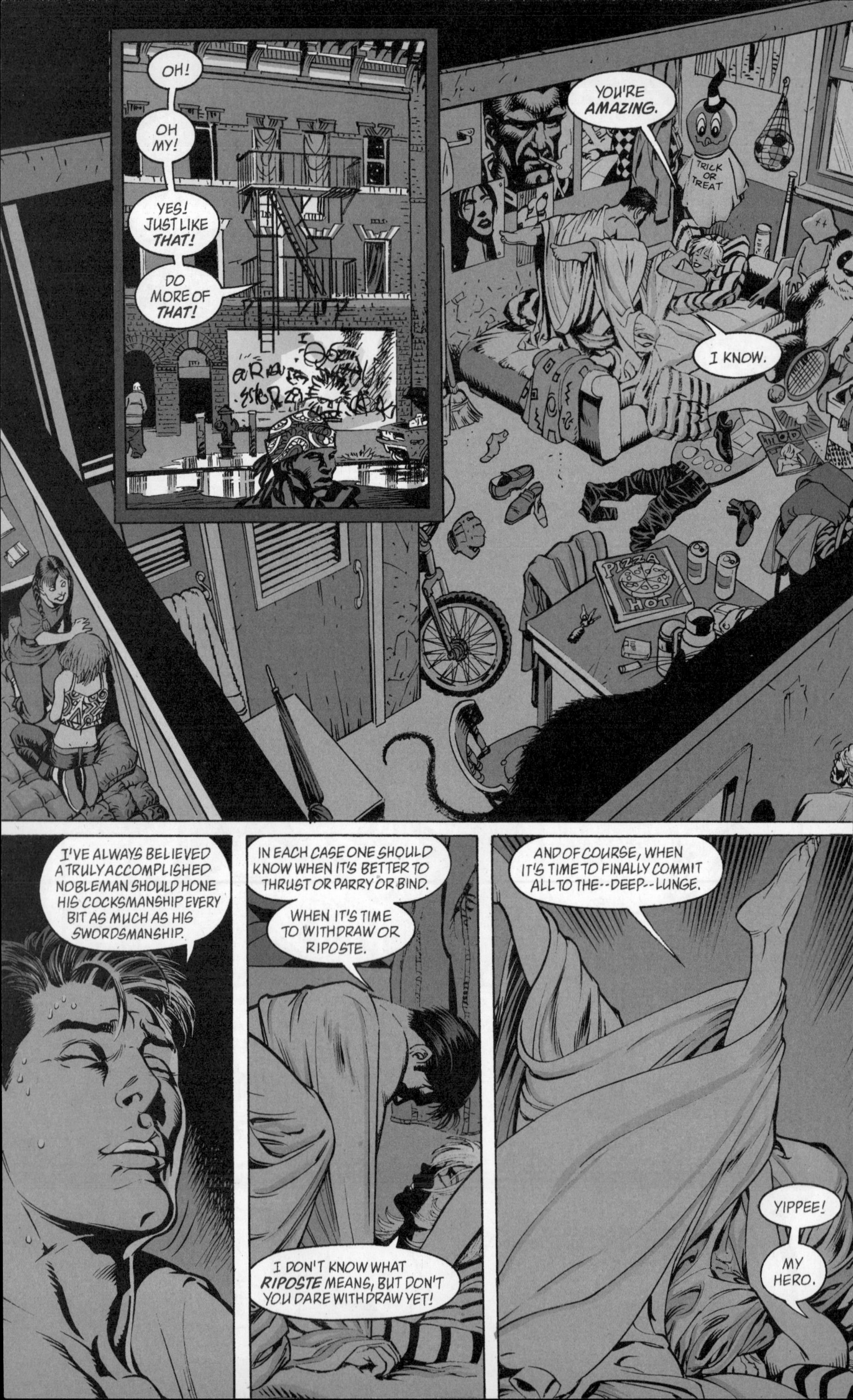
OH!
OH MY!
YES! JUST LIKE THAT!
DO MORE OF THAT!
YOU'RE AMAZING.
TRICK OR TREAT
I KNOW.
PIZZA HOT
I'VE ALWAYS BELIEVED A TRULY ACCOMPLISHED NOBLEMAN SHOULD HONE HIS COCKSMANSHIP EVERY BIT AS MUCH AS HIS SWORDSMANSHIP.
IN EACH CASE ONE SHOULD KNOW WHEN IT'S BETTER TO THRUST OR PARRY OR BIND.
WHEN IT'S TIME TO WITHDRAW OR RIPOSTE.
I DON'T KNOW WHAT RIPOSTE MEANS, BUT DON'T YOU DARE WITHDRAW YET!
AND OF COURSE, WHEN IT'S TIME TO FINALLY COMMIT ALL TO THE--DEEP--LUNGE.
YIPPEE!
MY HERO.

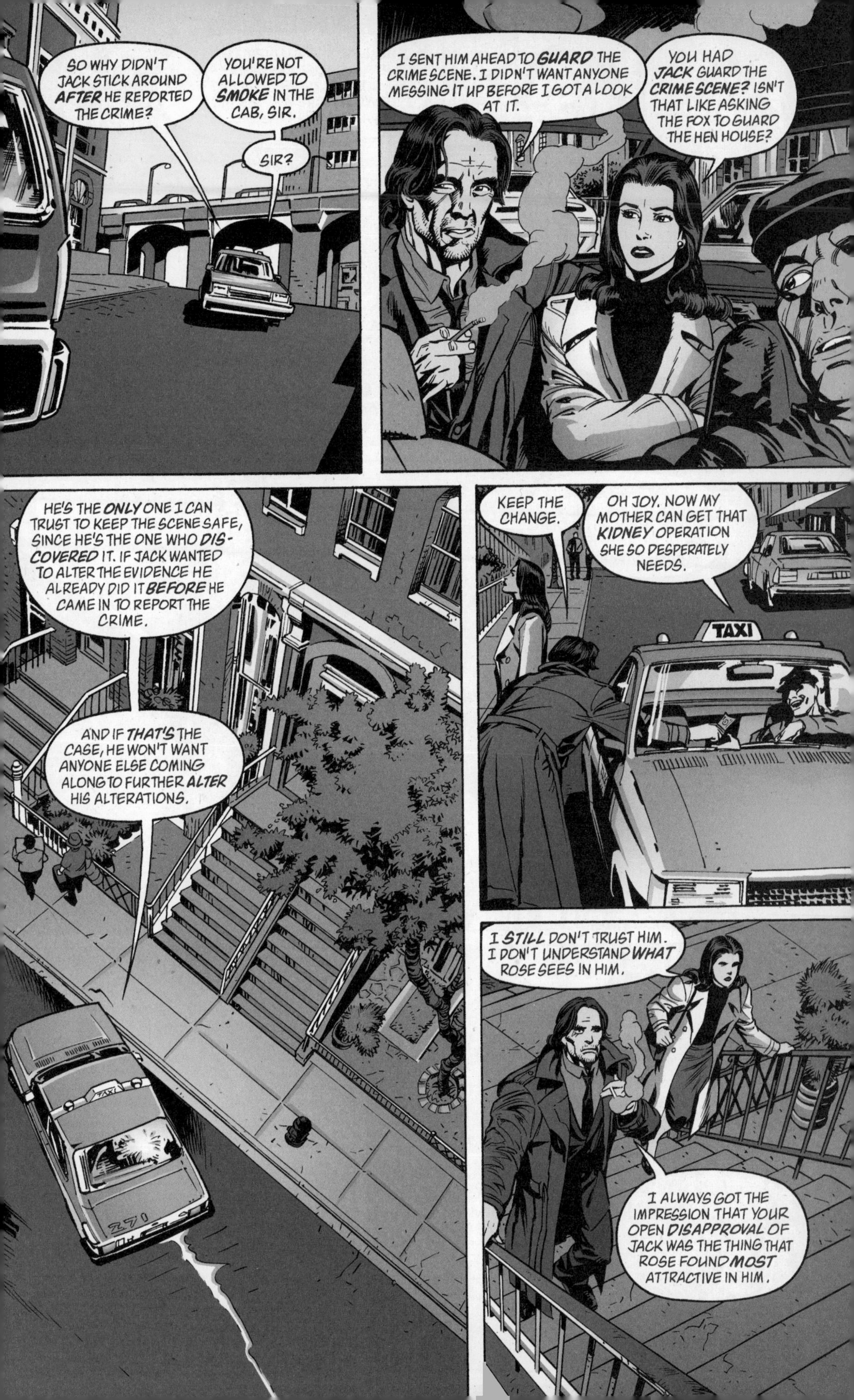

SO WHY DIDN'T JACK STICK AROUND AFTER HE REPORTED THE CRIME?
YOU'RE NOT ALLOWED TO SMOKE IN THE CAB, SIR.
SIR?
I SENT HIM AHEAD TO GUARD THE CRIME SCENE. I DIDN'T WANT ANYONE MESSING IT UP BEFORE I GOT A LOOK AT IT.
YOU HAD JACK GUARD THE CRIME SCENE? ISN'T THAT LIKE ASKING THE FOX TO GUARD THE HEN HOUSE?
HE'S THE ONLY ONE I CAN TRUST TO KEEP THE SCENE SAFE, SINCE HE'S THE ONE WHO DISCOVERED IT. IF JACK WANTED TO ALTER THE EVIDENCE HE ALREADY DID IT BEFORE HE CAME IN TO REPORT THE CRIME.
AND IF THAT'S THE CASE, HE WON'T WANT ANYONE ELSE COMING ALONG TO FURTHER ALTER HIS ALTERATIONS.
KEEP THE CHANGE.
OH JOY. NOW MY MOTHER CAN GET THAT KIDNEY OPERATION SHE SO DESPERATELY NEEDS.
TAXI
I STILL DON'T TRUST HIM. I DON'T UNDERSTAND WHAT ROSE SEES IN HIM.
I ALWAYS GOT THE IMPRESSION THAT YOUR OPEN DISAPPROVAL OF JACK WAS THE THING THAT ROSE FOUND MOST ATTRACTIVE IN HIM.

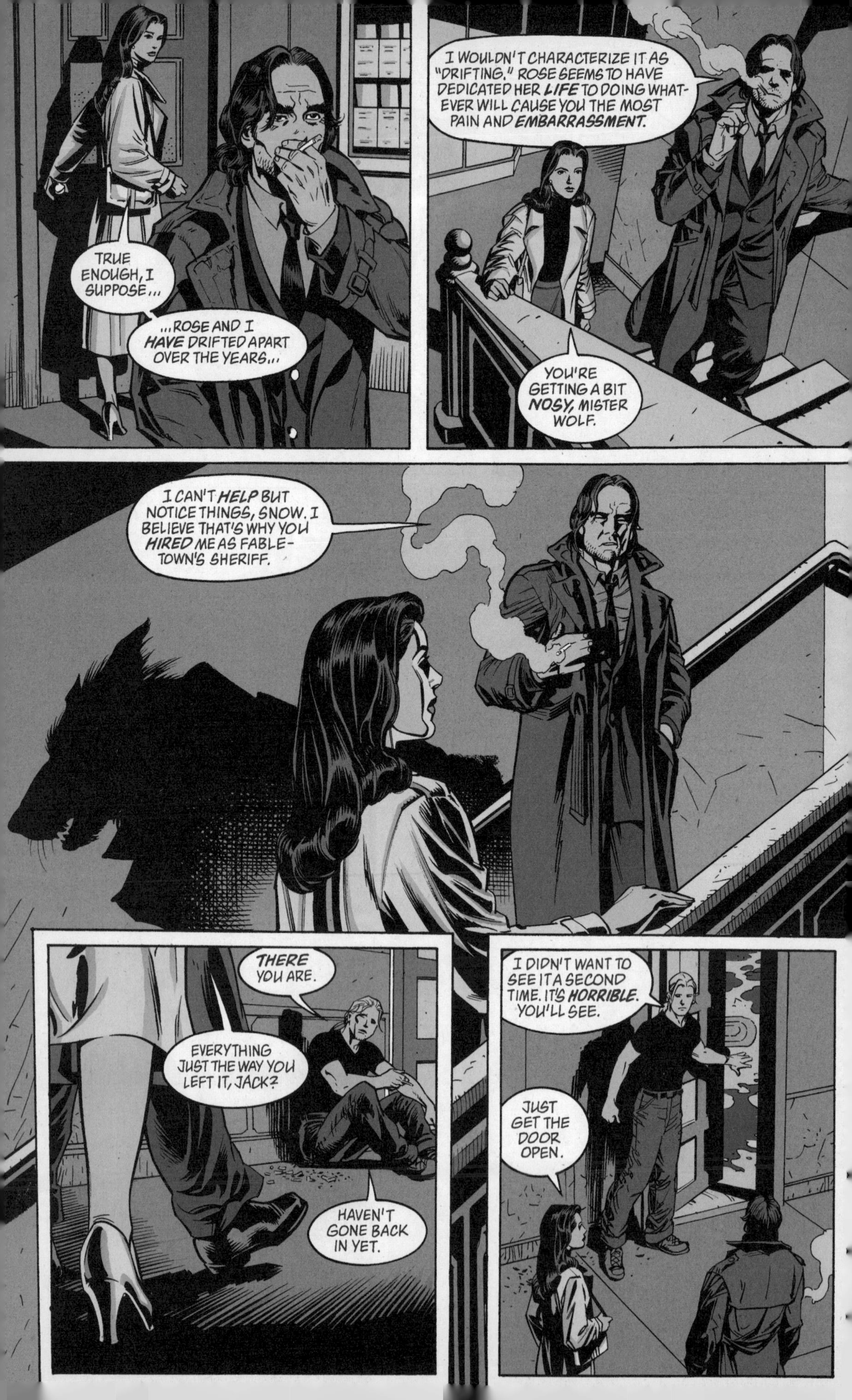
TRUE ENOUGH, I SUPPOSE...
...ROSE AND I HAVE DRIFTED APART OVER THE YEARS...
I WOULDN'T CHARACTERIZE IT AS "DRIFTING." ROSE SEEMS TO HAVE DEDICATED HER LIFE TO DOING WHATEVER WILL CAUSE YOU THE MOST PAIN AND EMBARRASSMENT.
YOU'RE GETTING A BIT NOSY, MISTER WOLF.
I CAN'T HELP BUT NOTICE THINGS, SNOW. I BELIEVE THAT'S WHY YOU HIRED ME AS FABLE-TOWN'S SHERIFF.
THERE YOU ARE.
EVERYTHING JUST THE WAY YOU LEFT IT, JACK?
HAVEN'T GONE BACK IN YET.
I DIDN'T WANT TO SEE IT A SECOND TIME. IT'S HORRIBLE. YOU'LL SEE.
JUST GET THE DOOR OPEN.

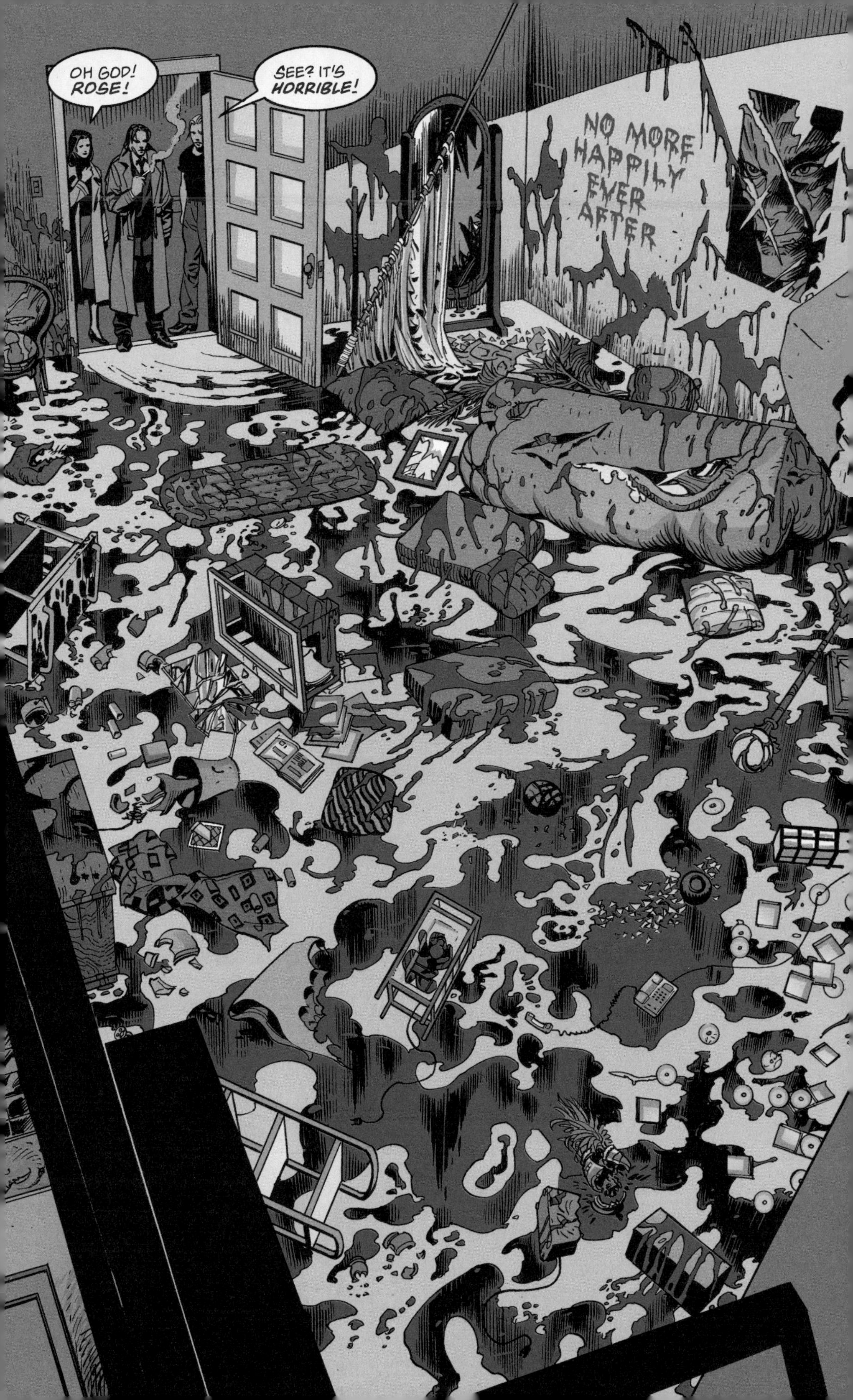
OH GOD! ROSE!
SEE? IT'S HORRIBLE!
NO MORE HAPPILY EVER AFTER

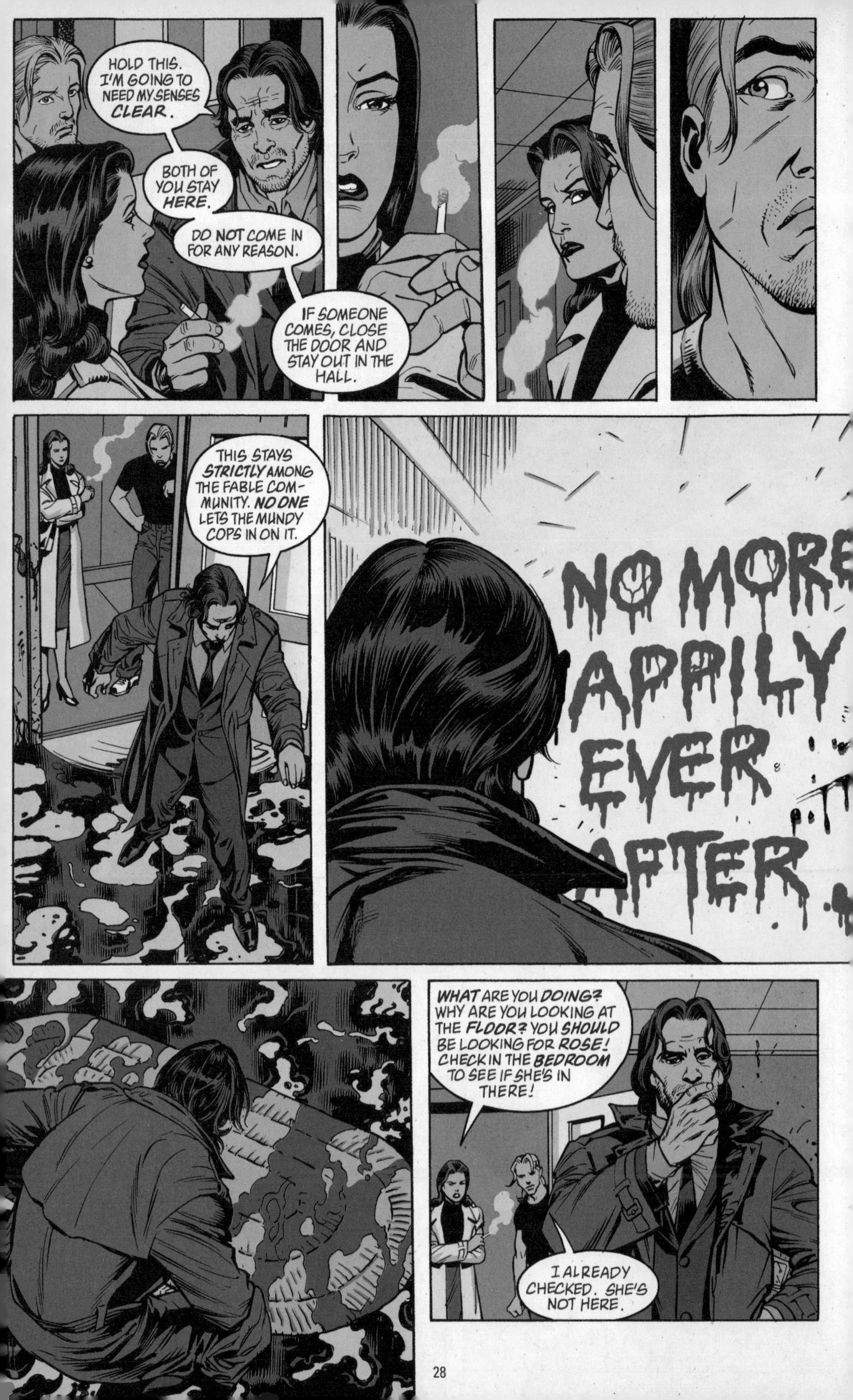
HOLD THIS. I'M GOING TO NEED MY SENSES CLEAR.
BOTH OF YOU STAY HERE.
DO NOT COME IN FOR ANY REASON.
IF SOMEONE COMES, CLOSE THE DOOR AND STAY OUT IN THE HALL.
THIS STAYS STRICTLY AMONG THE FABLE COMMUNITY. NO ONE LETS THE MUNDY COPS IN ON IT.
NO MORE APPILY EVER AFTER
WHAT ARE YOU DOING? WHY ARE YOU LOOKING AT THE FLOOR? YOU SHOULD BE LOOKING FOR ROSE! CHECK IN THE BEDROOM TO SEE IF SHE'S IN THERE!
I ALREADY CHECKED. SHE'S NOT HERE.

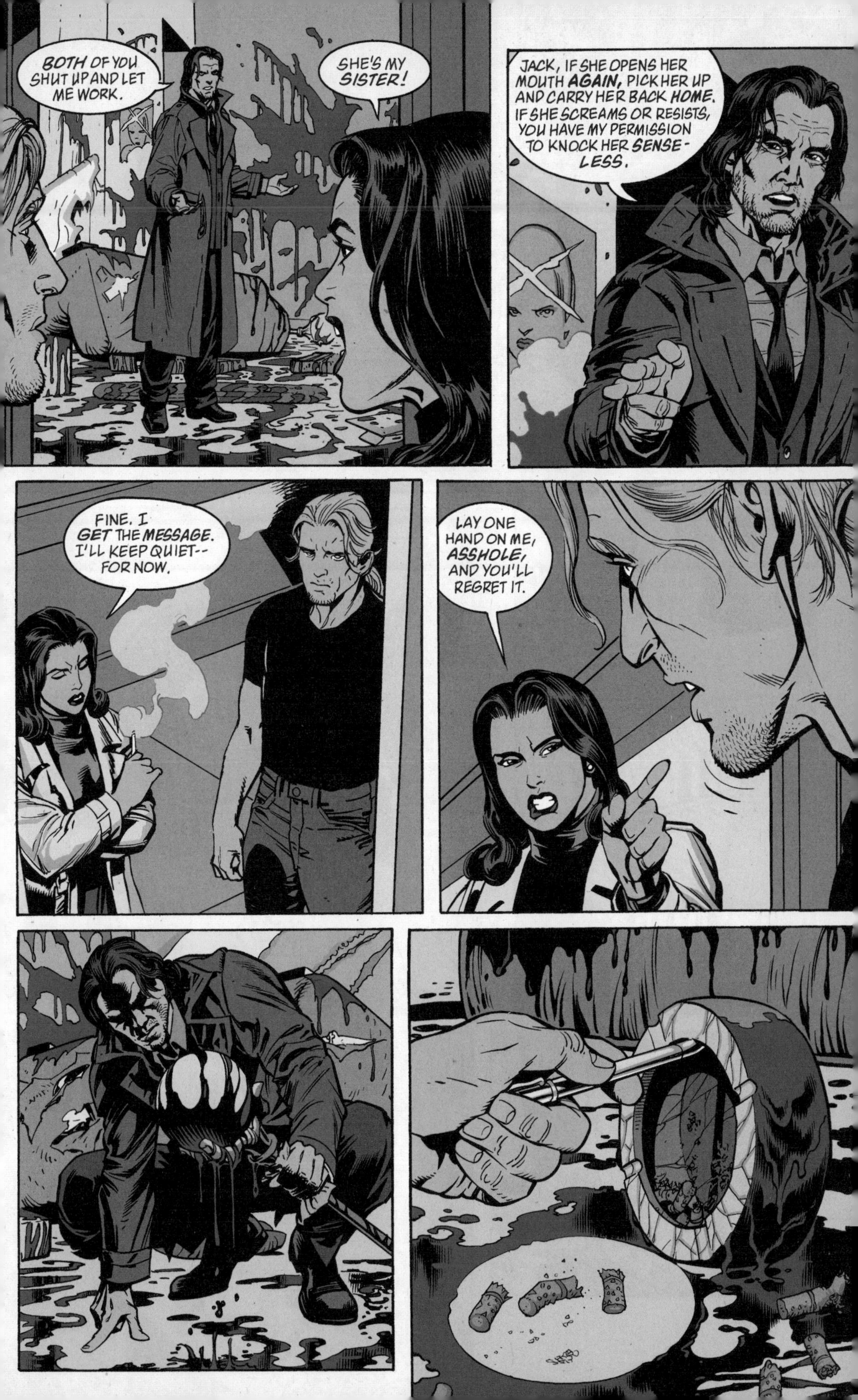
BOTH OF YOU SHUT UP AND LET ME WORK.
SHE'S MY SISTER!
JACK, IF SHE OPENS HER MOUTH AGAIN, PICK HER UP AND CARRY HER BACK HOME. IF SHE SCREAMS OR RESISTS, YOU HAVE MY PERMISSION TO KNOCK HER SENSE-LESS.
FINE. I GET THE MESSAGE. I'LL KEEP QUIET-- FOR NOW.
LAY ONE HAND ON ME, ASSHOLE, AND YOU'LL REGRET IT.

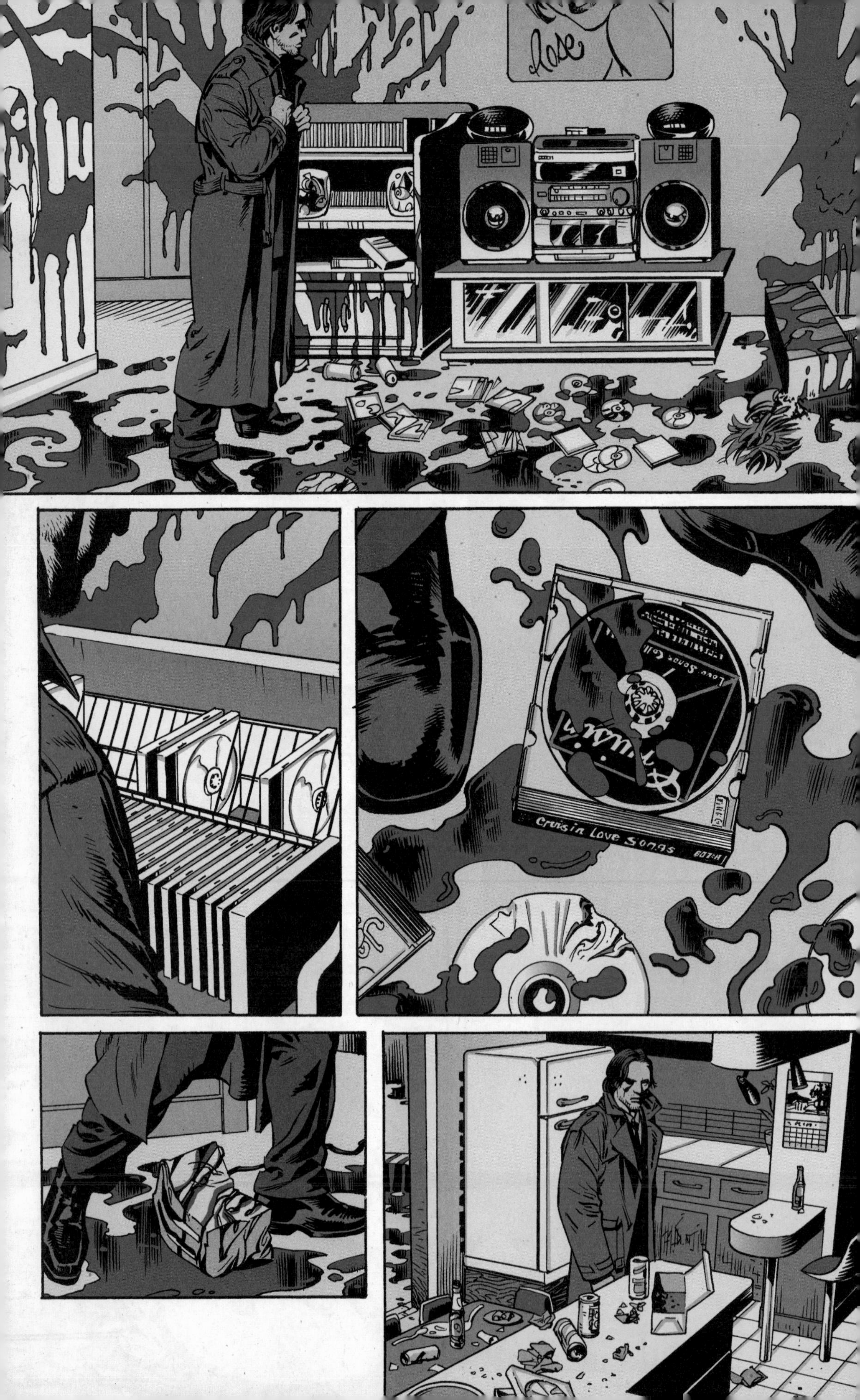
Rose
Cruisin Love Songs

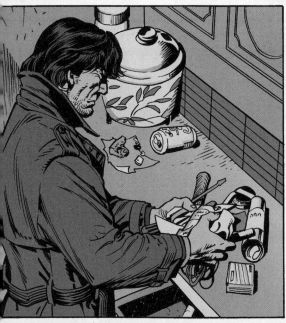

AH *HA.*

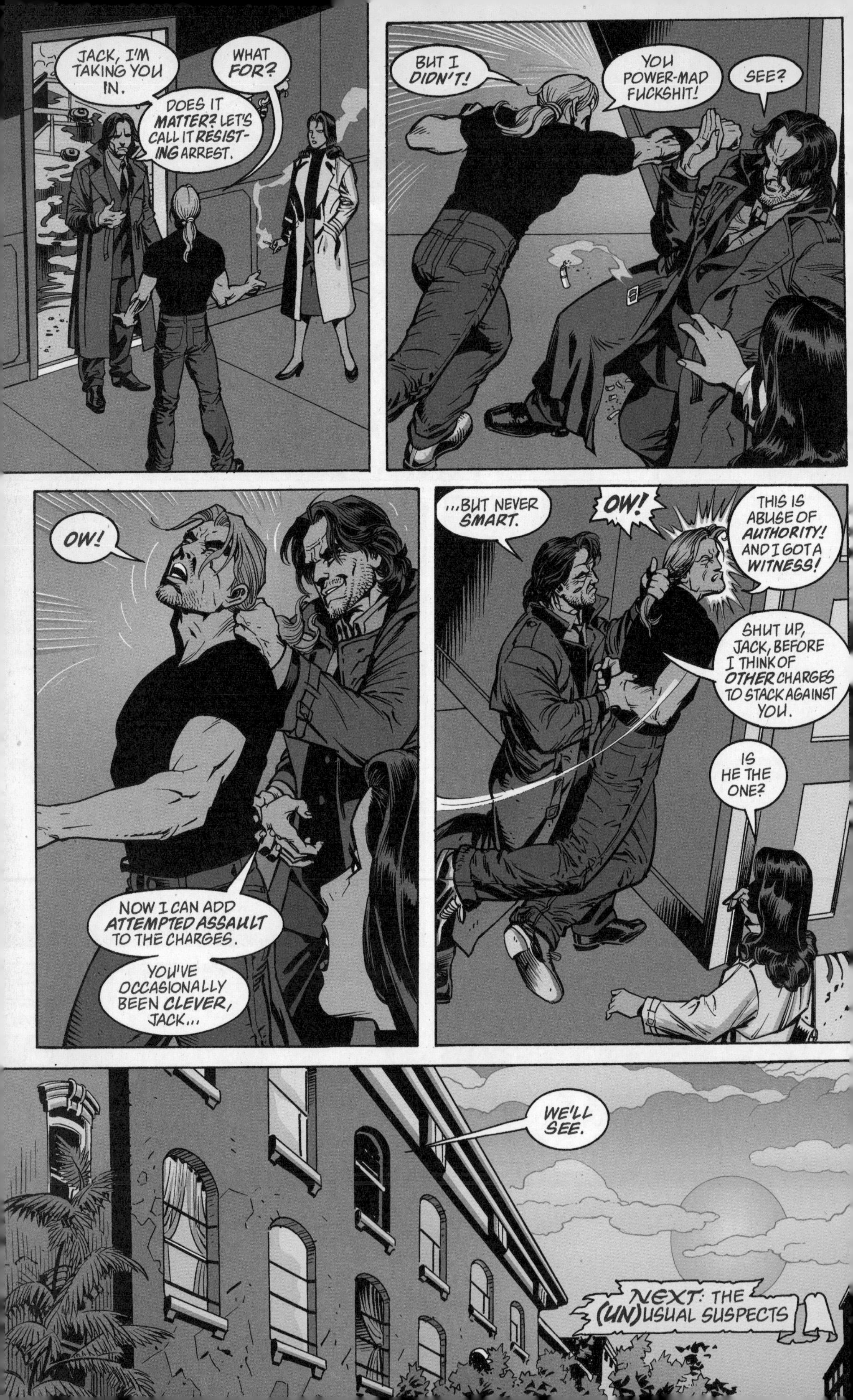
JACK, I'M TAKING YOU IN.
WHAT FOR?
DOES IT MATTER? LET'S CALL IT RESISTING ARREST.
BUT I DIDN'T!
YOU POWER-MAD FUCKSHIT!
SEE?
OW!
NOW I CAN ADD ATTEMPTED ASSAULT TO THE CHARGES.
YOU'VE OCCASIONALLY BEEN CLEVER, JACK...
...BUT NEVER SMART.
OW!
THIS IS ABUSE OF AUTHORITY! AND I GOT A WITNESS!
SHUT UP, JACK, BEFORE I THINK OF OTHER CHARGES TO STACK AGAINST YOU.
IS HE THE ONE?
WE'LL SEE.
NEXT: THE (UN)USUAL SUSPECTS

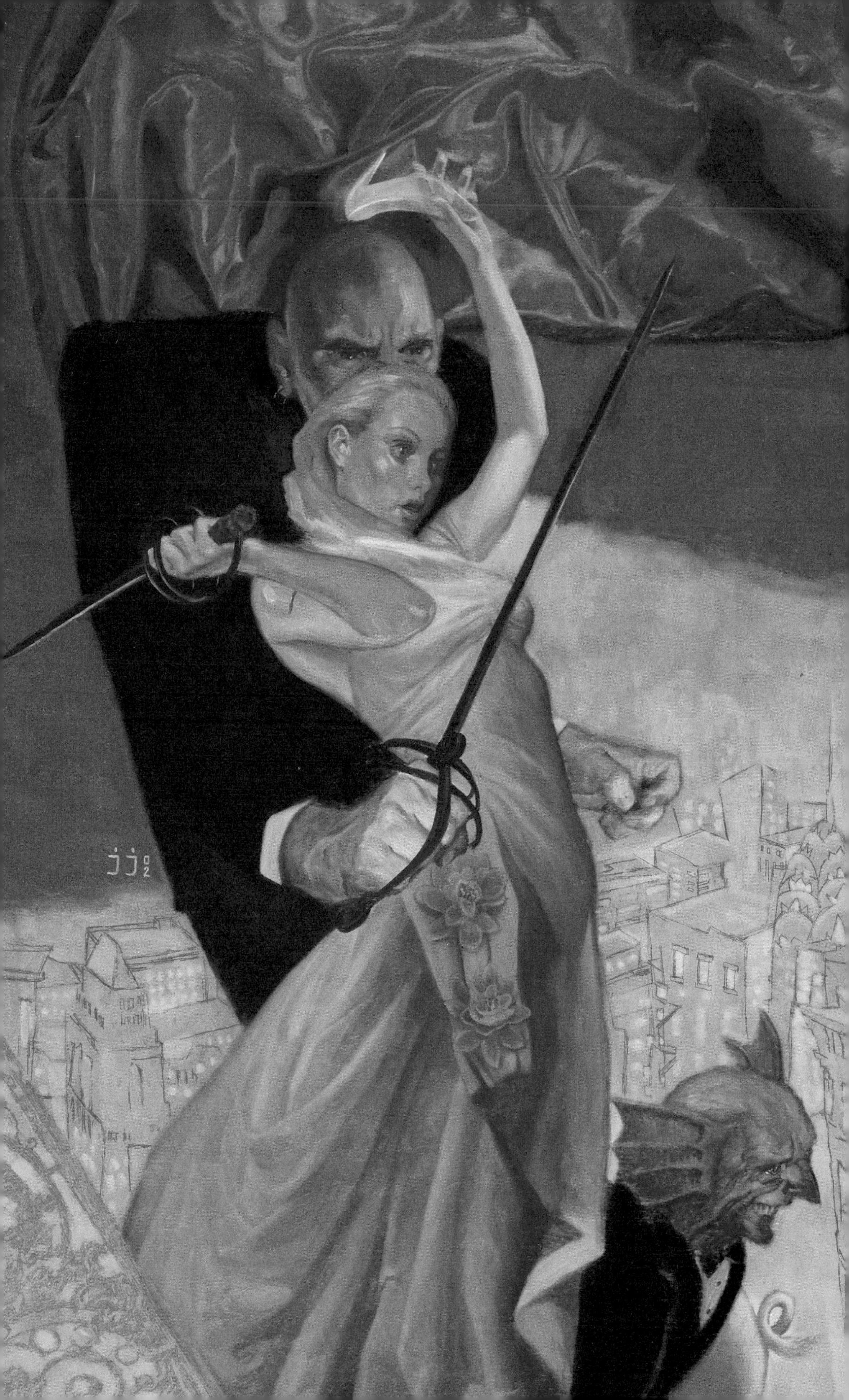

CHAPTER TWO:
THE (UN)USUAL SUSPECTS

In which our intrepid detective delves deeper into the mystery of the missing Fable, and a prince is reunited with his old lady love.

Written by	Pencilled by	Inked by
Bill Willingham	Lan Medina	Steve Leialoha
Lettered by	Colored by Sherilyn	Separated
Todd Klein	van Valkenburgh	by Zylonol
Cover art by	Assistant Editor	Editor
James Jean	Mariah Huehner	Shelly Bond

FABLES is created by Bill Willingham

THE NEXT DAY.

THE WOODLAND. THE SECRET "CITY HALL" OF THE UNDERGROUND COMMUNITY KNOWN TO ITS MEMBERS AS FABLETOWN.

FROG WENT A-COURTIN'--

--HE DID RIGHT--

--UH-HUH.

GOOD MORNING, MISS WHITE.

GRAND DAY, ISN'T IT?

LOVELY.

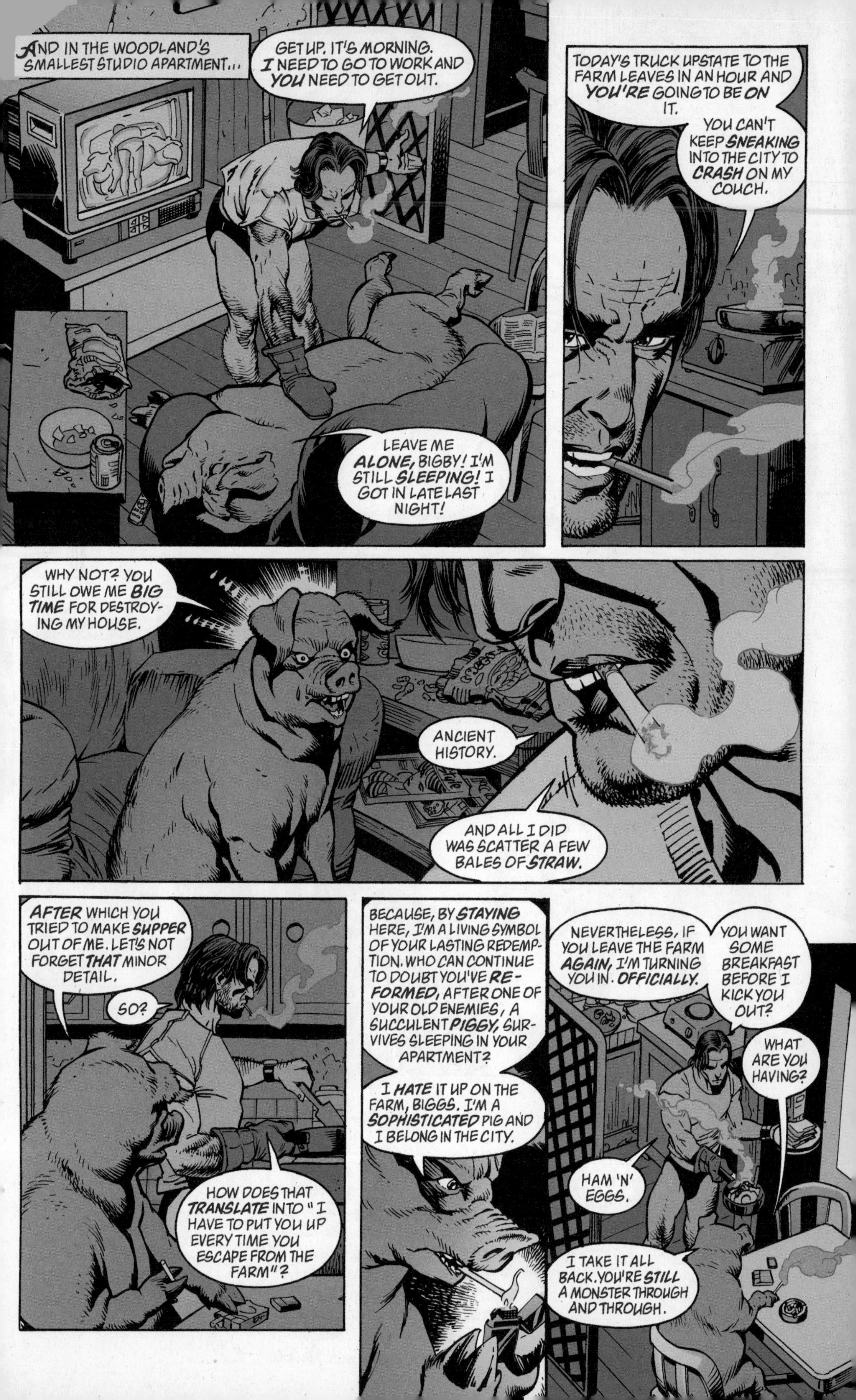
AND IN THE WOODLAND'S SMALLEST STUDIO APARTMENT...
GET UP. IT'S MORNING. I NEED TO GO TO WORK AND YOU NEED TO GET OUT.
LEAVE ME ALONE, BIGBY! I'M STILL SLEEPING! I GOT IN LATE LAST NIGHT!
TODAY'S TRUCK UPSTATE TO THE FARM LEAVES IN AN HOUR AND YOU'RE GOING TO BE ON IT.
YOU CAN'T KEEP SNEAKING INTO THE CITY TO CRASH ON MY COUCH.
WHY NOT? YOU STILL OWE ME BIG TIME FOR DESTROYING MY HOUSE.
ANCIENT HISTORY.
AND ALL I DID WAS SCATTER A FEW BALES OF STRAW.
AFTER WHICH YOU TRIED TO MAKE SUPPER OUT OF ME. LET'S NOT FORGET THAT MINOR DETAIL.
SO?
HOW DOES THAT TRANSLATE INTO "I HAVE TO PUT YOU UP EVERY TIME YOU ESCAPE FROM THE FARM"?
BECAUSE, BY STAYING HERE, I'M A LIVING SYMBOL OF YOUR LASTING REDEMPTION. WHO CAN CONTINUE TO DOUBT YOU'VE REFORMED, AFTER ONE OF YOUR OLD ENEMIES, A SUCCULENT PIGGY, SURVIVES SLEEPING IN YOUR APARTMENT?
I HATE IT UP ON THE FARM, BIGGS. I'M A SOPHISTICATED PIG AND I BELONG IN THE CITY.
NEVERTHELESS, IF YOU LEAVE THE FARM AGAIN, I'M TURNING YOU IN. OFFICIALLY.
YOU WANT SOME BREAKFAST BEFORE I KICK YOU OUT?
WHAT ARE YOU HAVING?
HAM 'N' EGGS.
I TAKE IT ALL BACK. YOU'RE STILL A MONSTER THROUGH AND THROUGH.

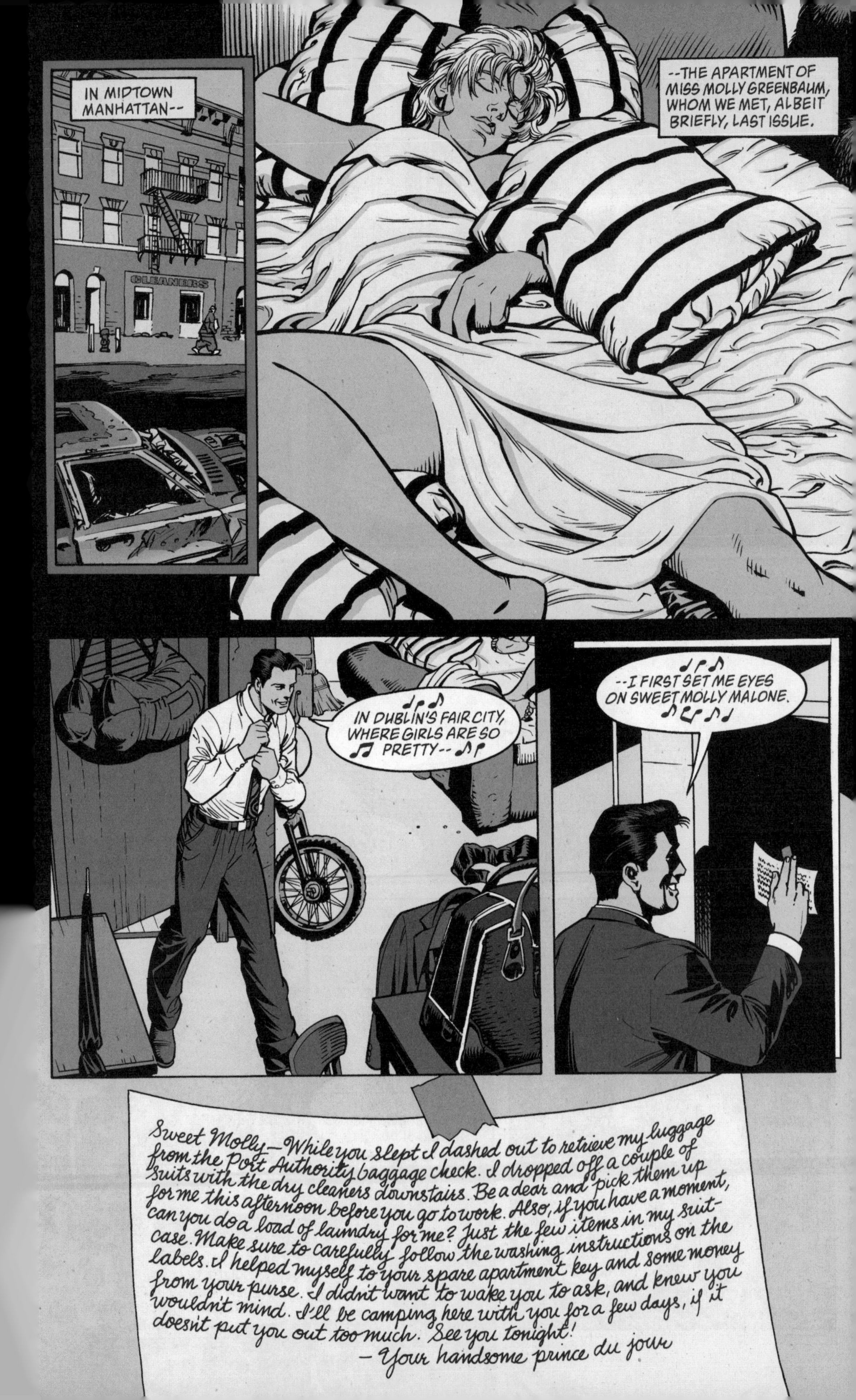

IN MIDTOWN MANHATTAN--
CLEANERS
--THE APARTMENT OF MISS MOLLY GREENBAUM, WHOM WE MET, ALBEIT BRIEFLY, LAST ISSUE.
IN DUBLIN'S FAIR CITY, WHERE GIRLS ARE SO PRETTY--
--I FIRST SET ME EYES ON SWEET MOLLY MALONE.
Sweet Molly— While you slept I dashed out to retrieve my luggage from the Port Authority baggage check. I dropped off a couple of suits with the dry cleaners downstairs. Be a dear and pick them up for me this afternoon before you go to work. Also, if you have a moment, can you do a load of laundry for me? Just the few items in my suit-case. Make sure to carefully follow the washing instructions on the labels. I helped myself to your spare apartment key and some money from your purse. I didn't want to wake you to ask, and knew you wouldn't mind. I'll be camping here with you for a few days, if it doesn't put you out too much. See you tonight!
— Your handsome prince du jour

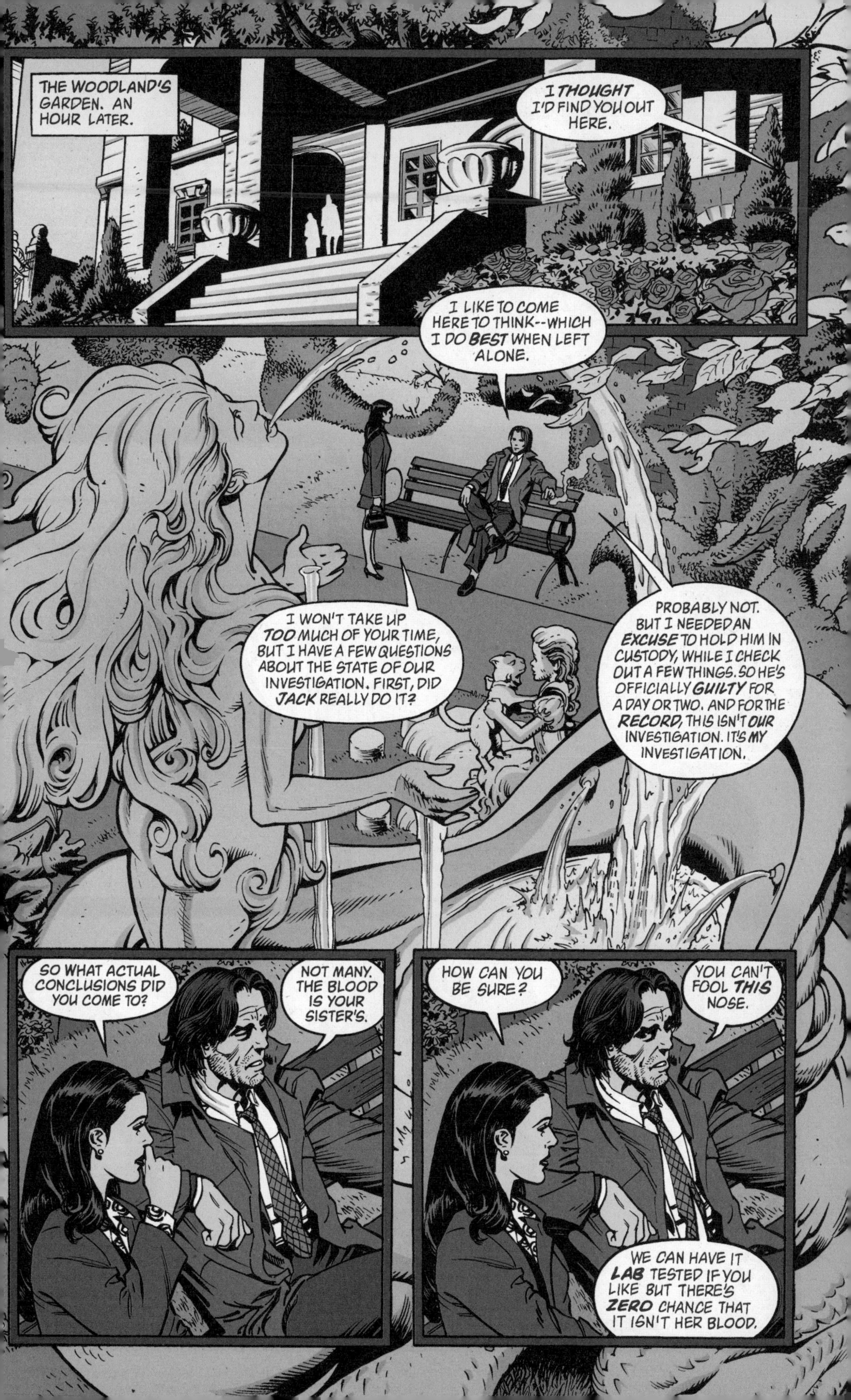
THE WOODLAND'S GARDEN. AN HOUR LATER.
I THOUGHT I'D FIND YOU OUT HERE.
I LIKE TO COME HERE TO THINK--WHICH I DO BEST WHEN LEFT ALONE.
I WON'T TAKE UP TOO MUCH OF YOUR TIME, BUT I HAVE A FEW QUESTIONS ABOUT THE STATE OF OUR INVESTIGATION. FIRST, DID JACK REALLY DO IT?
PROBABLY NOT. BUT I NEEDED AN EXCUSE TO HOLD HIM IN CUSTODY, WHILE I CHECK OUT A FEW THINGS. SO HE'S OFFICIALLY GUILTY FOR A DAY OR TWO. AND FOR THE RECORD, THIS ISN'T OUR INVESTIGATION. IT'S MY INVESTIGATION.
SO WHAT ACTUAL CONCLUSIONS DID YOU COME TO?
NOT MANY. THE BLOOD IS YOUR SISTER'S.
HOW CAN YOU BE SURE?
YOU CAN'T FOOL THIS NOSE.
WE CAN HAVE IT LAB TESTED IF YOU LIKE BUT THERE'S ZERO CHANCE THAT IT ISN'T HER BLOOD.

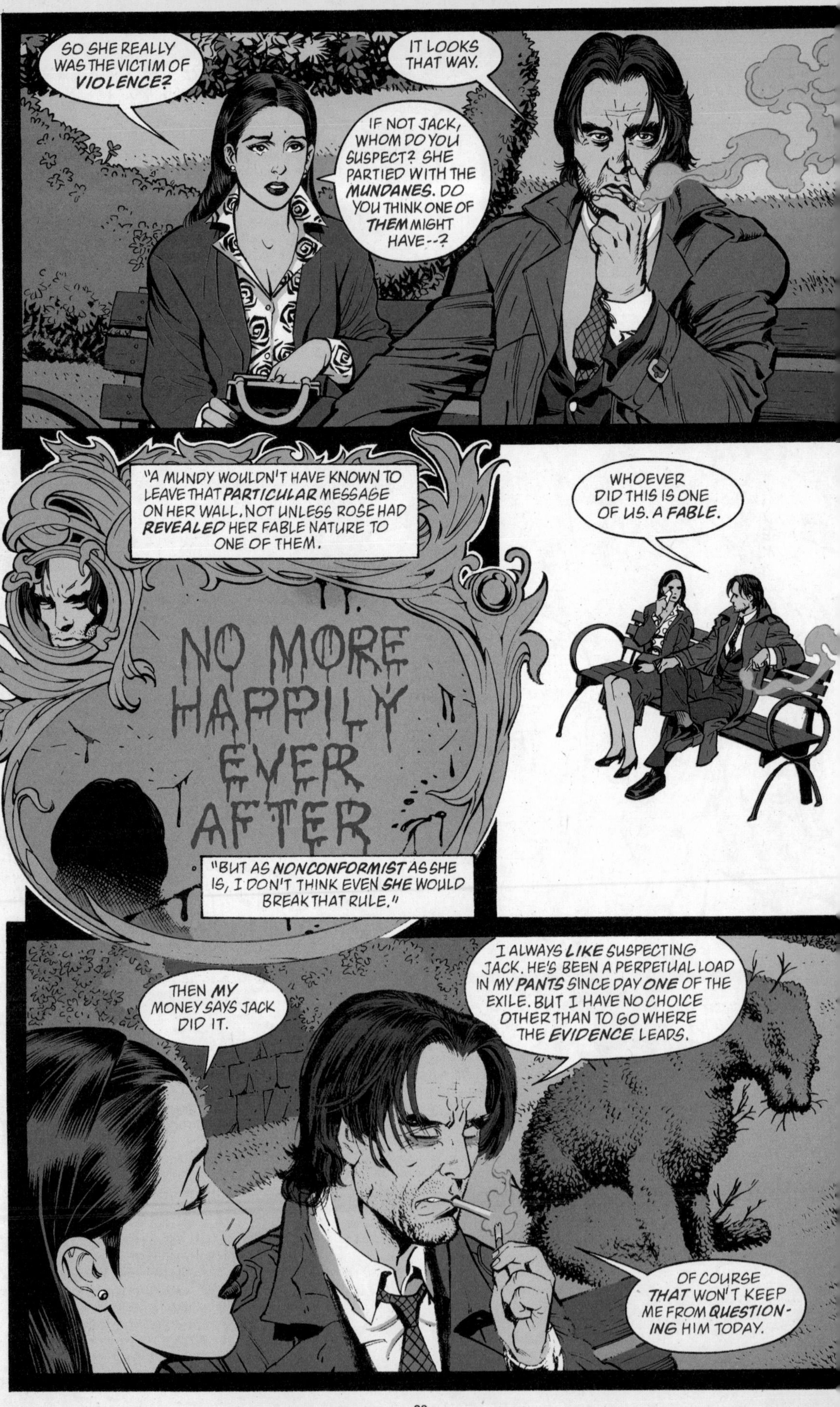

SO SHE REALLY WAS THE VICTIM OF VIOLENCE?
IT LOOKS THAT WAY.
IF NOT JACK, WHOM DO YOU SUSPECT? SHE PARTIED WITH THE MUNDANES. DO YOU THINK ONE OF THEM MIGHT HAVE--?
"A MUNDY WOULDN'T HAVE KNOWN TO LEAVE THAT PARTICULAR MESSAGE ON HER WALL, NOT UNLESS ROSE HAD REVEALED HER FABLE NATURE TO ONE OF THEM.
NO MORE HAPPILY EVER AFTER
"BUT AS NONCONFORMIST AS SHE IS, I DON'T THINK EVEN SHE WOULD BREAK THAT RULE."
WHOEVER DID THIS IS ONE OF US. A FABLE.
THEN MY MONEY SAYS JACK DID IT.
I ALWAYS LIKE SUSPECTING JACK. HE'S BEEN A PERPETUAL LOAD IN MY PANTS SINCE DAY ONE OF THE EXILE. BUT I HAVE NO CHOICE OTHER THAN TO GO WHERE THE EVIDENCE LEADS.
OF COURSE THAT WON'T KEEP ME FROM QUESTIONING HIM TODAY.

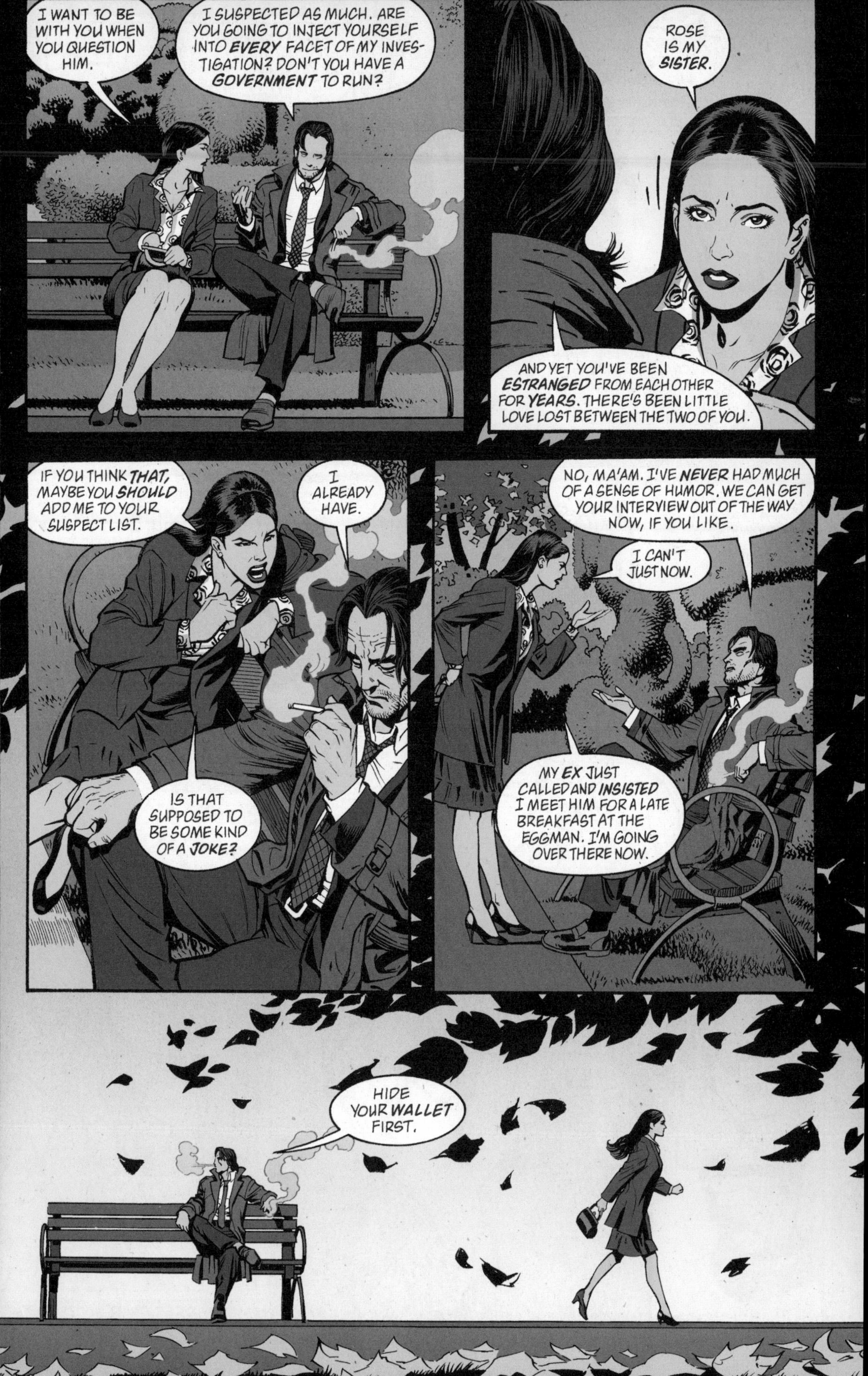
I WANT TO BE WITH YOU WHEN YOU QUESTION HIM.
I SUSPECTED AS MUCH. ARE YOU GOING TO INJECT YOURSELF INTO EVERY FACET OF MY INVESTIGATION? DON'T YOU HAVE A GOVERNMENT TO RUN?
ROSE IS MY SISTER.
AND YET YOU'VE BEEN ESTRANGED FROM EACH OTHER FOR YEARS. THERE'S BEEN LITTLE LOVE LOST BETWEEN THE TWO OF YOU.
IF YOU THINK THAT, MAYBE YOU SHOULD ADD ME TO YOUR SUSPECT LIST.
I ALREADY HAVE.
IS THAT SUPPOSED TO BE SOME KIND OF A JOKE?
NO, MA'AM. I'VE NEVER HAD MUCH OF A SENSE OF HUMOR. WE CAN GET YOUR INTERVIEW OUT OF THE WAY NOW, IF YOU LIKE.
I CAN'T JUST NOW.
MY EX JUST CALLED AND INSISTED I MEET HIM FOR A LATE BREAKFAST AT THE EGGMAN. I'M GOING OVER THERE NOW.
HIDE YOUR WALLET FIRST.

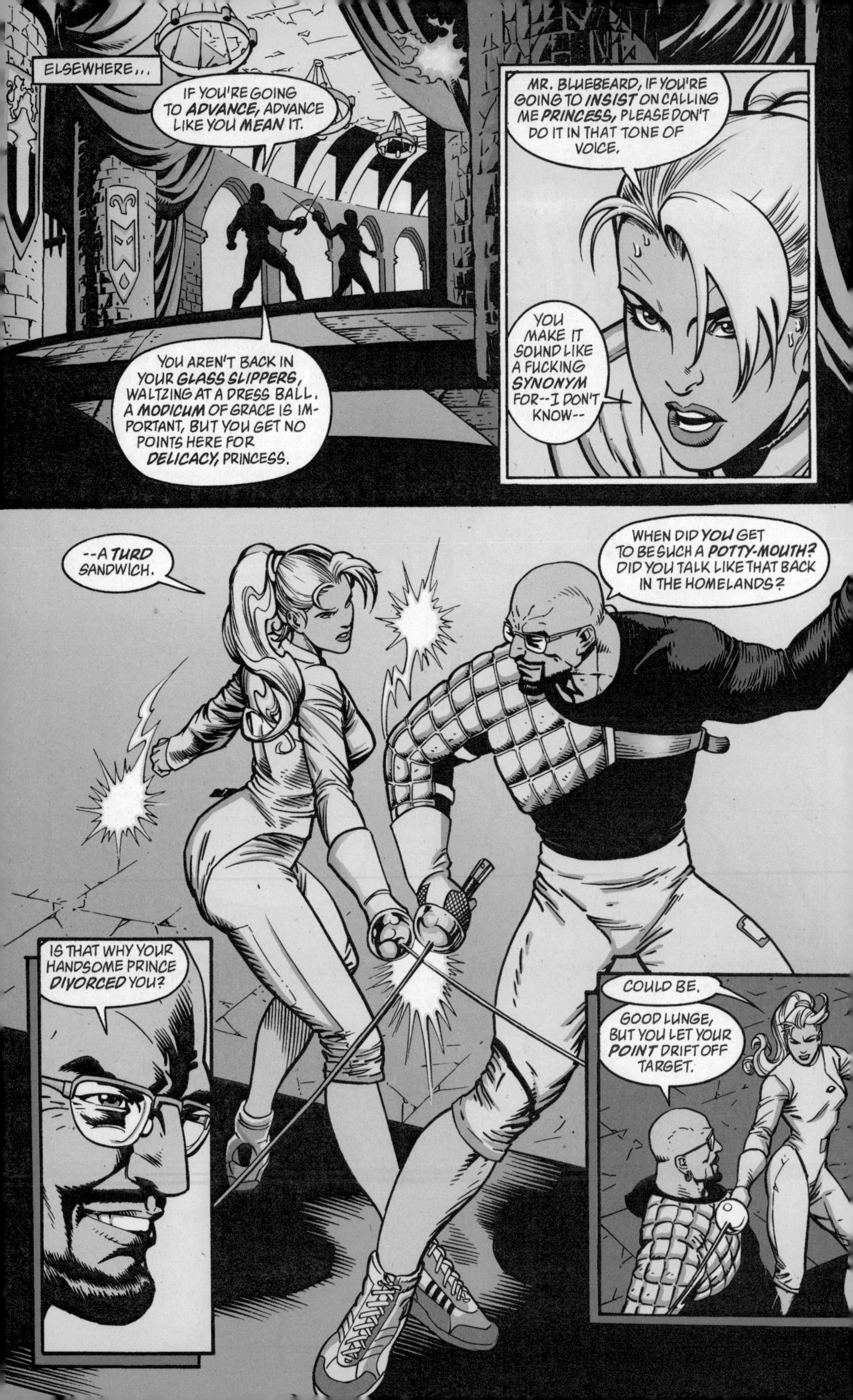
ELSEWHERE...
IF YOU'RE GOING TO ADVANCE, ADVANCE LIKE YOU MEAN IT.
YOU AREN'T BACK IN YOUR GLASS SLIPPERS, WALTZING AT A DRESS BALL. A MODICUM OF GRACE IS IMPORTANT, BUT YOU GET NO POINTS HERE FOR DELICACY, PRINCESS.
MR. BLUEBEARD, IF YOU'RE GOING TO INSIST ON CALLING ME PRINCESS, PLEASE DON'T DO IT IN THAT TONE OF VOICE.
YOU MAKE IT SOUND LIKE A FUCKING SYNONYM FOR--I DON'T KNOW--
--A TURD SANDWICH.
WHEN DID YOU GET TO BE SUCH A POTTY-MOUTH? DID YOU TALK LIKE THAT BACK IN THE HOMELANDS?
IS THAT WHY YOUR HANDSOME PRINCE DIVORCED YOU?
COULD BE.
GOOD LUNGE, BUT YOU LET YOUR POINT DRIFT OFF TARGET.

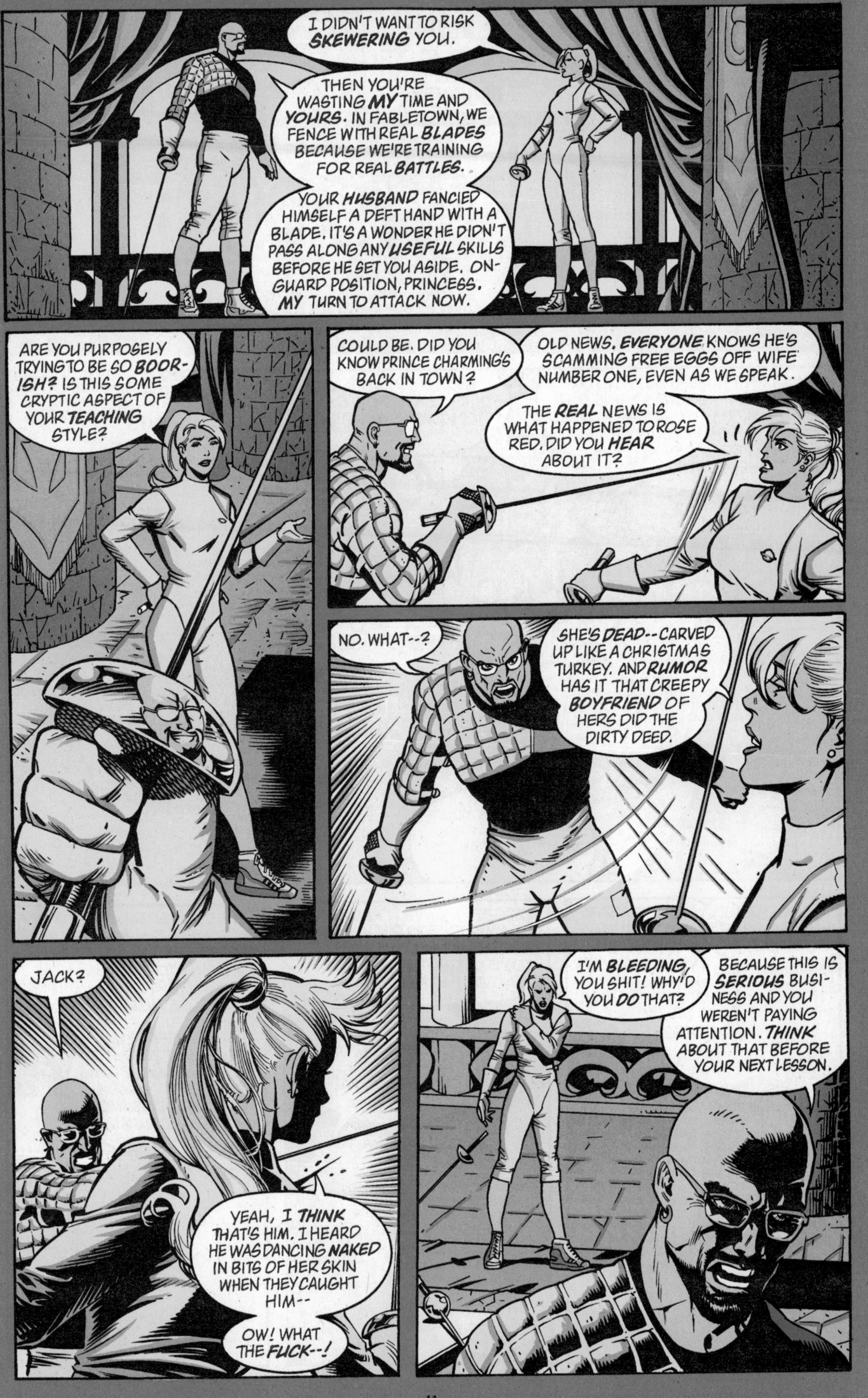
I DIDN'T WANT TO RISK SKEWERING YOU.
THEN YOU'RE WASTING MY TIME AND YOURS. IN FABLETOWN, WE FENCE WITH REAL BLADES BECAUSE WE'RE TRAINING FOR REAL BATTLES.
YOUR HUSBAND FANCIED HIMSELF A DEFT HAND WITH A BLADE. IT'S A WONDER HE DIDN'T PASS ALONG ANY USEFUL SKILLS BEFORE HE SET YOU ASIDE. ON-GUARD POSITION, PRINCESS. MY TURN TO ATTACK NOW.
ARE YOU PURPOSELY TRYING TO BE SO BOORISH? IS THIS SOME CRYPTIC ASPECT OF YOUR TEACHING STYLE?
COULD BE. DID YOU KNOW PRINCE CHARMING'S BACK IN TOWN?
OLD NEWS. EVERYONE KNOWS HE'S SCAMMING FREE EGGS OFF WIFE NUMBER ONE, EVEN AS WE SPEAK.
THE REAL NEWS IS WHAT HAPPENED TO ROSE RED. DID YOU HEAR ABOUT IT?
NO. WHAT--?
SHE'S DEAD--CARVED UP LIKE A CHRISTMAS TURKEY. AND RUMOR HAS IT THAT CREEPY BOYFRIEND OF HERS DID THE DIRTY DEED.
JACK?
YEAH, I THINK THAT'S HIM. I HEARD HE WAS DANCING NAKED IN BITS OF HER SKIN WHEN THEY CAUGHT HIM--
OW! WHAT THE FUCK--!
I'M BLEEDING, YOU SHIT! WHY'D YOU DO THAT?
BECAUSE THIS IS SERIOUS BUSINESS AND YOU WEREN'T PAYING ATTENTION. THINK ABOUT THAT BEFORE YOUR NEXT LESSON.

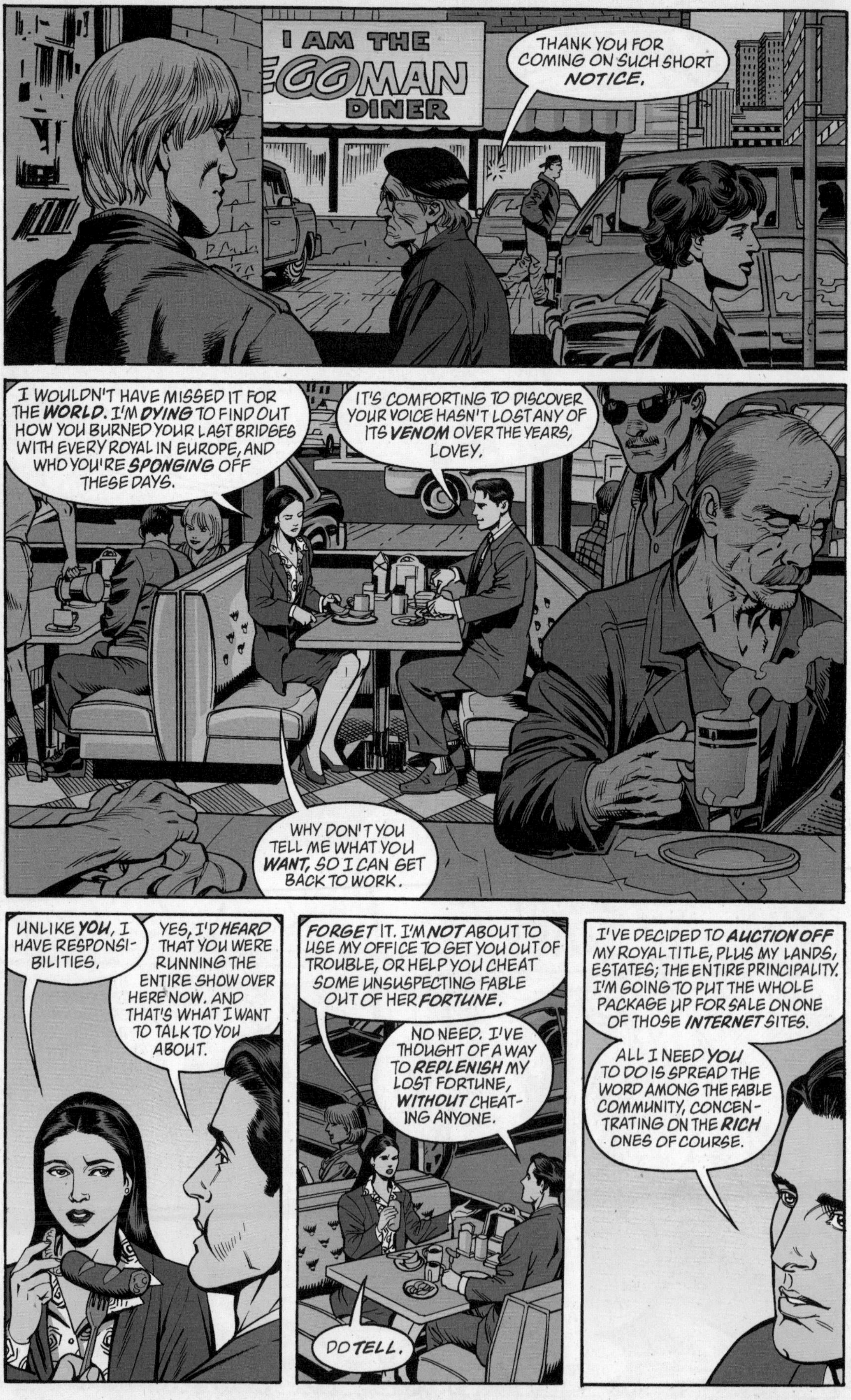
I AM THE EGGMAN DINER
THANK YOU FOR COMING ON SUCH SHORT NOTICE.
I WOULDN'T HAVE MISSED IT FOR THE WORLD. I'M DYING TO FIND OUT HOW YOU BURNED YOUR LAST BRIDGES WITH EVERY ROYAL IN EUROPE, AND WHO YOU'RE SPONGING OFF THESE DAYS.
IT'S COMFORTING TO DISCOVER YOUR VOICE HASN'T LOST ANY OF ITS VENOM OVER THE YEARS, LOVEY.
WHY DON'T YOU TELL ME WHAT YOU WANT, SO I CAN GET BACK TO WORK.
UNLIKE YOU, I HAVE RESPONSI-BILITIES.
YES, I'D HEARD THAT YOU WERE RUNNING THE ENTIRE SHOW OVER HERE NOW. AND THAT'S WHAT I WANT TO TALK TO YOU ABOUT.
FORGET IT. I'M NOT ABOUT TO USE MY OFFICE TO GET YOU OUT OF TROUBLE, OR HELP YOU CHEAT SOME UNSUSPECTING FABLE OUT OF HER FORTUNE.
NO NEED. I'VE THOUGHT OF A WAY TO REPLENISH MY LOST FORTUNE, WITHOUT CHEAT-ING ANYONE.
DO TELL.
I'VE DECIDED TO AUCTION OFF MY ROYAL TITLE, PLUS MY LANDS, ESTATES; THE ENTIRE PRINCIPALITY. I'M GOING TO PUT THE WHOLE PACKAGE UP FOR SALE ON ONE OF THOSE INTERNET SITES.
ALL I NEED YOU TO DO IS SPREAD THE WORD AMONG THE FABLE COMMUNITY, CONCEN-TRATING ON THE RICH ONES OF COURSE.

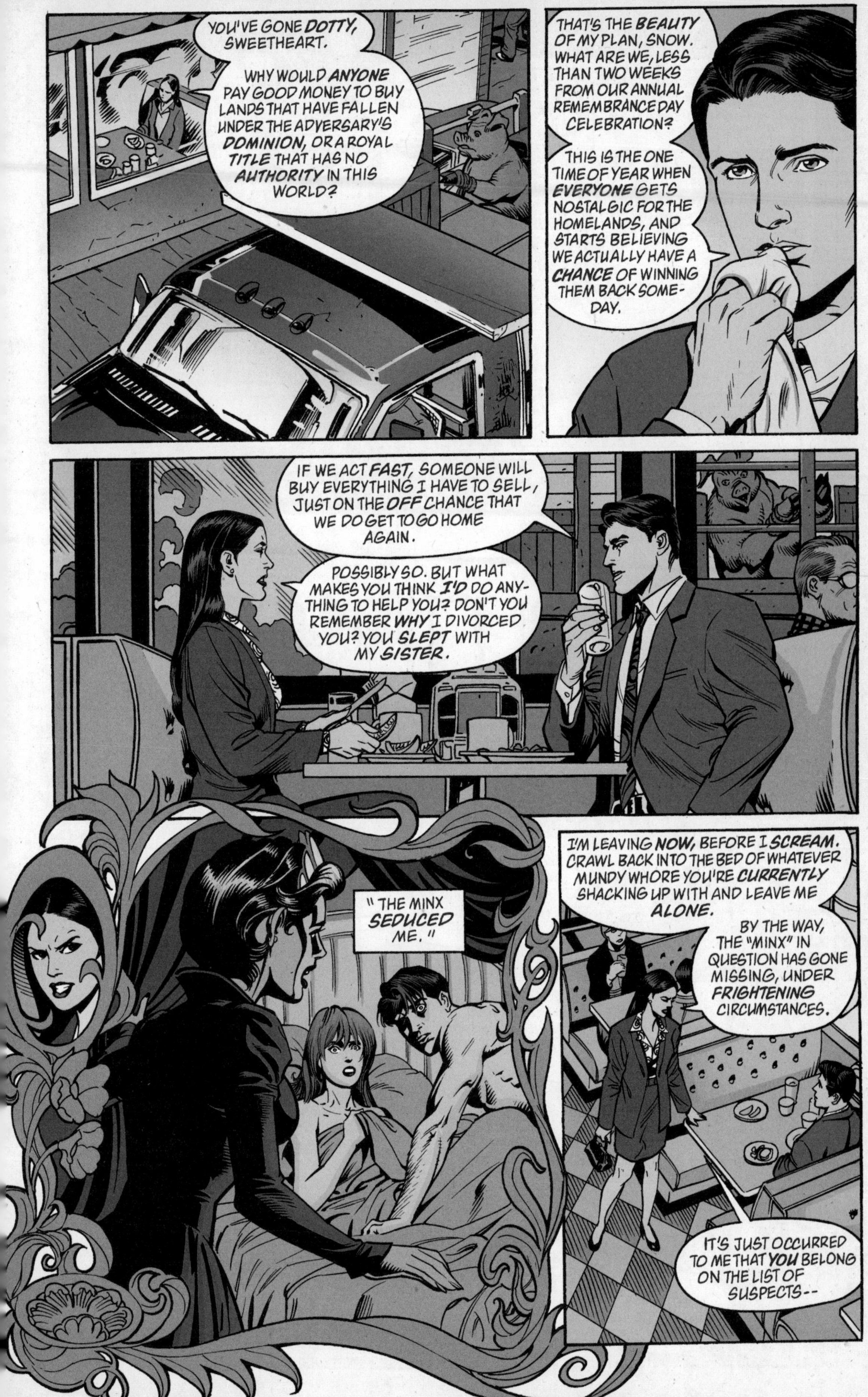

YOU'VE GONE DOTTY, SWEETHEART.
WHY WOULD ANYONE PAY GOOD MONEY TO BUY LANDS THAT HAVE FALLEN UNDER THE ADVERSARY'S DOMINION, OR A ROYAL TITLE THAT HAS NO AUTHORITY IN THIS WORLD?
THAT'S THE BEAUTY OF MY PLAN, SNOW. WHAT ARE WE, LESS THAN TWO WEEKS FROM OUR ANNUAL REMEMBRANCE DAY CELEBRATION?
THIS IS THE ONE TIME OF YEAR WHEN EVERYONE GETS NOSTALGIC FOR THE HOMELANDS, AND STARTS BELIEVING WE ACTUALLY HAVE A CHANCE OF WINNING THEM BACK SOME-DAY.
IF WE ACT FAST, SOMEONE WILL BUY EVERYTHING I HAVE TO SELL, JUST ON THE OFF CHANCE THAT WE DO GET TO GO HOME AGAIN.
POSSIBLY SO. BUT WHAT MAKES YOU THINK I'D DO ANYTHING TO HELP YOU? DON'T YOU REMEMBER WHY I DIVORCED YOU? YOU SLEPT WITH MY SISTER.
"THE MINX SEDUCED ME."
I'M LEAVING NOW, BEFORE I SCREAM. CRAWL BACK INTO THE BED OF WHATEVER MUNDY WHORE YOU'RE CURRENTLY SHACKING UP WITH AND LEAVE ME ALONE.
BY THE WAY, THE "MINX" IN QUESTION HAS GONE MISSING, UNDER FRIGHTENING CIRCUMSTANCES.
IT'S JUST OCCURRED TO ME THAT YOU BELONG ON THE LIST OF SUSPECTS--

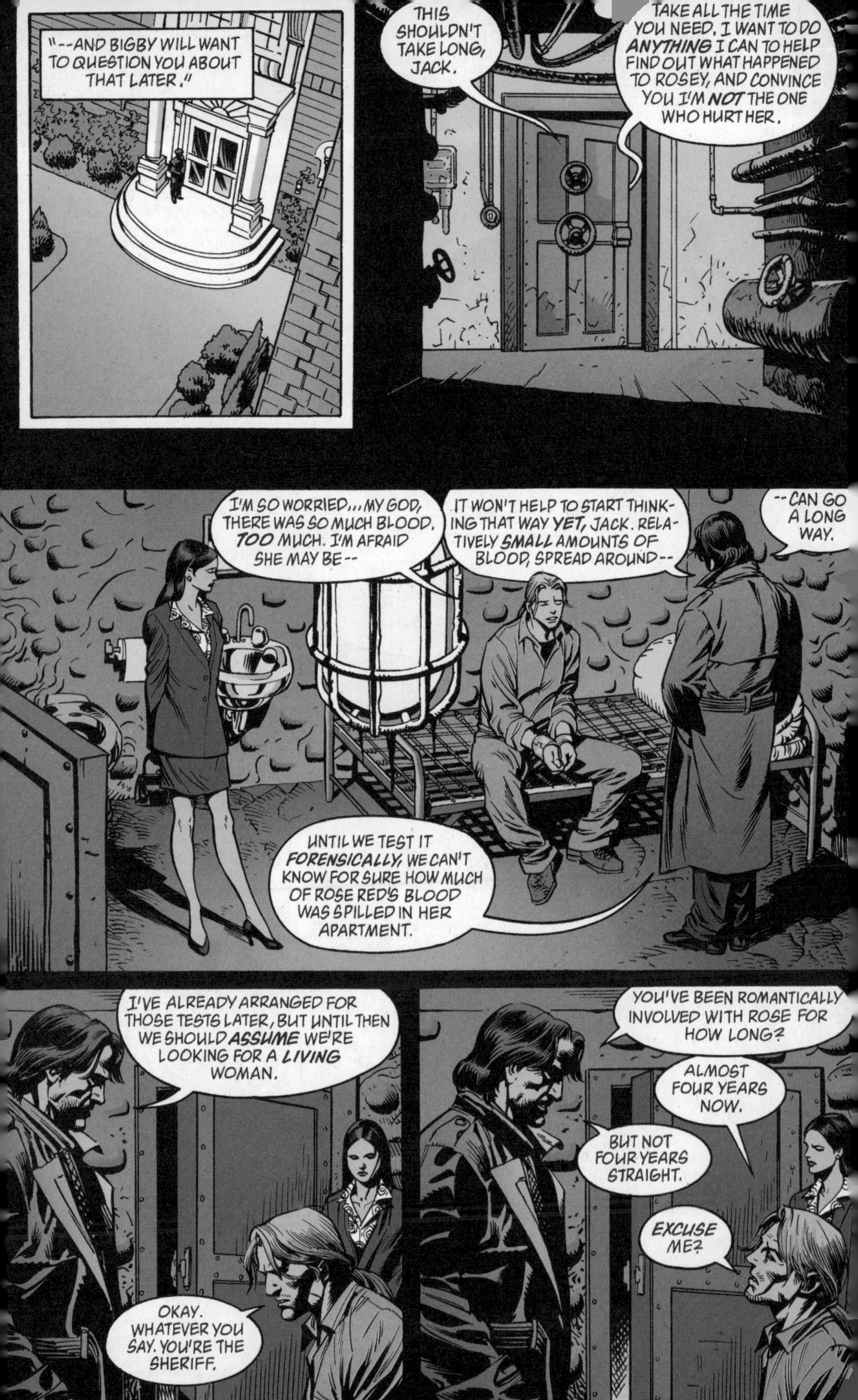
"--AND BIGBY WILL WANT TO QUESTION YOU ABOUT THAT LATER."
THIS SHOULDN'T TAKE LONG, JACK.
TAKE ALL THE TIME YOU NEED. I WANT TO DO ANYTHING I CAN TO HELP FIND OUT WHAT HAPPENED TO ROSEY, AND CONVINCE YOU I'M NOT THE ONE WHO HURT HER.
I'M SO WORRIED... MY GOD, THERE WAS SO MUCH BLOOD. TOO MUCH. I'M AFRAID SHE MAY BE--
IT WON'T HELP TO START THINKING THAT WAY YET, JACK. RELATIVELY SMALL AMOUNTS OF BLOOD, SPREAD AROUND--
--CAN GO A LONG WAY.
UNTIL WE TEST IT FORENSICALLY, WE CAN'T KNOW FOR SURE HOW MUCH OF ROSE RED'S BLOOD WAS SPILLED IN HER APARTMENT.
I'VE ALREADY ARRANGED FOR THOSE TESTS LATER, BUT UNTIL THEN WE SHOULD ASSUME WE'RE LOOKING FOR A LIVING WOMAN.
OKAY. WHATEVER YOU SAY. YOU'RE THE SHERIFF.
YOU'VE BEEN ROMANTICALLY INVOLVED WITH ROSE FOR HOW LONG?
ALMOST FOUR YEARS NOW.
BUT NOT FOUR YEARS STRAIGHT.
EXCUSE ME?

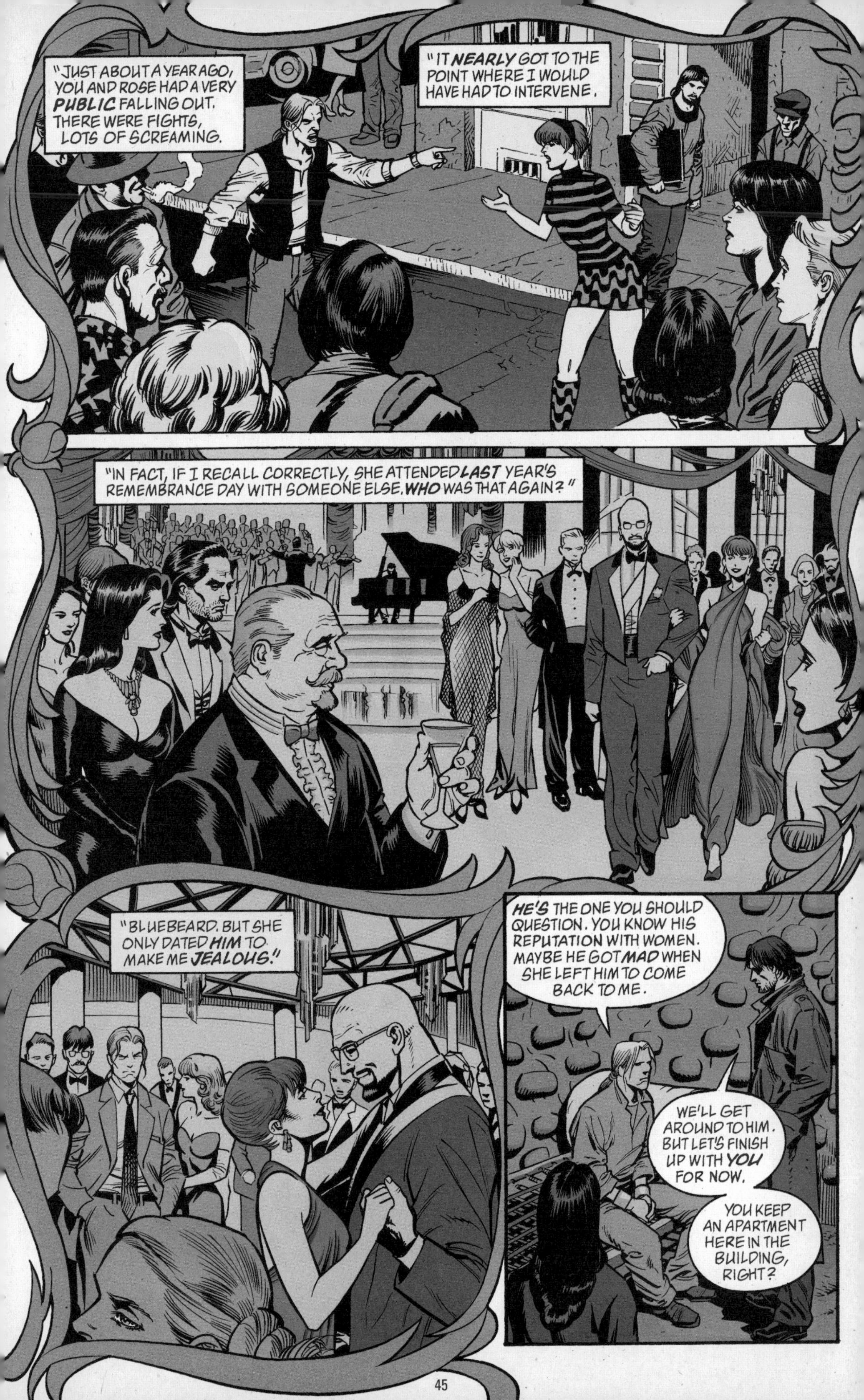

"JUST ABOUT A YEAR AGO, YOU AND ROSE HAD A VERY PUBLIC FALLING OUT. THERE WERE FIGHTS, LOTS OF SCREAMING.
"IT NEARLY GOT TO THE POINT WHERE I WOULD HAVE HAD TO INTERVENE.
"IN FACT, IF I RECALL CORRECTLY, SHE ATTENDED LAST YEAR'S REMEMBRANCE DAY WITH SOMEONE ELSE. WHO WAS THAT AGAIN?"
"BLUEBEARD. BUT SHE ONLY DATED HIM TO MAKE ME JEALOUS."
HE'S THE ONE YOU SHOULD QUESTION. YOU KNOW HIS REPUTATION WITH WOMEN. MAYBE HE GOT MAD WHEN SHE LEFT HIM TO COME BACK TO ME.
WE'LL GET AROUND TO HIM. BUT LET'S FINISH UP WITH YOU FOR NOW.
YOU KEEP AN APARTMENT HERE IN THE BUILDING, RIGHT?

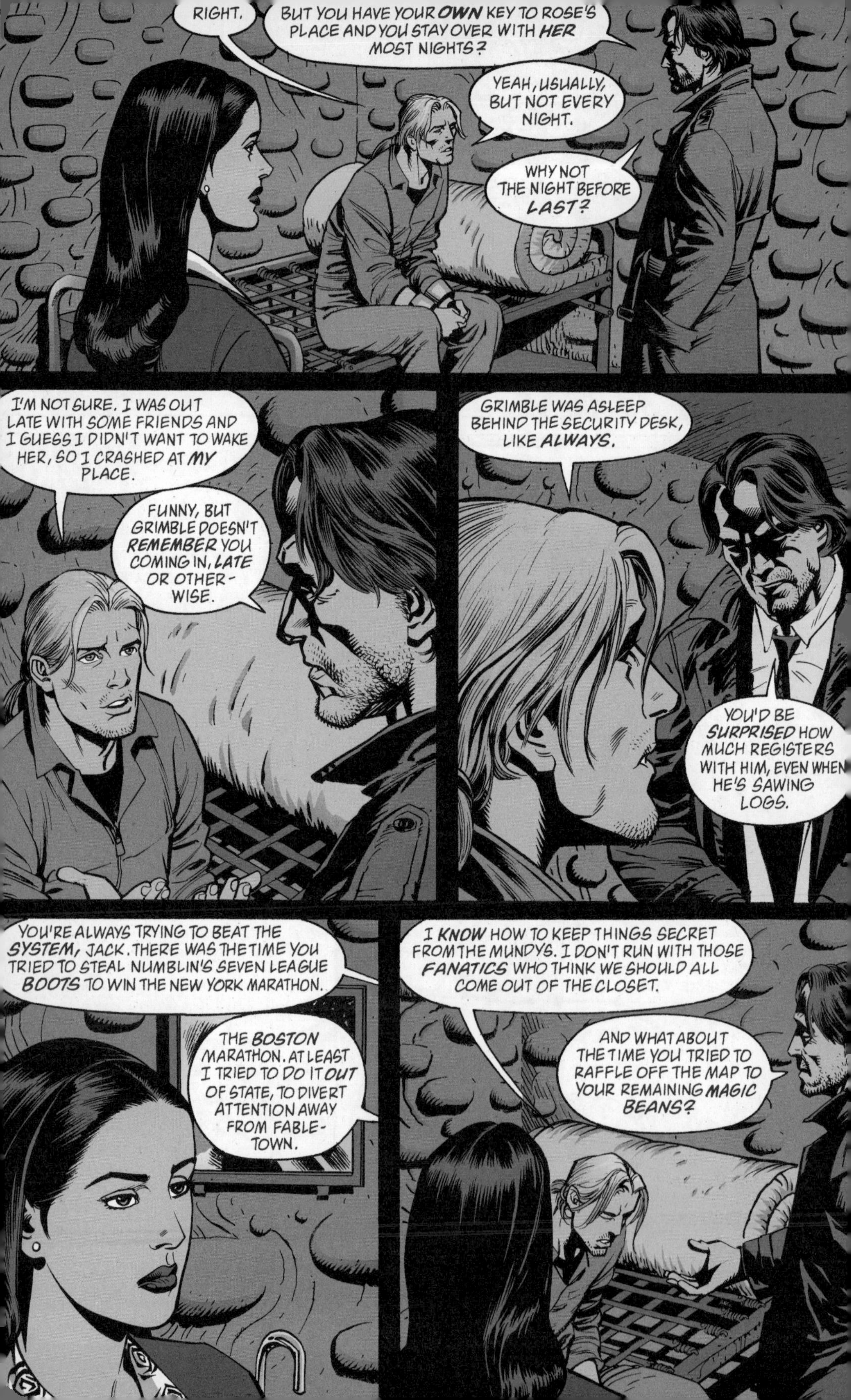
RIGHT.
BUT YOU HAVE YOUR OWN KEY TO ROSE'S PLACE AND YOU STAY OVER WITH HER MOST NIGHTS?
YEAH, USUALLY, BUT NOT EVERY NIGHT.
WHY NOT THE NIGHT BEFORE LAST?
I'M NOT SURE. I WAS OUT LATE WITH SOME FRIENDS AND I GUESS I DIDN'T WANT TO WAKE HER, SO I CRASHED AT MY PLACE.
FUNNY, BUT GRIMBLE DOESN'T REMEMBER YOU COMING IN, LATE OR OTHER-WISE.
GRIMBLE WAS ASLEEP BEHIND THE SECURITY DESK, LIKE ALWAYS.
YOU'D BE SURPRISED HOW MUCH REGISTERS WITH HIM, EVEN WHEN HE'S SAWING LOGS.
YOU'RE ALWAYS TRYING TO BEAT THE SYSTEM, JACK. THERE WAS THE TIME YOU TRIED TO STEAL NUMBLIN'S SEVEN LEAGUE BOOTS TO WIN THE NEW YORK MARATHON.
THE BOSTON MARATHON. AT LEAST I TRIED TO DO IT OUT OF STATE, TO DIVERT ATTENTION AWAY FROM FABLE-TOWN.
I KNOW HOW TO KEEP THINGS SECRET FROM THE MUNDYS. I DON'T RUN WITH THOSE FANATICS WHO THINK WE SHOULD ALL COME OUT OF THE CLOSET.
AND WHAT ABOUT THE TIME YOU TRIED TO RAFFLE OFF THE MAP TO YOUR REMAINING MAGIC BEANS?

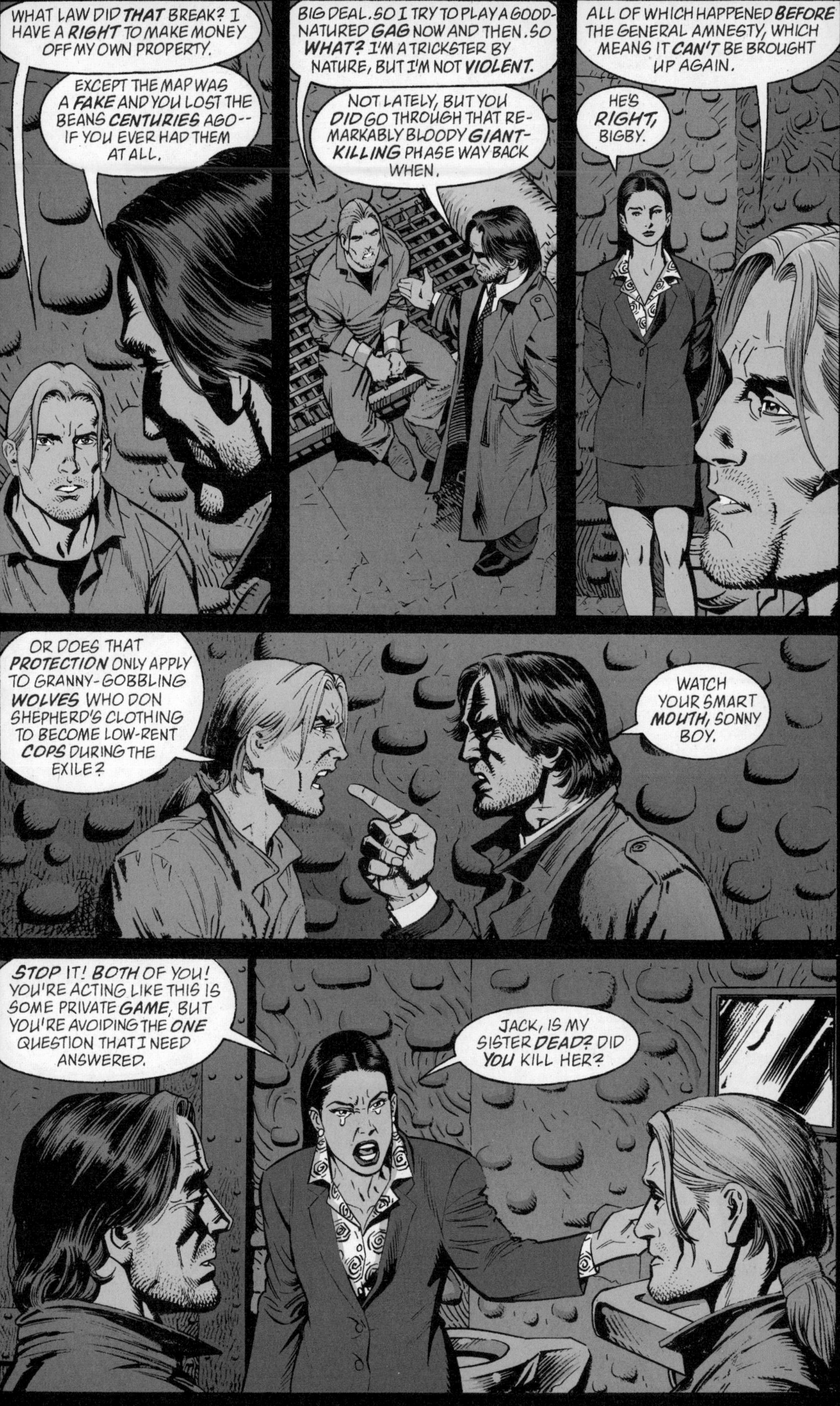
WHAT LAW DID THAT BREAK? I HAVE A RIGHT TO MAKE MONEY OFF MY OWN PROPERTY.
EXCEPT THE MAP WAS A FAKE AND YOU LOST THE BEANS CENTURIES AGO-- IF YOU EVER HAD THEM AT ALL.
BIG DEAL. SO I TRY TO PLAY A GOOD-NATURED GAG NOW AND THEN. SO WHAT? I'M A TRICKSTER BY NATURE, BUT I'M NOT VIOLENT.
NOT LATELY, BUT YOU DID GO THROUGH THAT REMARKABLY BLOODY GIANT-KILLING PHASE WAY BACK WHEN.
ALL OF WHICH HAPPENED BEFORE THE GENERAL AMNESTY, WHICH MEANS IT CAN'T BE BROUGHT UP AGAIN.
HE'S RIGHT, BIGBY.
OR DOES THAT PROTECTION ONLY APPLY TO GRANNY-GOBBLING WOLVES WHO DON SHEPHERD'S CLOTHING TO BECOME LOW-RENT COPS DURING THE EXILE?
WATCH YOUR SMART MOUTH, SONNY BOY.
STOP IT! BOTH OF YOU! YOU'RE ACTING LIKE THIS IS SOME PRIVATE GAME, BUT YOU'RE AVOIDING THE ONE QUESTION THAT I NEED ANSWERED.
JACK, IS MY SISTER DEAD? DID YOU KILL HER?

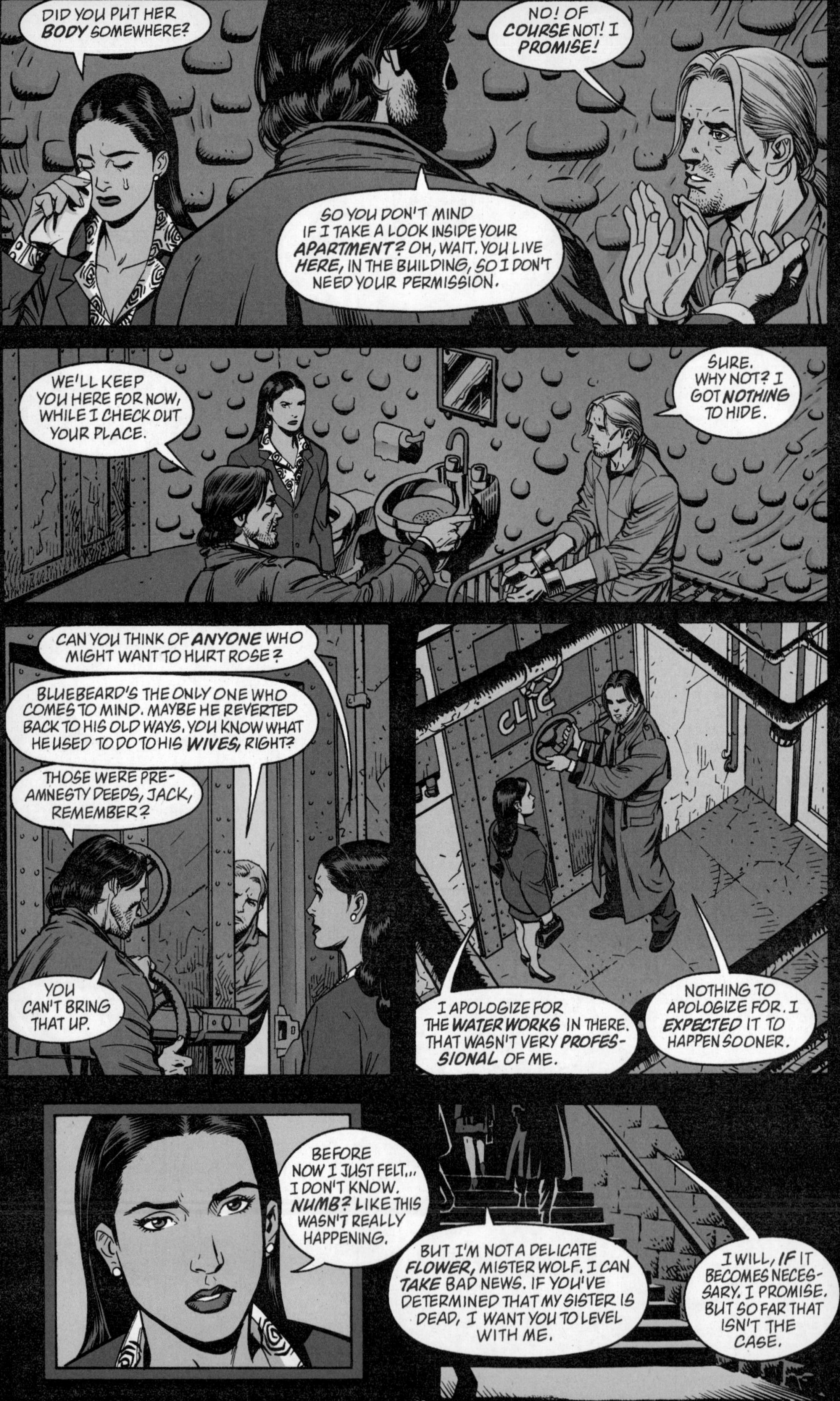
DID YOU PUT HER BODY SOMEWHERE?
NO! OF COURSE NOT! I PROMISE!
SO YOU DON'T MIND IF I TAKE A LOOK INSIDE YOUR APARTMENT? OH, WAIT. YOU LIVE HERE, IN THE BUILDING, SO I DON'T NEED YOUR PERMISSION.
WE'LL KEEP YOU HERE FOR NOW, WHILE I CHECK OUT YOUR PLACE.
SURE. WHY NOT? I GOT NOTHING TO HIDE.
CAN YOU THINK OF ANYONE WHO MIGHT WANT TO HURT ROSE?
BLUEBEARD'S THE ONLY ONE WHO COMES TO MIND. MAYBE HE REVERTED BACK TO HIS OLD WAYS. YOU KNOW WHAT HE USED TO DO TO HIS WIVES, RIGHT?
THOSE WERE PRE-AMNESTY DEEDS, JACK, REMEMBER?
YOU CAN'T BRING THAT UP.
CLIC
I APOLOGIZE FOR THE WATER WORKS IN THERE. THAT WASN'T VERY PROFES-SIONAL OF ME.
NOTHING TO APOLOGIZE FOR. I EXPECTED IT TO HAPPEN SOONER.
BEFORE NOW I JUST FELT... I DON'T KNOW. NUMB? LIKE THIS WASN'T REALLY HAPPENING.
BUT I'M NOT A DELICATE FLOWER, MISTER WOLF. I CAN TAKE BAD NEWS. IF YOU'VE DETERMINED THAT MY SISTER IS DEAD, I WANT YOU TO LEVEL WITH ME.
I WILL, IF IT BECOMES NECES-SARY. I PROMISE. BUT SO FAR THAT ISN'T THE CASE.

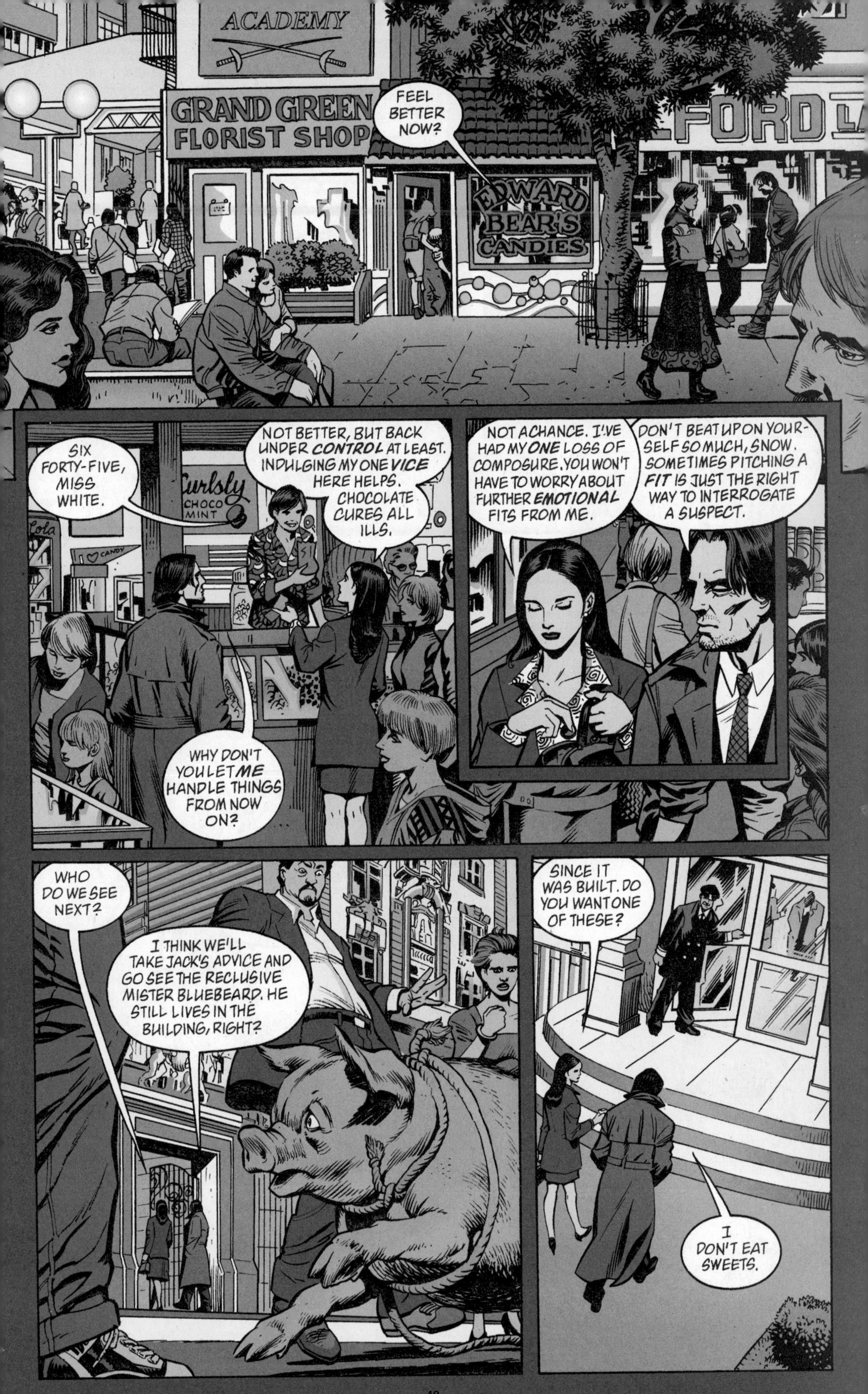
ACADEMY
GRAND GREEN FLORIST SHOP
FEEL BETTER NOW?
EDWARD BEAR'S CANDIES
FORD
SIX FORTY-FIVE, MISS WHITE.
NOT BETTER, BUT BACK UNDER CONTROL AT LEAST. INDULGING MY ONE VICE HERE HELPS. CHOCOLATE CURES ALL ILLS.
Curlsly CHOCO MINT
WHY DON'T YOU LET ME HANDLE THINGS FROM NOW ON?
NOT A CHANCE. I'VE HAD MY ONE LOSS OF COMPOSURE. YOU WON'T HAVE TO WORRY ABOUT FURTHER EMOTIONAL FITS FROM ME.
DON'T BEAT UP ON YOURSELF SO MUCH, SNOW. SOMETIMES PITCHING A FIT IS JUST THE RIGHT WAY TO INTERROGATE A SUSPECT.
WHO DO WE SEE NEXT?
I THINK WE'LL TAKE JACK'S ADVICE AND GO SEE THE RECLUSIVE MISTER BLUEBEARD. HE STILL LIVES IN THE BUILDING, RIGHT?
SINCE IT WAS BUILT. DO YOU WANT ONE OF THESE?
I DON'T EAT SWEETS.

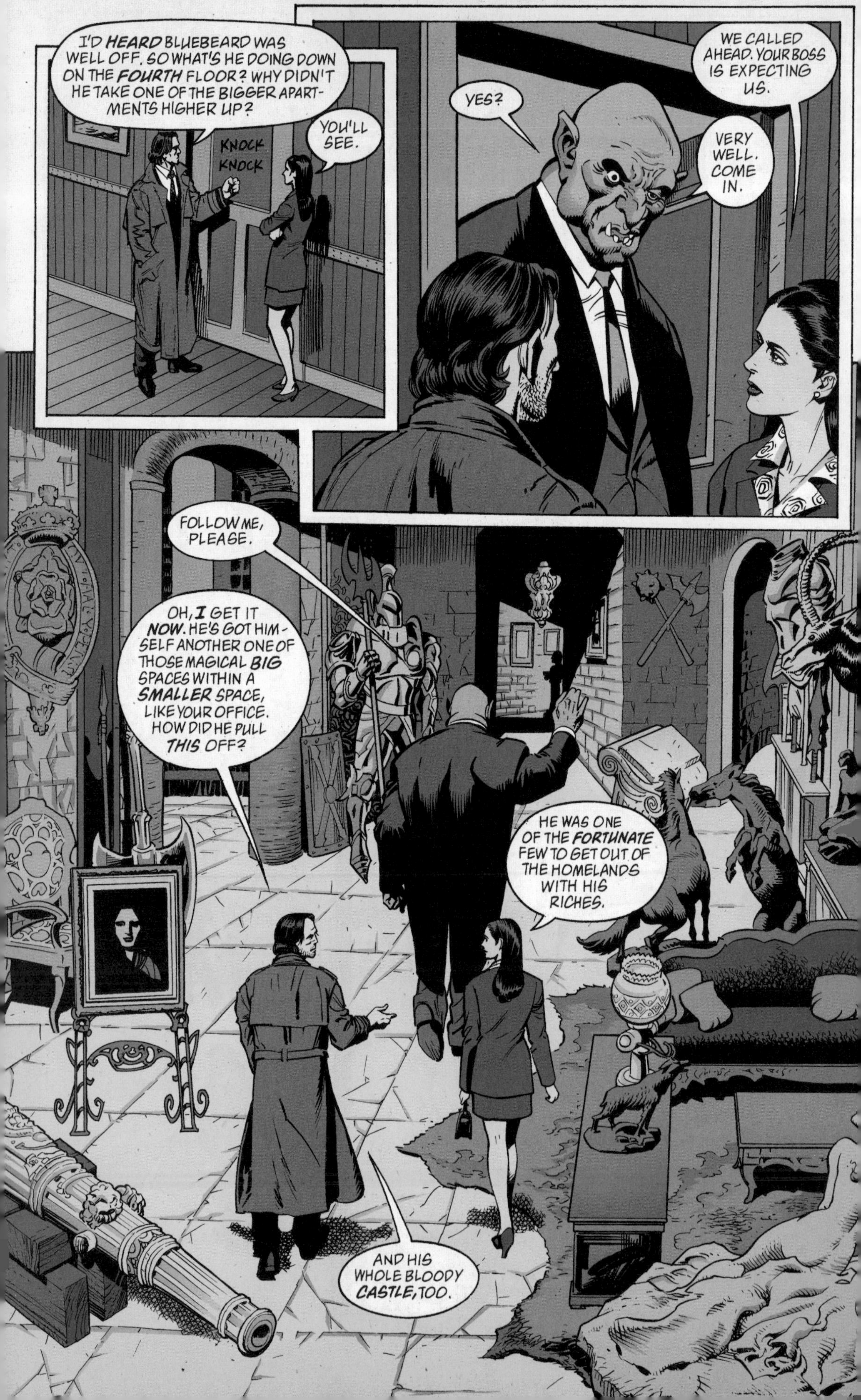
I'D HEARD BLUEBEARD WAS WELL OFF. SO WHAT'S HE DOING DOWN ON THE FOURTH FLOOR? WHY DIDN'T HE TAKE ONE OF THE BIGGER APARTMENTS HIGHER UP?
KNOCK KNOCK
YOU'LL SEE.
YES?
WE CALLED AHEAD. YOUR BOSS IS EXPECTING US.
VERY WELL. COME IN.
FOLLOW ME, PLEASE.
OH, I GET IT NOW. HE'S GOT HIMSELF ANOTHER ONE OF THOSE MAGICAL BIG SPACES WITHIN A SMALLER SPACE, LIKE YOUR OFFICE. HOW DID HE PULL THIS OFF?
HE WAS ONE OF THE FORTUNATE FEW TO GET OUT OF THE HOMELANDS WITH HIS RICHES.
AND HIS WHOLE BLOODY CASTLE, TOO.

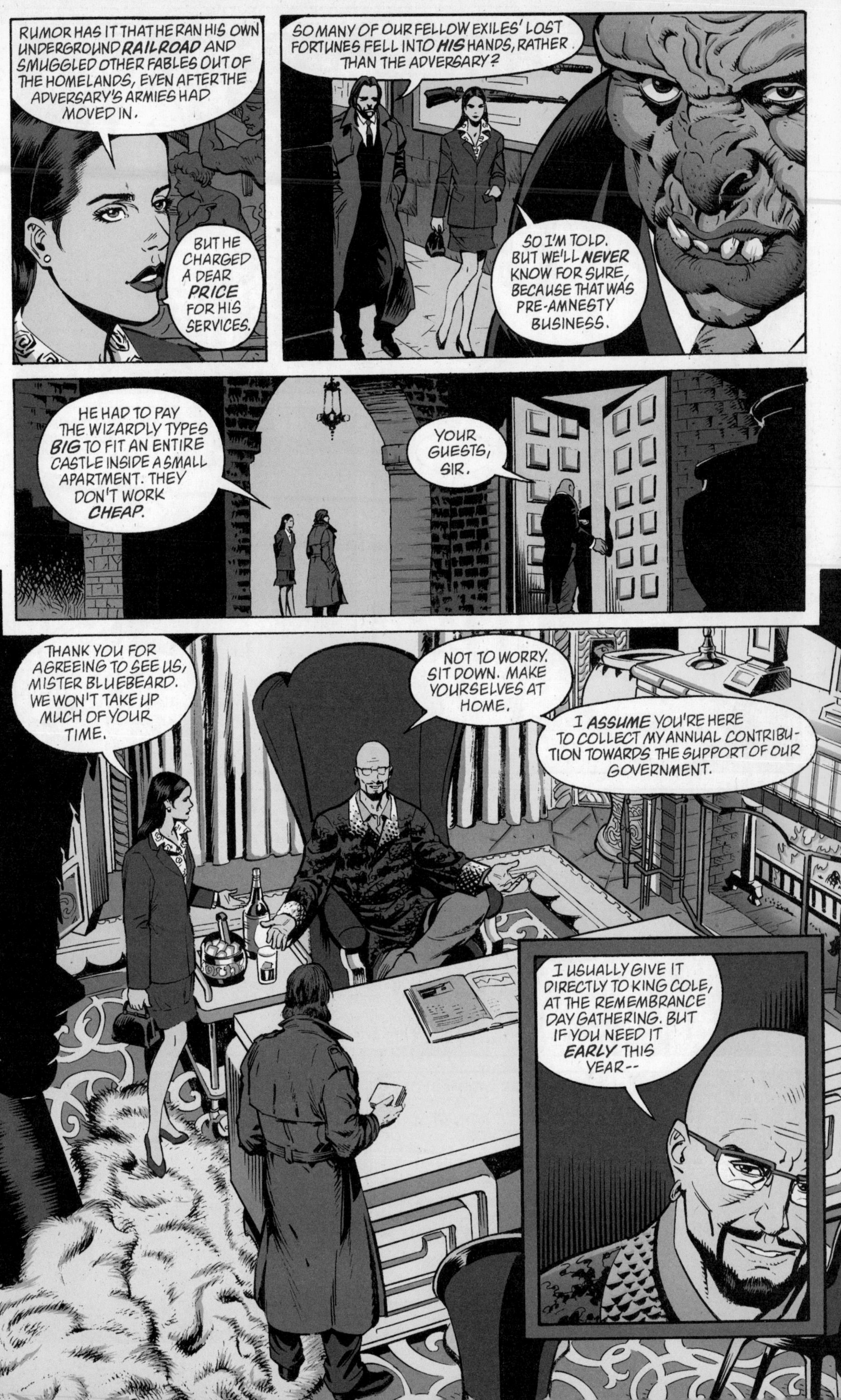
RUMOR HAS IT THAT HE RAN HIS OWN UNDERGROUND **RAILROAD** AND SMUGGLED OTHER FABLES OUT OF THE HOMELANDS, EVEN AFTER THE ADVERSARY'S ARMIES HAD MOVED IN.
BUT HE CHARGED A DEAR **PRICE** FOR HIS SERVICES.
SO MANY OF OUR FELLOW EXILES' LOST FORTUNES FELL INTO **HIS** HANDS, RATHER THAN THE ADVERSARY?
SO I'M TOLD. BUT WE'LL **NEVER** KNOW FOR SURE, BECAUSE THAT WAS PRE-AMNESTY BUSINESS.
HE HAD TO PAY THE WIZARDLY TYPES **BIG** TO FIT AN ENTIRE CASTLE INSIDE A SMALL APARTMENT. THEY DON'T WORK **CHEAP**.
YOUR GUESTS, SIR.
THANK YOU FOR AGREEING TO SEE US, MISTER BLUEBEARD. WE WON'T TAKE UP MUCH OF YOUR TIME.
NOT TO WORRY. SIT DOWN. MAKE YOURSELVES AT HOME.
I **ASSUME** YOU'RE HERE TO COLLECT MY ANNUAL CONTRIBU-TION TOWARDS THE SUPPORT OF OUR GOVERNMENT.
I USUALLY GIVE IT DIRECTLY TO KING COLE, AT THE REMEMBRANCE DAY GATHERING. BUT IF YOU NEED IT **EARLY** THIS YEAR--

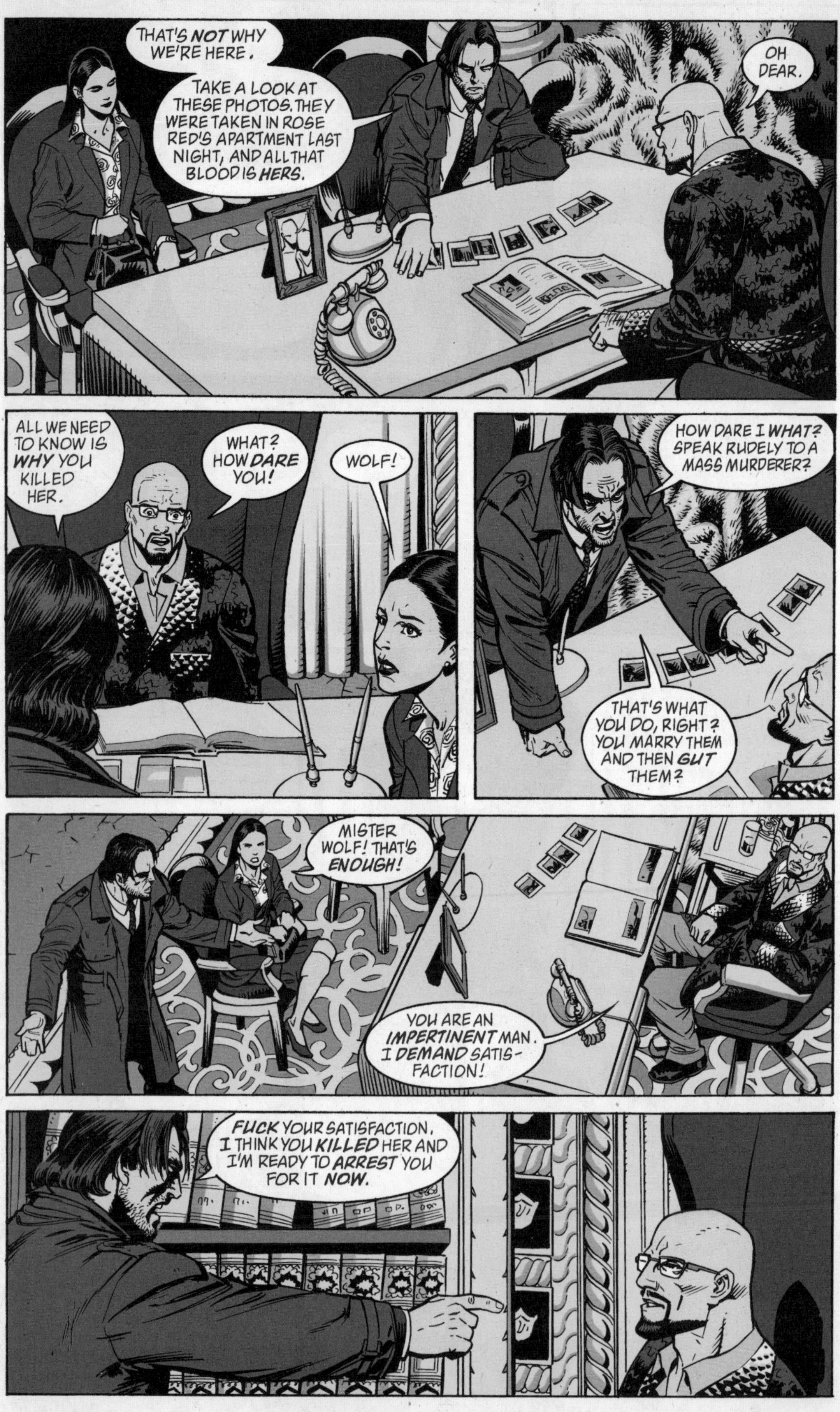
THAT'S NOT WHY WE'RE HERE.
TAKE A LOOK AT THESE PHOTOS. THEY WERE TAKEN IN ROSE RED'S APARTMENT LAST NIGHT, AND ALL THAT BLOOD IS HERS.
OH DEAR.
ALL WE NEED TO KNOW IS WHY YOU KILLED HER.
WHAT? HOW DARE YOU!
WOLF!
HOW DARE I WHAT? SPEAK RUDELY TO A MASS MURDERER?
THAT'S WHAT YOU DO, RIGHT? YOU MARRY THEM AND THEN GUT THEM?
MISTER WOLF! THAT'S ENOUGH!
YOU ARE AN IMPERTINENT MAN. I DEMAND SATIS-FACTION!
FUCK YOUR SATISFACTION. I THINK YOU KILLED HER AND I'M READY TO ARREST YOU FOR IT NOW.

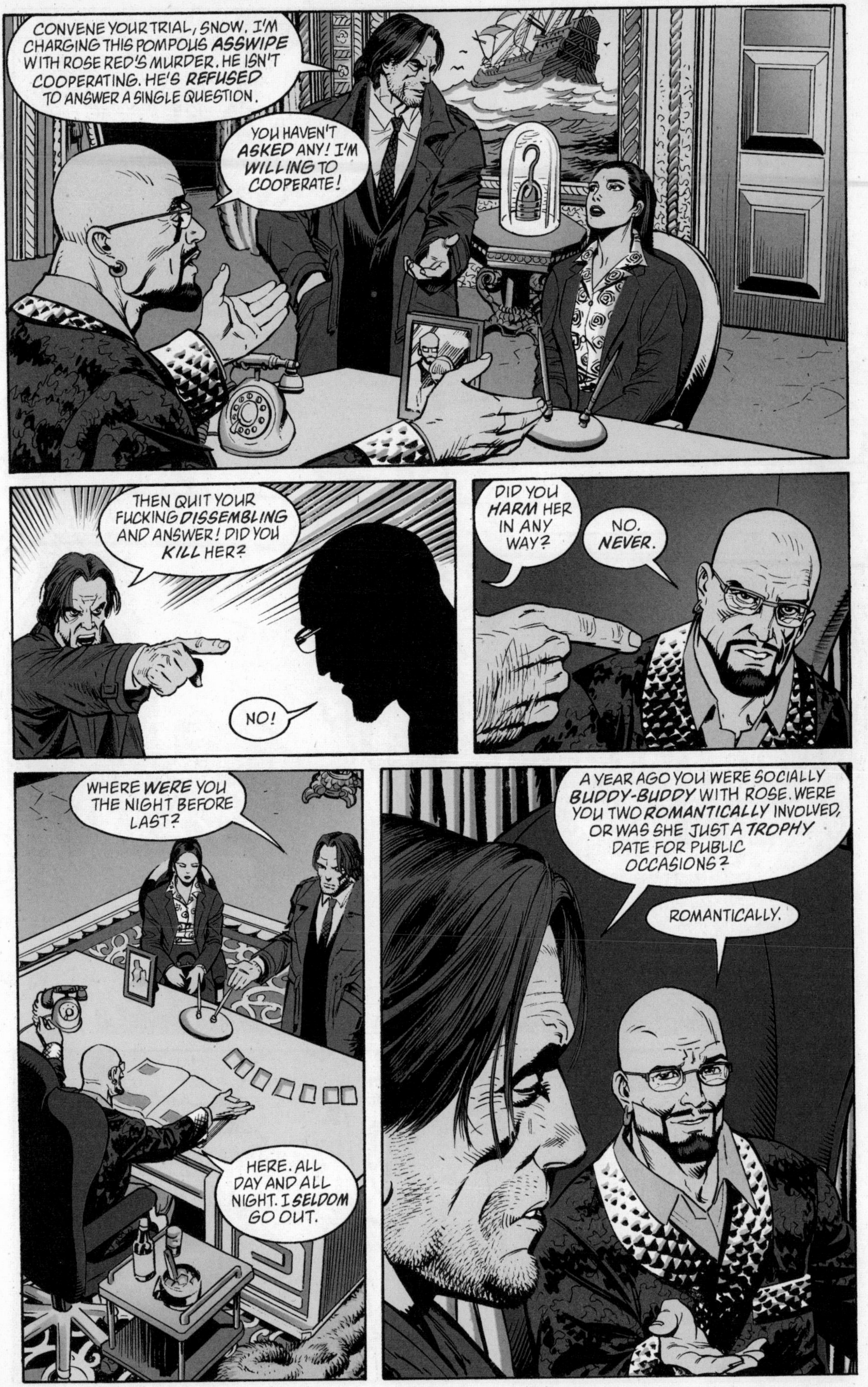
CONVENE YOUR TRIAL, SNOW. I'M CHARGING THIS POMPOUS ASSWIPE WITH ROSE RED'S MURDER. HE ISN'T COOPERATING. HE'S REFUSED TO ANSWER A SINGLE QUESTION.
YOU HAVEN'T ASKED ANY! I'M WILLING TO COOPERATE!
THEN QUIT YOUR FUCKING DISSEMBLING AND ANSWER! DID YOU KILL HER?
NO!
DID YOU HARM HER IN ANY WAY?
NO. NEVER.
WHERE WERE YOU THE NIGHT BEFORE LAST?
HERE. ALL DAY AND ALL NIGHT. I SELDOM GO OUT.
A YEAR AGO YOU WERE SOCIALLY BUDDY-BUDDY WITH ROSE. WERE YOU TWO ROMANTICALLY INVOLVED, OR WAS SHE JUST A TROPHY DATE FOR PUBLIC OCCASIONS?
ROMANTICALLY.

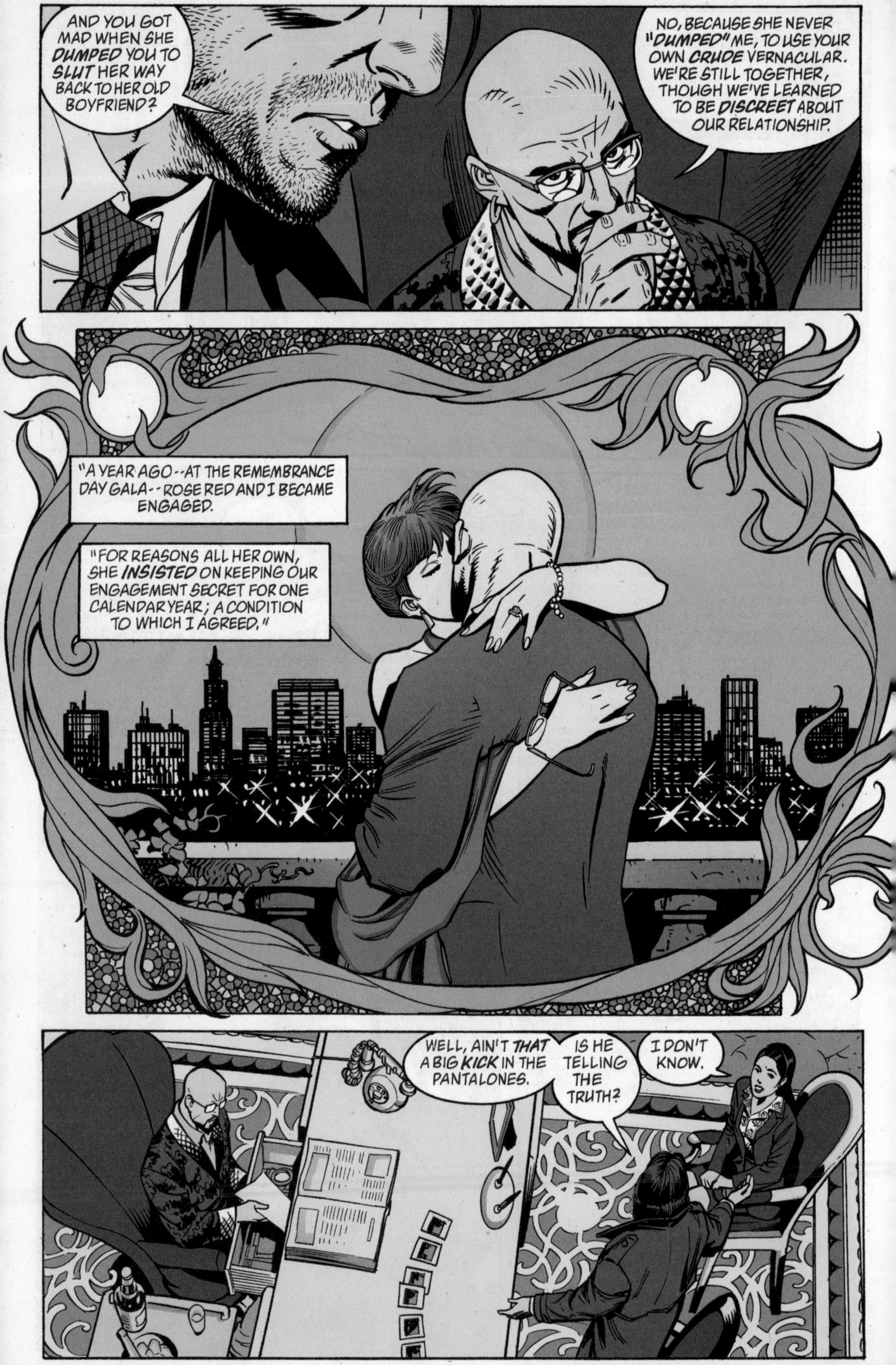

AND YOU GOT MAD WHEN SHE DUMPED YOU TO SLUT HER WAY BACK TO HER OLD BOYFRIEND?
NO, BECAUSE SHE NEVER "DUMPED" ME, TO USE YOUR OWN CRUDE VERNACULAR. WE'RE STILL TOGETHER, THOUGH WE'VE LEARNED TO BE DISCREET ABOUT OUR RELATIONSHIP.
"A YEAR AGO--AT THE REMEMBRANCE DAY GALA--ROSE RED AND I BECAME ENGAGED.
"FOR REASONS ALL HER OWN, SHE INSISTED ON KEEPING OUR ENGAGEMENT SECRET FOR ONE CALENDAR YEAR; A CONDITION TO WHICH I AGREED."
WELL, AIN'T THAT A BIG KICK IN THE PANTALONES.
IS HE TELLING THE TRUTH?
I DON'T KNOW.

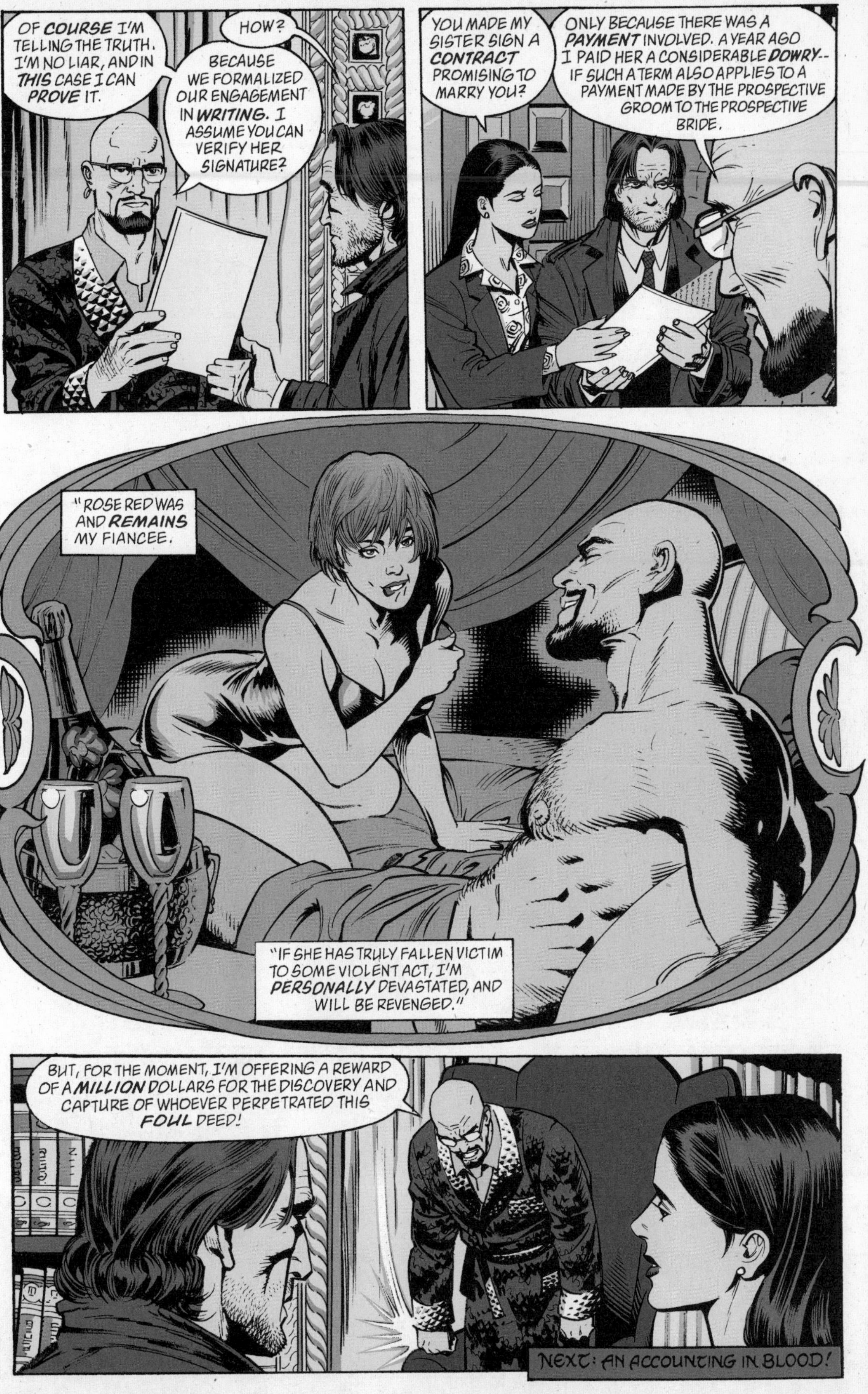
OF COURSE I'M TELLING THE TRUTH. I'M NO LIAR, AND IN THIS CASE I CAN PROVE IT.
HOW?
BECAUSE WE FORMALIZED OUR ENGAGEMENT IN WRITING. I ASSUME YOU CAN VERIFY HER SIGNATURE?
YOU MADE MY SISTER SIGN A CONTRACT PROMISING TO MARRY YOU?
ONLY BECAUSE THERE WAS A PAYMENT INVOLVED. A YEAR AGO I PAID HER A CONSIDERABLE DOWRY-- IF SUCH A TERM ALSO APPLIES TO A PAYMENT MADE BY THE PROSPECTIVE GROOM TO THE PROSPECTIVE BRIDE.
"ROSE RED WAS AND REMAINS MY FIANCEE.
"IF SHE HAS TRULY FALLEN VICTIM TO SOME VIOLENT ACT, I'M PERSONALLY DEVASTATED, AND WILL BE REVENGED."
BUT, FOR THE MOMENT, I'M OFFERING A REWARD OF A MILLION DOLLARS FOR THE DISCOVERY AND CAPTURE OF WHOEVER PERPETRATED THIS FOUL DEED!
NEXT: AN ACCOUNTING IN BLOOD!

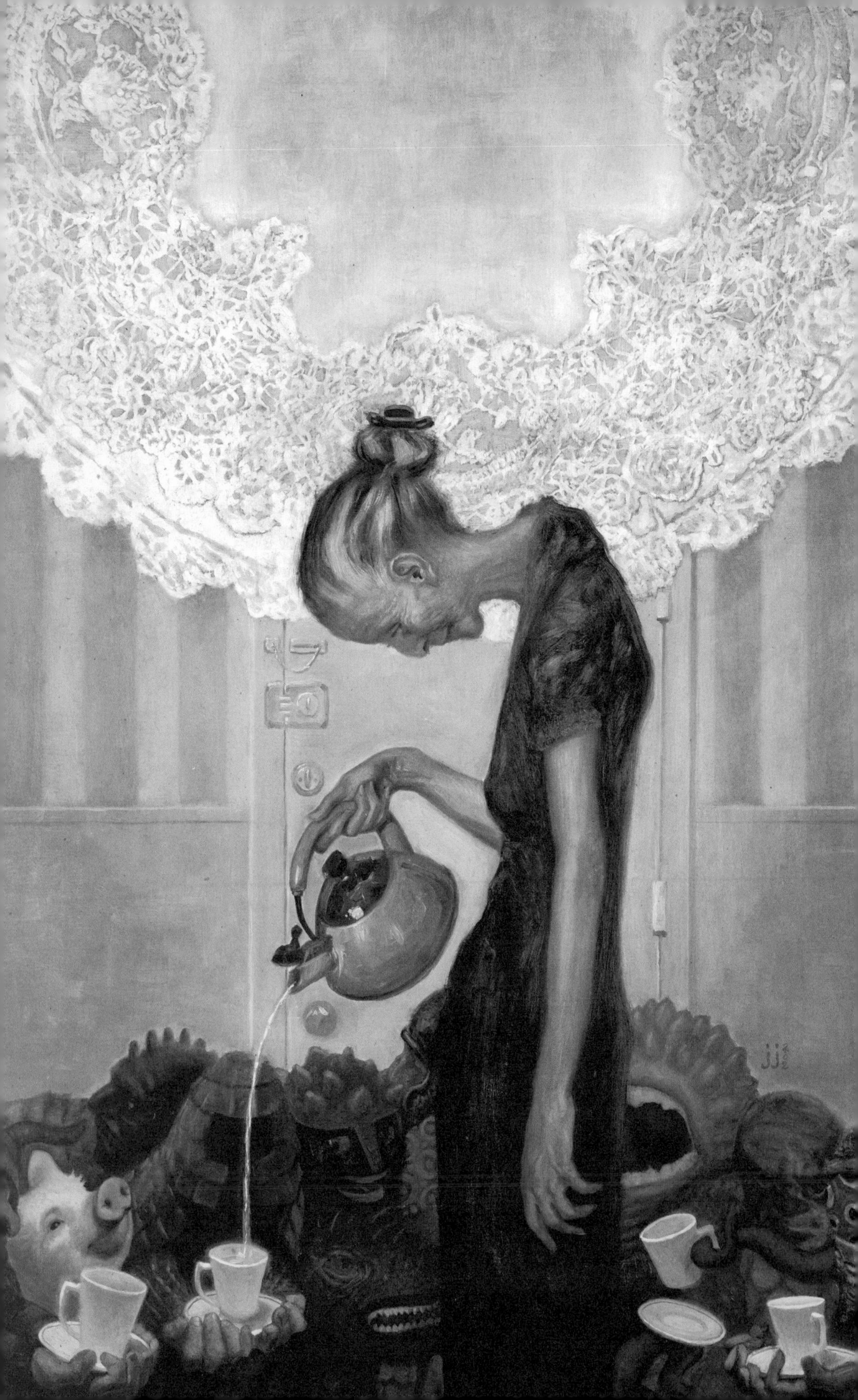

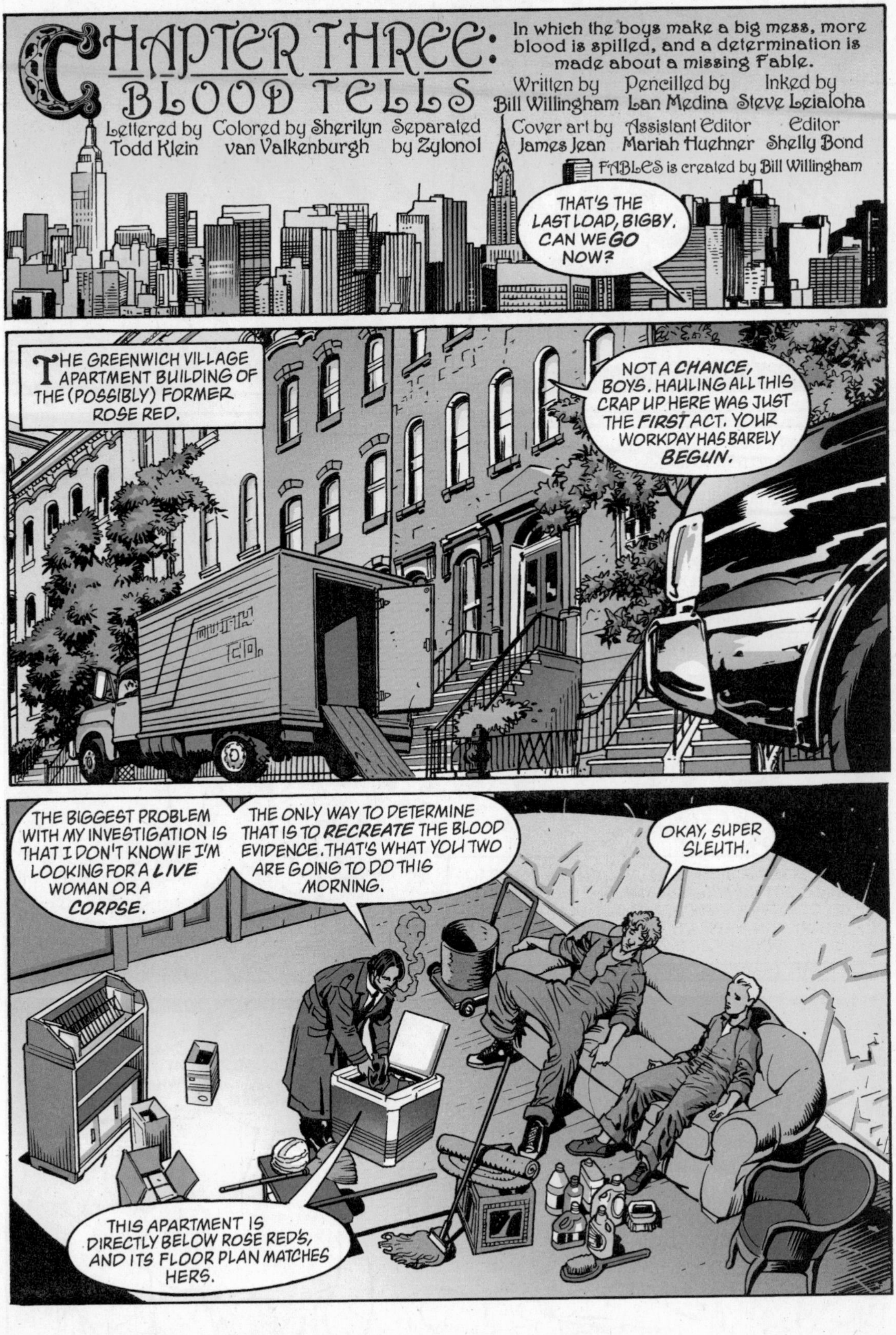
CHAPTER THREE: BLOOD TELLS
In which the boys make a big mess, more blood is spilled, and a determination is made about a missing Fable.
Written by Bill Willingham
Pencilled by Lan Medina
Inked by Steve Leialoha
Lettered by Todd Klein
Colored by Sherilyn van Valkenburgh
Separated by Zylonol
Cover art by James Jean
Assistant Editor Mariah Huehner
Editor Shelly Bond
FABLES is created by Bill Willingham
THAT'S THE LAST LOAD, BIGBY. CAN WE GO NOW?
THE GREENWICH VILLAGE APARTMENT BUILDING OF THE (POSSIBLY) FORMER ROSE RED.
NOT A CHANCE, BOYS. HAULING ALL THIS CRAP UP HERE WAS JUST THE FIRST ACT. YOUR WORKDAY HAS BARELY BEGUN.
THE BIGGEST PROBLEM WITH MY INVESTIGATION IS THAT I DON'T KNOW IF I'M LOOKING FOR A LIVE WOMAN OR A CORPSE.
THE ONLY WAY TO DETERMINE THAT IS TO RECREATE THE BLOOD EVIDENCE. THAT'S WHAT YOU TWO ARE GOING TO DO THIS MORNING.
OKAY, SUPER SLEUTH.
THIS APARTMENT IS DIRECTLY BELOW ROSE RED'S, AND ITS FLOOR PLAN MATCHES HERS.

FIRST, YOU'RE GOING TO SET UP THIS JUNK TO *DUPLICATE* -- AS MUCH AS POSSIBLE -- HER FURNITURE LAYOUT.

THEN COMES THE FUN PART I PROMISED. YOU GET TO MAKE A BIG *MESS.*

USING THESE PRE-MEASURED PACKETS OF *BLOOD,* YOU'RE GOING TO RECREATE THE SPATTER PATTERNS OF THE APARTMENT ABOVE.

COOL.

"KEEP AN *EXACT* COUNT OF HOW MUCH BLOOD YOU HAVE TO USE TO MATCH THE SCENE UPSTAIRS. THEN WE'LL KNOW HOW MUCH OF ROSE RED'S BLOOD WAS ACTUALLY SPILLED.

"USE THESE PHOTOS FROM THE REAL CRIME SCENE TO MAKE YOUR RE-CREATION AS ACCURATE AS POSSIBLE.

"IF YOU ABSOLUTELY *HAVE* TO, YOU CAN GO UP TO CHECK OUT THE ACTUAL SCENE, BUT DON'T TRAMP ALL OVER THE EVIDENCE, AND GOD HELP YOU IF YOU LET ANY MUNDY SEE ANYTHING, OR IF YOU FORGET TO LOCK UP AFTER YOURSELVES."

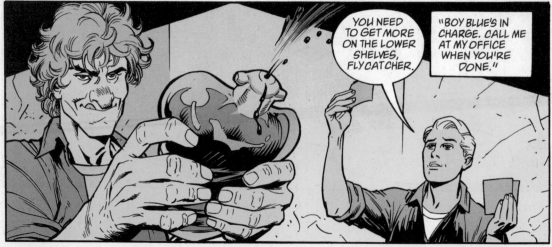

YOU NEED TO GET MORE ON THE LOWER SHELVES, FLYCATCHER.

"BOY BLUE'S IN CHARGE. CALL ME AT MY OFFICE WHEN YOU'RE DONE."

THE WOODLAND BUILDING ON THE UPPER WEST SIDE.

YOU WANTED TO SEE ME, YOUR HONOR?

THE PENTHOUSE RESIDENCE OF KING COLE, UNOFFICIAL MAYOR-FOR-LIFE OF FABLETOWN.

OH, WE DON'T NEED TO STAND ON *FORMALITIES*, SNOW, NOT WHEN IT'S JUST YOU AND ME. COME IN.

THANK YOU, SIR. WHAT CAN I DO FOR YOU THIS MORNING?

I'M *TROUBLED* BY THIS UNFORTUNATE SITUATION WITH YOUR SISTER. TRAGIC, *AWFUL* BUSINESS. I UNDERSTAND YOU'RE ASSISTING BIGBY WITH HIS INVESTIGATION.

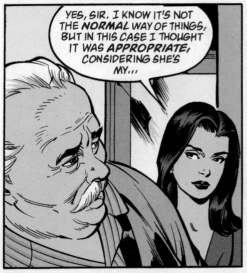

YES, SIR. I KNOW IT'S NOT THE *NORMAL* WAY OF THINGS, BUT IN THIS CASE I THOUGHT IT WAS *APPROPRIATE*, CONSIDERING SHE'S MY...

YES, OF *COURSE*. NO TROUBLE THERE. *ENTIRELY* UNDERSTANDABLE. BLOOD RELATIONS NEED TO LOOK AFTER EACH OTHER. WE CAN LET *OTHER* BUSINESS SLIDE FOR A DAY OR TWO, ONLY...

SIR?

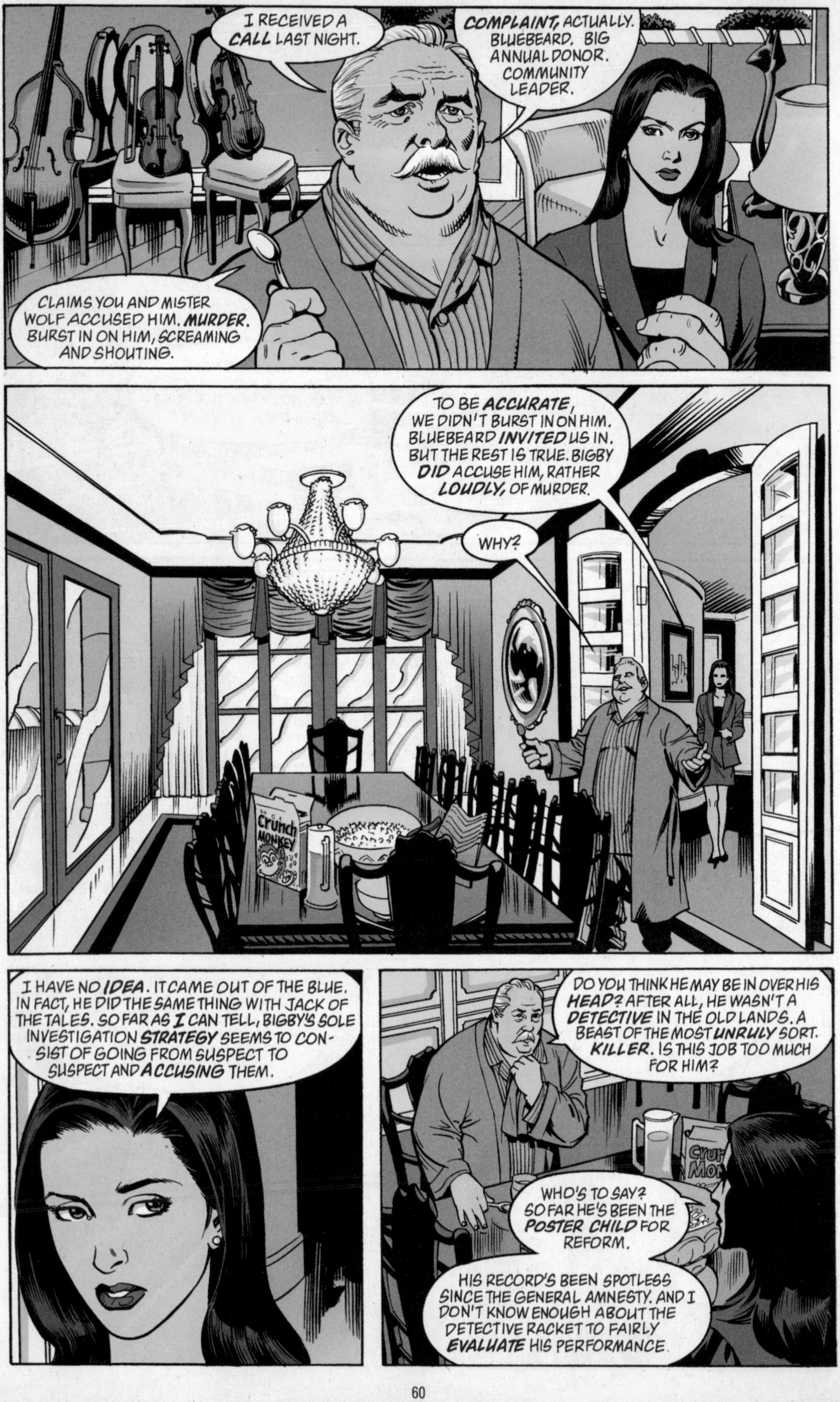
I RECEIVED A CALL LAST NIGHT.
COMPLAINT, ACTUALLY. BLUEBEARD. BIG ANNUAL DONOR. COMMUNITY LEADER.
CLAIMS YOU AND MISTER WOLF ACCUSED HIM. MURDER. BURST IN ON HIM, SCREAMING AND SHOUTING.
TO BE ACCURATE, WE DIDN'T BURST IN ON HIM. BLUEBEARD INVITED US IN. BUT THE REST IS TRUE. BIGBY DID ACCUSE HIM, RATHER LOUDLY, OF MURDER.
WHY?
Crunch MONKEY
I HAVE NO IDEA. IT CAME OUT OF THE BLUE. IN FACT, HE DID THE SAME THING WITH JACK OF THE TALES. SO FAR AS I CAN TELL, BIGBY'S SOLE INVESTIGATION STRATEGY SEEMS TO CONSIST OF GOING FROM SUSPECT TO SUSPECT AND ACCUSING THEM.
DO YOU THINK HE MAY BE IN OVER HIS HEAD? AFTER ALL, HE WASN'T A DETECTIVE IN THE OLD LANDS. A BEAST OF THE MOST UNRULY SORT. KILLER. IS THIS JOB TOO MUCH FOR HIM?
WHO'S TO SAY? SO FAR HE'S BEEN THE POSTER CHILD FOR REFORM.
HIS RECORD'S BEEN SPOTLESS SINCE THE GENERAL AMNESTY. AND I DON'T KNOW ENOUGH ABOUT THE DETECTIVE RACKET TO FAIRLY EVALUATE HIS PERFORMANCE.

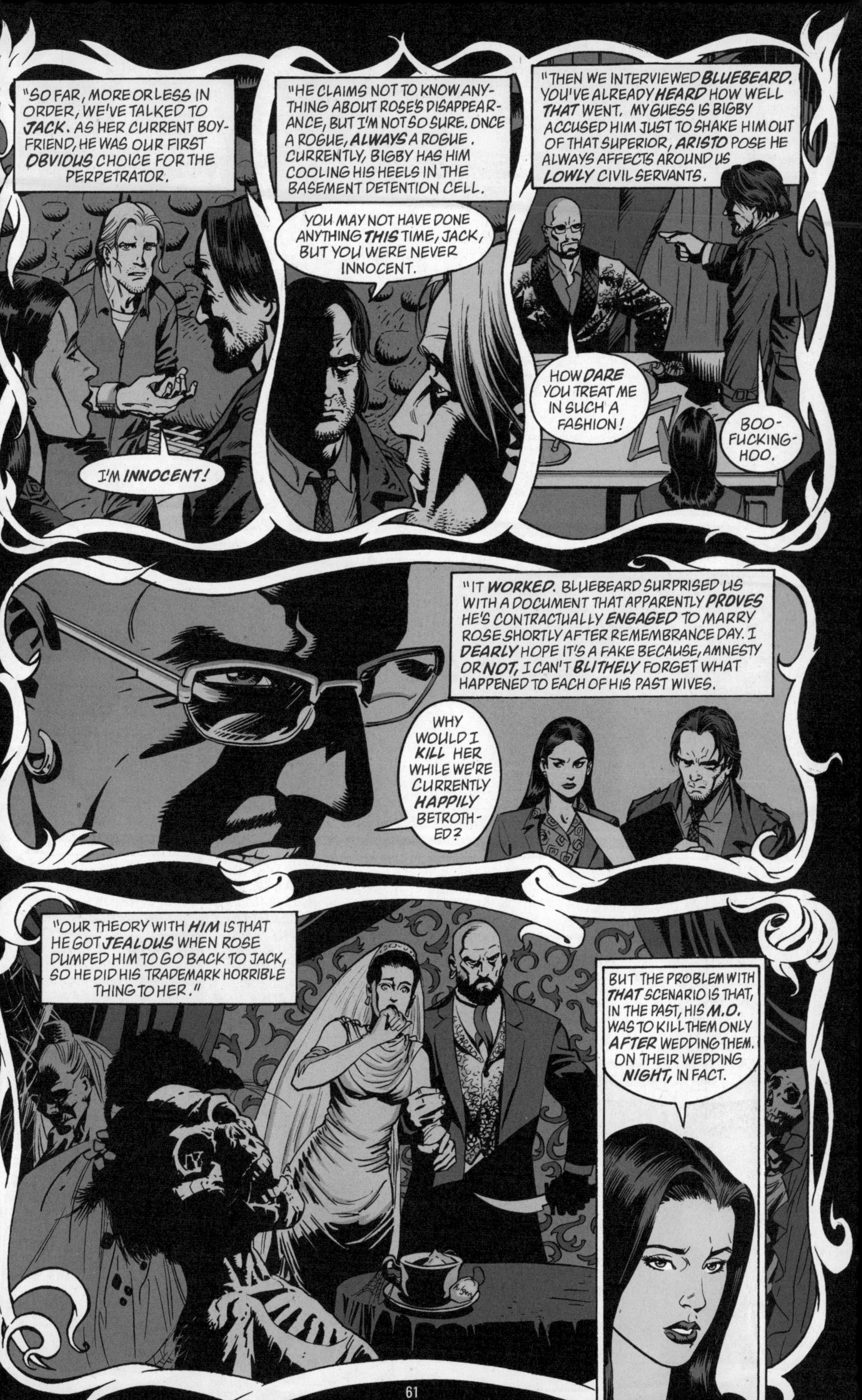
"SO FAR, MORE OR LESS IN ORDER, WE'VE TALKED TO JACK. AS HER CURRENT BOY-FRIEND, HE WAS OUR FIRST OBVIOUS CHOICE FOR THE PERPETRATOR.
I'M INNOCENT!
"HE CLAIMS NOT TO KNOW ANY-THING ABOUT ROSE'S DISAPPEAR-ANCE, BUT I'M NOT SO SURE. ONCE A ROGUE, ALWAYS A ROGUE. CURRENTLY, BIGBY HAS HIM COOLING HIS HEELS IN THE BASEMENT DETENTION CELL.
YOU MAY NOT HAVE DONE ANYTHING THIS TIME, JACK, BUT YOU WERE NEVER INNOCENT.
"THEN WE INTERVIEWED BLUEBEARD. YOU'VE ALREADY HEARD HOW WELL THAT WENT. MY GUESS IS BIGBY ACCUSED HIM JUST TO SHAKE HIM OUT OF THAT SUPERIOR, ARISTO POSE HE ALWAYS AFFECTS AROUND US LOWLY CIVIL SERVANTS.
HOW DARE YOU TREAT ME IN SUCH A FASHION!
BOO-FUCKING-HOO.
"IT WORKED. BLUEBEARD SURPRISED US WITH A DOCUMENT THAT APPARENTLY PROVES HE'S CONTRACTUALLY ENGAGED TO MARRY ROSE SHORTLY AFTER REMEMBRANCE DAY. I DEARLY HOPE IT'S A FAKE BECAUSE, AMNESTY OR NOT, I CAN'T BLITHELY FORGET WHAT HAPPENED TO EACH OF HIS PAST WIVES.
WHY WOULD I KILL HER WHILE WE'RE CURRENTLY HAPPILY BETROTH-ED?
"OUR THEORY WITH HIM IS THAT HE GOT JEALOUS WHEN ROSE DUMPED HIM TO GO BACK TO JACK, SO HE DID HIS TRADEMARK HORRIBLE THING TO HER."
BUT THE PROBLEM WITH THAT SCENARIO IS THAT, IN THE PAST, HIS M.O. WAS TO KILL THEM ONLY AFTER WEDDING THEM. ON THEIR WEDDING NIGHT, IN FACT.

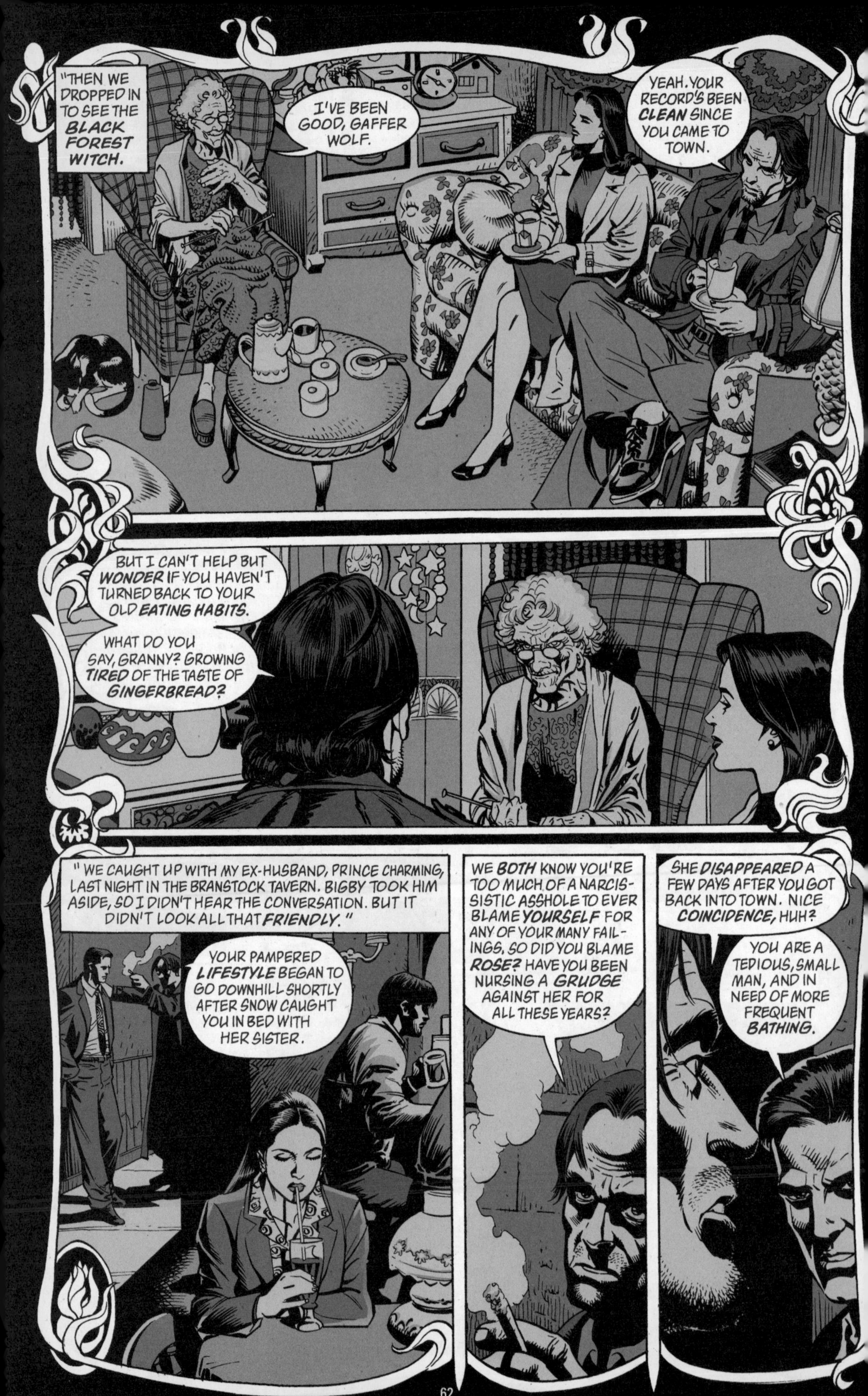
"THEN WE DROPPED IN TO SEE THE BLACK FOREST WITCH.
I'VE BEEN GOOD, GAFFER WOLF.
YEAH. YOUR RECORD'S BEEN CLEAN SINCE YOU CAME TO TOWN.
BUT I CAN'T HELP BUT WONDER IF YOU HAVEN'T TURNED BACK TO YOUR OLD EATING HABITS.
WHAT DO YOU SAY, GRANNY? GROWING TIRED OF THE TASTE OF GINGERBREAD?
" WE CAUGHT UP WITH MY EX-HUSBAND, PRINCE CHARMING, LAST NIGHT IN THE BRANSTOCK TAVERN. BIGBY TOOK HIM ASIDE, SO I DIDN'T HEAR THE CONVERSATION. BUT IT DIDN'T LOOK ALL THAT FRIENDLY."
YOUR PAMPERED LIFESTYLE BEGAN TO GO DOWNHILL SHORTLY AFTER SNOW CAUGHT YOU IN BED WITH HER SISTER.
WE BOTH KNOW YOU'RE TOO MUCH OF A NARCISSISTIC ASSHOLE TO EVER BLAME YOURSELF FOR ANY OF YOUR MANY FAILINGS, SO DID YOU BLAME ROSE? HAVE YOU BEEN NURSING A GRUDGE AGAINST HER FOR ALL THESE YEARS?
SHE DISAPPEARED A FEW DAYS AFTER YOU GOT BACK INTO TOWN. NICE COINCIDENCE, HUH?
YOU ARE A TEDIOUS, SMALL MAN, AND IN NEED OF MORE FREQUENT BATHING.

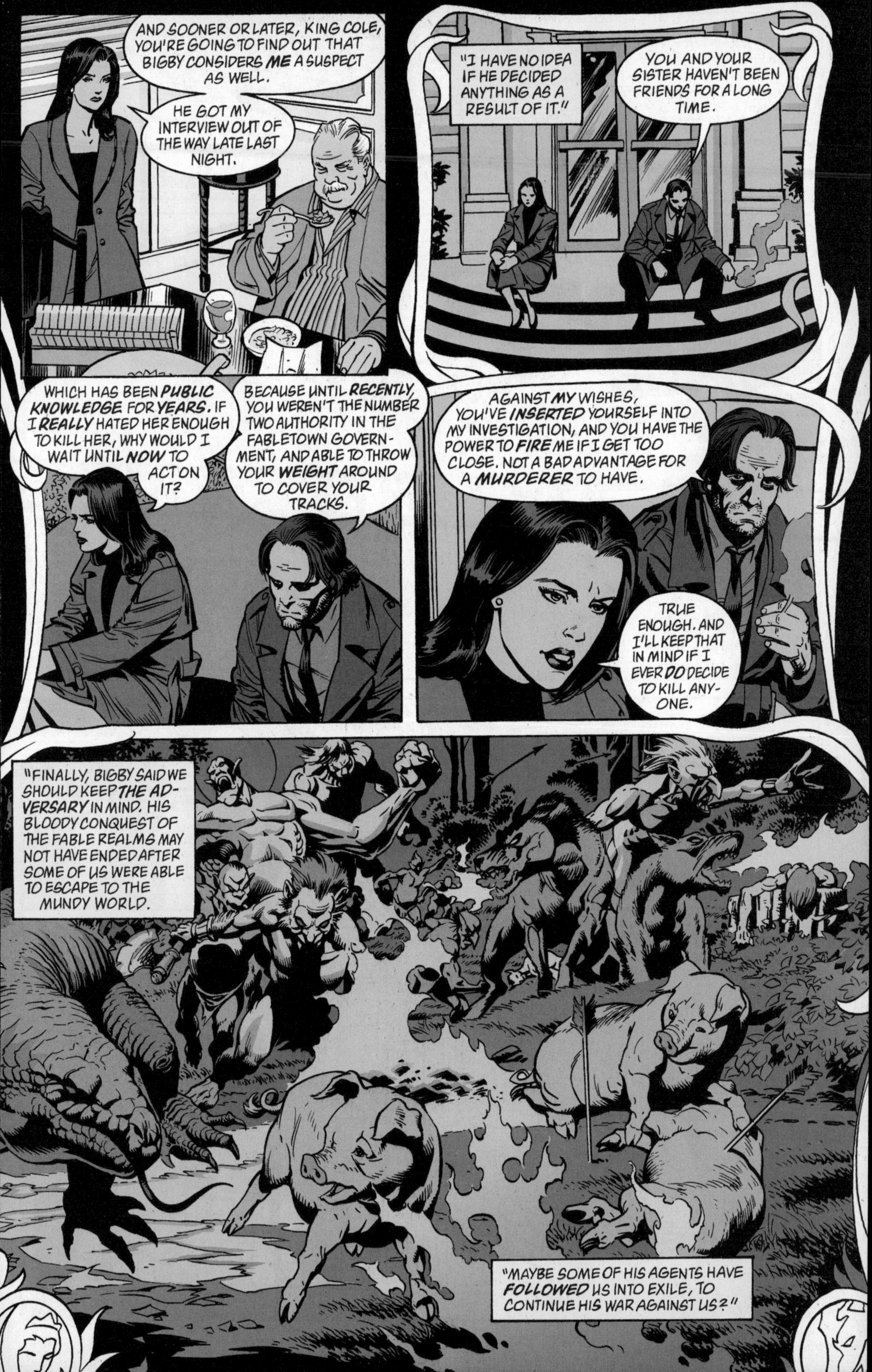
AND SOONER OR LATER, KING COLE, YOU'RE GOING TO FIND OUT THAT BIGBY CONSIDERS ME A SUSPECT AS WELL.
HE GOT MY INTERVIEW OUT OF THE WAY LATE LAST NIGHT.
"I HAVE NO IDEA IF HE DECIDED ANYTHING AS A RESULT OF IT."
YOU AND YOUR SISTER HAVEN'T BEEN FRIENDS FOR A LONG TIME.
WHICH HAS BEEN PUBLIC KNOWLEDGE FOR YEARS. IF I REALLY HATED HER ENOUGH TO KILL HER, WHY WOULD I WAIT UNTIL NOW TO ACT ON IT?
BECAUSE UNTIL RECENTLY, YOU WEREN'T THE NUMBER TWO AUTHORITY IN THE FABLETOWN GOVERNMENT, AND ABLE TO THROW YOUR WEIGHT AROUND TO COVER YOUR TRACKS.
AGAINST MY WISHES, YOU'VE INSERTED YOURSELF INTO MY INVESTIGATION, AND YOU HAVE THE POWER TO FIRE ME IF I GET TOO CLOSE. NOT A BAD ADVANTAGE FOR A MURDERER TO HAVE.
TRUE ENOUGH. AND I'LL KEEP THAT IN MIND IF I EVER DO DECIDE TO KILL ANYONE.
"FINALLY, BIGBY SAID WE SHOULD KEEP THE ADVERSARY IN MIND. HIS BLOODY CONQUEST OF THE FABLE REALMS MAY NOT HAVE ENDED AFTER SOME OF US WERE ABLE TO ESCAPE TO THE MUNDY WORLD.
"MAYBE SOME OF HIS AGENTS HAVE FOLLOWED US INTO EXILE, TO CONTINUE HIS WAR AGAINST US?"

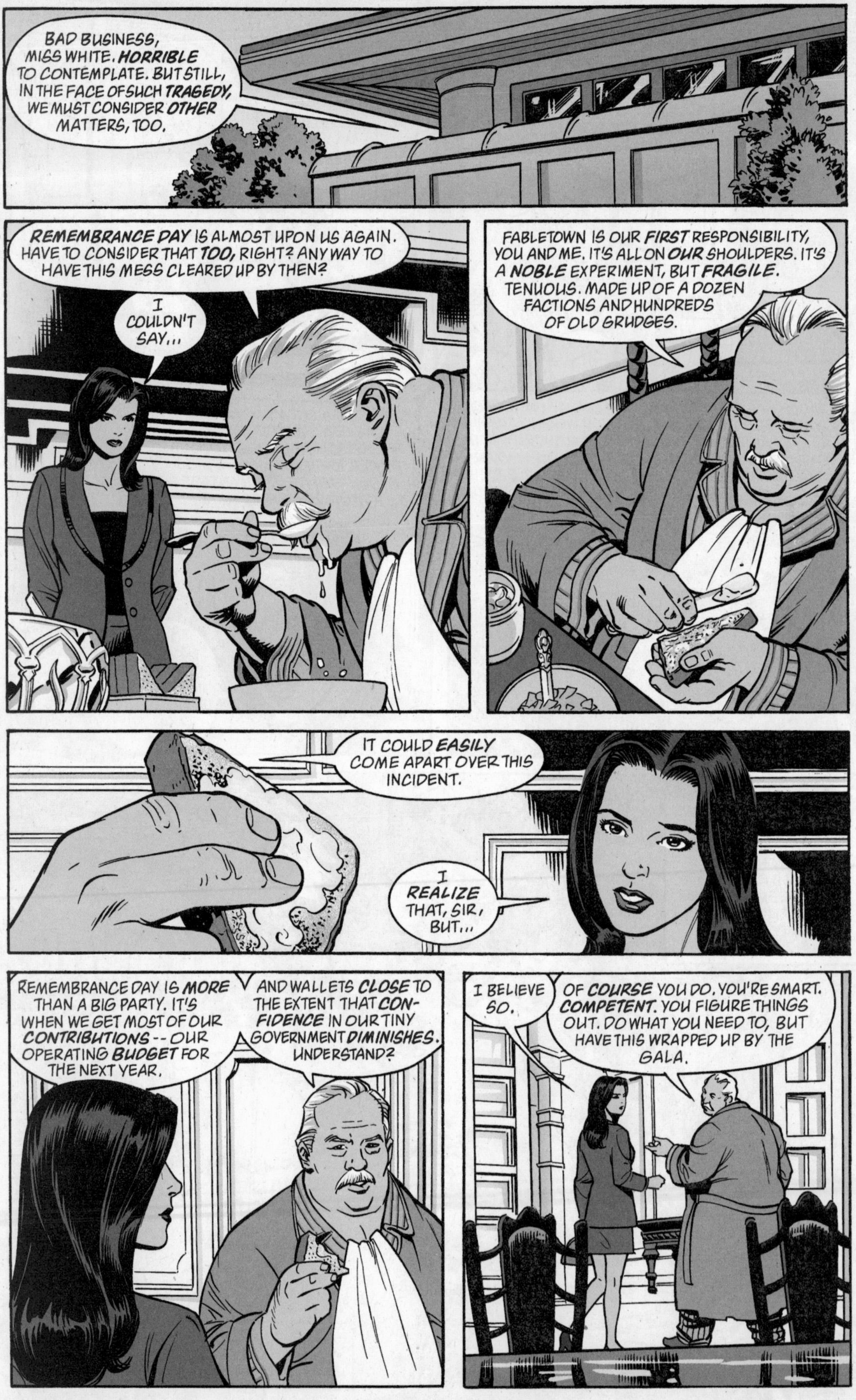
BAD BUSINESS, MISS WHITE. HORRIBLE TO CONTEMPLATE. BUT STILL, IN THE FACE OF SUCH TRAGEDY, WE MUST CONSIDER OTHER MATTERS, TOO.
REMEMBRANCE DAY IS ALMOST UPON US AGAIN. HAVE TO CONSIDER THAT TOO, RIGHT? ANY WAY TO HAVE THIS MESS CLEARED UP BY THEN?
I COULDN'T SAY...
FABLETOWN IS OUR FIRST RESPONSIBILITY, YOU AND ME. IT'S ALL ON OUR SHOULDERS. IT'S A NOBLE EXPERIMENT, BUT FRAGILE. TENUOUS. MADE UP OF A DOZEN FACTIONS AND HUNDREDS OF OLD GRUDGES.
IT COULD EASILY COME APART OVER THIS INCIDENT.
I REALIZE THAT, SIR, BUT...
REMEMBRANCE DAY IS MORE THAN A BIG PARTY. IT'S WHEN WE GET MOST OF OUR CONTRIBUTIONS -- OUR OPERATING BUDGET FOR THE NEXT YEAR.
AND WALLETS CLOSE TO THE EXTENT THAT CONFIDENCE IN OUR TINY GOVERNMENT DIMINISHES. UNDERSTAND?
I BELIEVE SO.
OF COURSE YOU DO. YOU'RE SMART. COMPETENT. YOU FIGURE THINGS OUT. DO WHAT YOU NEED TO, BUT HAVE THIS WRAPPED UP BY THE GALA.

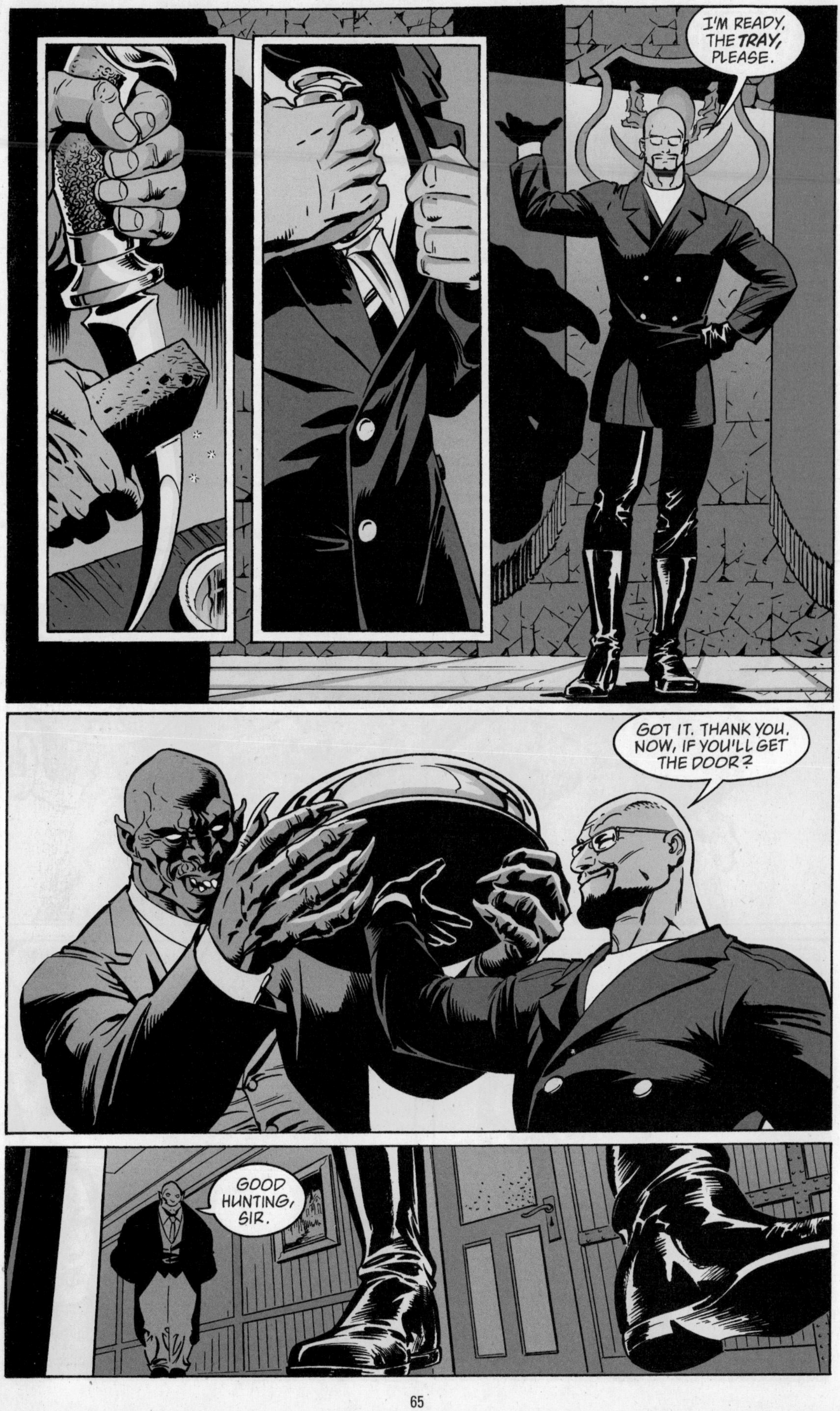
I'M READY. THE TRAY, PLEASE.
GOT IT. THANK YOU. NOW, IF YOU'LL GET THE DOOR?
GOOD HUNTING, SIR.

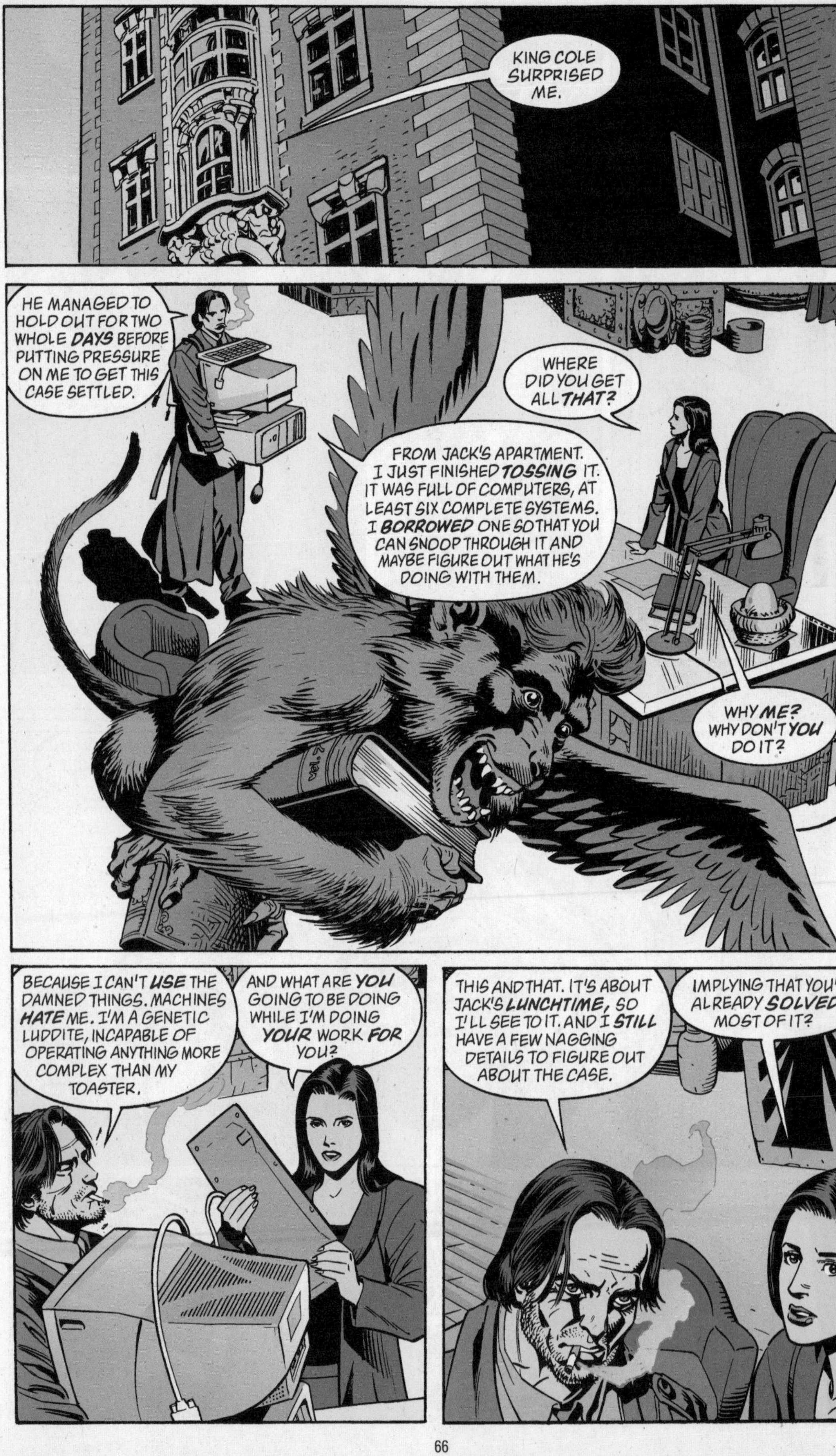
KING COLE SURPRISED ME.
HE MANAGED TO HOLD OUT FOR TWO WHOLE **DAYS** BEFORE PUTTING PRESSURE ON ME TO GET THIS CASE SETTLED.
WHERE DID YOU GET ALL **THAT?**
FROM JACK'S APARTMENT. I JUST FINISHED **TOSSING** IT. IT WAS FULL OF COMPUTERS, AT LEAST SIX COMPLETE SYSTEMS. I **BORROWED** ONE SO THAT YOU CAN SNOOP THROUGH IT AND MAYBE FIGURE OUT WHAT HE'S DOING WITH THEM.
WHY **ME?** WHY DON'T **YOU** DO IT?
BECAUSE I CAN'T **USE** THE DAMNED THINGS. MACHINES **HATE** ME. I'M A GENETIC LUDDITE, INCAPABLE OF OPERATING ANYTHING MORE COMPLEX THAN MY TOASTER.
AND WHAT ARE **YOU** GOING TO BE DOING WHILE I'M DOING **YOUR** WORK **FOR** YOU?
THIS AND THAT. IT'S ABOUT JACK'S **LUNCHTIME,** SO I'LL SEE TO IT. AND I **STILL** HAVE A FEW NAGGING DETAILS TO FIGURE OUT ABOUT THE CASE.
IMPLYING THAT YOU'VE ALREADY **SOLVED** MOST OF IT?

YUP. I SOLVED THE BULK OF IT WITHIN THE FIRST *HOUR.* I PRETTY MUCH KNOW *WHAT* HAPPENED, AND MOST OF *HOW,* BUT I'M STILL SHORT ON SOME OF THE *WHO* AND *WHY.*

AND WHEN *EXACTLY* ARE YOU PLANNING TO CLUE *ME* IN?

THE VERY MOMENT I'M CONVINCED YOU AREN'T THE *VILLAIN* IN THIS MYSTERY.

AT *LEAST* TELL ME IF SHE'S *DEAD* OR ALIVE.

WE'LL SEE.

YOU CAN BE ONE *FRUSTRATING* SON OF A BITCH!

LITERALLY, IN *MY* CASE, BUT SHE WAS NEVER LESS THAN LOVING AND NURTURING. THE BEST *MOTHER* ANY BOY COULD WANT.

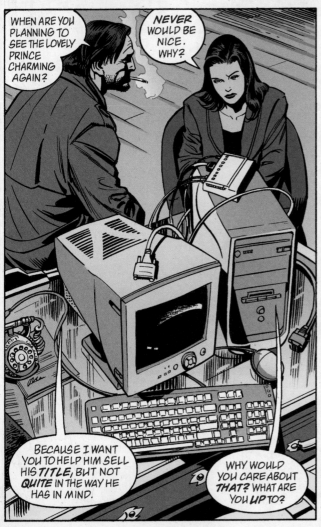

WHEN ARE YOU PLANNING TO SEE THE LOVELY PRINCE CHARMING AGAIN?

NEVER WOULD BE NICE. WHY?

BECAUSE I WANT YOU TO HELP HIM SELL HIS *TITLE,* BUT NOT *QUITE* IN THE WAY HE HAS IN MIND.

WHY WOULD YOU CARE ABOUT *THAT?* WHAT ARE YOU *UP* TO?

A MAD BUT *IMPROBABLE* SCHEME TO MAKE EVERYTHING COME OUT RIGHT IN THE END, WITHOUT ANY *FURTHER* BLOOD-SHED. AND JUST *MAYBE* THE FABLE COMMUNITY DOESN'T DISINTEGRATE IN THE PROCESS.

PROBABLY WON'T WORK, THOUGH.

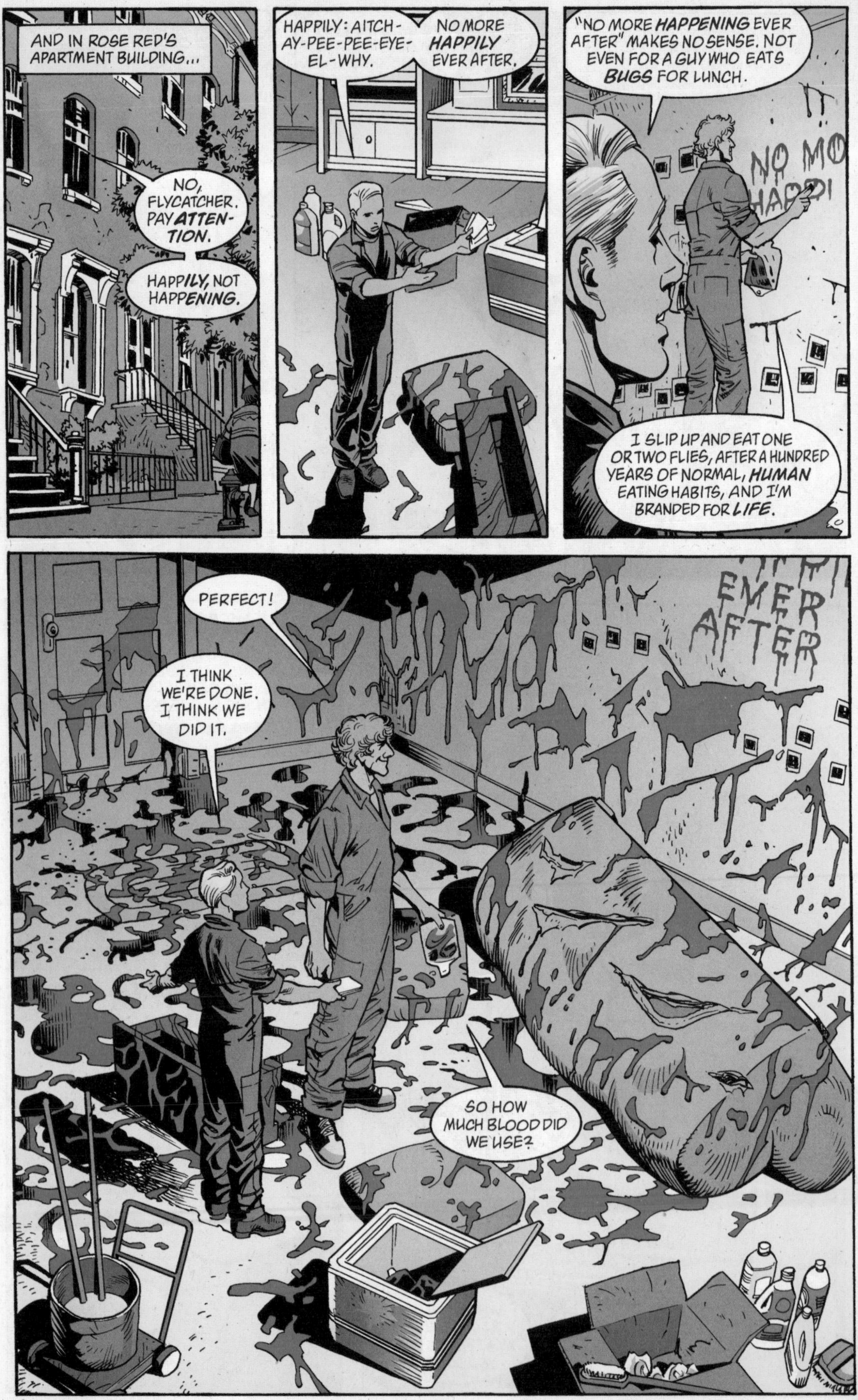
AND IN ROSE RED'S APARTMENT BUILDING...
NO, FLYCATCHER. PAY ATTENTION.
HAPPILY, NOT HAPPENING.
HAPPILY: AITCH-AY-PEE-PEE-EYE-EL-WHY.
NO MORE HAPPILY EVER AFTER.
"NO MORE HAPPENING EVER AFTER" MAKES NO SENSE. NOT EVEN FOR A GUY WHO EATS BUGS FOR LUNCH.
I SLIP UP AND EAT ONE OR TWO FLIES, AFTER A HUNDRED YEARS OF NORMAL, HUMAN EATING HABITS, AND I'M BRANDED FOR LIFE.
PERFECT!
I THINK WE'RE DONE. I THINK WE DID IT.
EVER AFTER
SO HOW MUCH BLOOD DID WE USE?

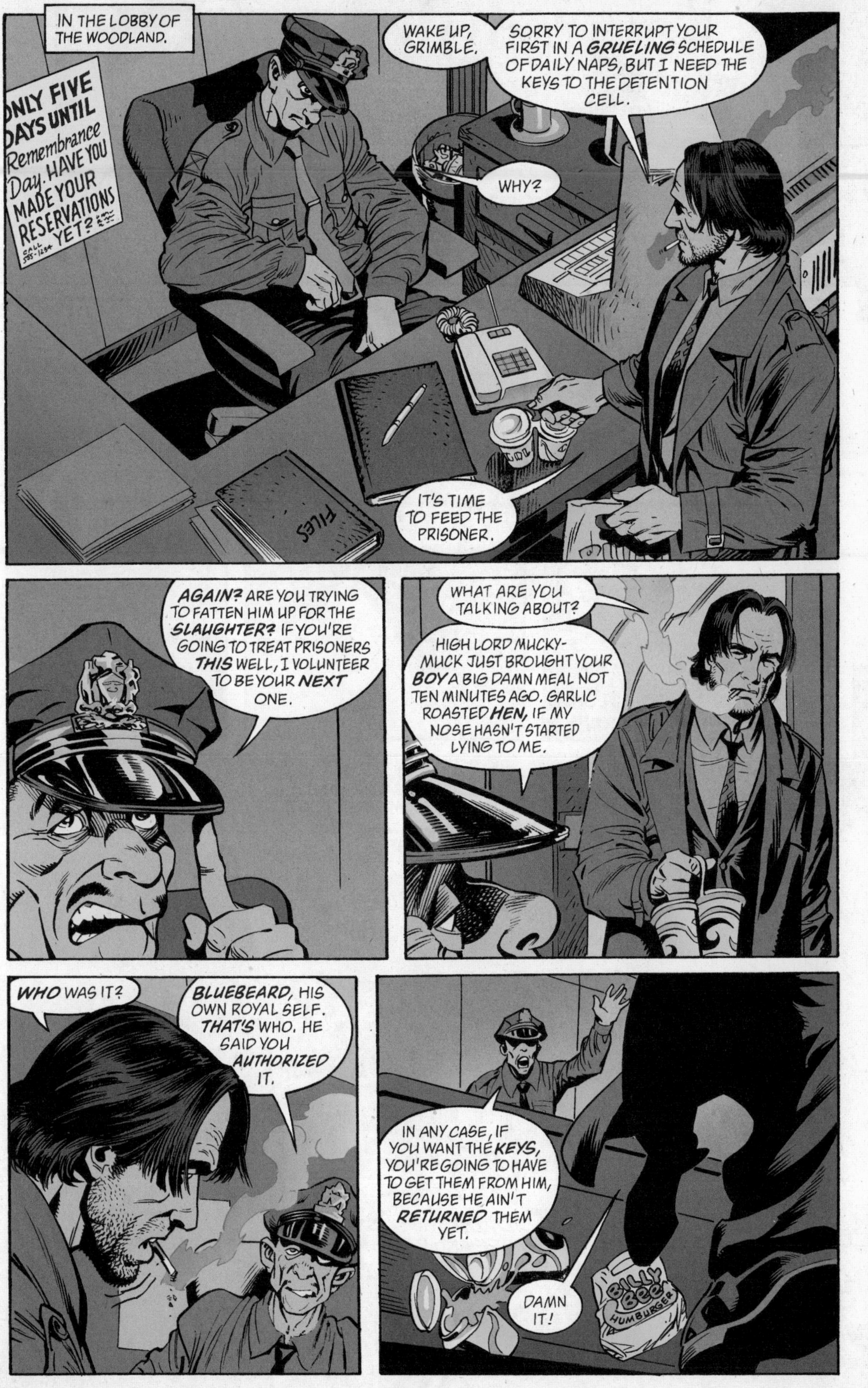
IN THE LOBBY OF THE WOODLAND.
ONLY FIVE DAYS UNTIL Remembrance Day. HAVE YOU MADE YOUR RESERVATIONS YET?
CALL 555-1234
WAKE UP, GRIMBLE.
SORRY TO INTERRUPT YOUR FIRST IN A GRUELING SCHEDULE OF DAILY NAPS, BUT I NEED THE KEYS TO THE DETENTION CELL.
WHY?
IT'S TIME TO FEED THE PRISONER.
FILES
AGAIN? ARE YOU TRYING TO FATTEN HIM UP FOR THE SLAUGHTER? IF YOU'RE GOING TO TREAT PRISONERS THIS WELL, I VOLUNTEER TO BE YOUR NEXT ONE.
WHAT ARE YOU TALKING ABOUT?
HIGH LORD MUCKY-MUCK JUST BROUGHT YOUR BOY A BIG DAMN MEAL NOT TEN MINUTES AGO. GARLIC ROASTED HEN, IF MY NOSE HASN'T STARTED LYING TO ME.
WHO WAS IT?
BLUEBEARD, HIS OWN ROYAL SELF. THAT'S WHO. HE SAID YOU AUTHORIZED IT.
IN ANY CASE, IF YOU WANT THE KEYS, YOU'RE GOING TO HAVE TO GET THEM FROM HIM, BECAUSE HE AIN'T RETURNED THEM YET.
BILLY Bee HUMBURGER
DAMN IT!

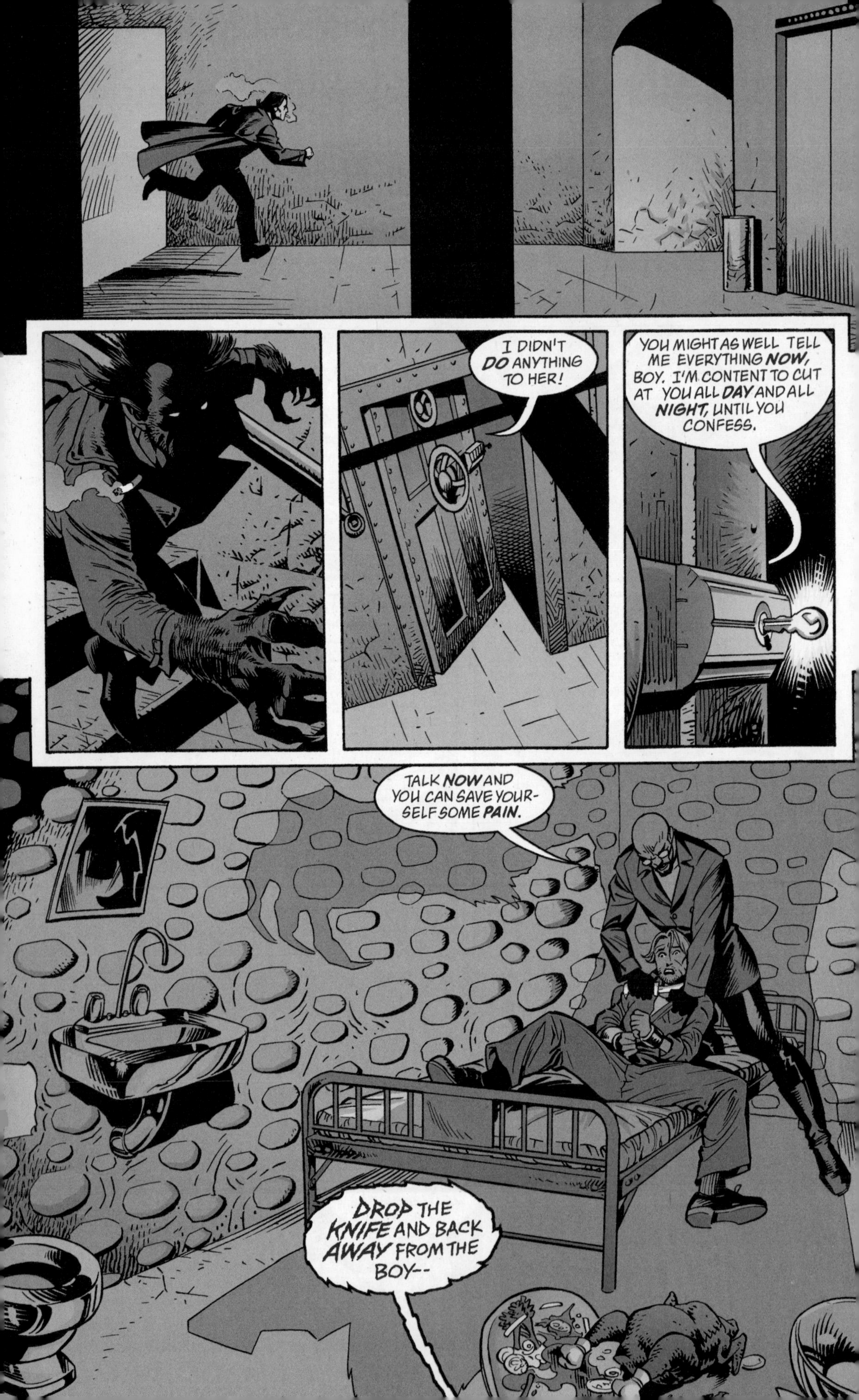
I DIDN'T DO ANYTHING TO HER!
YOU MIGHT AS WELL TELL ME EVERYTHING NOW, BOY. I'M CONTENT TO CUT AT YOU ALL DAY AND ALL NIGHT, UNTIL YOU CONFESS.
TALK NOW AND YOU CAN SAVE YOURSELF SOME PAIN.
DROP THE KNIFE AND BACK AWAY FROM THE BOY--

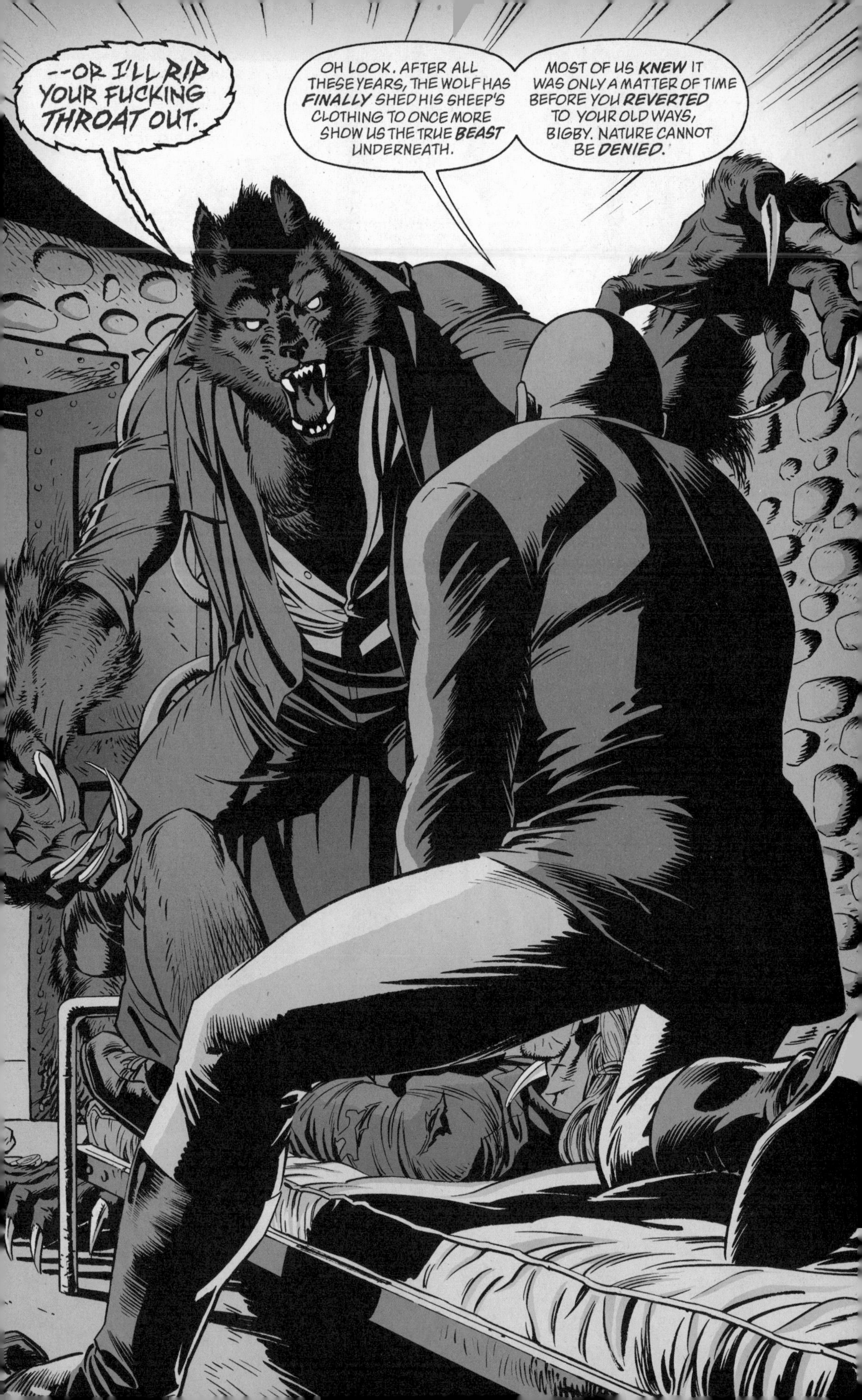
--OR I'LL RIP YOUR FUCKING THROAT OUT.
OH LOOK. AFTER ALL THESE YEARS, THE WOLF HAS FINALLY SHED HIS SHEEP'S CLOTHING TO ONCE MORE SHOW US THE TRUE BEAST UNDERNEATH.
MOST OF US KNEW IT WAS ONLY A MATTER OF TIME BEFORE YOU REVERTED TO YOUR OLD WAYS, BIGBY. NATURE CANNOT BE DENIED.

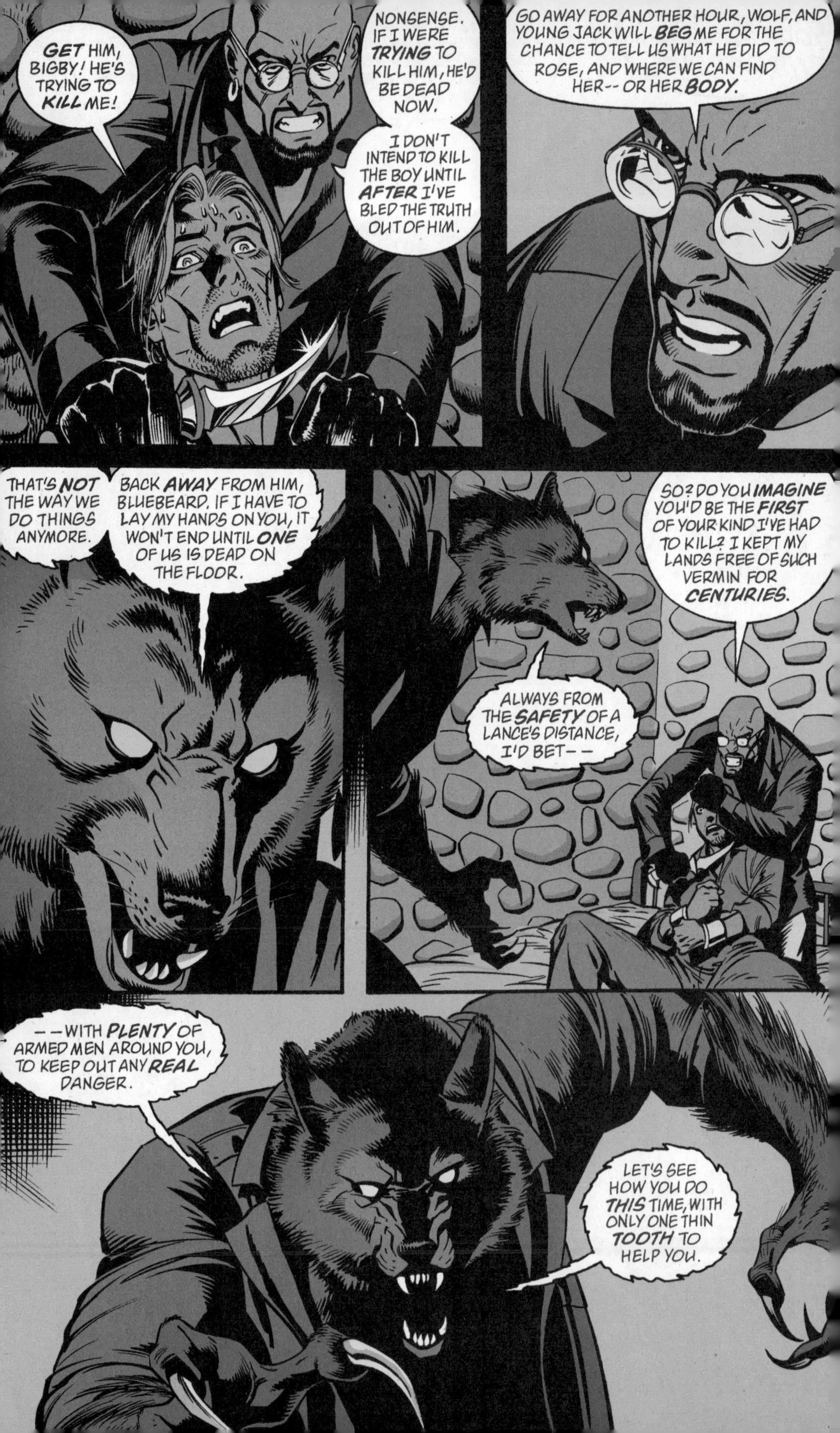
GET HIM, BIGBY! HE'S TRYING TO KILL ME!
NONSENSE. IF I WERE TRYING TO KILL HIM, HE'D BE DEAD NOW.
I DON'T INTEND TO KILL THE BOY UNTIL AFTER I'VE BLED THE TRUTH OUT OF HIM.
GO AWAY FOR ANOTHER HOUR, WOLF, AND YOUNG JACK WILL BEG ME FOR THE CHANCE TO TELL US WHAT HE DID TO ROSE, AND WHERE WE CAN FIND HER-- OR HER BODY.
THAT'S NOT THE WAY WE DO THINGS ANYMORE.
BACK AWAY FROM HIM, BLUEBEARD. IF I HAVE TO LAY MY HANDS ON YOU, IT WON'T END UNTIL ONE OF US IS DEAD ON THE FLOOR.
SO? DO YOU IMAGINE YOU'D BE THE FIRST OF YOUR KIND I'VE HAD TO KILL? I KEPT MY LANDS FREE OF SUCH VERMIN FOR CENTURIES.
ALWAYS FROM THE SAFETY OF A LANCE'S DISTANCE, I'D BET--
--WITH PLENTY OF ARMED MEN AROUND YOU, TO KEEP OUT ANY REAL DANGER.
LET'S SEE HOW YOU DO THIS TIME, WITH ONLY ONE THIN TOOTH TO HELP YOU.

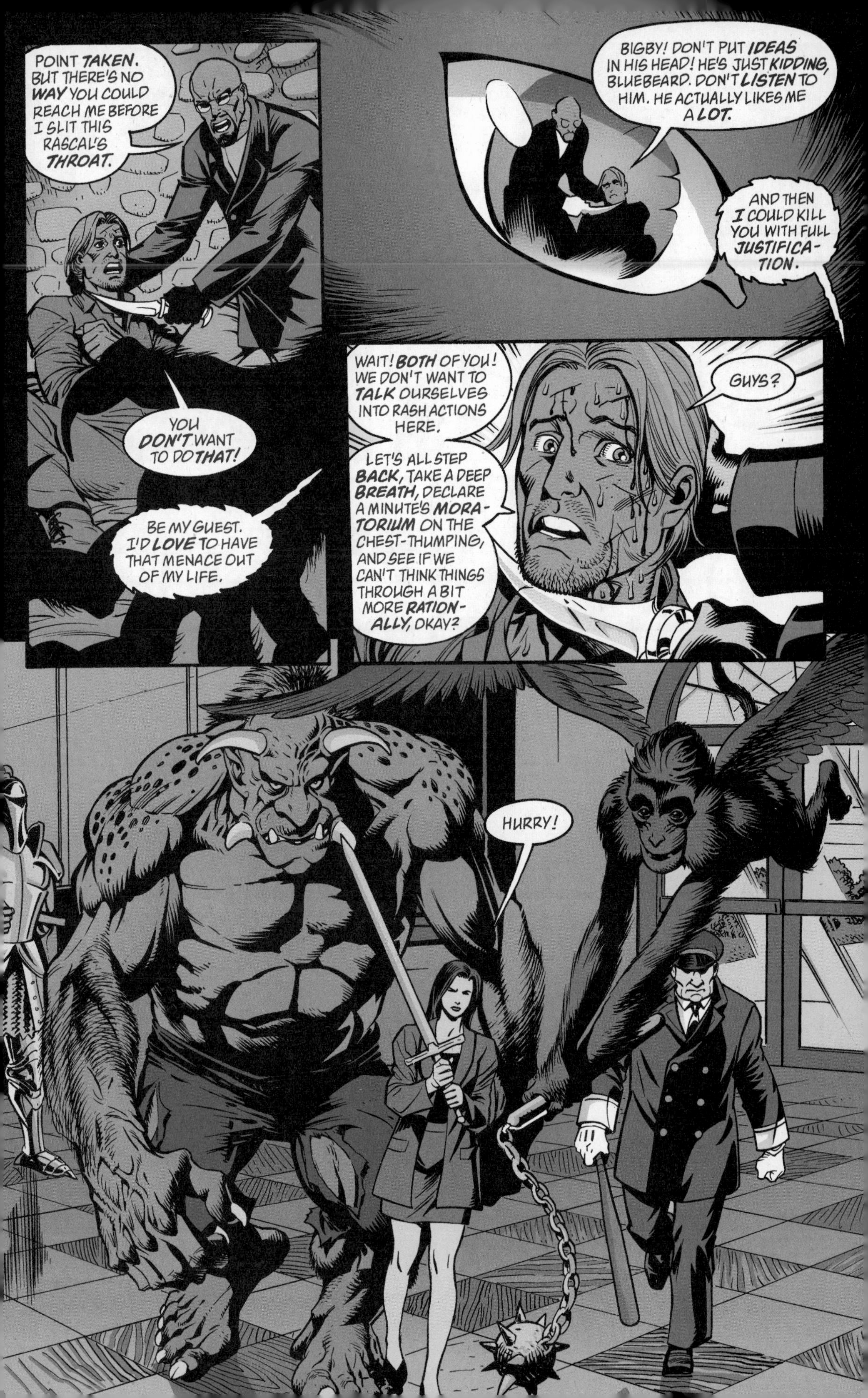

POINT TAKEN. BUT THERE'S NO WAY YOU COULD REACH ME BEFORE I SLIT THIS RASCAL'S THROAT.
YOU DON'T WANT TO DO THAT!
BE MY GUEST. I'D LOVE TO HAVE THAT MENACE OUT OF MY LIFE.
BIGBY! DON'T PUT IDEAS IN HIS HEAD! HE'S JUST KIDDING, BLUEBEARD. DON'T LISTEN TO HIM. HE ACTUALLY LIKES ME A LOT.
AND THEN I COULD KILL YOU WITH FULL JUSTIFICA-TION.
WAIT! BOTH OF YOU! WE DON'T WANT TO TALK OURSELVES INTO RASH ACTIONS HERE.
LET'S ALL STEP BACK, TAKE A DEEP BREATH, DECLARE A MINUTE'S MORA-TORIUM ON THE CHEST-THUMPING, AND SEE IF WE CAN'T THINK THINGS THROUGH A BIT MORE RATION-ALLY, OKAY?
GUYS?
HURRY!

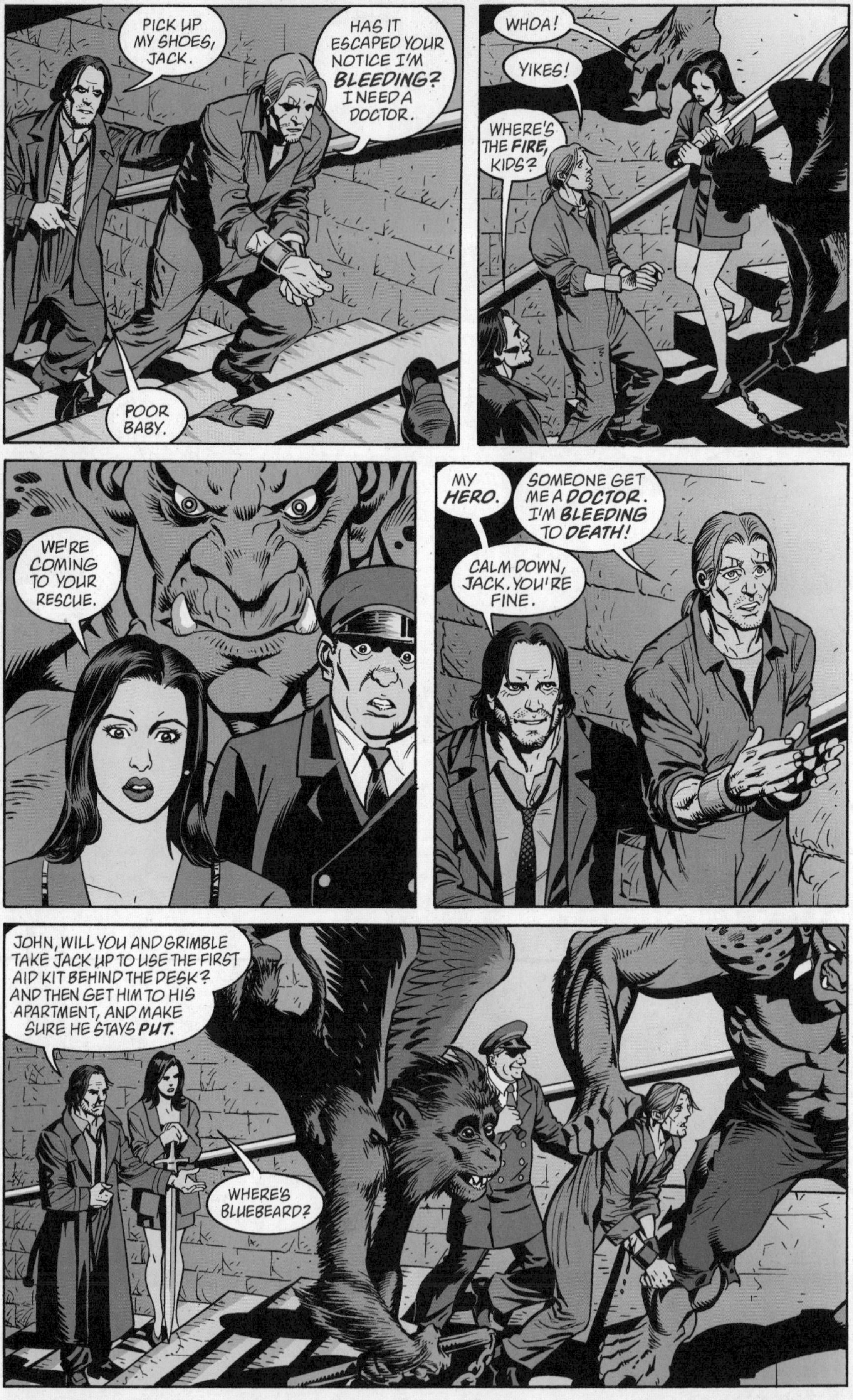

PICK UP MY SHOES, JACK.
HAS IT ESCAPED YOUR NOTICE I'M BLEEDING? I NEED A DOCTOR.
POOR BABY.
WHOA!
YIKES!
WHERE'S THE FIRE, KIDS?
WE'RE COMING TO YOUR RESCUE.
MY HERO.
SOMEONE GET ME A DOCTOR. I'M BLEEDING TO DEATH!
CALM DOWN, JACK. YOU'RE FINE.
JOHN, WILL YOU AND GRIMBLE TAKE JACK UP TO USE THE FIRST AID KIT BEHIND THE DESK? AND THEN GET HIM TO HIS APARTMENT, AND MAKE SURE HE STAYS PUT.
WHERE'S BLUEBEARD?

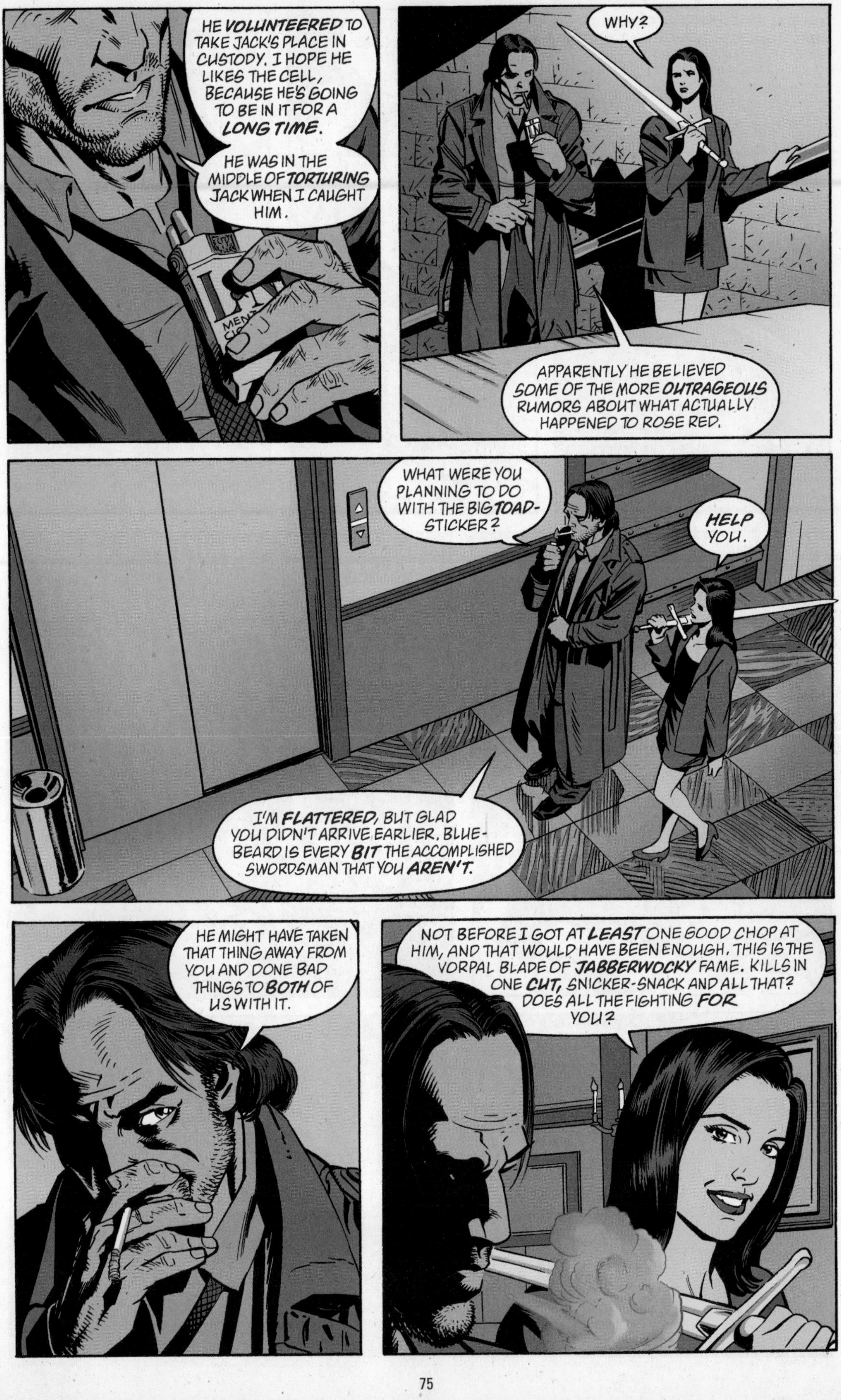
HE VOLUNTEERED TO TAKE JACK'S PLACE IN CUSTODY. I HOPE HE LIKES THE CELL, BECAUSE HE'S GOING TO BE IN IT FOR A LONG TIME.
HE WAS IN THE MIDDLE OF TORTURING JACK WHEN I CAUGHT HIM.
WHY?
APPARENTLY HE BELIEVED SOME OF THE MORE OUTRAGEOUS RUMORS ABOUT WHAT ACTUALLY HAPPENED TO ROSE RED.
WHAT WERE YOU PLANNING TO DO WITH THE BIG TOAD-STICKER?
HELP YOU.
I'M FLATTERED, BUT GLAD YOU DIDN'T ARRIVE EARLIER. BLUE-BEARD IS EVERY BIT THE ACCOMPLISHED SWORDSMAN THAT YOU AREN'T.
HE MIGHT HAVE TAKEN THAT THING AWAY FROM YOU AND DONE BAD THINGS TO BOTH OF US WITH IT.
NOT BEFORE I GOT AT LEAST ONE GOOD CHOP AT HIM, AND THAT WOULD HAVE BEEN ENOUGH. THIS IS THE VORPAL BLADE OF JABBERWOCKY FAME. KILLS IN ONE CUT, SNICKER-SNACK AND ALL THAT? DOES ALL THE FIGHTING FOR YOU?

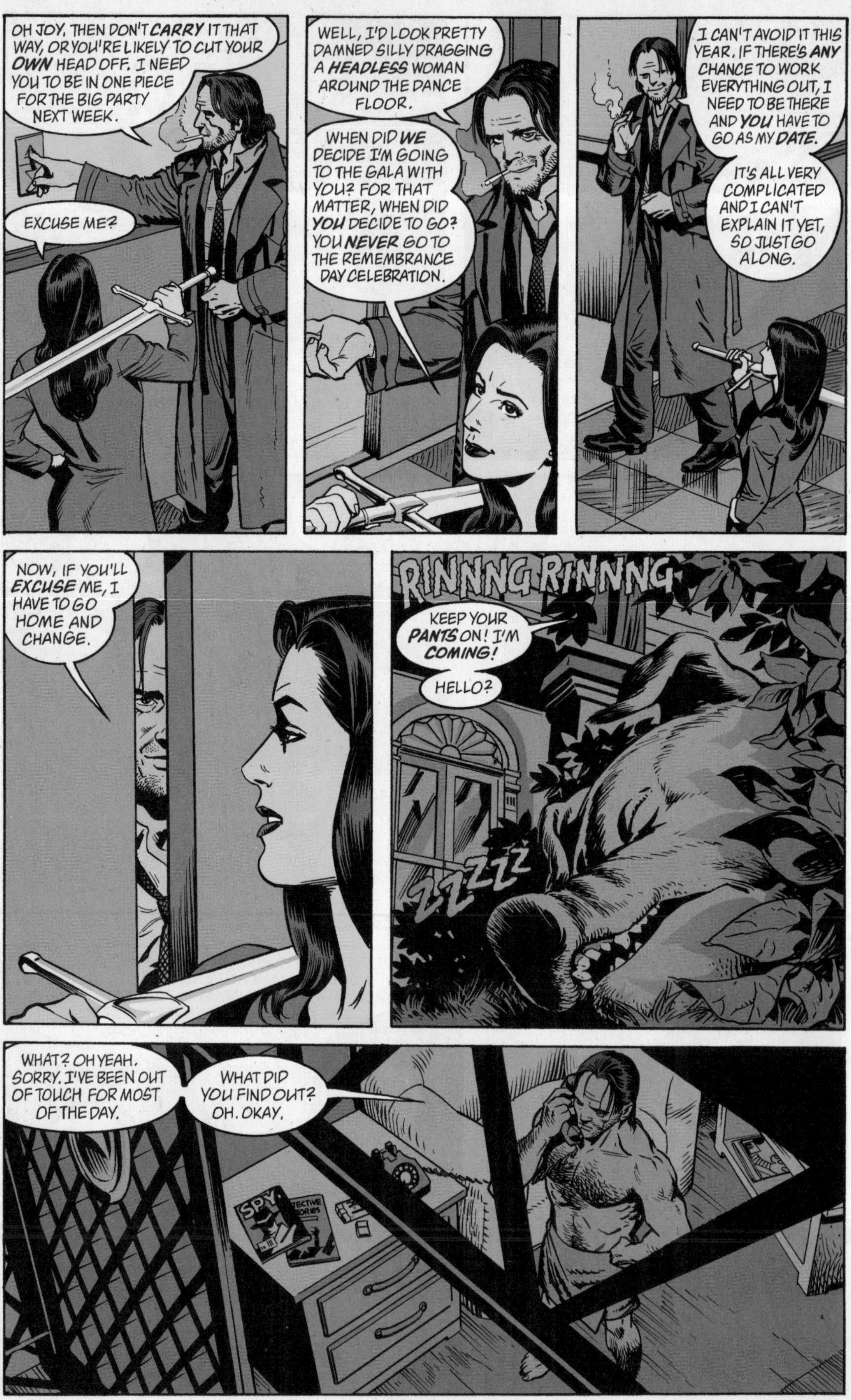
OH JOY, THEN DON'T CARRY IT THAT WAY, OR YOU'RE LIKELY TO CUT YOUR OWN HEAD OFF. I NEED YOU TO BE IN ONE PIECE FOR THE BIG PARTY NEXT WEEK.
EXCUSE ME?
WELL, I'D LOOK PRETTY DAMNED SILLY DRAGGING A HEADLESS WOMAN AROUND THE DANCE FLOOR.
WHEN DID WE DECIDE I'M GOING TO THE GALA WITH YOU? FOR THAT MATTER, WHEN DID YOU DECIDE TO GO? YOU NEVER GO TO THE REMEMBRANCE DAY CELEBRATION.
I CAN'T AVOID IT THIS YEAR. IF THERE'S ANY CHANCE TO WORK EVERYTHING OUT, I NEED TO BE THERE AND YOU HAVE TO GO AS MY DATE.
IT'S ALL VERY COMPLICATED AND I CAN'T EXPLAIN IT YET, SO JUST GO ALONG.
NOW, IF YOU'LL EXCUSE ME, I HAVE TO GO HOME AND CHANGE.
RINNNG RINNNG
KEEP YOUR PANTS ON! I'M COMING!
HELLO?
ZZZZZ
WHAT? OH YEAH. SORRY. I'VE BEEN OUT OF TOUCH FOR MOST OF THE DAY.
WHAT DID YOU FIND OUT? OH. OKAY.

NOT YET. I'VE GOT **MORE** BAD NEWS FOR THE TWO OF YOU. YOU NEED TO CLEAN UP THE PLACE. MOP, WAX, SCRUB AND PAINT UNTIL YOU RETURN IT TO **PRISTINE** CONDITION.

AND YOU NEED TO WORK FAST, BECAUSE WE COULD ONLY **AFFORD** TO RENT THE PLACE FOR TWO DAYS.

WHEN YOU'RE DONE WITH THAT, GO UP TO ROSE RED'S PLACE AND DO THE SAME THING, FROM TOP TO BOTTOM.

NOPE. I NO LONGER NEED TO **PRESERVE** THE EVIDENCE.

THEN, LAST OF ALL, TAKE THE RUINED FURNITURE FROM BOTH APARTMENTS OUT TO THE DUMP AND **BURN** IT.

AND DON'T LET THE **MUNDYS** CATCH YOU.

WHEN YOU'VE DONE ALL OF THAT, AND **ONLY** THEN, YOU CAN COME HOME.

YEAH, WELL MY HEART **BLEEDS** FOR YOU. YOU KNOW WHAT THEY SAY. THE ONLY **EASY** DAY WAS **YESTERDAY**.

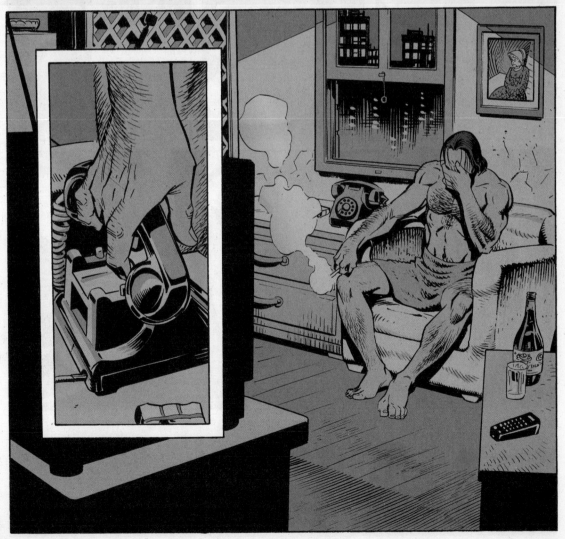

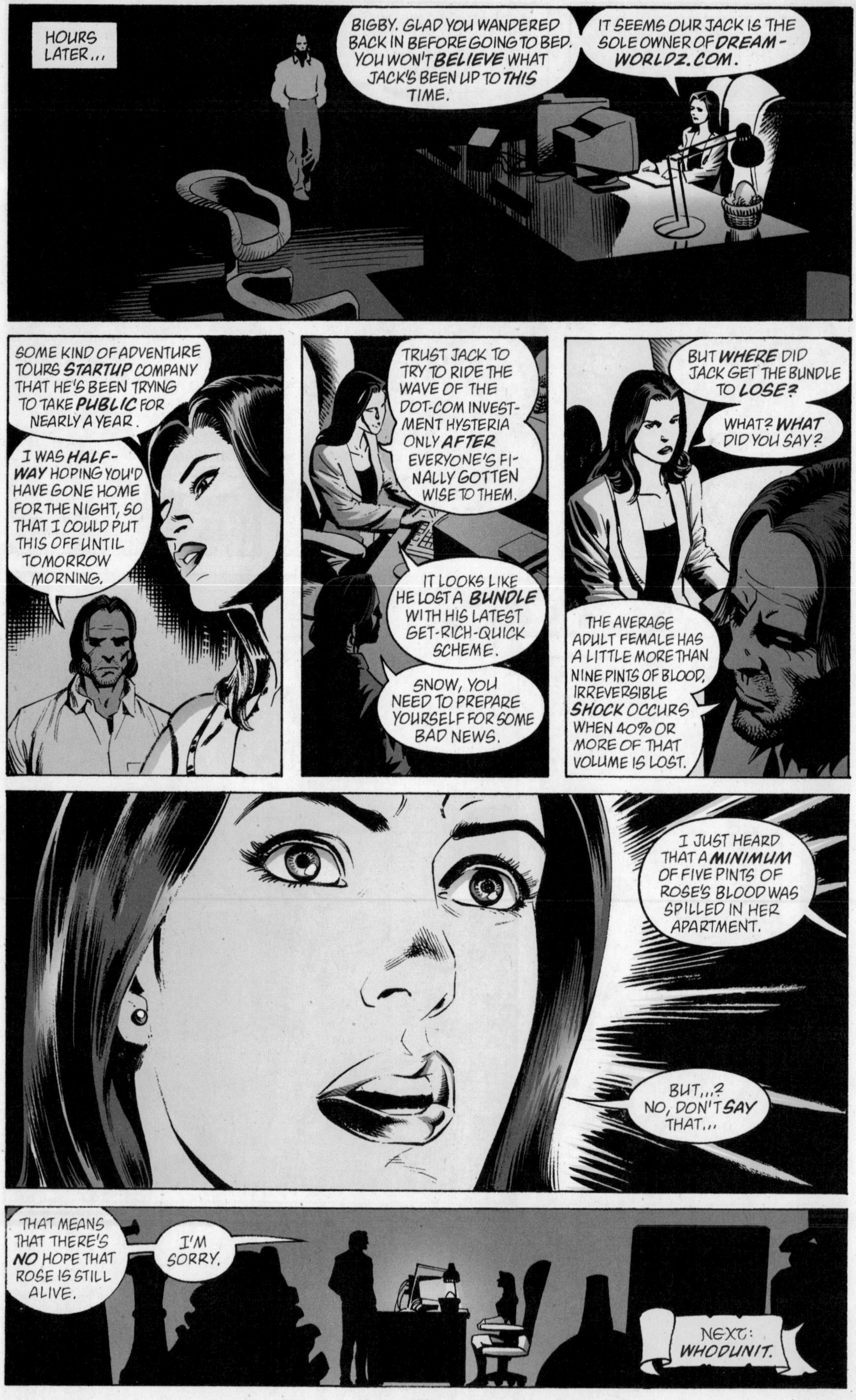
HOURS LATER...
BIGBY. GLAD YOU WANDERED BACK IN BEFORE GOING TO BED. YOU WON'T BELIEVE WHAT JACK'S BEEN UP TO THIS TIME.
IT SEEMS OUR JACK IS THE SOLE OWNER OF DREAM-WORLDZ.COM.
SOME KIND OF ADVENTURE TOURS STARTUP COMPANY THAT HE'S BEEN TRYING TO TAKE PUBLIC FOR NEARLY A YEAR.
I WAS HALF-WAY HOPING YOU'D HAVE GONE HOME FOR THE NIGHT, SO THAT I COULD PUT THIS OFF UNTIL TOMORROW MORNING.
TRUST JACK TO TRY TO RIDE THE WAVE OF THE DOT-COM INVEST-MENT HYSTERIA ONLY AFTER EVERYONE'S FI-NALLY GOTTEN WISE TO THEM.
IT LOOKS LIKE HE LOST A BUNDLE WITH HIS LATEST GET-RICH-QUICK SCHEME.
SNOW, YOU NEED TO PREPARE YOURSELF FOR SOME BAD NEWS.
BUT WHERE DID JACK GET THE BUNDLE TO LOSE?
WHAT? WHAT DID YOU SAY?
THE AVERAGE ADULT FEMALE HAS A LITTLE MORE THAN NINE PINTS OF BLOOD. IRREVERSIBLE SHOCK OCCURS WHEN 40% OR MORE OF THAT VOLUME IS LOST.
I JUST HEARD THAT A MINIMUM OF FIVE PINTS OF ROSE'S BLOOD WAS SPILLED IN HER APARTMENT.
BUT...? NO, DON'T SAY THAT...
THAT MEANS THAT THERE'S NO HOPE THAT ROSE IS STILL ALIVE.
I'M SORRY.
NEXT: WHODUNIT.

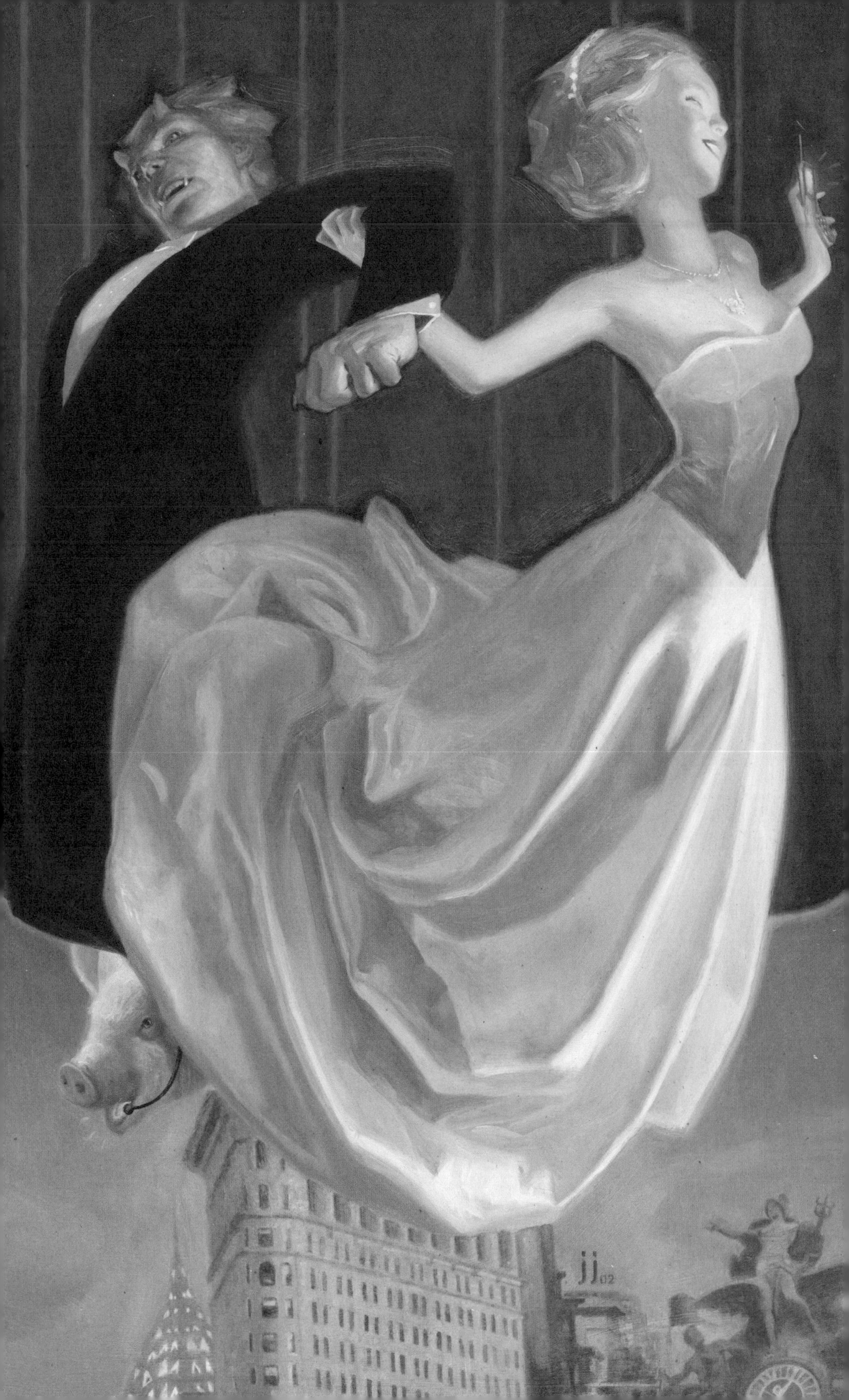
jj02

ND JUST LIKE THAT, THE BIG DAY ARRIVED.

FABLETOWN'S GRANDEST EVENT OF THE YEAR, LIKE CHRISTMAS AND FOURTH OF JULY MULTIPLIED MANY TIMES OVER.

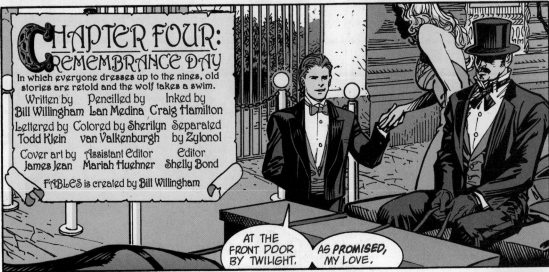

CHAPTER FOUR: REMEMBRANCE DAY

In which everyone dresses up to the nines, old stories are retold and the wolf takes a swim.

Written by
Bill Willingham

Pencilled by
Lan Medina

Inked by
Craig Hamilton

Lettered by
Todd Klein

Colored by
Sherilyn van Valkenburgh

Separated by Zylonol

Cover art by
James Jean

Assistant Editor
Mariah Huehner

Editor
Shelly Bond

FABLES is created by Bill Willingham

AT THE FRONT DOOR BY TWILIGHT.

AS PROMISED, MY LOVE.

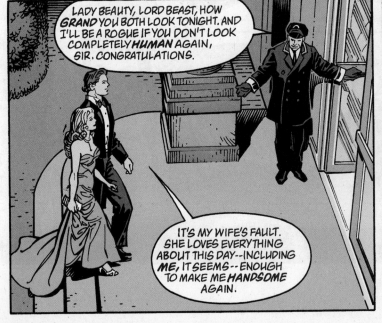

LADY BEAUTY, LORD BEAST, HOW GRAND YOU BOTH LOOK TONIGHT. AND I'LL BE A ROGUE IF YOU DON'T LOOK COMPLETELY HUMAN AGAIN, SIR. CONGRATULATIONS.

IT'S MY WIFE'S FAULT. SHE LOVES EVERYTHING ABOUT THIS DAY--INCLUDING ME, IT SEEMS--ENOUGH TO MAKE ME HANDSOME AGAIN.

DON'T START.

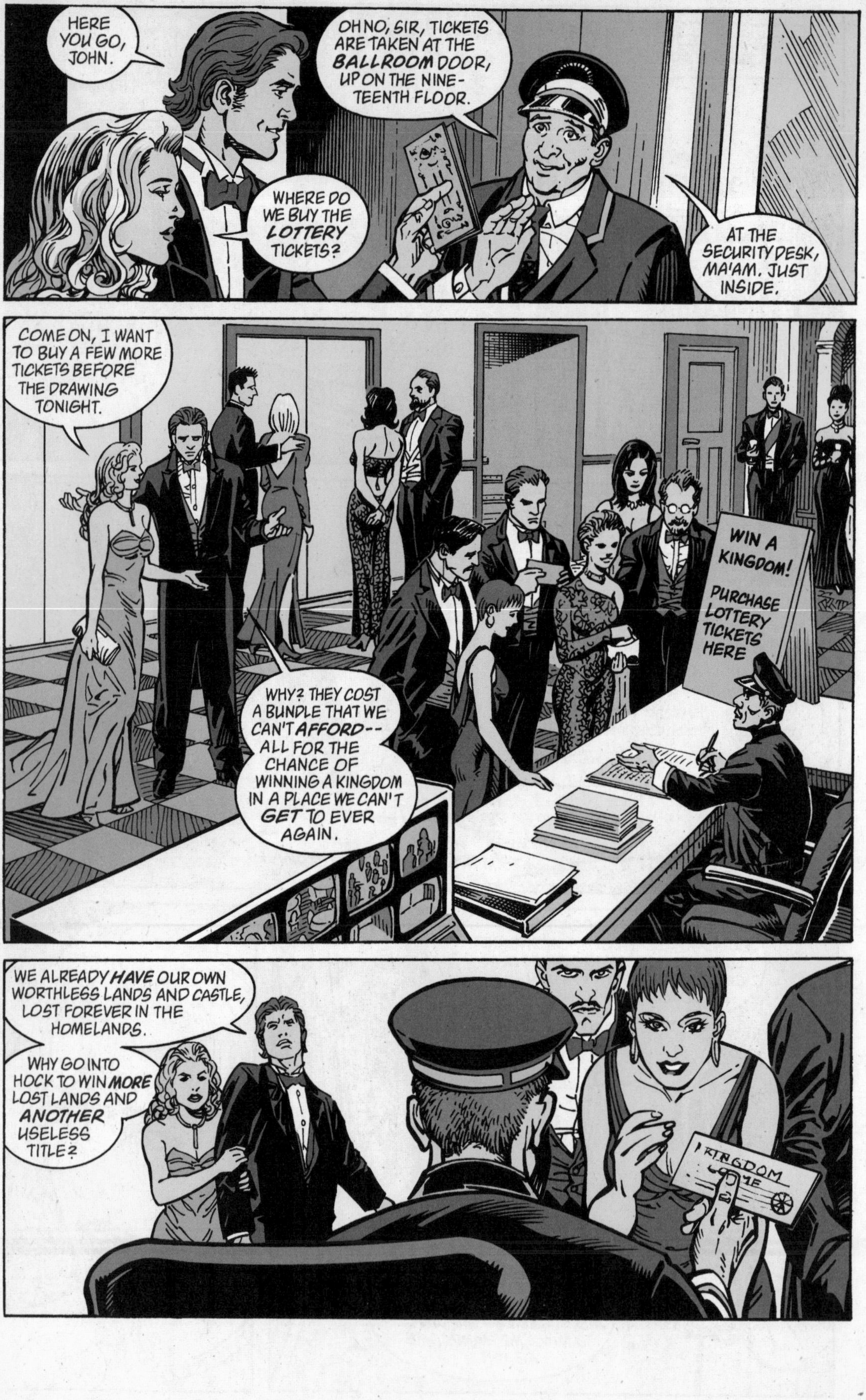
HERE YOU GO, JOHN.
OH NO, SIR, TICKETS ARE TAKEN AT THE BALLROOM DOOR, UP ON THE NINETEENTH FLOOR.
WHERE DO WE BUY THE LOTTERY TICKETS?
AT THE SECURITY DESK, MA'AM. JUST INSIDE.
COME ON, I WANT TO BUY A FEW MORE TICKETS BEFORE THE DRAWING TONIGHT.
WIN A KINGDOM!
PURCHASE LOTTERY TICKETS HERE
WHY? THEY COST A BUNDLE THAT WE CAN'T AFFORD-- ALL FOR THE CHANCE OF WINNING A KINGDOM IN A PLACE WE CAN'T GET TO EVER AGAIN.
WE ALREADY HAVE OUR OWN WORTHLESS LANDS AND CASTLE, LOST FOREVER IN THE HOMELANDS.
WHY GO INTO HOCK TO WIN MORE LOST LANDS AND ANOTHER USELESS TITLE?
KINGDOM

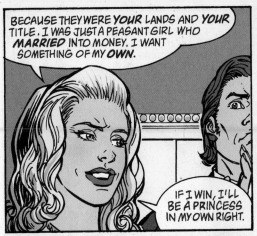

BECAUSE THEY WERE **YOUR** LANDS AND **YOUR** TITLE. I WAS JUST A PEASANT GIRL WHO **MARRIED** INTO MONEY. I WANT SOMETHING OF MY **OWN**.

IF I WIN, I'LL BE A PRINCESS IN MY OWN RIGHT.

BUT STILL WORKING FOR MINIMUM WAGE IN A **BOOKSTORE**.

DON'T **SPOIL** THE EVENING, DARLING.

A HUNDRED DOLLARS A TICKET, BUT FIFTY DOLLARS **OFF** IF YOU BUY FIVE AT A TIME.

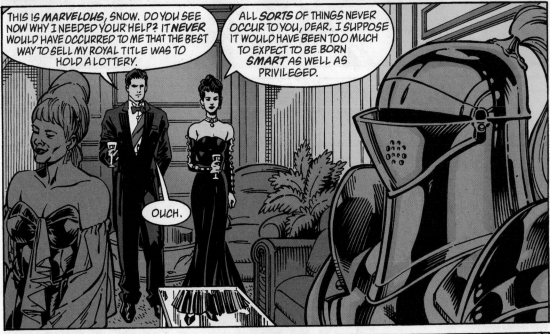

THIS IS **MARVELOUS**, SNOW. DO YOU SEE NOW WHY I NEEDED YOUR HELP? IT **NEVER** WOULD HAVE OCCURRED TO ME THAT THE BEST WAY TO SELL MY ROYAL TITLE WAS TO HOLD A LOTTERY.

ALL **SORTS** OF THINGS NEVER OCCUR TO YOU, DEAR. I SUPPOSE IT WOULD HAVE BEEN TOO MUCH TO EXPECT TO BE BORN **SMART** AS WELL AS PRIVILEGED.

OUCH.

HOW MUCH HAVE WE MADE SO FAR?

AS OF THIS MORNING, WE WERE CLOSING IN ON THREE HUNDRED **GRAND**, BUT SALES HAVE PICKED UP TODAY. I'D BE SURPRISED IF WE HAVEN'T **DOUBLED** THAT AMOUNT BY NOW.

LOVELY. WHO WOULD HAVE THOUGHT THAT SO **MANY** WOULD WILLINGLY SPEND SO **MUCH** FOR A SLIGHT CHANCE TO WIN ABSOLUTELY **NOTHING** OF SUBSTANCE?

NO WONDER THEY CALL LOTTERIES **TAXES** ON STUPID PEOPLE.

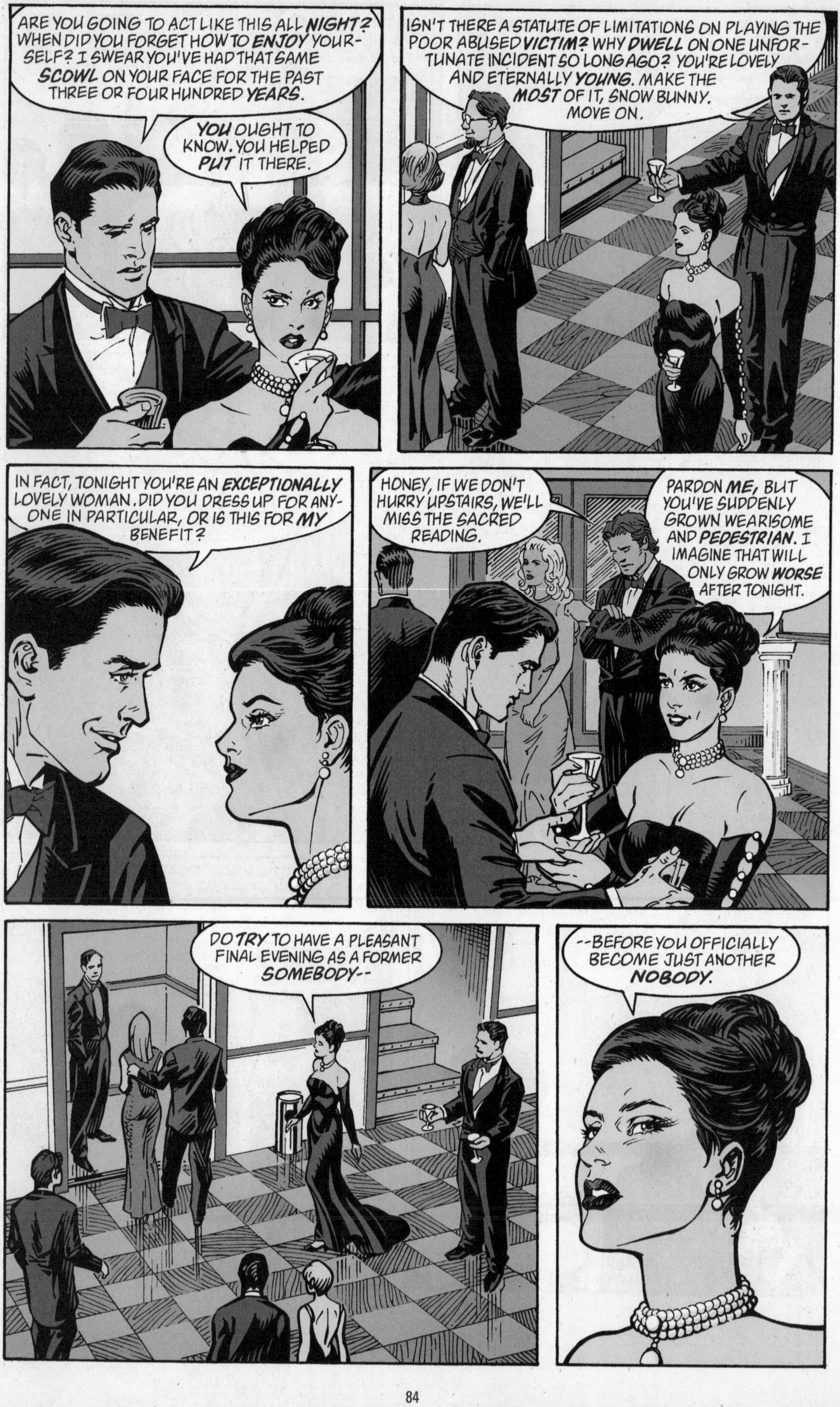
ARE YOU GOING TO ACT LIKE THIS ALL NIGHT? WHEN DID YOU FORGET HOW TO ENJOY YOURSELF? I SWEAR YOU'VE HAD THAT SAME SCOWL ON YOUR FACE FOR THE PAST THREE OR FOUR HUNDRED YEARS.
YOU OUGHT TO KNOW. YOU HELPED PUT IT THERE.
ISN'T THERE A STATUTE OF LIMITATIONS ON PLAYING THE POOR ABUSED VICTIM? WHY DWELL ON ONE UNFORTUNATE INCIDENT SO LONG AGO? YOU'RE LOVELY AND ETERNALLY YOUNG. MAKE THE MOST OF IT, SNOW BUNNY. MOVE ON.
IN FACT, TONIGHT YOU'RE AN EXCEPTIONALLY LOVELY WOMAN. DID YOU DRESS UP FOR ANYONE IN PARTICULAR, OR IS THIS FOR MY BENEFIT?
HONEY, IF WE DON'T HURRY UPSTAIRS, WE'LL MISS THE SACRED READING.
PARDON ME, BUT YOU'VE SUDDENLY GROWN WEARISOME AND PEDESTRIAN. I IMAGINE THAT WILL ONLY GROW WORSE AFTER TONIGHT.
DO TRY TO HAVE A PLEASANT FINAL EVENING AS A FORMER SOMEBODY--
--BEFORE YOU OFFICIALLY BECOME JUST ANOTHER NOBODY.

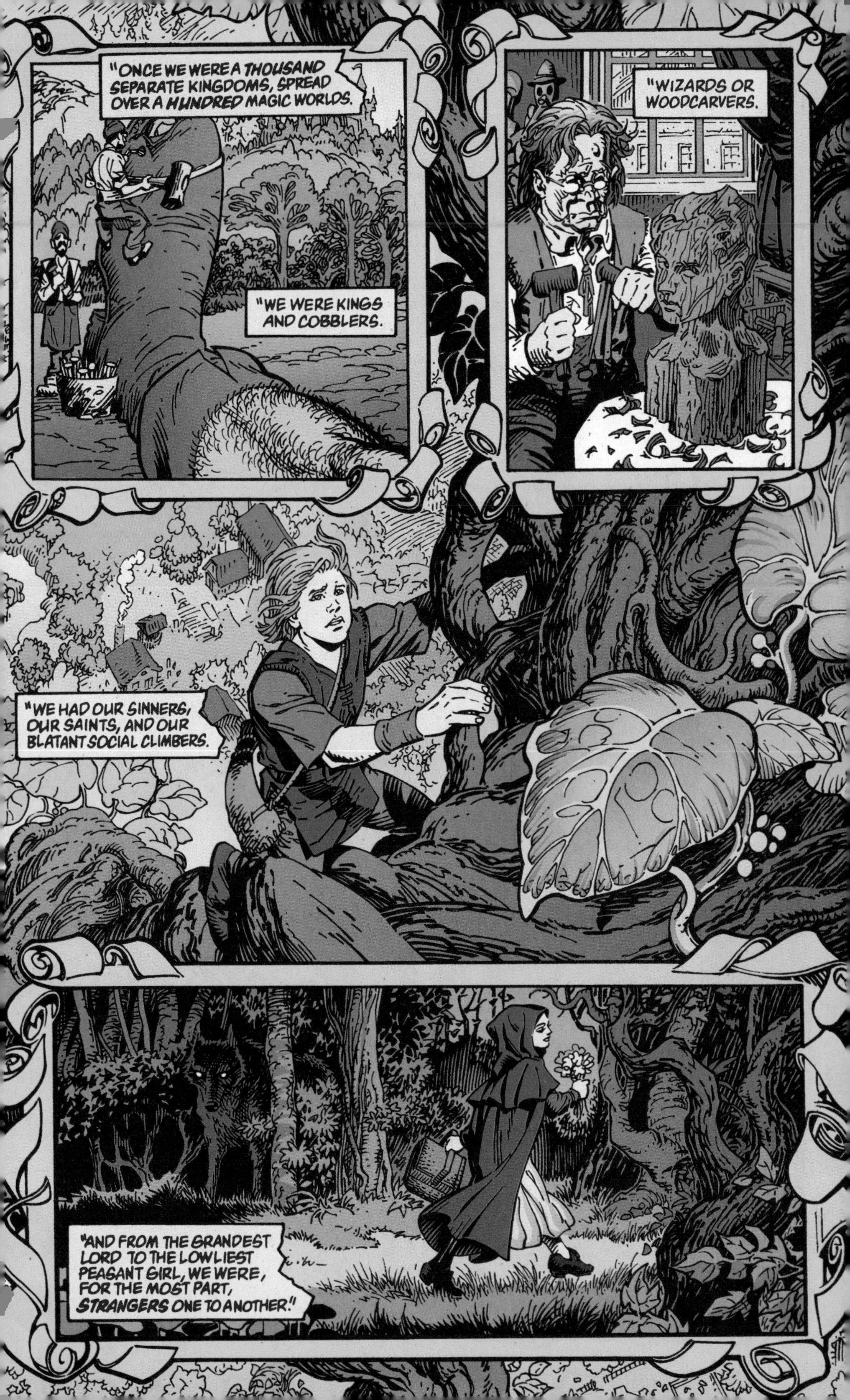
"ONCE WE WERE A THOUSAND SEPARATE KINGDOMS, SPREAD OVER A HUNDRED MAGIC WORLDS.
"WE WERE KINGS AND COBBLERS.
"WIZARDS OR WOODCARVERS.
"WE HAD OUR SINNERS, OUR SAINTS, AND OUR BLATANT SOCIAL CLIMBERS.
"AND FROM THE GRANDEST LORD TO THE LOWLIEST PEASANT GIRL, WE WERE, FOR THE MOST PART, STRANGERS ONE TO ANOTHER."

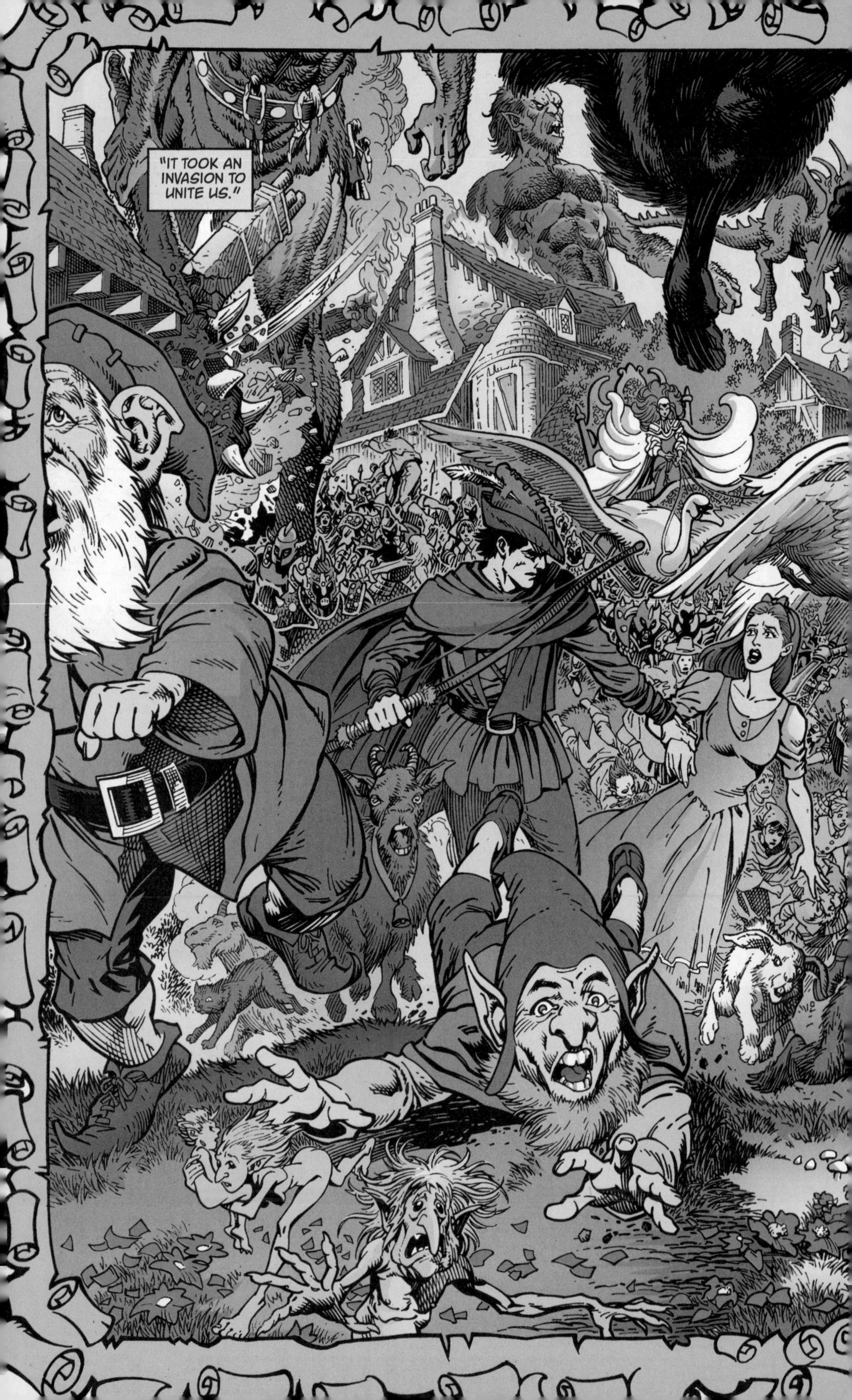
"IT TOOK AN INVASION TO UNITE US."

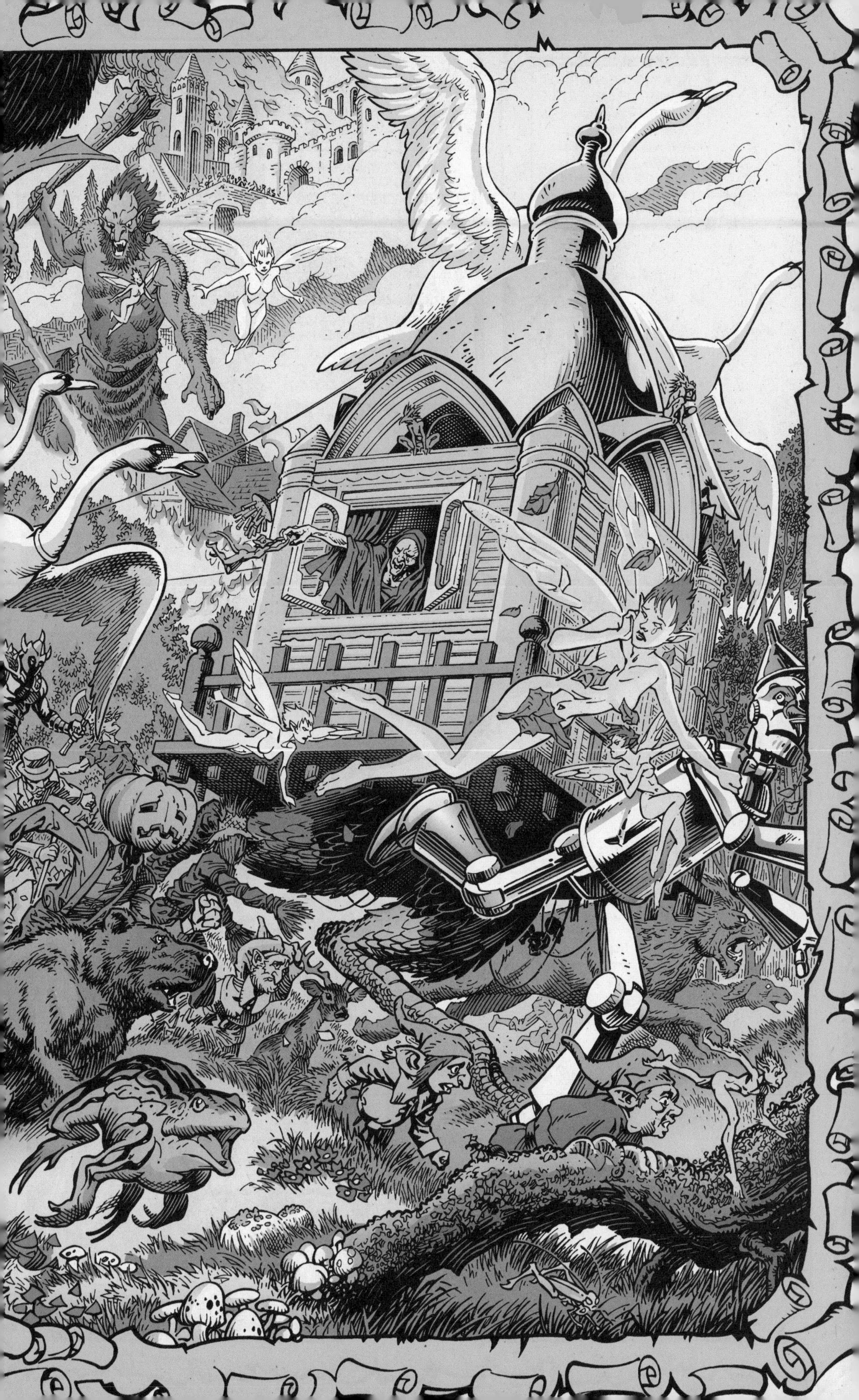

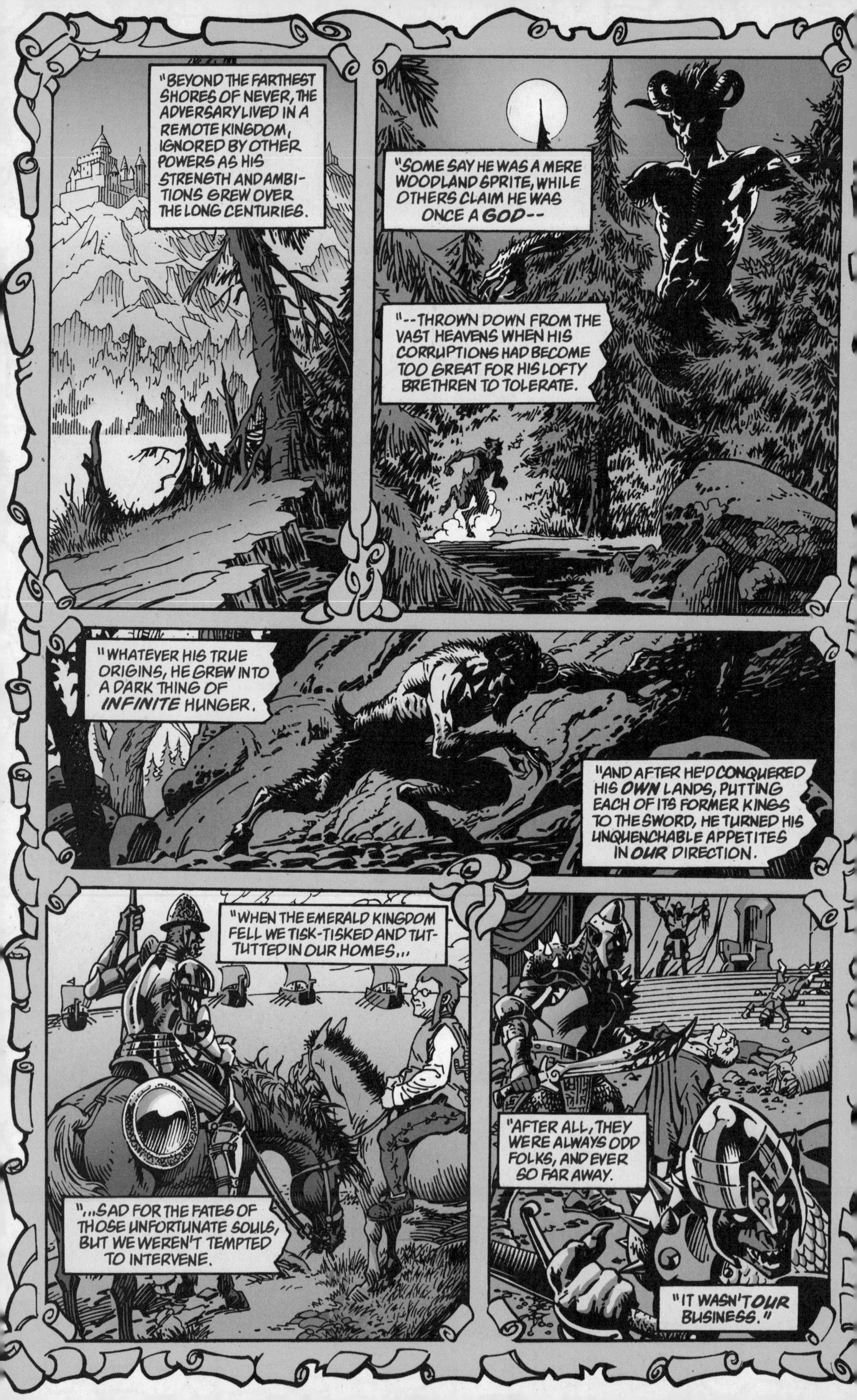
"BEYOND THE FARTHEST SHORES OF NEVER, THE ADVERSARY LIVED IN A REMOTE KINGDOM, IGNORED BY OTHER POWERS AS HIS STRENGTH AND AMBITIONS GREW OVER THE LONG CENTURIES.
"SOME SAY HE WAS A MERE WOODLAND SPRITE, WHILE OTHERS CLAIM HE WAS ONCE A GOD--
"--THROWN DOWN FROM THE VAST HEAVENS WHEN HIS CORRUPTIONS HAD BECOME TOO GREAT FOR HIS LOFTY BRETHREN TO TOLERATE.
"WHATEVER HIS TRUE ORIGINS, HE GREW INTO A DARK THING OF INFINITE HUNGER.
"AND AFTER HE'D CONQUERED HIS OWN LANDS, PUTTING EACH OF ITS FORMER KINGS TO THE SWORD, HE TURNED HIS UNQUENCHABLE APPETITES IN OUR DIRECTION.
"WHEN THE EMERALD KINGDOM FELL WE TISK-TISKED AND TUT-TUTTED IN OUR HOMES...
"...SAD FOR THE FATES OF THOSE UNFORTUNATE SOULS, BUT WE WEREN'T TEMPTED TO INTERVENE.
"AFTER ALL, THEY WERE ALWAYS ODD FOLKS, AND EVER SO FAR AWAY.
"IT WASN'T OUR BUSINESS."

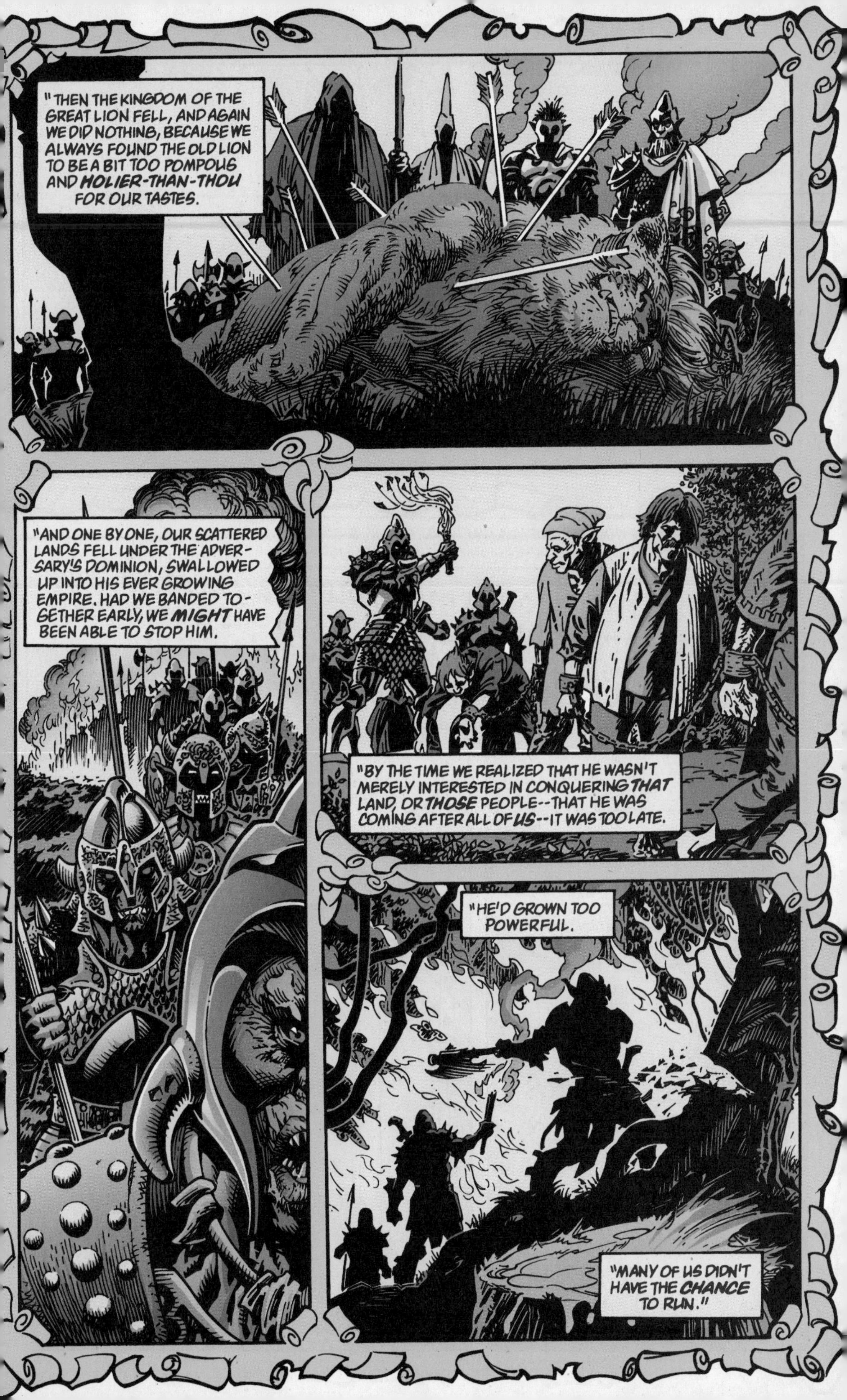
"THEN THE KINGDOM OF THE GREAT LION FELL, AND AGAIN WE DID NOTHING, BECAUSE WE ALWAYS FOUND THE OLD LION TO BE A BIT TOO POMPOUS AND HOLIER-THAN-THOU FOR OUR TASTES.
"AND ONE BY ONE, OUR SCATTERED LANDS FELL UNDER THE ADVERSARY'S DOMINION, SWALLOWED UP INTO HIS EVER GROWING EMPIRE. HAD WE BANDED TOGETHER EARLY, WE MIGHT HAVE BEEN ABLE TO STOP HIM.
"BY THE TIME WE REALIZED THAT HE WASN'T MERELY INTERESTED IN CONQUERING THAT LAND, OR THOSE PEOPLE--THAT HE WAS COMING AFTER ALL OF US--IT WAS TOO LATE.
"HE'D GROWN TOO POWERFUL.
"MANY OF US DIDN'T HAVE THE CHANCE TO RUN."

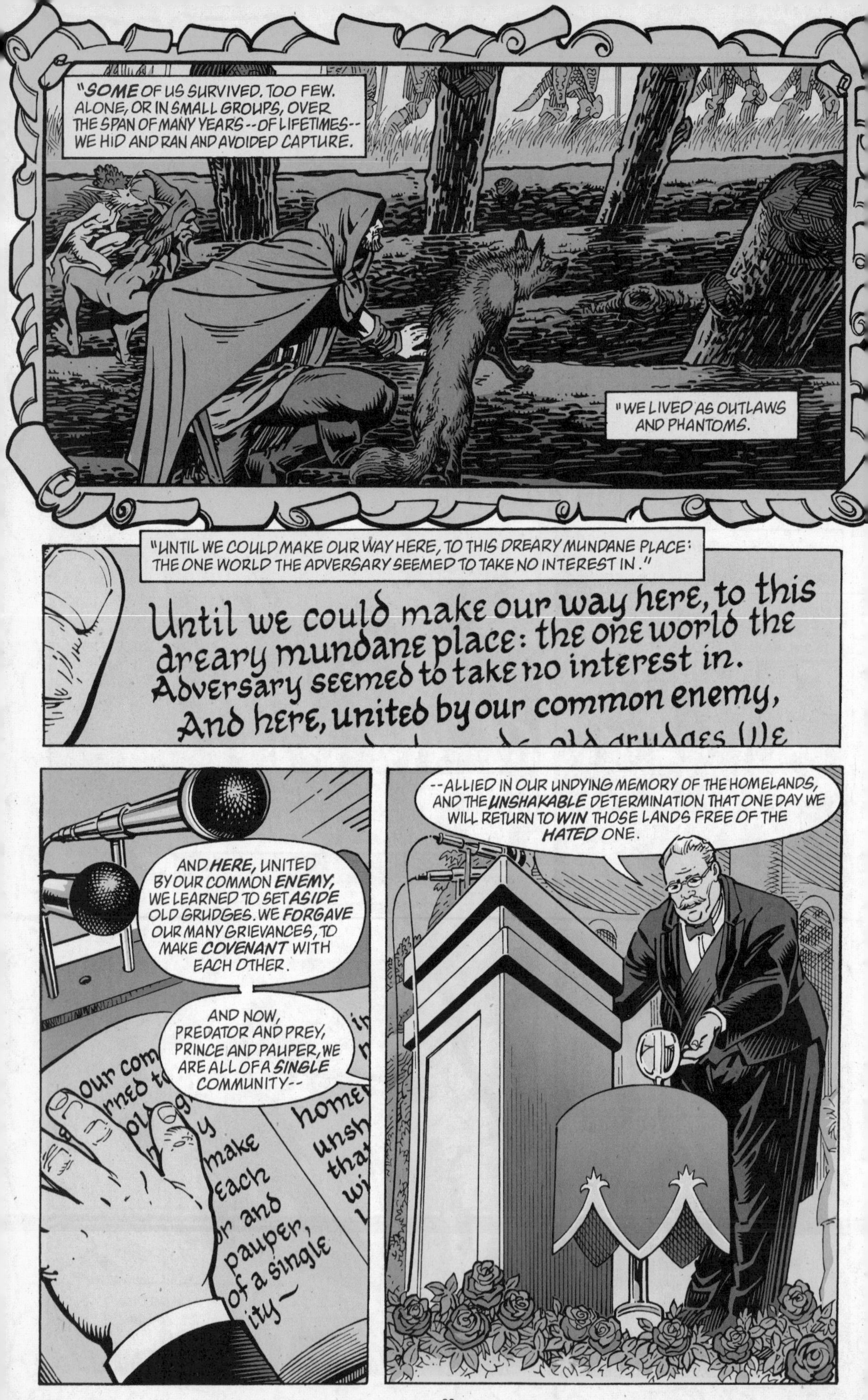
"SOME OF US SURVIVED. TOO FEW. ALONE, OR IN SMALL GROUPS, OVER THE SPAN OF MANY YEARS--OF LIFETIMES--WE HID AND RAN AND AVOIDED CAPTURE.
"WE LIVED AS OUTLAWS AND PHANTOMS.
"UNTIL WE COULD MAKE OUR WAY HERE, TO THIS DREARY MUNDANE PLACE: THE ONE WORLD THE ADVERSARY SEEMED TO TAKE NO INTEREST IN."
Until we could make our way here, to this
dreary mundane place: the one world the
Adversary seemed to take no interest in.
And here, united by our common enemy,
AND HERE, UNITED BY OUR COMMON ENEMY, WE LEARNED TO SET ASIDE OLD GRUDGES. WE FORGAVE OUR MANY GRIEVANCES, TO MAKE COVENANT WITH EACH OTHER.
AND NOW, PREDATOR AND PREY, PRINCE AND PAUPER, WE ARE ALL OF A SINGLE COMMUNITY--
--ALLIED IN OUR UNDYING MEMORY OF THE HOMELANDS, AND THE UNSHAKABLE DETERMINATION THAT ONE DAY WE WILL RETURN TO WIN THOSE LANDS FREE OF THE HATED ONE.

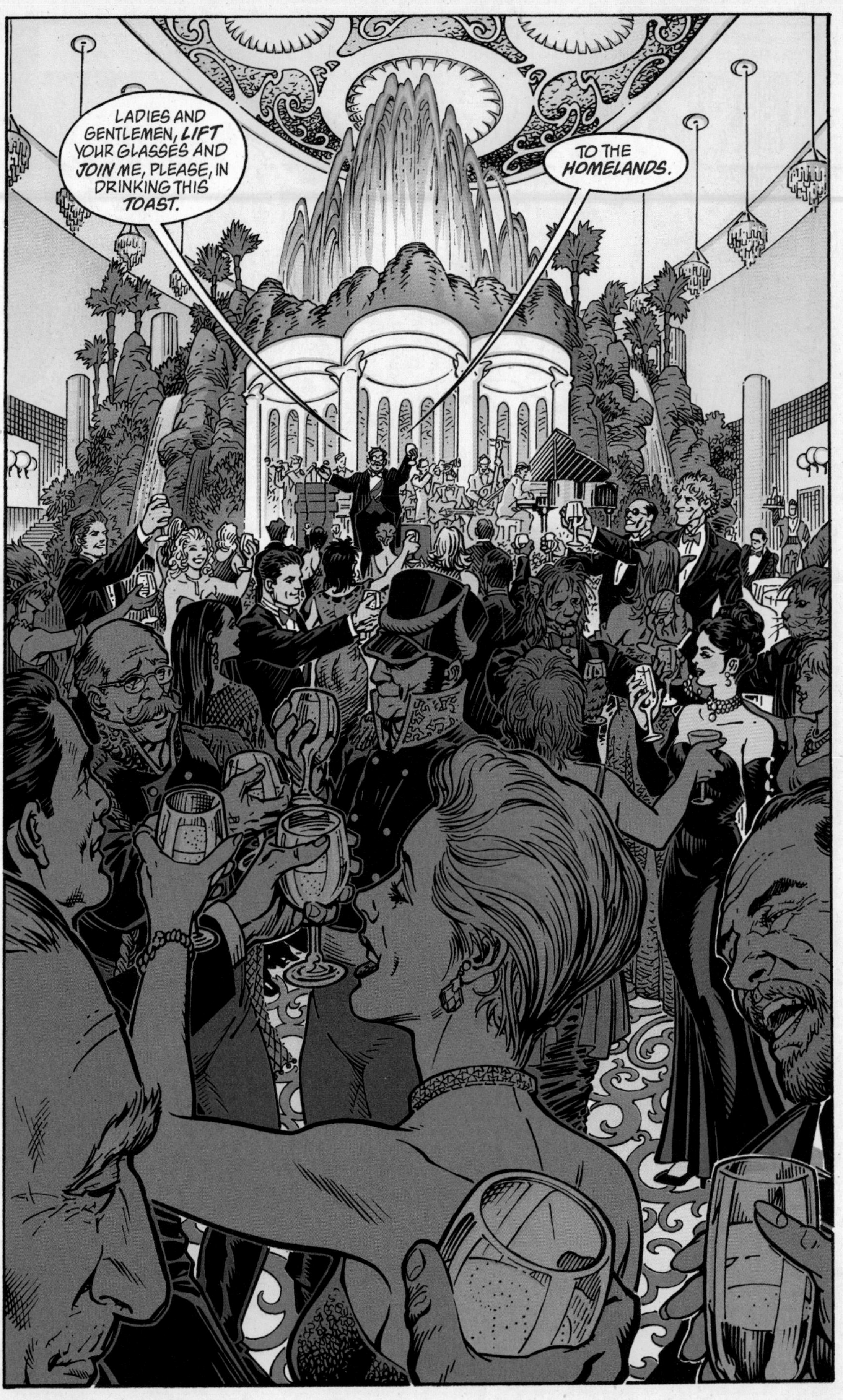
LADIES AND GENTLEMEN, LIFT YOUR GLASSES AND JOIN ME, PLEASE, IN DRINKING THIS TOAST.
TO THE HOMELANDS.

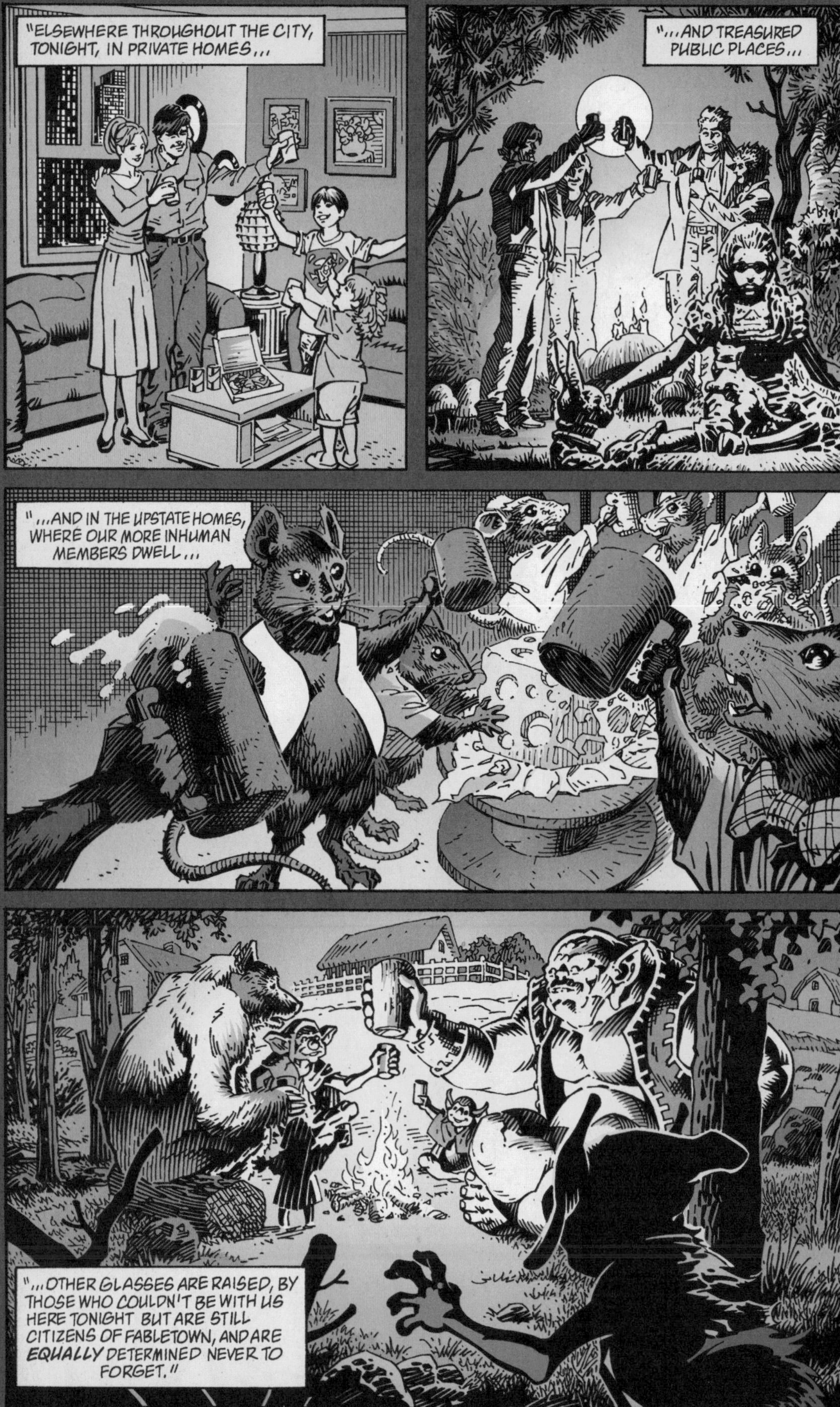
"ELSEWHERE THROUGHOUT THE CITY, TONIGHT, IN PRIVATE HOMES...
"...AND TREASURED PUBLIC PLACES...
"...AND IN THE UPSTATE HOMES, WHERE OUR MORE INHUMAN MEMBERS DWELL...
"...OTHER GLASSES ARE RAISED, BY THOSE WHO COULDN'T BE WITH US HERE TONIGHT BUT ARE STILL CITIZENS OF FABLETOWN, AND ARE **EQUALLY** DETERMINED NEVER TO FORGET."

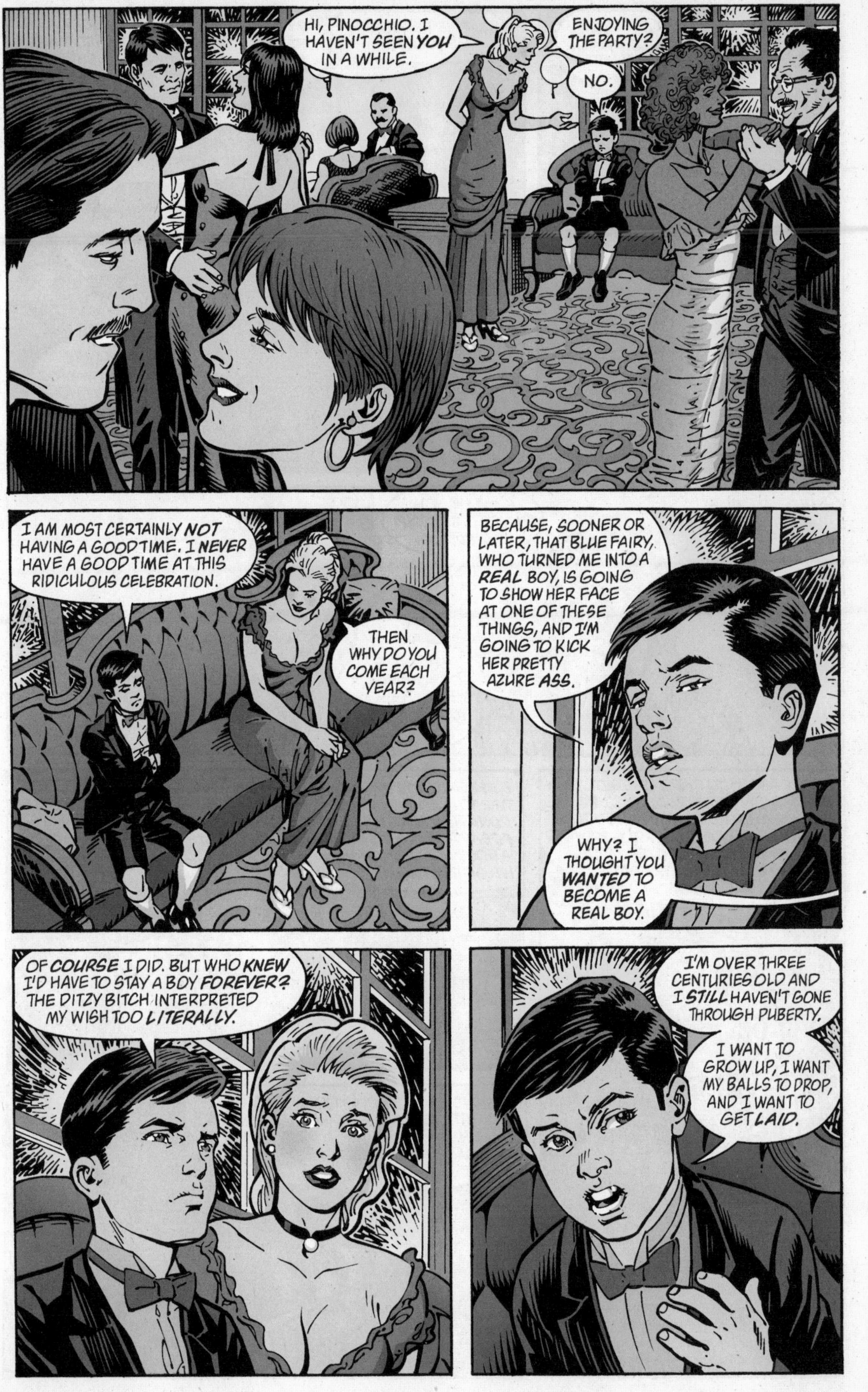
HI, PINOCCHIO. I HAVEN'T SEEN YOU IN A WHILE.
ENJOYING THE PARTY?
NO.
I AM MOST CERTAINLY NOT HAVING A GOOD TIME. I NEVER HAVE A GOOD TIME AT THIS RIDICULOUS CELEBRATION.
THEN WHY DO YOU COME EACH YEAR?
BECAUSE, SOONER OR LATER, THAT BLUE FAIRY, WHO TURNED ME INTO A REAL BOY, IS GOING TO SHOW HER FACE AT ONE OF THESE THINGS, AND I'M GOING TO KICK HER PRETTY AZURE ASS.
WHY? I THOUGHT YOU WANTED TO BECOME A REAL BOY.
OF COURSE I DID. BUT WHO KNEW I'D HAVE TO STAY A BOY FOREVER? THE DITZY BITCH INTERPRETED MY WISH TOO LITERALLY.
I'M OVER THREE CENTURIES OLD AND I STILL HAVEN'T GONE THROUGH PUBERTY.
I WANT TO GROW UP, I WANT MY BALLS TO DROP, AND I WANT TO GET LAID.

SECURITY OFFICE
B. WOLF

BOTH OF YOU, QUIT YOUR DAMNED BITCHING AND CRYING.

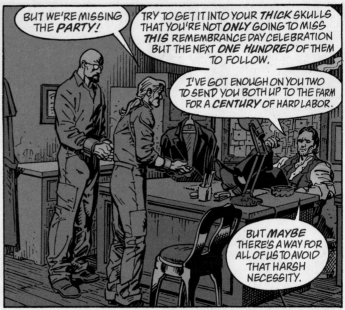

BUT WE'RE MISSING THE *PARTY!*

TRY TO GET IT INTO YOUR *THICK* SKULLS THAT YOU'RE NOT *ONLY* GOING TO MISS *THIS* REMEMBRANCE DAY CELEBRATION BUT THE NEXT *ONE HUNDRED* OF THEM TO FOLLOW.

I'VE GOT ENOUGH ON YOU TWO TO SEND YOU BOTH UP TO THE FARM FOR A *CENTURY* OF HARD LABOR.

BUT *MAYBE* THERE'S A WAY FOR ALL OF US TO AVOID THAT HARSH NECESSITY.

BULLSHIT, BIGBY! SURE, YOU GOT BLUE-BEARD HERE BECAUSE YOU CAUGHT HIM RED-HANDED TORTURING ME...

SHUT UP, YOU PATHETIC, BLEATING *CHILD.*

...BUT YOU'VE GOT NOTHING ON ME -- NOTHING YOU CAN *PROVE,* ANYWAY.

YOU'RE ABOUT TO FIND OUT EXACTLY HOW *MUCH* I CAN PROVE. BUT UNTIL I BRING THE *HAMMER* DOWN, YOU CAN BOTH GO TO WHAT'S *LEFT* OF THE PARTY--PROVIDED YOU STAY AT LEAST A DOZEN YARDS AWAY FROM EACH OTHER AT ALL TIMES.

BLUEBEARD, YOU'VE GOT JUST ENOUGH TIME TO CLEAN UP AND GET YOUR ANNUAL *DONATION* INTO OUR BELOVED MAYOR'S POCKET-- WHICH WILL REMIND US WHAT A GOOD AND *SUPPORTIVE* CITIZEN YOU ARE.

AND *THIS* TIME LEAVE THE GUNS, DAGGERS AND BATTLE AXES AT HOME, PLEASE.

AND JACK, WE'RE GOING TO TALK *PRIVATELY* FOR A BIT. THEN YOU'RE GOING TO DEMONSTRATE YOUR *HELPFUL* NATURE BY DELIVERING A MESSAGE FROM ME TO ONE OF THE PARTY GUESTS.

WHY DON'T YOU RUN YOUR *OWN* DAMNED ERRANDS?

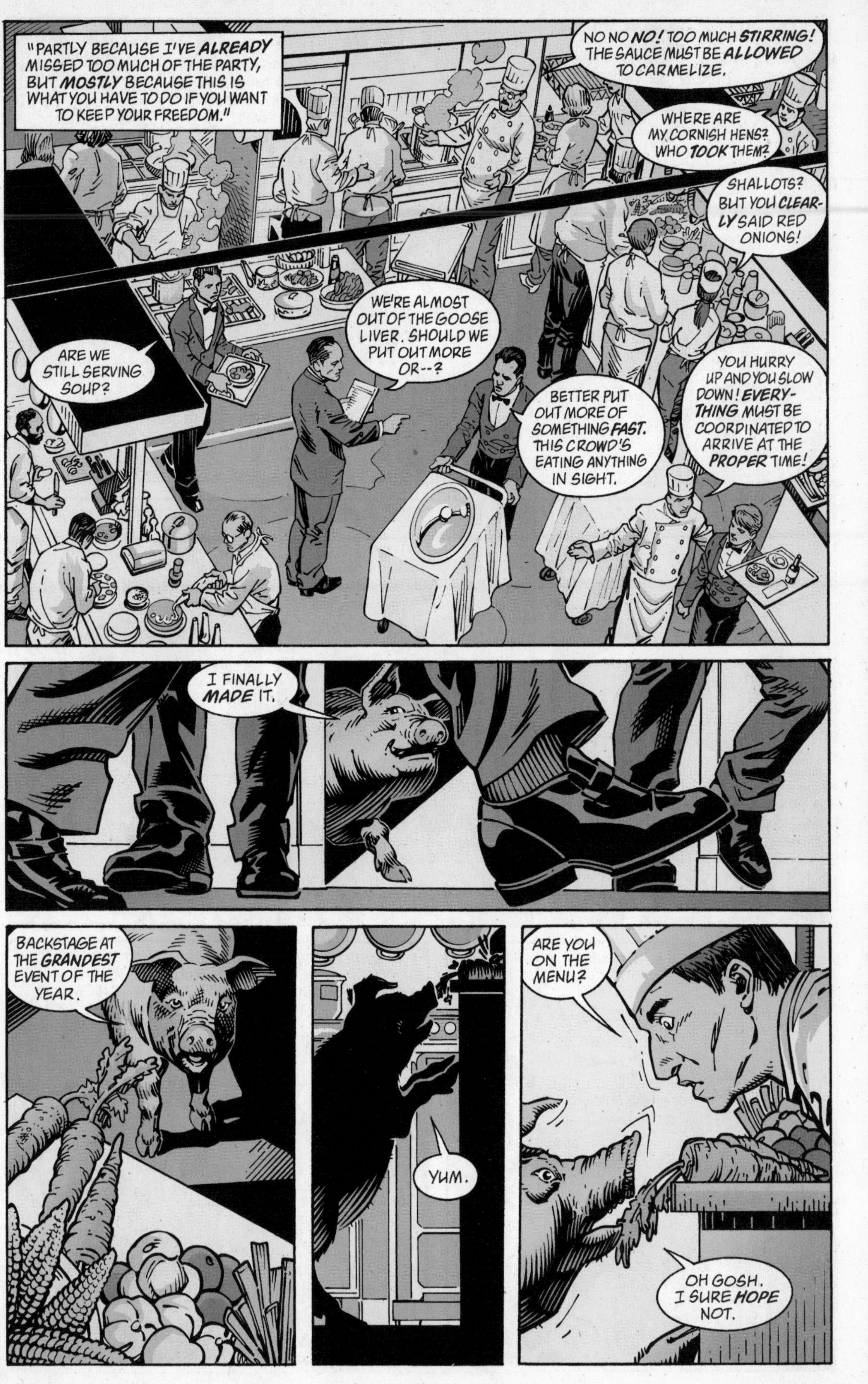
"PARTLY BECAUSE I'VE ALREADY MISSED TOO MUCH OF THE PARTY, BUT MOSTLY BECAUSE THIS IS WHAT YOU HAVE TO DO IF YOU WANT TO KEEP YOUR FREEDOM."
NO NO NO! TOO MUCH STIRRING! THE SAUCE MUST BE ALLOWED TO CARMELIZE.
WHERE ARE MY CORNISH HENS? WHO TOOK THEM?
SHALLOTS? BUT YOU CLEARLY SAID RED ONIONS!
ARE WE STILL SERVING SOUP?
WE'RE ALMOST OUT OF THE GOOSE LIVER. SHOULD WE PUT OUT MORE OR--?
BETTER PUT OUT MORE OF SOMETHING FAST. THIS CROWD'S EATING ANYTHING IN SIGHT.
YOU HURRY UP AND YOU SLOW DOWN! EVERYTHING MUST BE COORDINATED TO ARRIVE AT THE PROPER TIME!
I FINALLY MADE IT.
BACKSTAGE AT THE GRANDEST EVENT OF THE YEAR.
YUM.
ARE YOU ON THE MENU?
OH GOSH. I SURE HOPE NOT.

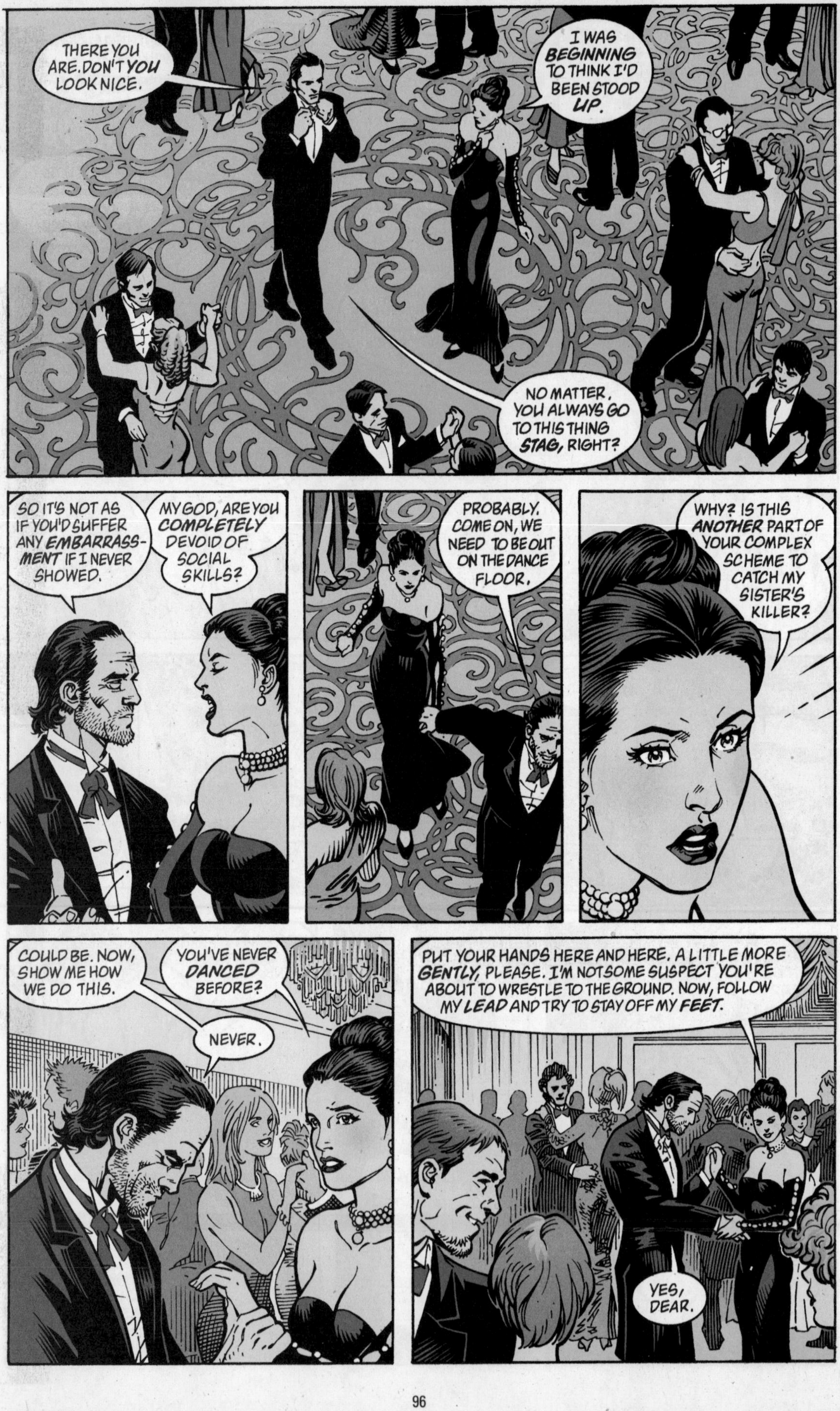
THERE YOU ARE. DON'T YOU LOOK NICE.
I WAS BEGINNING TO THINK I'D BEEN STOOD UP.
NO MATTER, YOU ALWAYS GO TO THIS THING STAG, RIGHT?
SO IT'S NOT AS IF YOU'D SUFFER ANY EMBARRASS-MENT IF I NEVER SHOWED.
MY GOD, ARE YOU COMPLETELY DEVOID OF SOCIAL SKILLS?
PROBABLY. COME ON, WE NEED TO BE OUT ON THE DANCE FLOOR.
WHY? IS THIS ANOTHER PART OF YOUR COMPLEX SCHEME TO CATCH MY SISTER'S KILLER?
COULD BE. NOW, SHOW ME HOW WE DO THIS.
YOU'VE NEVER DANCED BEFORE?
NEVER.
PUT YOUR HANDS HERE AND HERE. A LITTLE MORE GENTLY, PLEASE. I'M NOT SOME SUSPECT YOU'RE ABOUT TO WRESTLE TO THE GROUND. NOW, FOLLOW MY LEAD AND TRY TO STAY OFF MY FEET.
YES, DEAR.

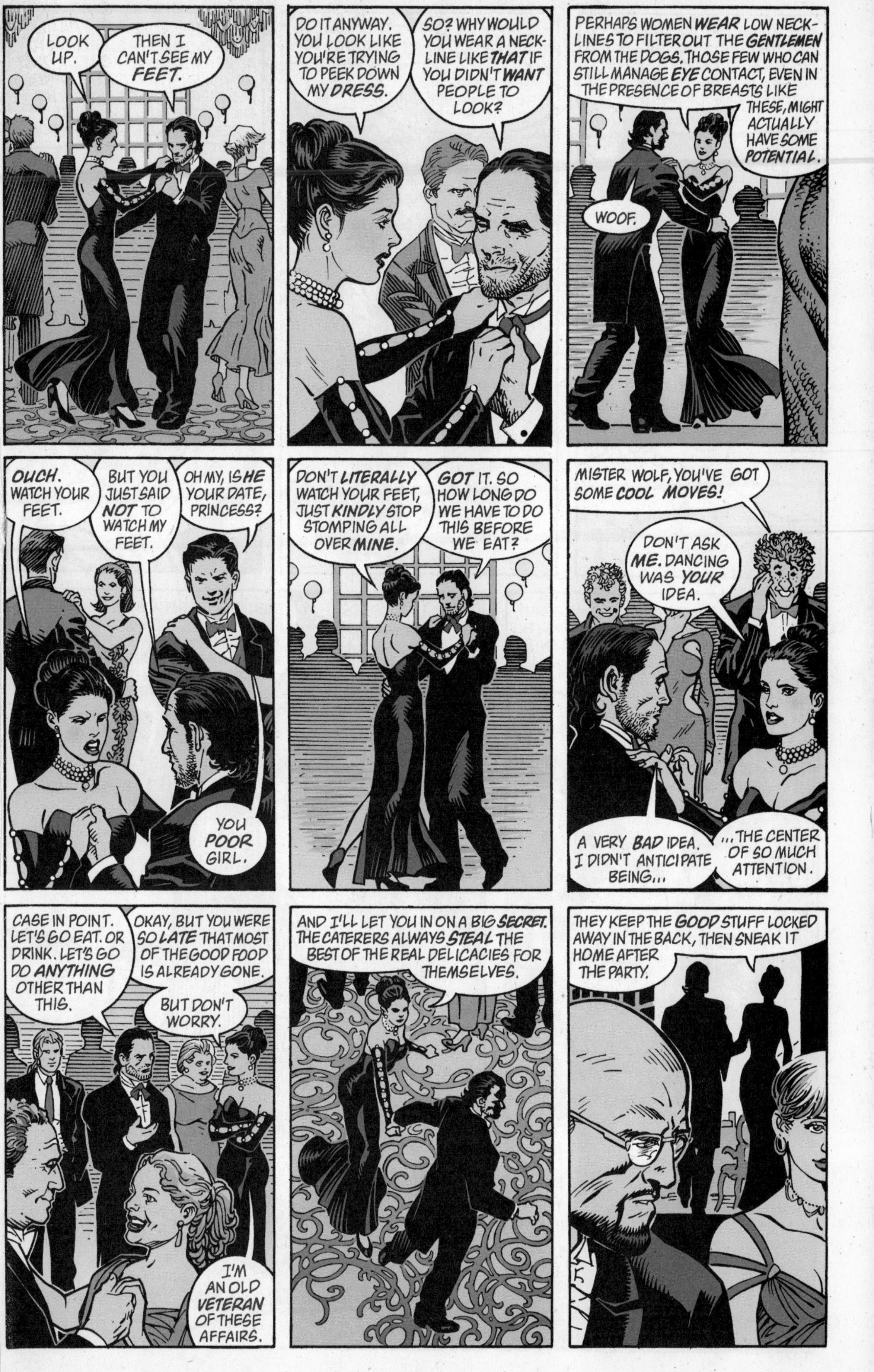
LOOK UP.
THEN I CAN'T SEE MY FEET.
DO IT ANYWAY. YOU LOOK LIKE YOU'RE TRYING TO PEEK DOWN MY DRESS.
SO? WHY WOULD YOU WEAR A NECKLINE LIKE THAT IF YOU DIDN'T WANT PEOPLE TO LOOK?
PERHAPS WOMEN WEAR LOW NECKLINES TO FILTER OUT THE GENTLEMEN FROM THE DOGS. THOSE FEW WHO CAN STILL MANAGE EYE CONTACT, EVEN IN THE PRESENCE OF BREASTS LIKE THESE, MIGHT ACTUALLY HAVE SOME POTENTIAL.
WOOF.
OUCH. WATCH YOUR FEET.
BUT YOU JUST SAID NOT TO WATCH MY FEET.
OH MY, IS HE YOUR DATE, PRINCESS?
YOU POOR GIRL.
DON'T LITERALLY WATCH YOUR FEET, JUST KINDLY STOP STOMPING ALL OVER MINE.
GOT IT. SO HOW LONG DO WE HAVE TO DO THIS BEFORE WE EAT?
MISTER WOLF, YOU'VE GOT SOME COOL MOVES!
DON'T ASK ME. DANCING WAS YOUR IDEA.
A VERY BAD IDEA. I DIDN'T ANTICIPATE BEING...
...THE CENTER OF SO MUCH ATTENTION.
CASE IN POINT. LET'S GO EAT. OR DRINK. LET'S GO DO ANYTHING OTHER THAN THIS.
OKAY, BUT YOU WERE SO LATE THAT MOST OF THE GOOD FOOD IS ALREADY GONE.
BUT DON'T WORRY.
I'M AN OLD VETERAN OF THESE AFFAIRS.
AND I'LL LET YOU IN ON A BIG SECRET. THE CATERERS ALWAYS STEAL THE BEST OF THE REAL DELICACIES FOR THEMSELVES.
THEY KEEP THE GOOD STUFF LOCKED AWAY IN THE BACK, THEN SNEAK IT HOME AFTER THE PARTY.

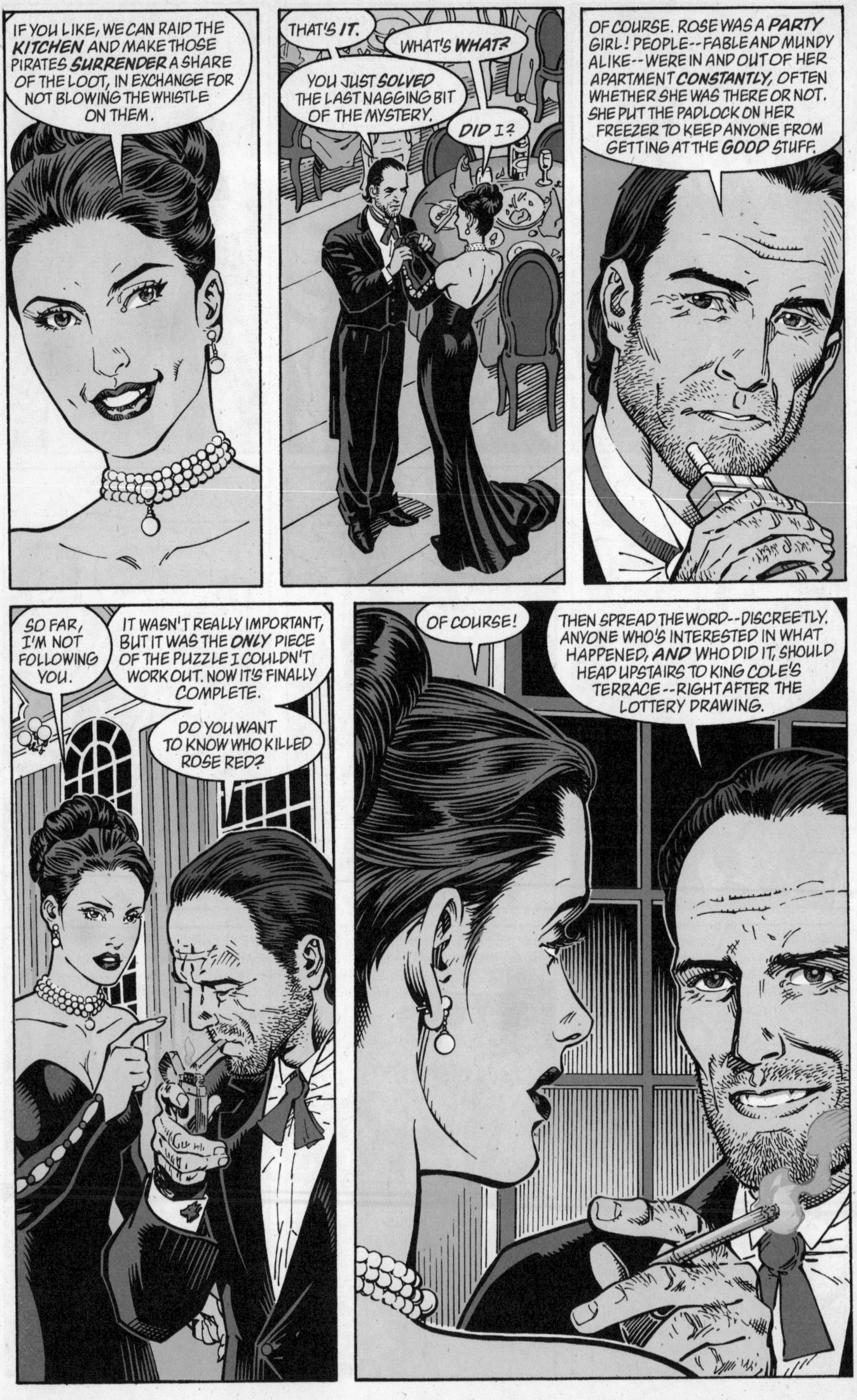
IF YOU LIKE, WE CAN RAID THE KITCHEN AND MAKE THOSE PIRATES SURRENDER A SHARE OF THE LOOT, IN EXCHANGE FOR NOT BLOWING THE WHISTLE ON THEM.
THAT'S IT.
WHAT'S WHAT?
YOU JUST SOLVED THE LAST NAGGING BIT OF THE MYSTERY.
DID I?
OF COURSE. ROSE WAS A PARTY GIRL! PEOPLE--FABLE AND MUNDY ALIKE--WERE IN AND OUT OF HER APARTMENT CONSTANTLY, OFTEN WHETHER SHE WAS THERE OR NOT. SHE PUT THE PADLOCK ON HER FREEZER TO KEEP ANYONE FROM GETTING AT THE GOOD STUFF.
SO FAR, I'M NOT FOLLOWING YOU.
IT WASN'T REALLY IMPORTANT, BUT IT WAS THE ONLY PIECE OF THE PUZZLE I COULDN'T WORK OUT. NOW IT'S FINALLY COMPLETE.
DO YOU WANT TO KNOW WHO KILLED ROSE RED?
OF COURSE!
THEN SPREAD THE WORD--DISCREETLY. ANYONE WHO'S INTERESTED IN WHAT HAPPENED, AND WHO DID IT, SHOULD HEAD UPSTAIRS TO KING COLE'S TERRACE--RIGHT AFTER THE LOTTERY DRAWING.

AND THE *WINNING* TICKET IS...

DOES HIS *ROYAL NIBS* KNOW YOU SNEAK UP HERE TO USE HIS *POOL* WHEN HE'S NOT AROUND?

WHO KNOWS?

IF HE *DOES*, HE'S NEVER COMPLAINED.

MIND IF I BUM A SMOKE?

I GUESS NOT.

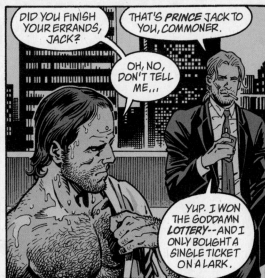

DID YOU FINISH YOUR ERRANDS, JACK?

THAT'S *PRINCE* JACK TO YOU, COMMONER.

OH, NO, DON'T TELL ME...

YUP. I WON THE GODDAMN *LOTTERY*--AND I ONLY BOUGHT A *SINGLE* TICKET ON A LARK.

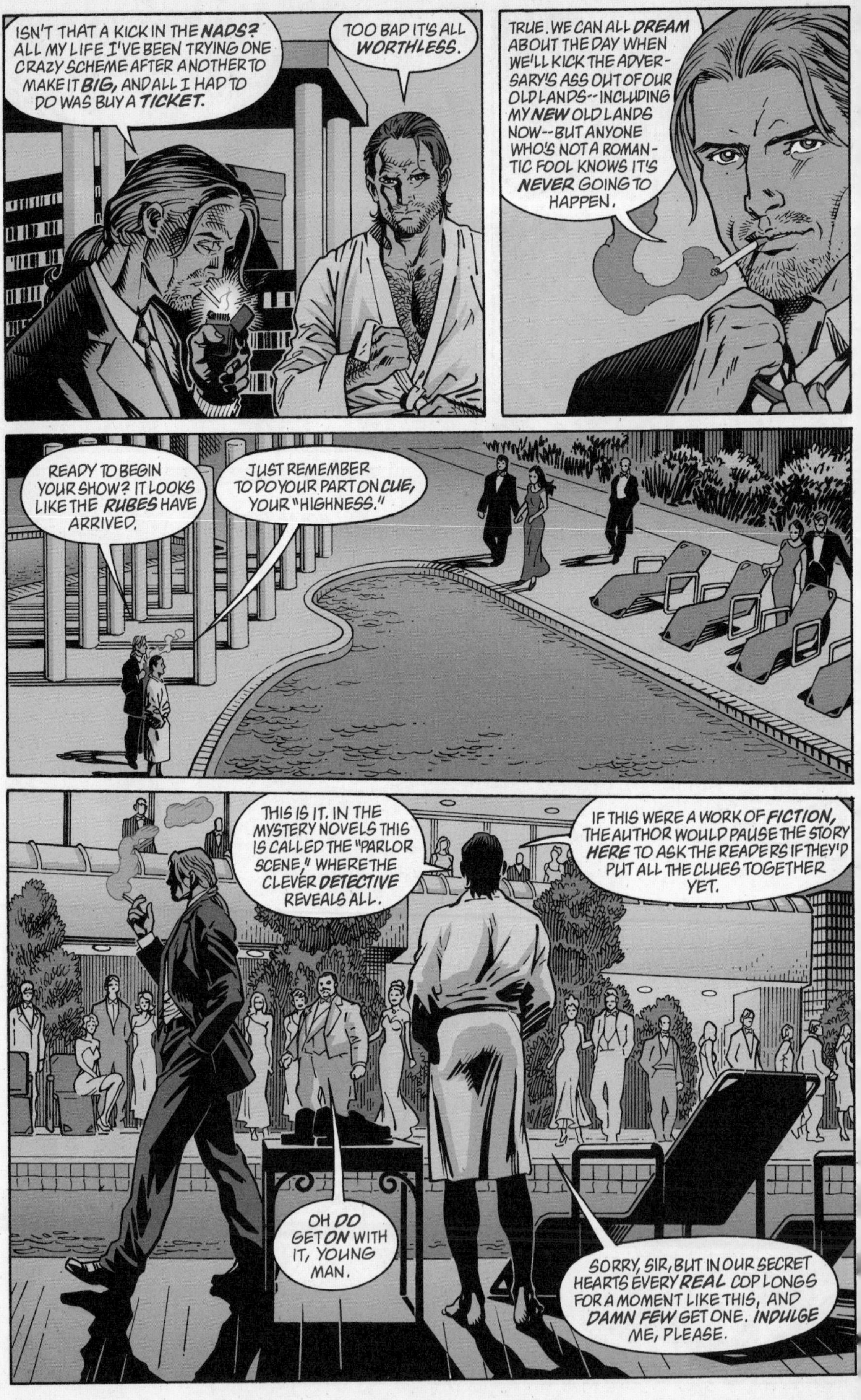
ISN'T THAT A KICK IN THE NADS? ALL MY LIFE I'VE BEEN TRYING ONE CRAZY SCHEME AFTER ANOTHER TO MAKE IT BIG, AND ALL I HAD TO DO WAS BUY A TICKET.
TOO BAD IT'S ALL WORTHLESS.
TRUE. WE CAN ALL DREAM ABOUT THE DAY WHEN WE'LL KICK THE ADVERSARY'S ASS OUT OF OUR OLD LANDS--INCLUDING MY NEW OLD LANDS NOW--BUT ANYONE WHO'S NOT A ROMANTIC FOOL KNOWS IT'S NEVER GOING TO HAPPEN.
READY TO BEGIN YOUR SHOW? IT LOOKS LIKE THE RUBES HAVE ARRIVED.
JUST REMEMBER TO DO YOUR PART ON CUE, YOUR "HIGHNESS."
THIS IS IT. IN THE MYSTERY NOVELS THIS IS CALLED THE "PARLOR SCENE," WHERE THE CLEVER DETECTIVE REVEALS ALL.
IF THIS WERE A WORK OF FICTION, THE AUTHOR WOULD PAUSE THE STORY HERE TO ASK THE READERS IF THEY'D PUT ALL THE CLUES TOGETHER YET.
OH DO GET ON WITH IT, YOUNG MAN.
SORRY, SIR, BUT IN OUR SECRET HEARTS EVERY REAL COP LONGS FOR A MOMENT LIKE THIS, AND DAMN FEW GET ONE. INDULGE ME, PLEASE.

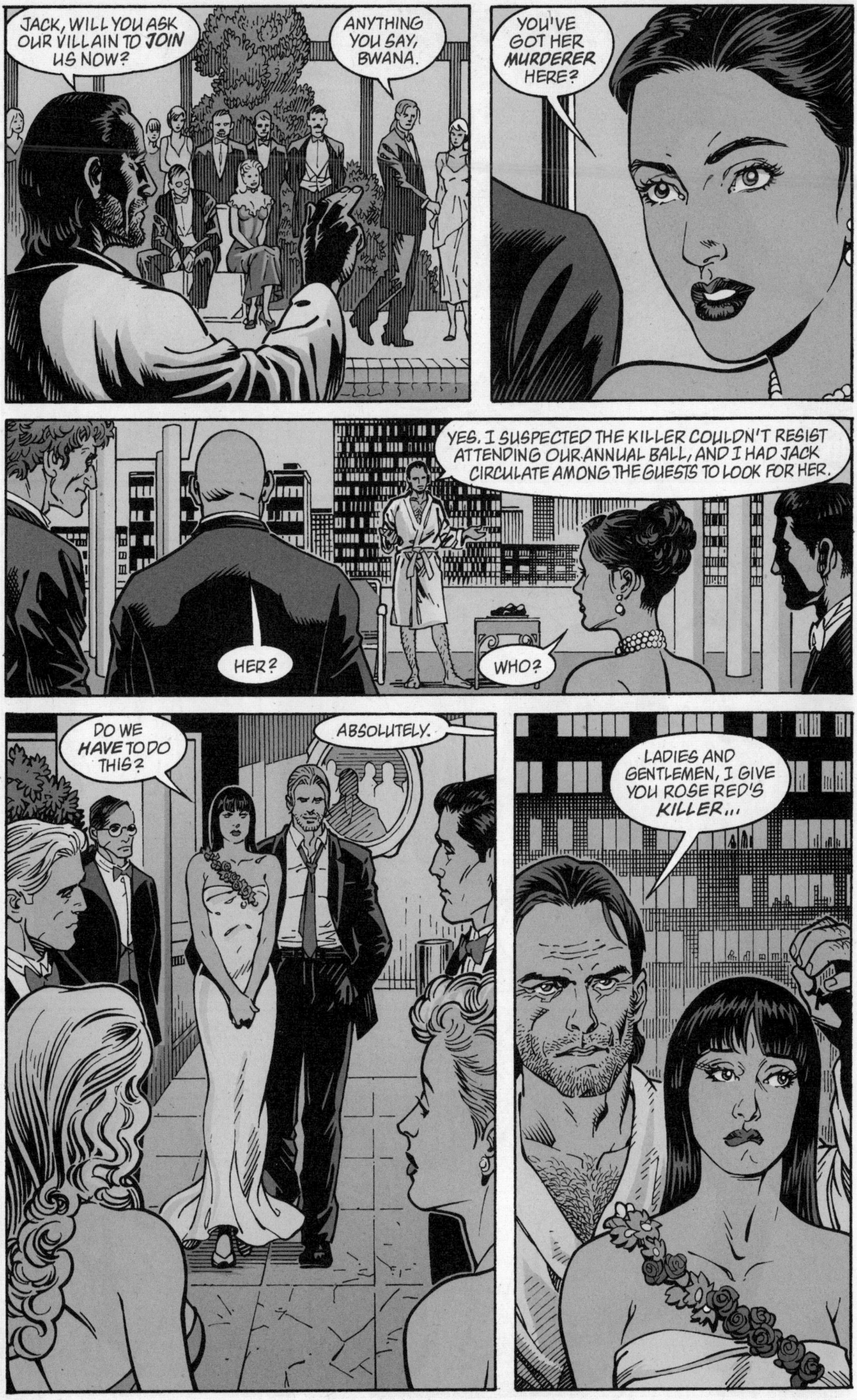
JACK, WILL YOU ASK OUR VILLAIN TO JOIN US NOW?
ANYTHING YOU SAY, BWANA.
YOU'VE GOT HER MURDERER HERE?
YES. I SUSPECTED THE KILLER COULDN'T RESIST ATTENDING OUR ANNUAL BALL, AND I HAD JACK CIRCULATE AMONG THE GUESTS TO LOOK FOR HER.
HER?
WHO?
DO WE HAVE TO DO THIS?
ABSOLUTELY.
LADIES AND GENTLEMEN, I GIVE YOU ROSE RED'S KILLER...

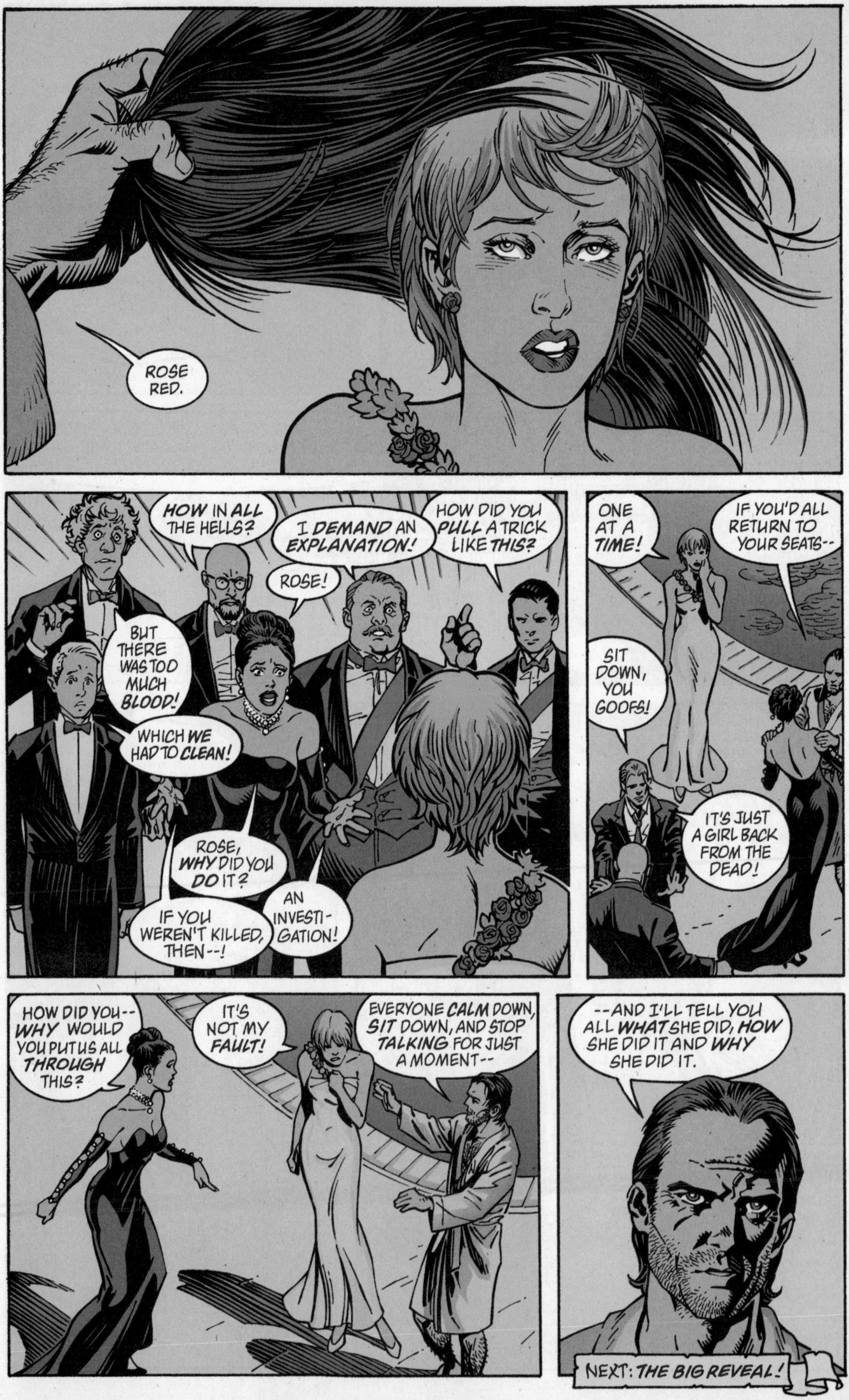
ROSE RED.
HOW IN ALL THE HELLS?
I DEMAND AN EXPLANATION!
HOW DID YOU PULL A TRICK LIKE THIS?
ROSE!
BUT THERE WAS TOO MUCH BLOOD!
WHICH WE HAD TO CLEAN!
ROSE, WHY DID YOU DO IT?
IF YOU WEREN'T KILLED, THEN--!
AN INVESTI-GATION!
ONE AT A TIME!
IF YOU'D ALL RETURN TO YOUR SEATS--
SIT DOWN, YOU GOOFS!
IT'S JUST A GIRL BACK FROM THE DEAD!
HOW DID YOU--WHY WOULD YOU PUT US ALL THROUGH THIS?
IT'S NOT MY FAULT!
EVERYONE CALM DOWN, SIT DOWN, AND STOP TALKING FOR JUST A MOMENT--
--AND I'LL TELL YOU ALL WHAT SHE DID, HOW SHE DID IT AND WHY SHE DID IT.
NEXT: THE BIG REVEAL!

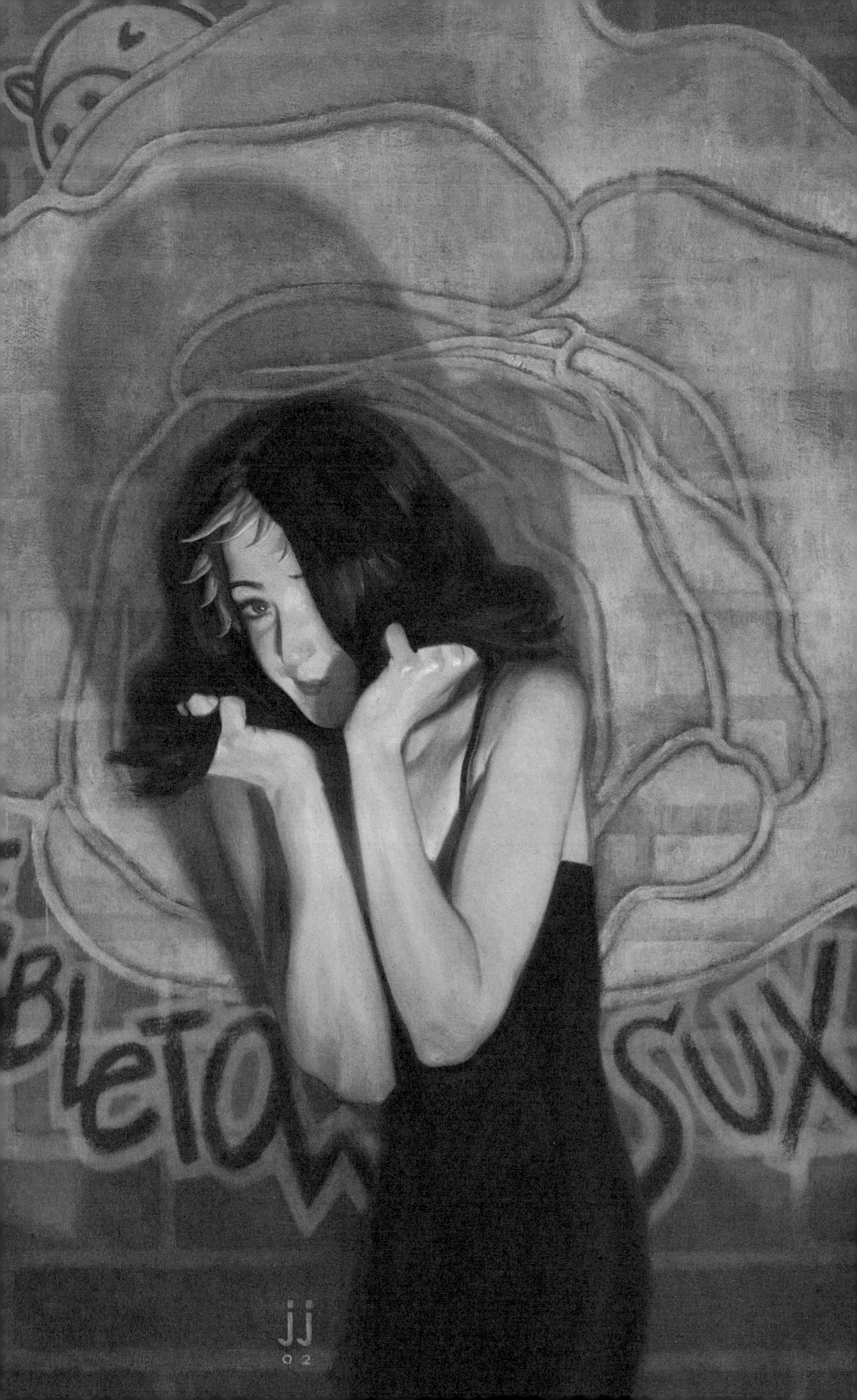
jj
02

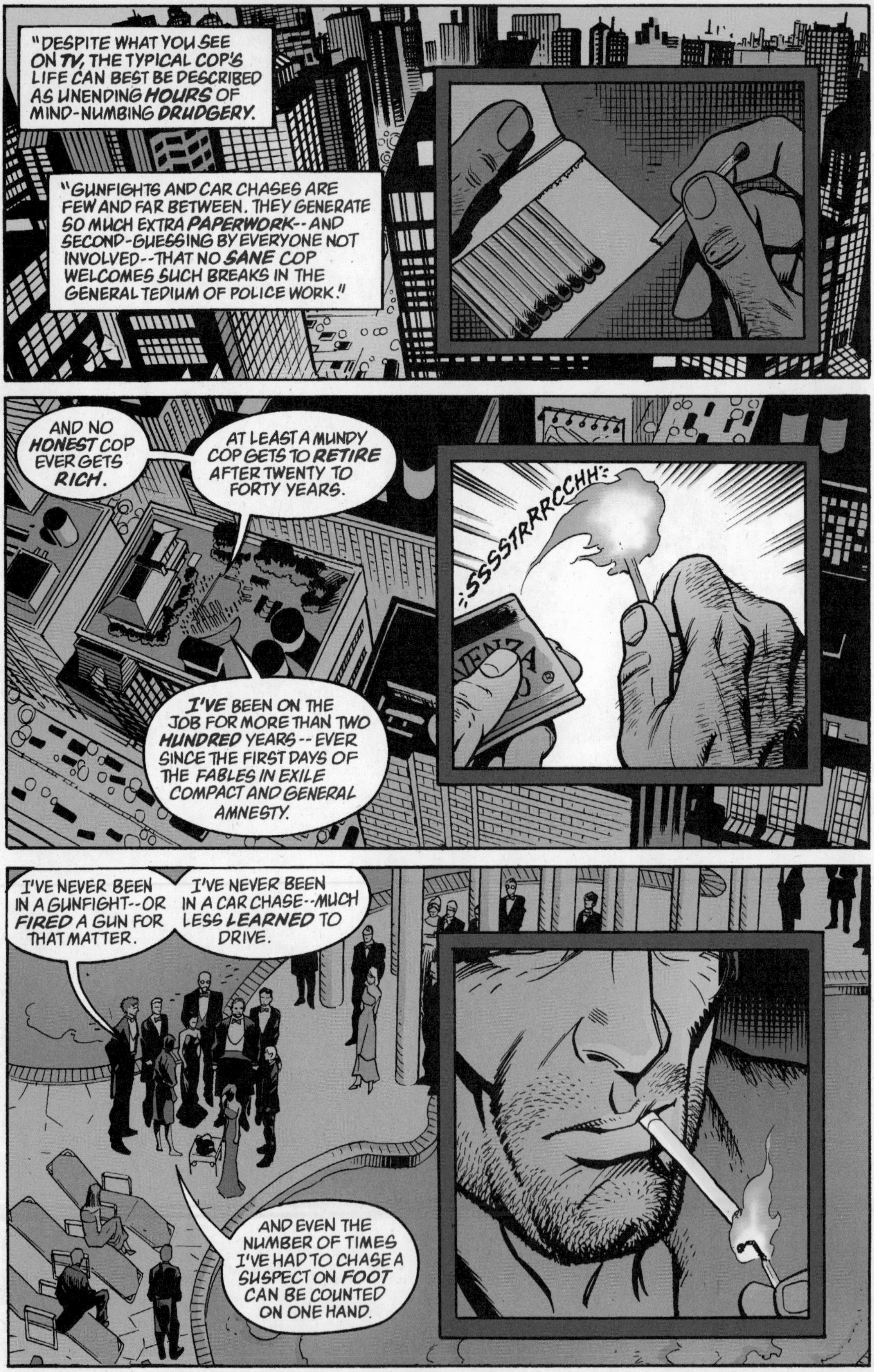
"DESPITE WHAT YOU SEE ON TV, THE TYPICAL COP'S LIFE CAN BEST BE DESCRIBED AS UNENDING HOURS OF MIND-NUMBING DRUDGERY.
"GUNFIGHTS AND CAR CHASES ARE FEW AND FAR BETWEEN. THEY GENERATE SO MUCH EXTRA PAPERWORK--AND SECOND-GUESSING BY EVERYONE NOT INVOLVED--THAT NO SANE COP WELCOMES SUCH BREAKS IN THE GENERAL TEDIUM OF POLICE WORK."
AND NO HONEST COP EVER GETS RICH.
AT LEAST A MUNDY COP GETS TO RETIRE AFTER TWENTY TO FORTY YEARS.
SSSSTRRRCCHH
I'VE BEEN ON THE JOB FOR MORE THAN TWO HUNDRED YEARS--EVER SINCE THE FIRST DAYS OF THE FABLES IN EXILE COMPACT AND GENERAL AMNESTY.
I'VE NEVER BEEN IN A GUNFIGHT--OR FIRED A GUN FOR THAT MATTER.
I'VE NEVER BEEN IN A CAR CHASE--MUCH LESS LEARNED TO DRIVE.
AND EVEN THE NUMBER OF TIMES I'VE HAD TO CHASE A SUSPECT ON FOOT CAN BE COUNTED ON ONE HAND.

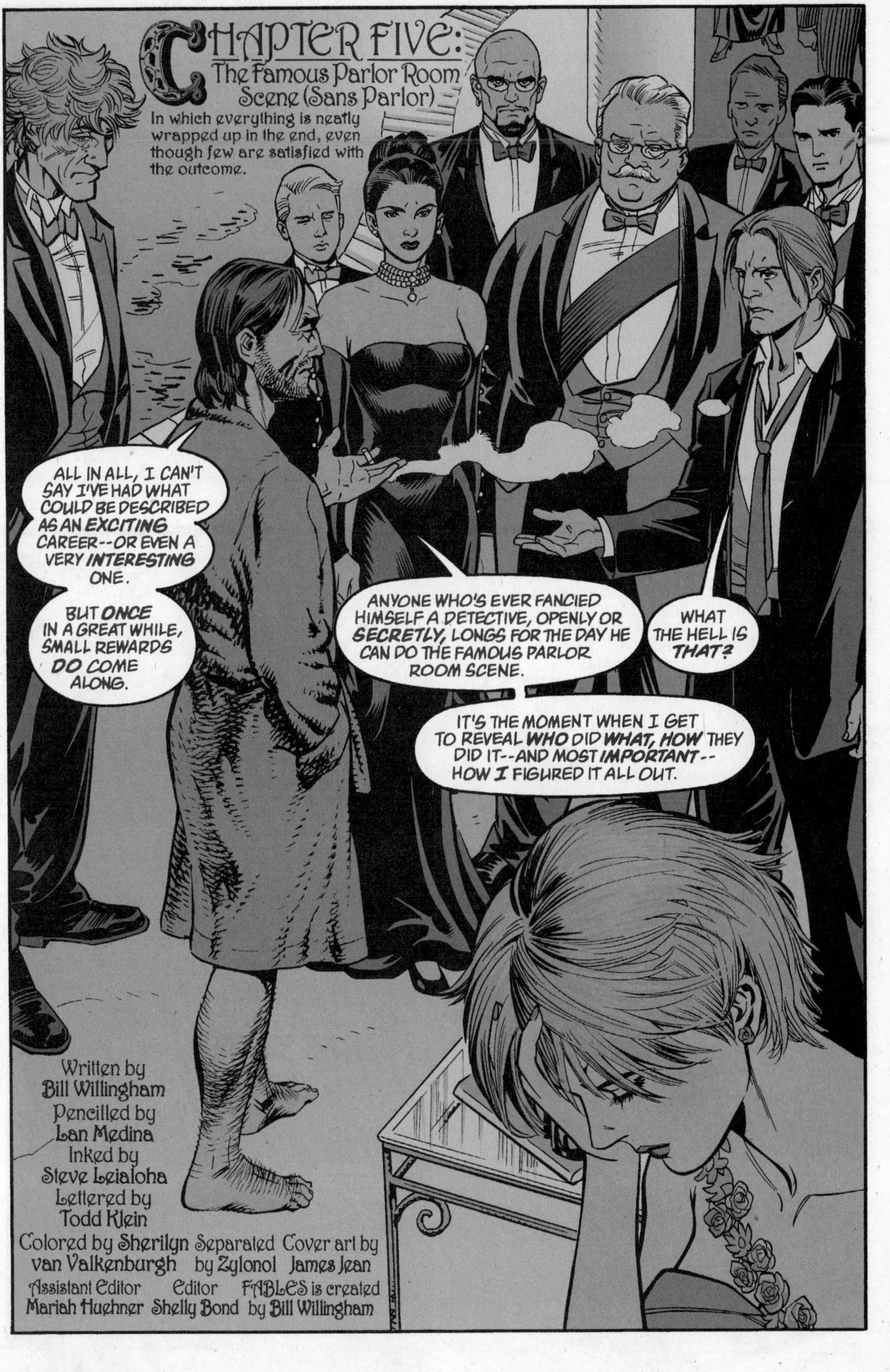

CHAPTER FIVE:
The Famous Parlor Room Scene (Sans Parlor)
In which everything is neatly wrapped up in the end, even though few are satisfied with the outcome.
ALL IN ALL, I CAN'T SAY I'VE HAD WHAT COULD BE DESCRIBED AS AN EXCITING CAREER--OR EVEN A VERY INTERESTING ONE.
BUT ONCE IN A GREAT WHILE, SMALL REWARDS DO COME ALONG.
ANYONE WHO'S EVER FANCIED HIMSELF A DETECTIVE, OPENLY OR SECRETLY, LONGS FOR THE DAY HE CAN DO THE FAMOUS PARLOR ROOM SCENE.
WHAT THE HELL IS THAT?
IT'S THE MOMENT WHEN I GET TO REVEAL WHO DID WHAT, HOW THEY DID IT--AND MOST IMPORTANT--HOW I FIGURED IT ALL OUT.
Written by Bill Willingham
Pencilled by Lan Medina
Inked by Steve Leialoha
Lettered by Todd Klein
Colored by Sherilyn van Valkenburgh
Separated by Zylonol
Cover art by James Jean
Assistant Editor Mariah Huehner
Editor Shelly Bond
FABLES is created by Bill Willingham

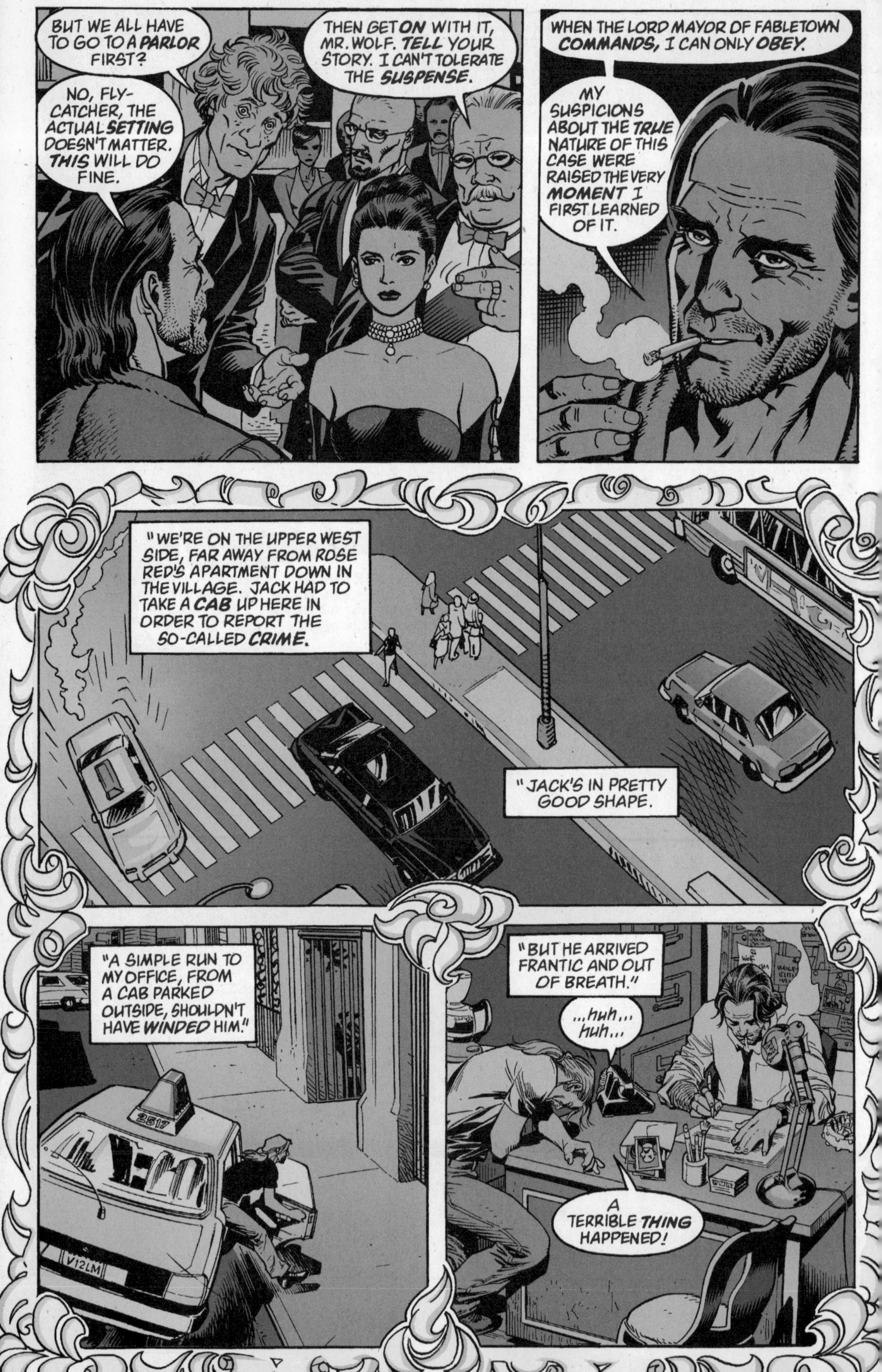
BUT WE ALL HAVE TO GO TO A PARLOR FIRST?
NO, FLY-CATCHER, THE ACTUAL SETTING DOESN'T MATTER. THIS WILL DO FINE.
THEN GET ON WITH IT, MR. WOLF. TELL YOUR STORY. I CAN'T TOLERATE THE SUSPENSE.
WHEN THE LORD MAYOR OF FABLETOWN COMMANDS, I CAN ONLY OBEY.
MY SUSPICIONS ABOUT THE TRUE NATURE OF THIS CASE WERE RAISED THE VERY MOMENT I FIRST LEARNED OF IT.
"WE'RE ON THE UPPER WEST SIDE, FAR AWAY FROM ROSE RED'S APARTMENT DOWN IN THE VILLAGE. JACK HAD TO TAKE A CAB UP HERE IN ORDER TO REPORT THE SO-CALLED CRIME.
"JACK'S IN PRETTY GOOD SHAPE.
"A SIMPLE RUN TO MY OFFICE, FROM A CAB PARKED OUTSIDE, SHOULDN'T HAVE WINDED HIM."
2517
V12LM
"BUT HE ARRIVED FRANTIC AND OUT OF BREATH."
...huh... huh...
A TERRIBLE THING HAPPENED!

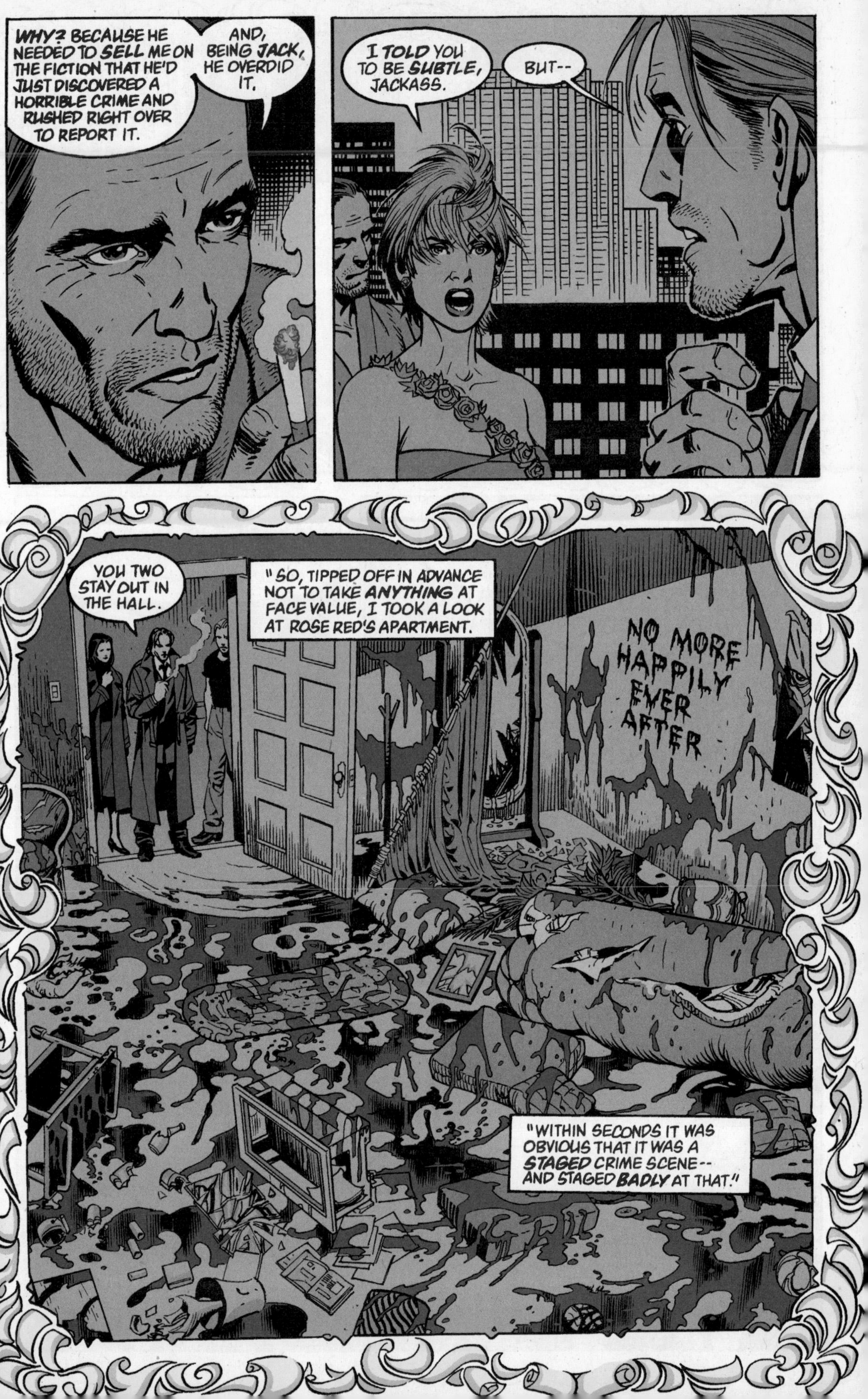
WHY? BECAUSE HE NEEDED TO SELL ME ON THE FICTION THAT HE'D JUST DISCOVERED A HORRIBLE CRIME AND RUSHED RIGHT OVER TO REPORT IT.
AND, BEING JACK, HE OVERDID IT.
I TOLD YOU TO BE SUBTLE, JACKASS.
BUT--
YOU TWO STAY OUT IN THE HALL.
"SO, TIPPED OFF IN ADVANCE NOT TO TAKE ANYTHING AT FACE VALUE, I TOOK A LOOK AT ROSE RED'S APARTMENT.
NO MORE HAPPILY EVER AFTER
"WITHIN SECONDS IT WAS OBVIOUS THAT IT WAS A STAGED CRIME SCENE-- AND STAGED BADLY AT THAT."

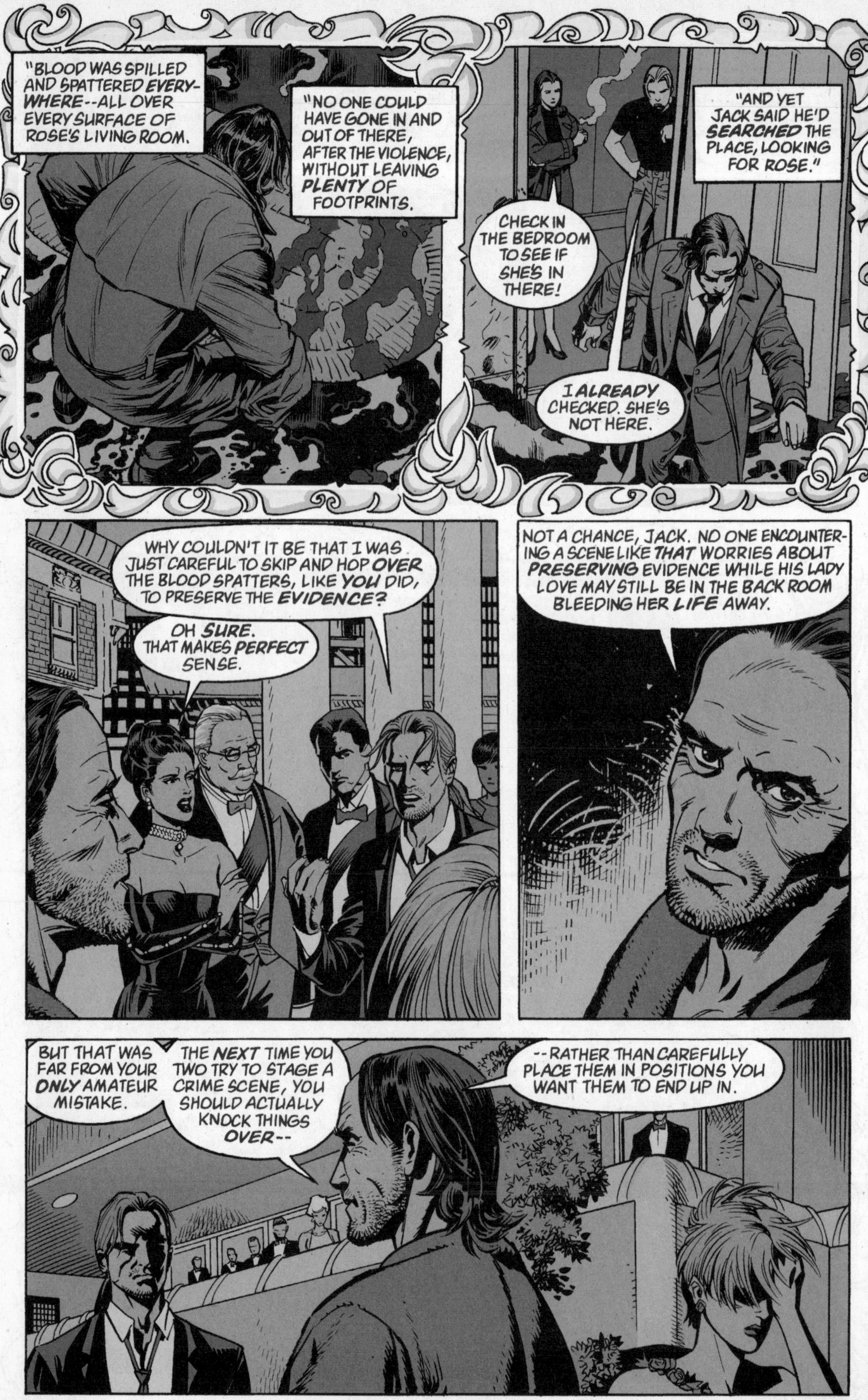
"BLOOD WAS SPILLED AND SPATTERED EVERY-WHERE--ALL OVER EVERY SURFACE OF ROSE'S LIVING ROOM.
"NO ONE COULD HAVE GONE IN AND OUT OF THERE, AFTER THE VIOLENCE, WITHOUT LEAVING PLENTY OF FOOTPRINTS.
"AND YET JACK SAID HE'D SEARCHED THE PLACE, LOOKING FOR ROSE."
CHECK IN THE BEDROOM TO SEE IF SHE'S IN THERE!
I ALREADY CHECKED. SHE'S NOT HERE.
WHY COULDN'T IT BE THAT I WAS JUST CAREFUL TO SKIP AND HOP OVER THE BLOOD SPATTERS, LIKE YOU DID, TO PRESERVE THE EVIDENCE?
OH SURE. THAT MAKES PERFECT SENSE.
NOT A CHANCE, JACK. NO ONE ENCOUNTERING A SCENE LIKE THAT WORRIES ABOUT PRESERVING EVIDENCE WHILE HIS LADY LOVE MAY STILL BE IN THE BACK ROOM BLEEDING HER LIFE AWAY.
BUT THAT WAS FAR FROM YOUR ONLY AMATEUR MISTAKE.
THE NEXT TIME YOU TWO TRY TO STAGE A CRIME SCENE, YOU SHOULD ACTUALLY KNOCK THINGS OVER--
--RATHER THAN CAREFULLY PLACE THEM IN POSITIONS YOU WANT THEM TO END UP IN.

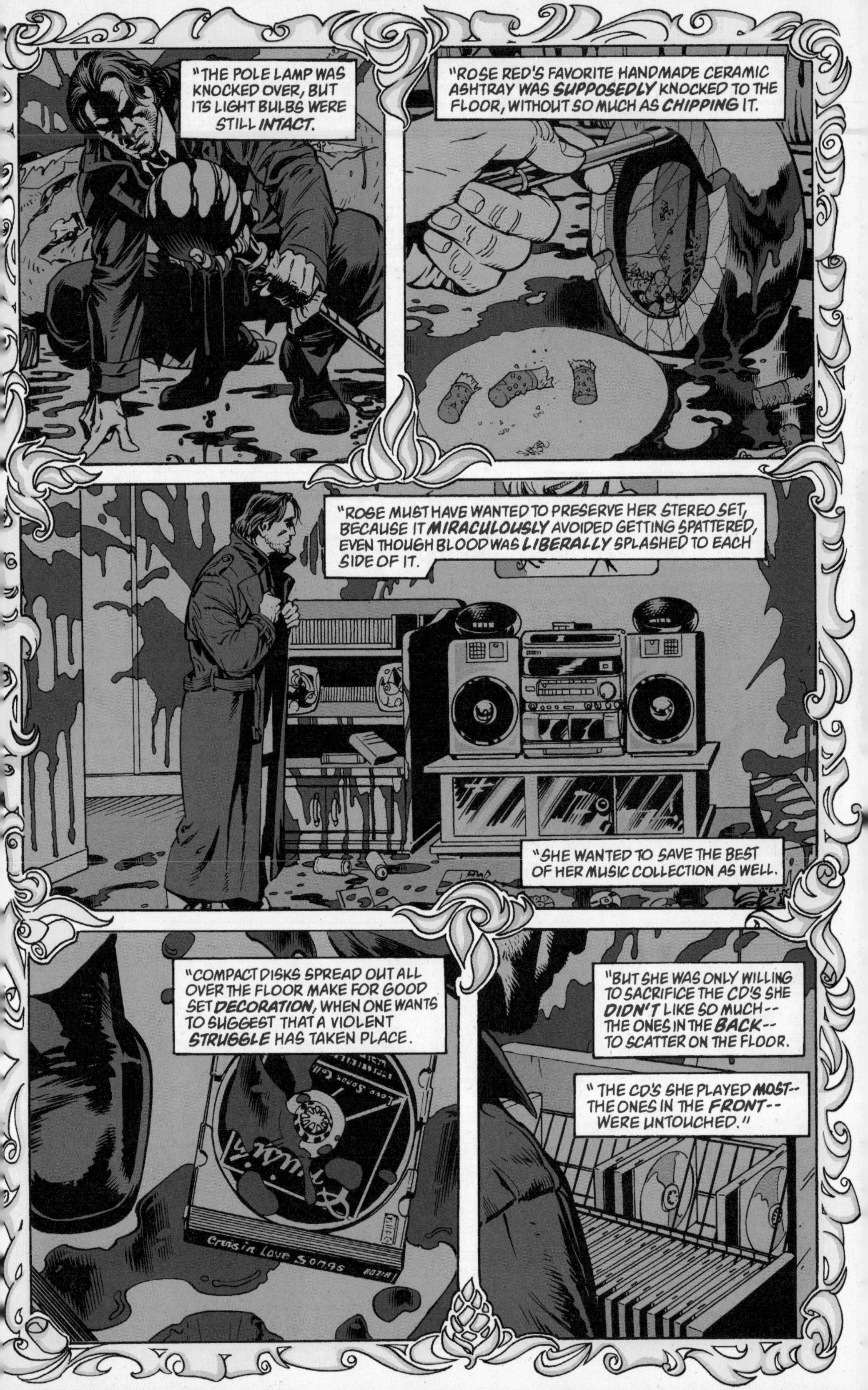
"THE POLE LAMP WAS KNOCKED OVER, BUT ITS LIGHT BULBS WERE STILL INTACT.
"ROSE RED'S FAVORITE HANDMADE CERAMIC ASHTRAY WAS SUPPOSEDLY KNOCKED TO THE FLOOR, WITHOUT SO MUCH AS CHIPPING IT.
"ROSE MUST HAVE WANTED TO PRESERVE HER STEREO SET, BECAUSE IT MIRACULOUSLY AVOIDED GETTING SPATTERED, EVEN THOUGH BLOOD WAS LIBERALLY SPLASHED TO EACH SIDE OF IT.
"SHE WANTED TO SAVE THE BEST OF HER MUSIC COLLECTION AS WELL.
"COMPACT DISKS SPREAD OUT ALL OVER THE FLOOR MAKE FOR GOOD SET DECORATION, WHEN ONE WANTS TO SUGGEST THAT A VIOLENT STRUGGLE HAS TAKEN PLACE.
Cruisin Love Songs
"BUT SHE WAS ONLY WILLING TO SACRIFICE THE CD'S SHE DIDN'T LIKE SO MUCH-- THE ONES IN THE BACK-- TO SCATTER ON THE FLOOR.
"THE CD'S SHE PLAYED MOST-- THE ONES IN THE FRONT-- WERE UNTOUCHED."

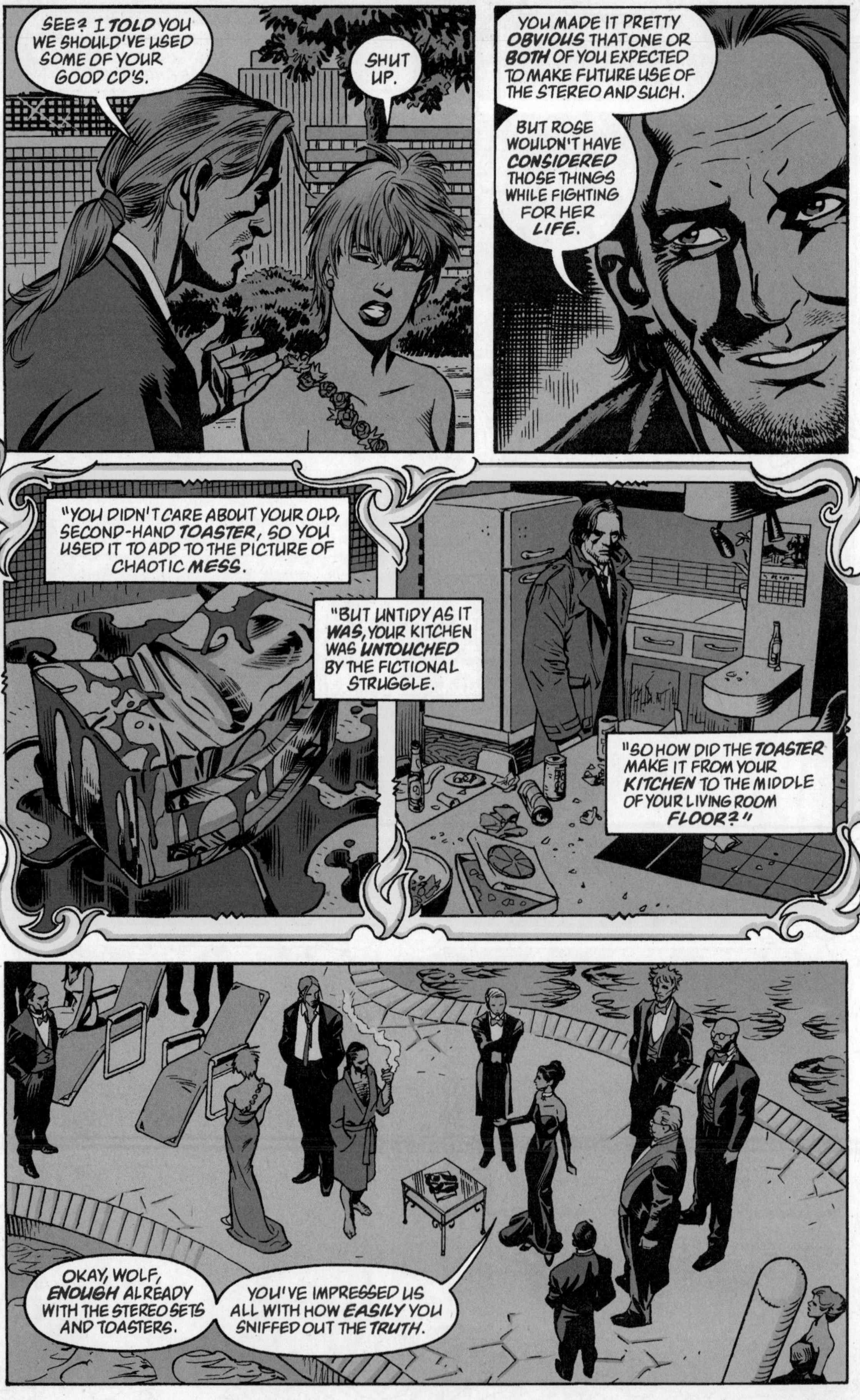
SEE? I TOLD YOU WE SHOULD'VE USED SOME OF YOUR GOOD CD'S.
SHUT UP.
YOU MADE IT PRETTY OBVIOUS THAT ONE OR BOTH OF YOU EXPECTED TO MAKE FUTURE USE OF THE STEREO AND SUCH.
BUT ROSE WOULDN'T HAVE CONSIDERED THOSE THINGS WHILE FIGHTING FOR HER LIFE.
"YOU DIDN'T CARE ABOUT YOUR OLD, SECOND-HAND TOASTER, SO YOU USED IT TO ADD TO THE PICTURE OF CHAOTIC MESS.
"BUT UNTIDY AS IT WAS, YOUR KITCHEN WAS UNTOUCHED BY THE FICTIONAL STRUGGLE.
"SO HOW DID THE TOASTER MAKE IT FROM YOUR KITCHEN TO THE MIDDLE OF YOUR LIVING ROOM FLOOR?"
OKAY, WOLF, ENOUGH ALREADY WITH THE STEREO SETS AND TOASTERS.
YOU'VE IMPRESSED US ALL WITH HOW EASILY YOU SNIFFED OUT THE TRUTH.

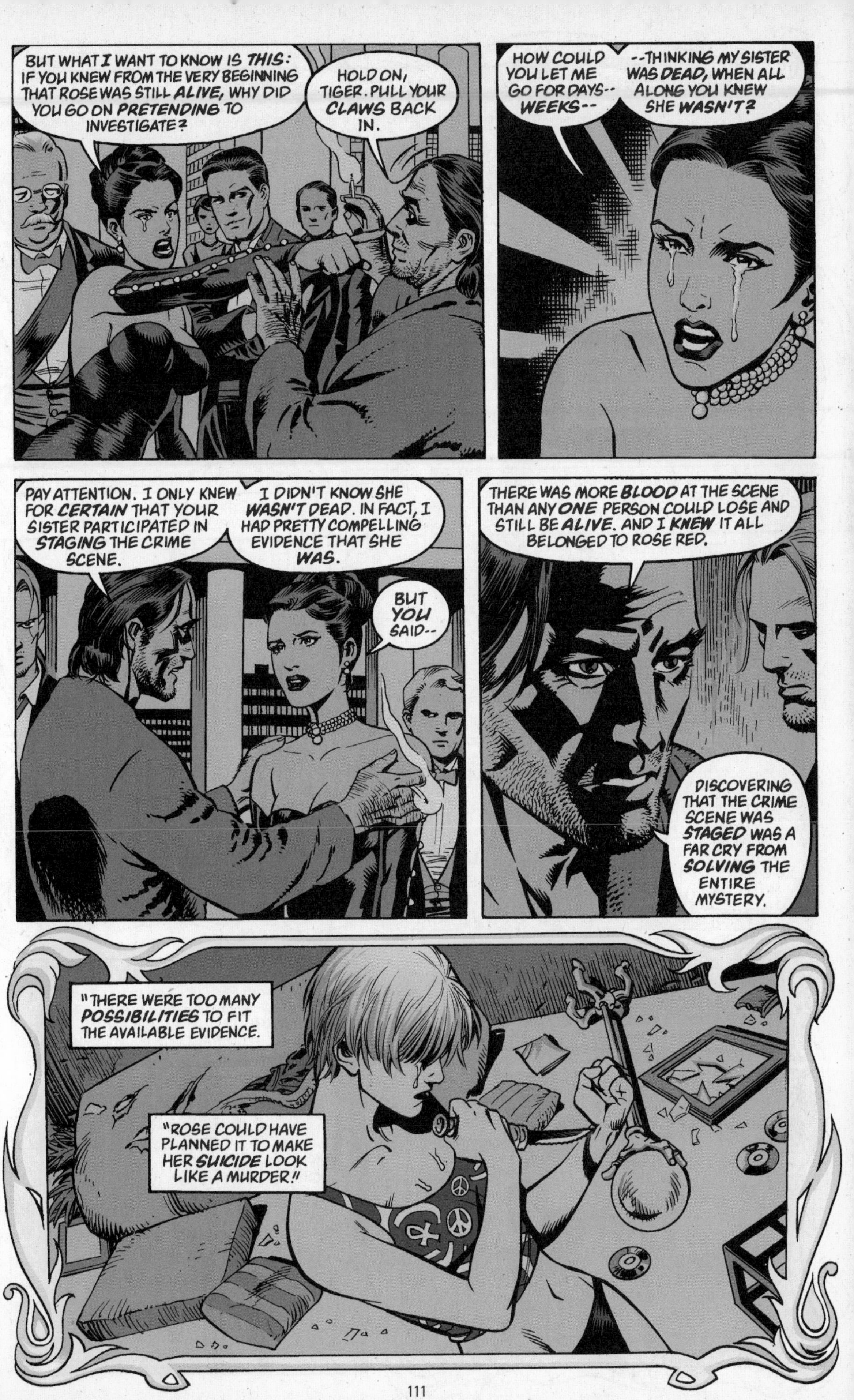
BUT WHAT I WANT TO KNOW IS THIS: IF YOU KNEW FROM THE VERY BEGINNING THAT ROSE WAS STILL ALIVE, WHY DID YOU GO ON PRETENDING TO INVESTIGATE?
HOLD ON, TIGER. PULL YOUR CLAWS BACK IN.
HOW COULD YOU LET ME GO FOR DAYS-- WEEKS--
--THINKING MY SISTER WAS DEAD, WHEN ALL ALONG YOU KNEW SHE WASN'T?
PAY ATTENTION. I ONLY KNEW FOR CERTAIN THAT YOUR SISTER PARTICIPATED IN STAGING THE CRIME SCENE.
I DIDN'T KNOW SHE WASN'T DEAD. IN FACT, I HAD PRETTY COMPELLING EVIDENCE THAT SHE WAS.
BUT YOU SAID--
THERE WAS MORE BLOOD AT THE SCENE THAN ANY ONE PERSON COULD LOSE AND STILL BE ALIVE. AND I KNEW IT ALL BELONGED TO ROSE RED.
DISCOVERING THAT THE CRIME SCENE WAS STAGED WAS A FAR CRY FROM SOLVING THE ENTIRE MYSTERY.
"THERE WERE TOO MANY POSSIBILITIES TO FIT THE AVAILABLE EVIDENCE.
"ROSE COULD HAVE PLANNED IT TO MAKE HER SUICIDE LOOK LIKE A MURDER!"

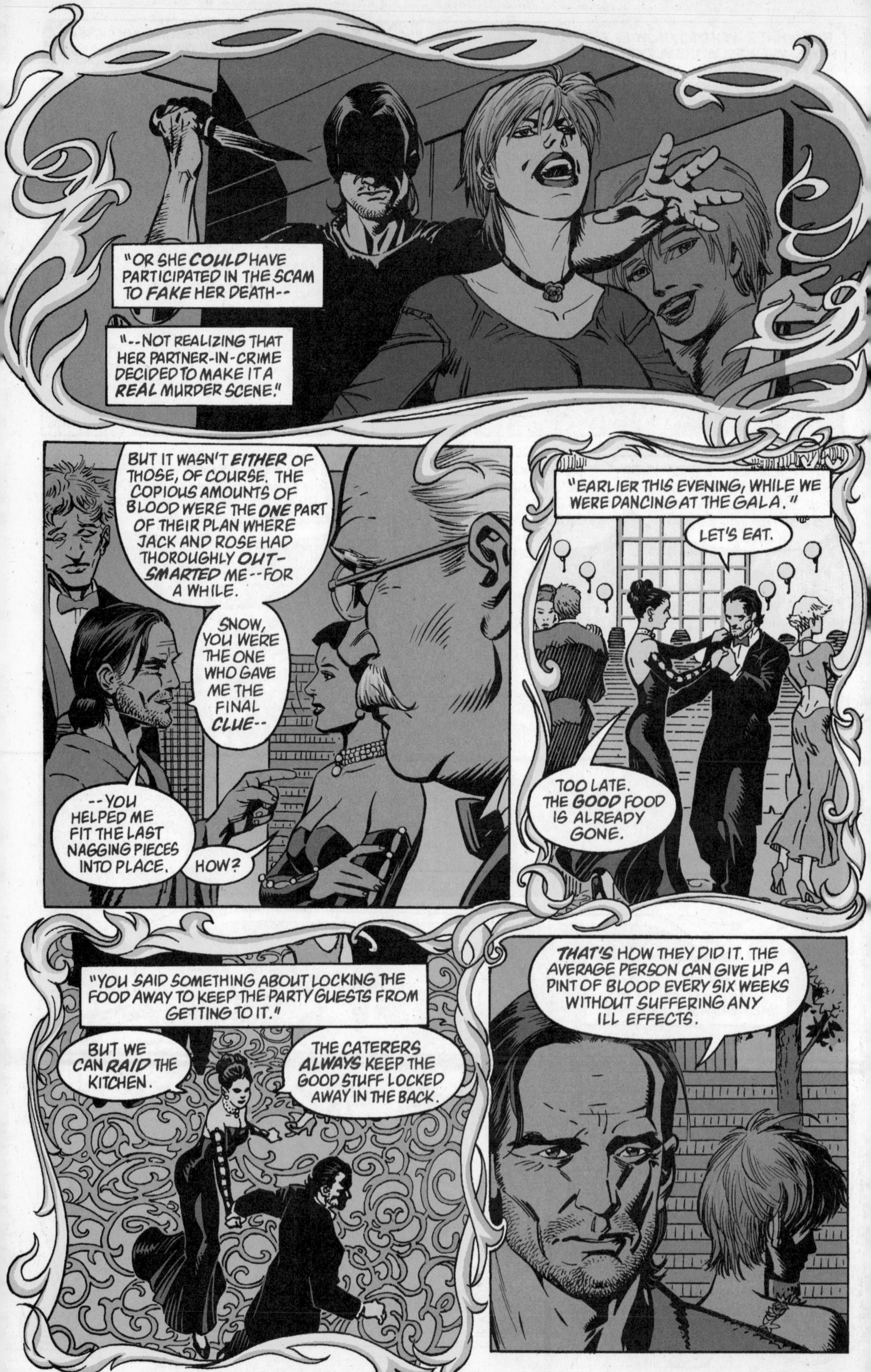

"OR SHE COULD HAVE PARTICIPATED IN THE SCAM TO FAKE HER DEATH--
"--NOT REALIZING THAT HER PARTNER-IN-CRIME DECIDED TO MAKE IT A REAL MURDER SCENE."
BUT IT WASN'T EITHER OF THOSE, OF COURSE. THE COPIOUS AMOUNTS OF BLOOD WERE THE ONE PART OF THEIR PLAN WHERE JACK AND ROSE HAD THOROUGHLY OUT-SMARTED ME--FOR A WHILE.
SNOW, YOU WERE THE ONE WHO GAVE ME THE FINAL CLUE--
--YOU HELPED ME FIT THE LAST NAGGING PIECES INTO PLACE.
HOW?
"EARLIER THIS EVENING, WHILE WE WERE DANCING AT THE GALA."
LET'S EAT.
TOO LATE. THE GOOD FOOD IS ALREADY GONE.
"YOU SAID SOMETHING ABOUT LOCKING THE FOOD AWAY TO KEEP THE PARTY GUESTS FROM GETTING TO IT."
BUT WE CAN RAID THE KITCHEN.
THE CATERERS ALWAYS KEEP THE GOOD STUFF LOCKED AWAY IN THE BACK.
THAT'S HOW THEY DID IT. THE AVERAGE PERSON CAN GIVE UP A PINT OF BLOOD EVERY SIX WEEKS WITHOUT SUFFERING ANY ILL EFFECTS.

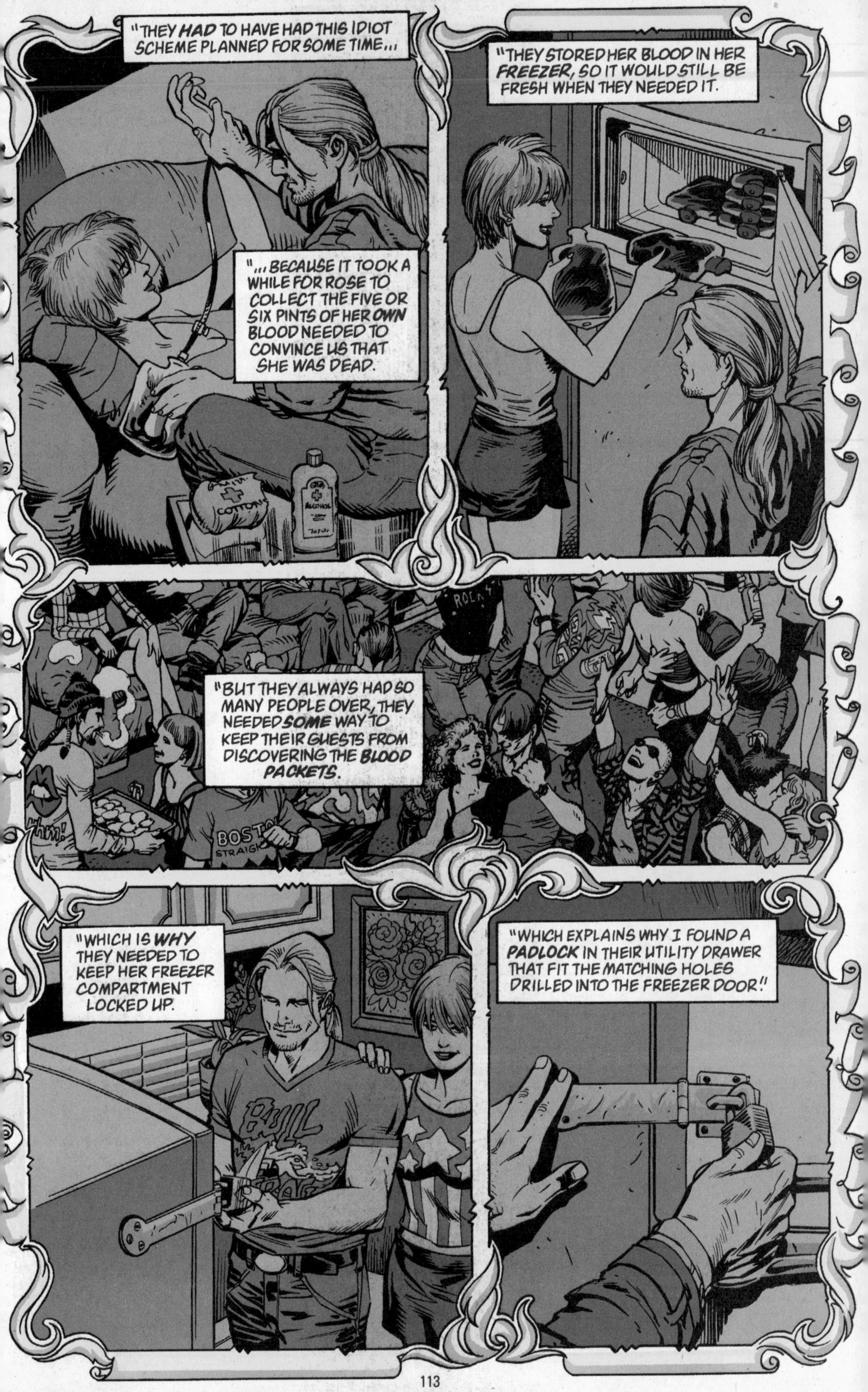
"THEY HAD TO HAVE HAD THIS IDIOT SCHEME PLANNED FOR SOME TIME...
"...BECAUSE IT TOOK A WHILE FOR ROSE TO COLLECT THE FIVE OR SIX PINTS OF HER OWN BLOOD NEEDED TO CONVINCE US THAT SHE WAS DEAD.
COTTON
ALCOHOL
"THEY STORED HER BLOOD IN HER FREEZER, SO IT WOULD STILL BE FRESH WHEN THEY NEEDED IT.
"BUT THEY ALWAYS HAD SO MANY PEOPLE OVER, THEY NEEDED SOME WAY TO KEEP THEIR GUESTS FROM DISCOVERING THE BLOOD PACKETS.
BOSTO
"WHICH IS WHY THEY NEEDED TO KEEP HER FREEZER COMPARTMENT LOCKED UP.
"WHICH EXPLAINS WHY I FOUND A PADLOCK IN THEIR UTILITY DRAWER THAT FIT THE MATCHING HOLES DRILLED INTO THE FREEZER DOOR."

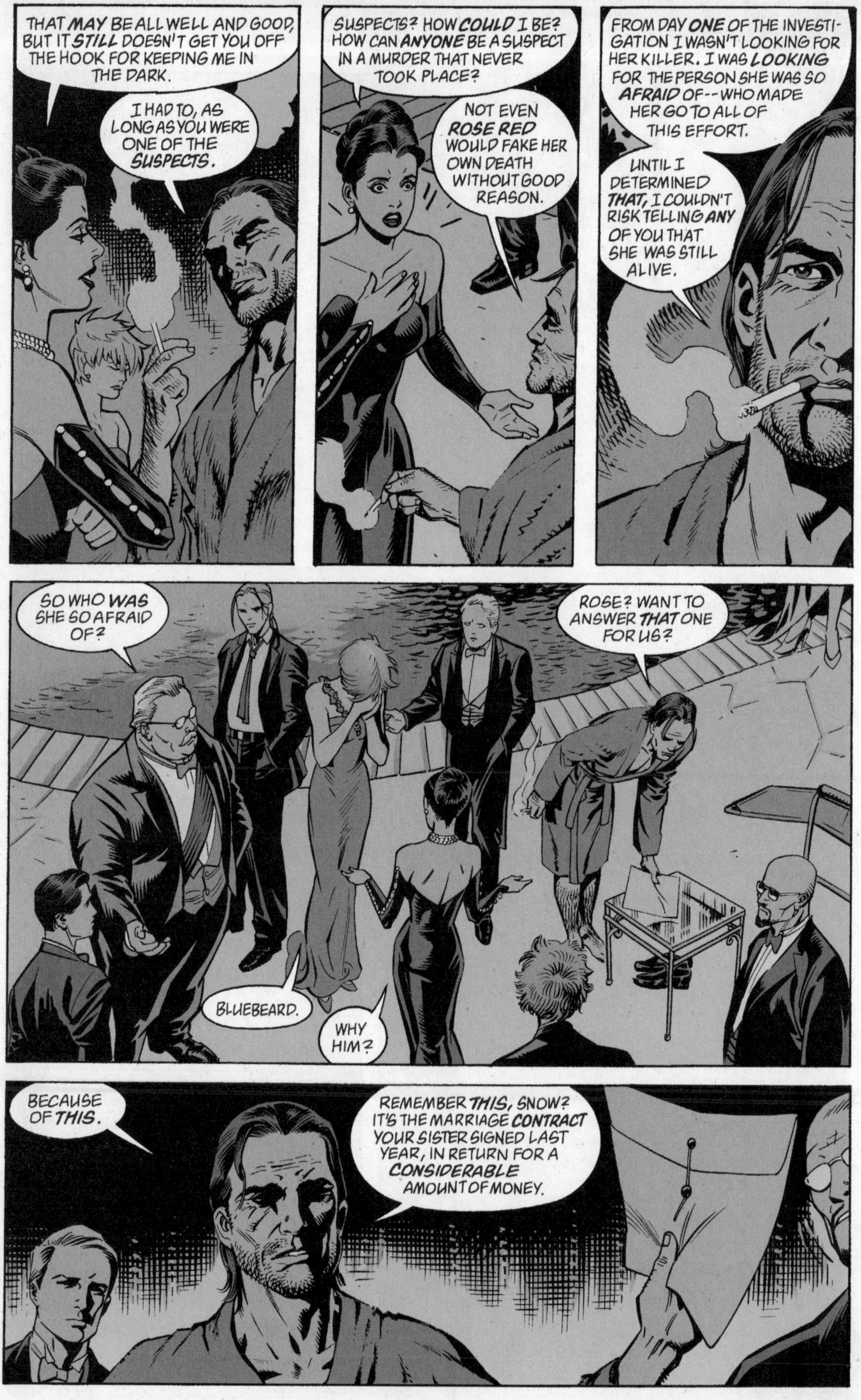
THAT MAY BE ALL WELL AND GOOD, BUT IT STILL DOESN'T GET YOU OFF THE HOOK FOR KEEPING ME IN THE DARK.
I HAD TO, AS LONG AS YOU WERE ONE OF THE SUSPECTS.
SUSPECTS? HOW COULD I BE? HOW CAN ANYONE BE A SUSPECT IN A MURDER THAT NEVER TOOK PLACE?
NOT EVEN ROSE RED WOULD FAKE HER OWN DEATH WITHOUT GOOD REASON.
FROM DAY ONE OF THE INVESTIGATION I WASN'T LOOKING FOR HER KILLER. I WAS LOOKING FOR THE PERSON SHE WAS SO AFRAID OF--WHO MADE HER GO TO ALL OF THIS EFFORT.
UNTIL I DETERMINED THAT, I COULDN'T RISK TELLING ANY OF YOU THAT SHE WAS STILL ALIVE.
SO WHO WAS SHE SO AFRAID OF?
ROSE? WANT TO ANSWER THAT ONE FOR US?
BLUEBEARD.
WHY HIM?
BECAUSE OF THIS.
REMEMBER THIS, SNOW? IT'S THE MARRIAGE CONTRACT YOUR SISTER SIGNED LAST YEAR, IN RETURN FOR A CONSIDERABLE AMOUNT OF MONEY.

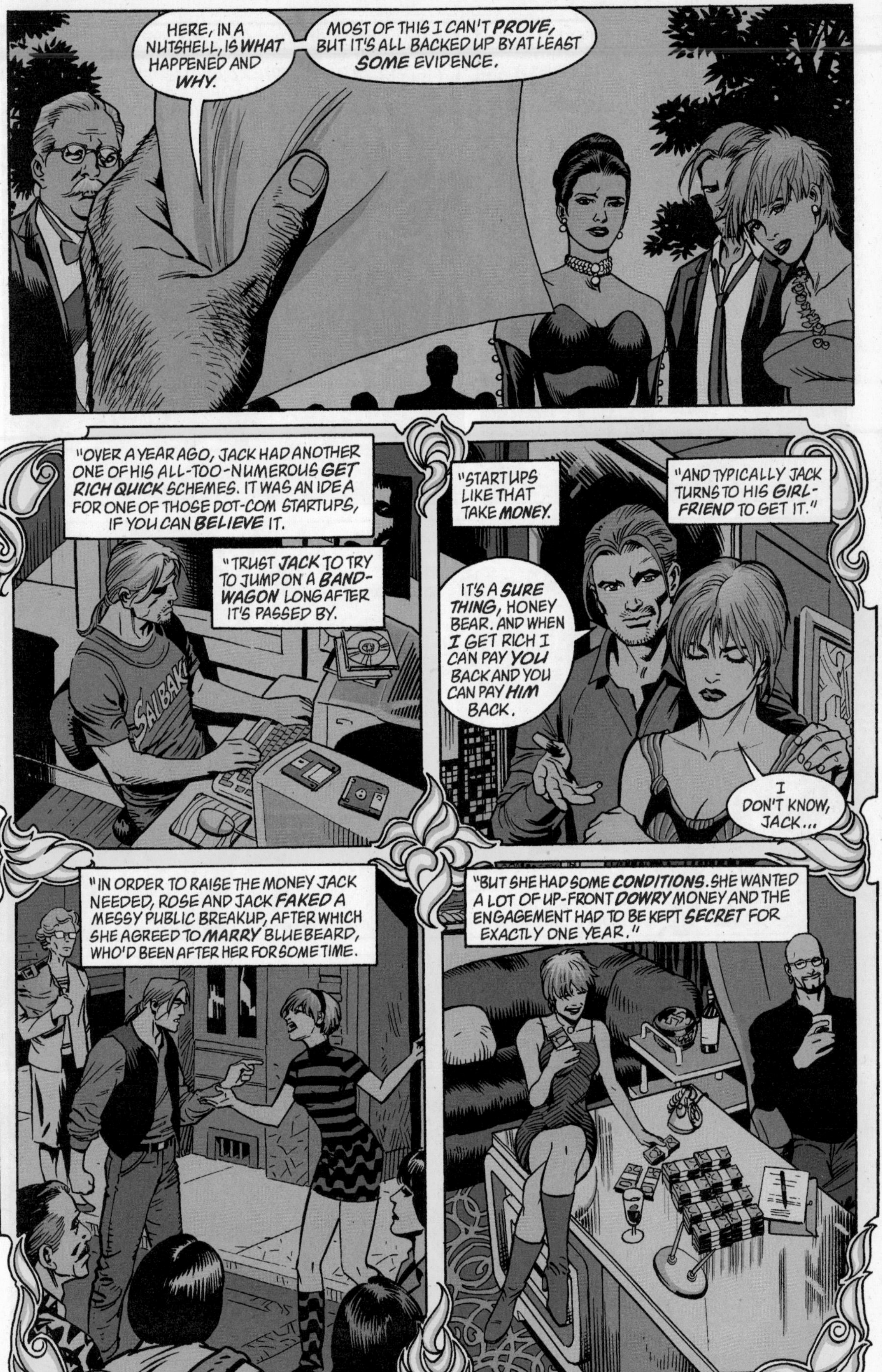
HERE, IN A NUTSHELL, IS WHAT HAPPENED AND WHY.
MOST OF THIS I CAN'T PROVE, BUT IT'S ALL BACKED UP BY AT LEAST SOME EVIDENCE.
"OVER A YEAR AGO, JACK HAD ANOTHER ONE OF HIS ALL-TOO-NUMEROUS GET RICH QUICK SCHEMES. IT WAS AN IDEA FOR ONE OF THOSE DOT-COM STARTUPS, IF YOU CAN BELIEVE IT.
"TRUST JACK TO TRY TO JUMP ON A BAND-WAGON LONG AFTER IT'S PASSED BY.
"STARTUPS LIKE THAT TAKE MONEY.
"AND TYPICALLY JACK TURNS TO HIS GIRL-FRIEND TO GET IT."
IT'S A SURE THING, HONEY BEAR. AND WHEN I GET RICH I CAN PAY YOU BACK AND YOU CAN PAY HIM BACK.
I DON'T KNOW, JACK...
"IN ORDER TO RAISE THE MONEY JACK NEEDED, ROSE AND JACK FAKED A MESSY PUBLIC BREAKUP, AFTER WHICH SHE AGREED TO MARRY BLUEBEARD, WHO'D BEEN AFTER HER FOR SOME TIME.
"BUT SHE HAD SOME CONDITIONS. SHE WANTED A LOT OF UP-FRONT DOWRY MONEY AND THE ENGAGEMENT HAD TO BE KEPT SECRET FOR EXACTLY ONE YEAR."

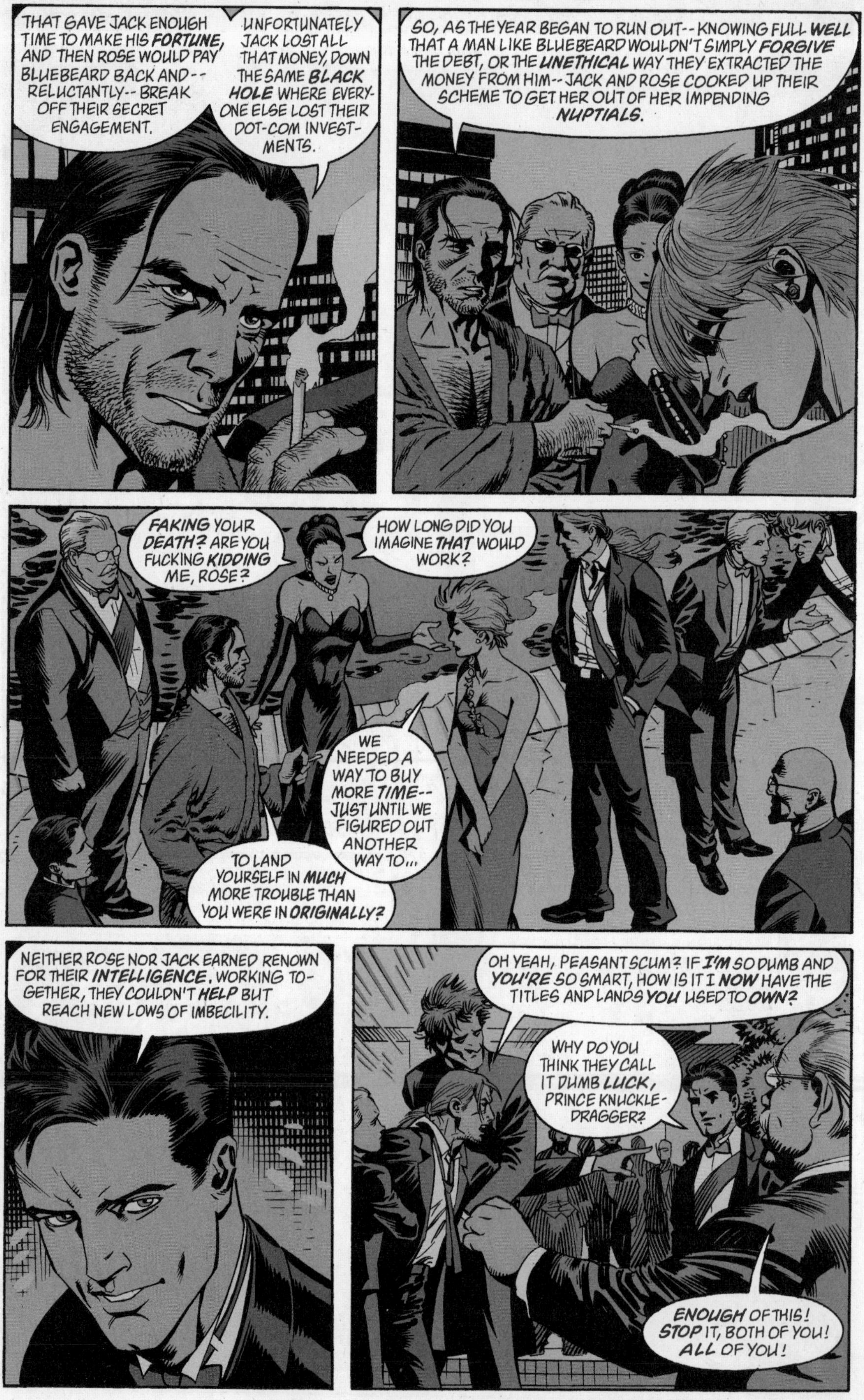
THAT GAVE JACK ENOUGH TIME TO MAKE HIS FORTUNE, AND THEN ROSE WOULD PAY BLUEBEARD BACK AND-- RELUCTANTLY-- BREAK OFF THEIR SECRET ENGAGEMENT.
UNFORTUNATELY JACK LOST ALL THAT MONEY, DOWN THE SAME BLACK HOLE WHERE EVERYONE ELSE LOST THEIR DOT-COM INVESTMENTS.
SO, AS THE YEAR BEGAN TO RUN OUT-- KNOWING FULL WELL THAT A MAN LIKE BLUEBEARD WOULDN'T SIMPLY FORGIVE THE DEBT, OR THE UNETHICAL WAY THEY EXTRACTED THE MONEY FROM HIM-- JACK AND ROSE COOKED UP THEIR SCHEME TO GET HER OUT OF HER IMPENDING NUPTIALS.
FAKING YOUR DEATH? ARE YOU FUCKING KIDDING ME, ROSE?
HOW LONG DID YOU IMAGINE THAT WOULD WORK?
WE NEEDED A WAY TO BUY MORE TIME-- JUST UNTIL WE FIGURED OUT ANOTHER WAY TO...
TO LAND YOURSELF IN MUCH MORE TROUBLE THAN YOU WERE IN ORIGINALLY?
NEITHER ROSE NOR JACK EARNED RENOWN FOR THEIR INTELLIGENCE. WORKING TOGETHER, THEY COULDN'T HELP BUT REACH NEW LOWS OF IMBECILITY.
OH YEAH, PEASANT SCUM? IF I'M SO DUMB AND YOU'RE SO SMART, HOW IS IT I NOW HAVE THE TITLES AND LANDS YOU USED TO OWN?
WHY DO YOU THINK THEY CALL IT DUMB LUCK, PRINCE KNUCKLE-DRAGGER?
ENOUGH OF THIS! STOP IT, BOTH OF YOU! ALL OF YOU!

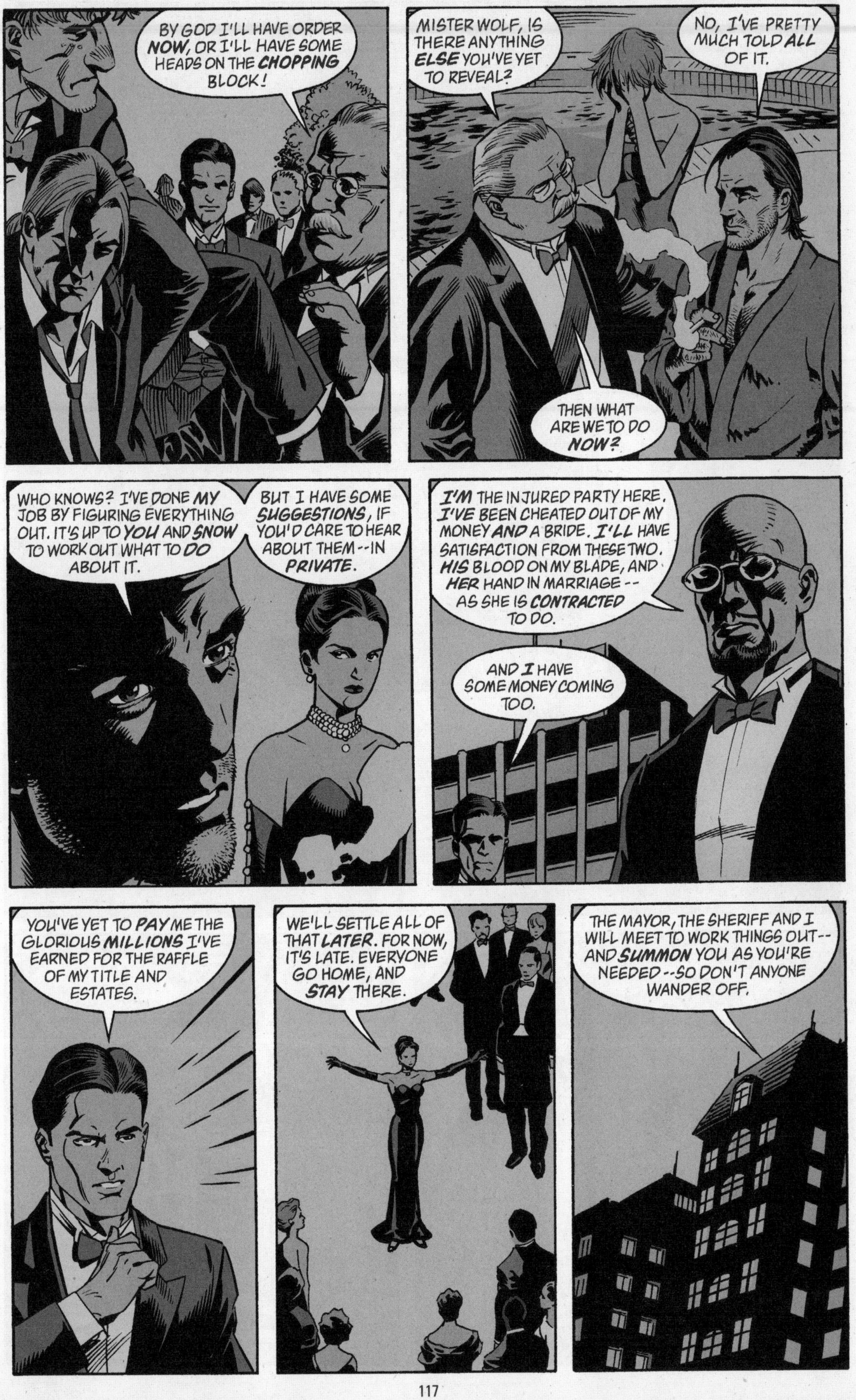
BY GOD I'LL HAVE ORDER NOW, OR I'LL HAVE SOME HEADS ON THE CHOPPING BLOCK!
MISTER WOLF, IS THERE ANYTHING ELSE YOU'VE YET TO REVEAL?
NO, I'VE PRETTY MUCH TOLD ALL OF IT.
THEN WHAT ARE WE TO DO NOW?
WHO KNOWS? I'VE DONE MY JOB BY FIGURING EVERYTHING OUT. IT'S UP TO YOU AND SNOW TO WORK OUT WHAT TO DO ABOUT IT.
BUT I HAVE SOME SUGGESTIONS, IF YOU'D CARE TO HEAR ABOUT THEM--IN PRIVATE.
I'M THE INJURED PARTY HERE. I'VE BEEN CHEATED OUT OF MY MONEY AND A BRIDE. I'LL HAVE SATISFACTION FROM THESE TWO. HIS BLOOD ON MY BLADE, AND HER HAND IN MARRIAGE -- AS SHE IS CONTRACTED TO DO.
AND I HAVE SOME MONEY COMING TOO.
YOU'VE YET TO PAY ME THE GLORIOUS MILLIONS I'VE EARNED FOR THE RAFFLE OF MY TITLE AND ESTATES.
WE'LL SETTLE ALL OF THAT LATER. FOR NOW, IT'S LATE. EVERYONE GO HOME, AND STAY THERE.
THE MAYOR, THE SHERIFF AND I WILL MEET TO WORK THINGS OUT-- AND SUMMON YOU AS YOU'RE NEEDED--SO DON'T ANYONE WANDER OFF.

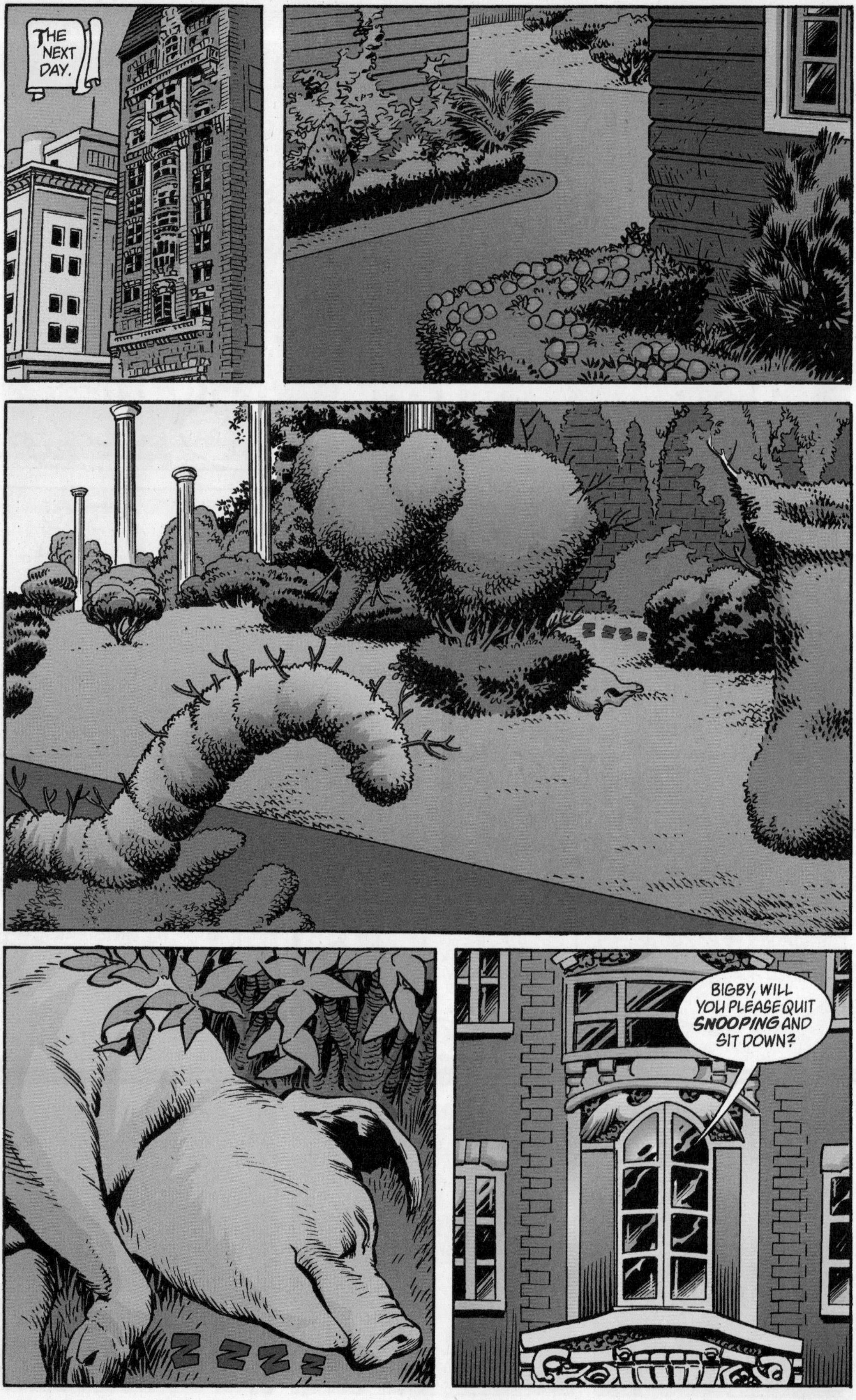
THE NEXT DAY.
ZZZ
ZZZZ
BIGBY, WILL YOU PLEASE QUIT SNOOPING AND SIT DOWN?

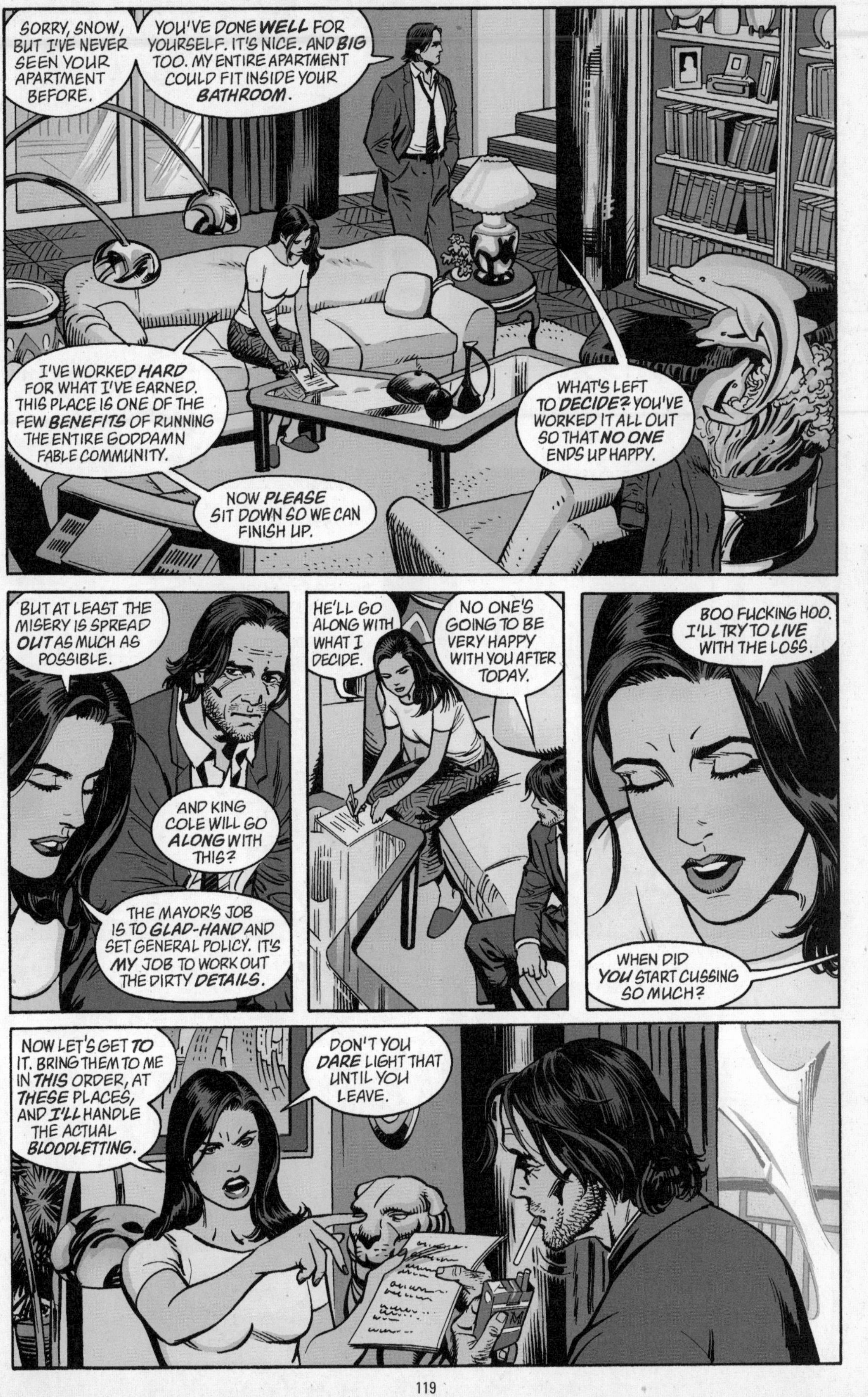
SORRY, SNOW, BUT I'VE NEVER SEEN YOUR APARTMENT BEFORE.
YOU'VE DONE WELL FOR YOURSELF. IT'S NICE. AND BIG TOO. MY ENTIRE APARTMENT COULD FIT INSIDE YOUR BATHROOM.
I'VE WORKED HARD FOR WHAT I'VE EARNED. THIS PLACE IS ONE OF THE FEW BENEFITS OF RUNNING THE ENTIRE GODDAMN FABLE COMMUNITY.
NOW PLEASE SIT DOWN SO WE CAN FINISH UP.
WHAT'S LEFT TO DECIDE? YOU'VE WORKED IT ALL OUT SO THAT NO ONE ENDS UP HAPPY.
BUT AT LEAST THE MISERY IS SPREAD OUT AS MUCH AS POSSIBLE.
AND KING COLE WILL GO ALONG WITH THIS?
THE MAYOR'S JOB IS TO GLAD-HAND AND SET GENERAL POLICY. IT'S MY JOB TO WORK OUT THE DIRTY DETAILS.
HE'LL GO ALONG WITH WHAT I DECIDE.
NO ONE'S GOING TO BE VERY HAPPY WITH YOU AFTER TODAY.
BOO FUCKING HOO. I'LL TRY TO LIVE WITH THE LOSS.
WHEN DID YOU START CUSSING SO MUCH?
NOW LET'S GET TO IT. BRING THEM TO ME IN THIS ORDER, AT THESE PLACES, AND I'LL HANDLE THE ACTUAL BLOODLETTING.
DON'T YOU DARE LIGHT THAT UNTIL YOU LEAVE.

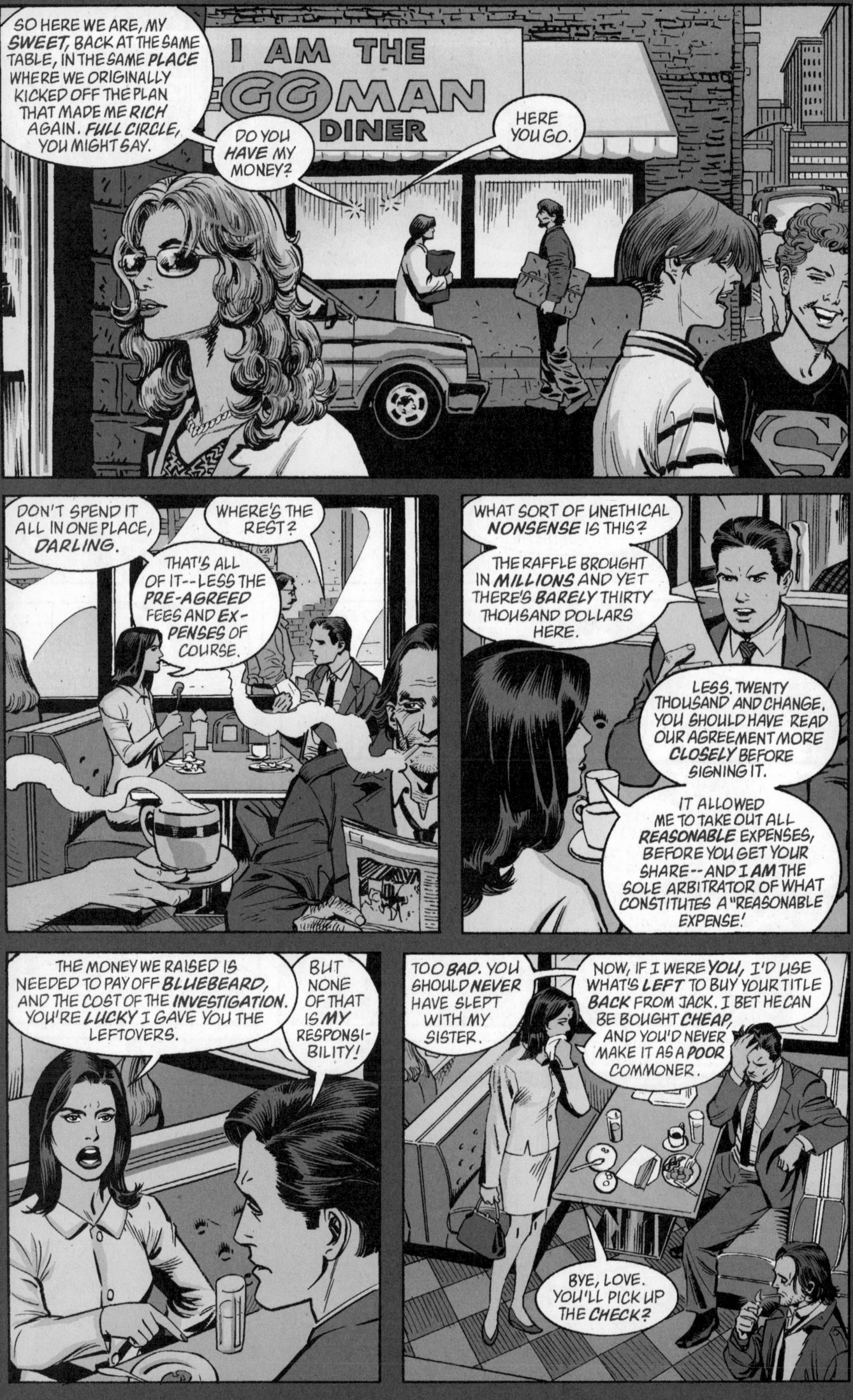
SO HERE WE ARE, MY SWEET, BACK AT THE SAME TABLE, IN THE SAME PLACE WHERE WE ORIGINALLY KICKED OFF THE PLAN THAT MADE ME RICH AGAIN. FULL CIRCLE, YOU MIGHT SAY.
I AM THE EGGMAN DINER
DO YOU HAVE MY MONEY?
HERE YOU GO.
DON'T SPEND IT ALL IN ONE PLACE, DARLING.
WHERE'S THE REST?
THAT'S ALL OF IT--LESS THE PRE-AGREED FEES AND EX-PENSES OF COURSE.
WHAT SORT OF UNETHICAL NONSENSE IS THIS?
THE RAFFLE BROUGHT IN MILLIONS AND YET THERE'S BARELY THIRTY THOUSAND DOLLARS HERE.
LESS. TWENTY THOUSAND AND CHANGE. YOU SHOULD HAVE READ OUR AGREEMENT MORE CLOSELY BEFORE SIGNING IT.
IT ALLOWED ME TO TAKE OUT ALL REASONABLE EXPENSES, BEFORE YOU GET YOUR SHARE--AND I AM THE SOLE ARBITRATOR OF WHAT CONSTITUTES A "REASONABLE EXPENSE.'
THE MONEY WE RAISED IS NEEDED TO PAY OFF BLUEBEARD, AND THE COST OF THE INVESTIGATION. YOU'RE LUCKY I GAVE YOU THE LEFTOVERS.
BUT NONE OF THAT IS MY RESPONSI-BILITY!
TOO BAD. YOU SHOULD NEVER HAVE SLEPT WITH MY SISTER.
NOW, IF I WERE YOU, I'D USE WHAT'S LEFT TO BUY YOUR TITLE BACK FROM JACK. I BET HE CAN BE BOUGHT CHEAP, AND YOU'D NEVER MAKE IT AS A POOR COMMONER.
BYE, LOVE. YOU'LL PICK UP THE CHECK?

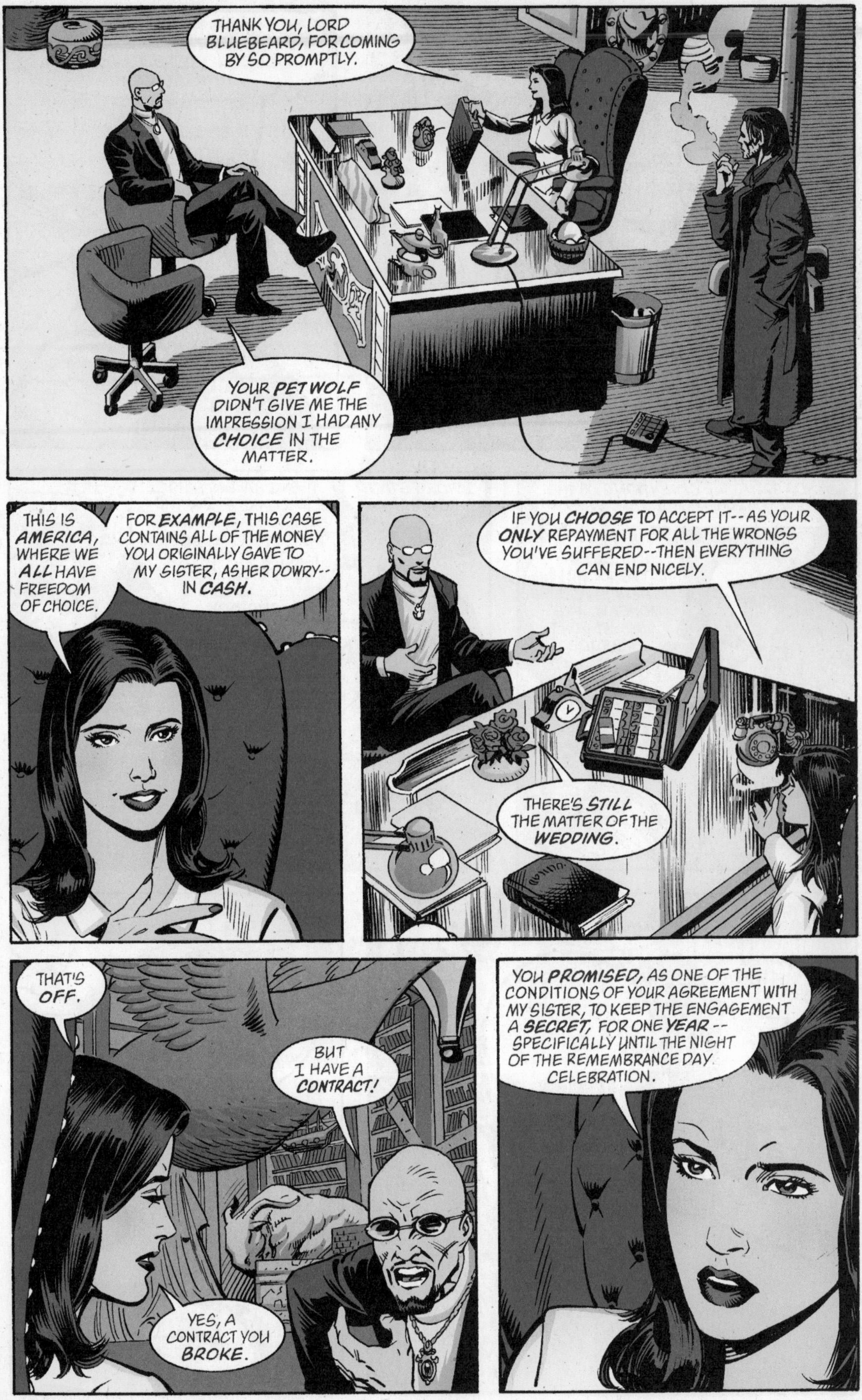
THANK YOU, LORD BLUEBEARD, FOR COMING BY SO PROMPTLY.
YOUR PET WOLF DIDN'T GIVE ME THE IMPRESSION I HAD ANY CHOICE IN THE MATTER.
THIS IS AMERICA, WHERE WE ALL HAVE FREEDOM OF CHOICE.
FOR EXAMPLE, THIS CASE CONTAINS ALL OF THE MONEY YOU ORIGINALLY GAVE TO MY SISTER, AS HER DOWRY-- IN CASH.
IF YOU CHOOSE TO ACCEPT IT--AS YOUR ONLY REPAYMENT FOR ALL THE WRONGS YOU'VE SUFFERED--THEN EVERYTHING CAN END NICELY.
THERE'S STILL THE MATTER OF THE WEDDING.
THAT'S OFF.
BUT I HAVE A CONTRACT!
YES, A CONTRACT YOU BROKE.
YOU PROMISED, AS ONE OF THE CONDITIONS OF YOUR AGREEMENT WITH MY SISTER, TO KEEP THE ENGAGEMENT A SECRET, FOR ONE YEAR -- SPECIFICALLY UNTIL THE NIGHT OF THE REMEMBRANCE DAY CELEBRATION.

SO?

SO YOU TOLD BIGBY AND ME ABOUT IT SEVERAL DAYS *BEFORE* THE CELEBRATION.

SNOW WHITE
DIRECTOR OF OPERATIONS

ONLY WHEN WE ALL THOUGHT SHE'D BEEN *MURDERED!* ONLY IN RESPONSE TO YOUR QUESTIONS, IN AN *OFFICIAL* INVESTIGATION!

SO? YOU BROKE THE *CONDITIONS* OF THE CONTRACT, MAKING IT *NULL* AND *VOID*.

YOU'RE LUCKY ENOUGH THAT WE'RE WILLING TO *REIMBURSE* THE MONEY YOU'VE LOST. WE DON'T *HAVE* TO.

I WON'T *STAND* FOR THIS!

THEN I HAVE NO CHOICE BUT TO TAKE *BACK* THE MONEY AND *REINSTATE* THE CHARGES AGAINST YOU, FOR THE *ATTEMPTED MURDER* OF JACK WHILE HE WAS IN *CUSTODY.*

SNOW WHITE
DIRECTOR OF OPERATIONS

UNFORTUNATELY, THAT MEANS YOUR *HEAD* GOES THE WAY OF SO MANY OF YOUR PAST *WIVES'* HEADS.

CHOPPY CHOPPY-- SO *SLOPPY.*

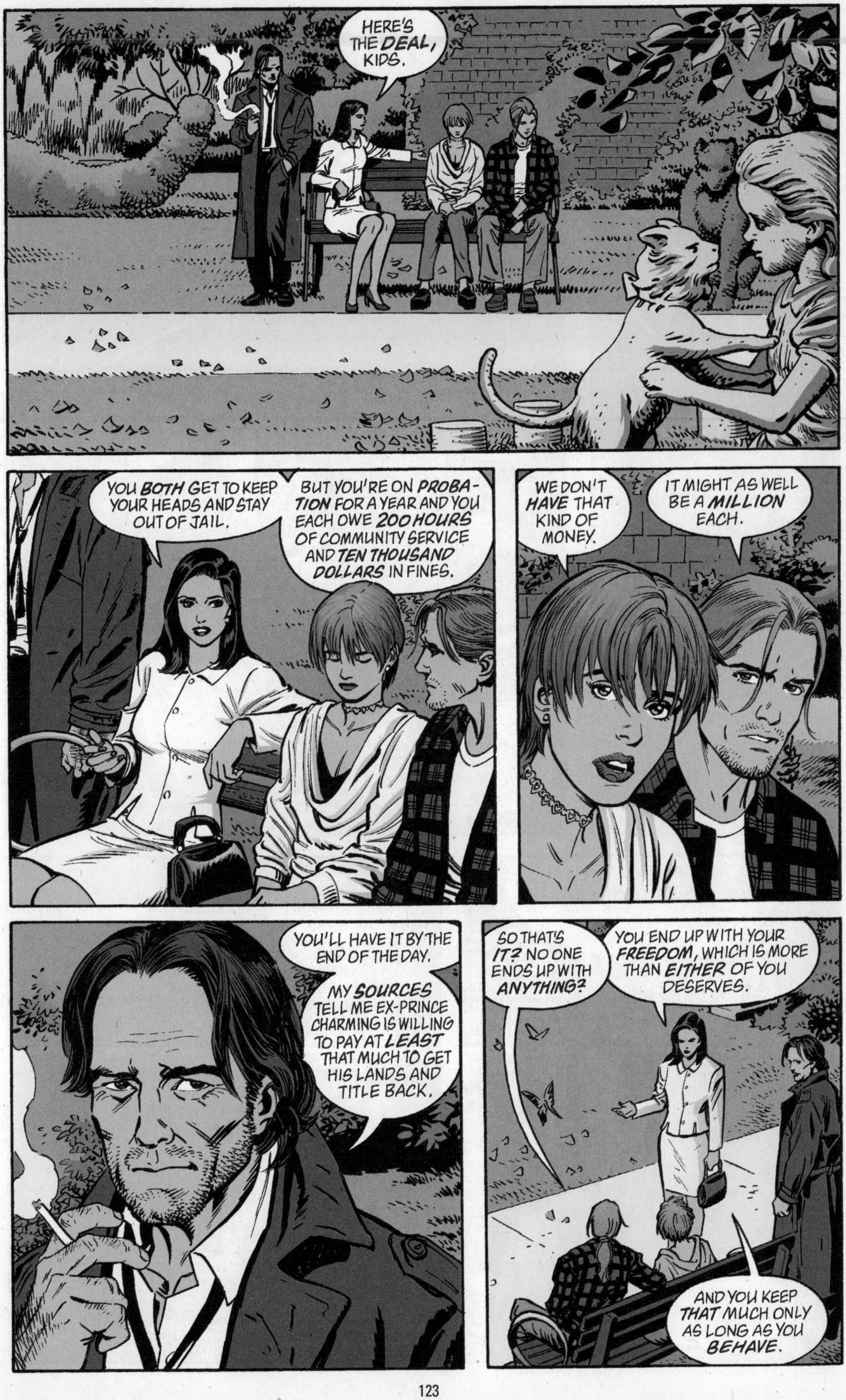
HERE'S THE DEAL, KIDS.
YOU BOTH GET TO KEEP YOUR HEADS AND STAY OUT OF JAIL.
BUT YOU'RE ON PROBATION FOR A YEAR AND YOU EACH OWE 200 HOURS OF COMMUNITY SERVICE AND TEN THOUSAND DOLLARS IN FINES.
WE DON'T HAVE THAT KIND OF MONEY.
IT MIGHT AS WELL BE A MILLION EACH.
YOU'LL HAVE IT BY THE END OF THE DAY.
MY SOURCES TELL ME EX-PRINCE CHARMING IS WILLING TO PAY AT LEAST THAT MUCH TO GET HIS LANDS AND TITLE BACK.
SO THAT'S IT? NO ONE ENDS UP WITH ANYTHING?
YOU END UP WITH YOUR FREEDOM, WHICH IS MORE THAN EITHER OF YOU DESERVES.
AND YOU KEEP THAT MUCH ONLY AS LONG AS YOU BEHAVE.

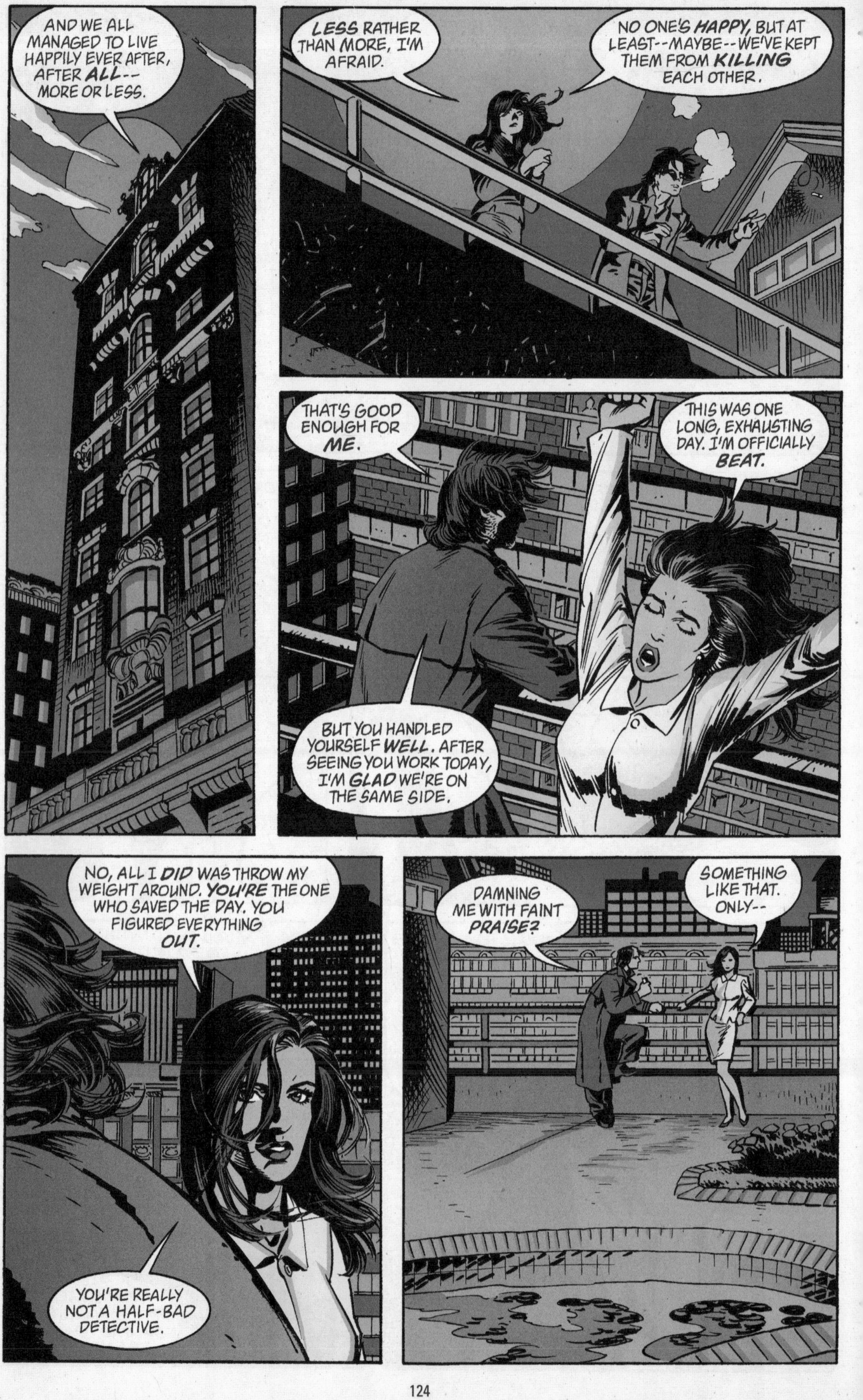
AND WE ALL MANAGED TO LIVE HAPPILY EVER AFTER, AFTER ALL-- MORE OR LESS.
LESS RATHER THAN MORE, I'M AFRAID.
NO ONE'S HAPPY, BUT AT LEAST--MAYBE--WE'VE KEPT THEM FROM KILLING EACH OTHER.
THAT'S GOOD ENOUGH FOR ME.
THIS WAS ONE LONG, EXHAUSTING DAY. I'M OFFICIALLY BEAT.
BUT YOU HANDLED YOURSELF WELL. AFTER SEEING YOU WORK TODAY, I'M GLAD WE'RE ON THE SAME SIDE.
NO, ALL I DID WAS THROW MY WEIGHT AROUND. YOU'RE THE ONE WHO SAVED THE DAY. YOU FIGURED EVERYTHING OUT.
YOU'RE REALLY NOT A HALF-BAD DETECTIVE.
DAMNING ME WITH FAINT PRAISE?
SOMETHING LIKE THAT. ONLY--

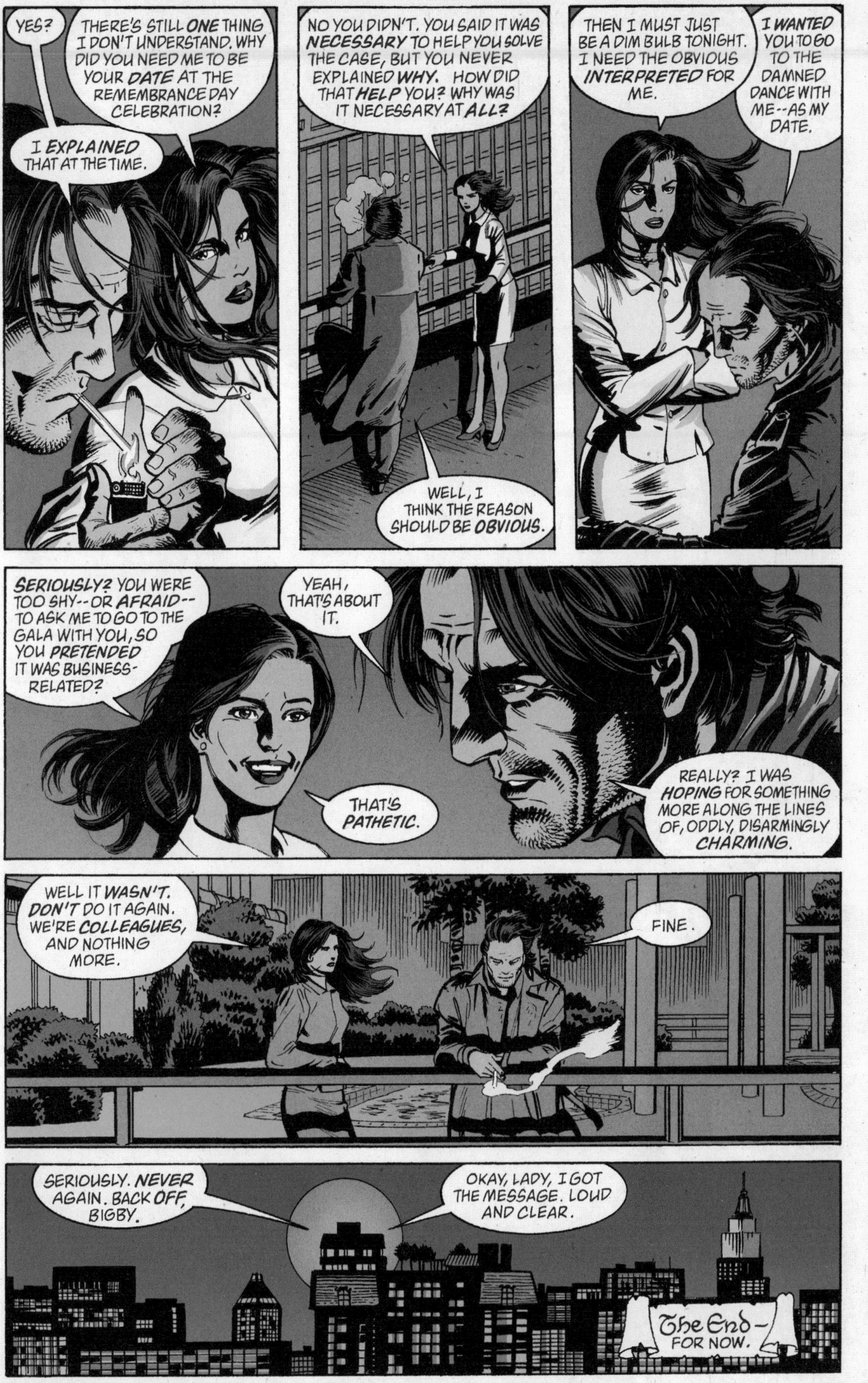
YES?
THERE'S STILL ONE THING I DON'T UNDERSTAND. WHY DID YOU NEED ME TO BE YOUR DATE AT THE REMEMBRANCE DAY CELEBRATION?
I EXPLAINED THAT AT THE TIME.
NO YOU DIDN'T. YOU SAID IT WAS NECESSARY TO HELP YOU SOLVE THE CASE, BUT YOU NEVER EXPLAINED WHY. HOW DID THAT HELP YOU? WHY WAS IT NECESSARY AT ALL?
WELL, I THINK THE REASON SHOULD BE OBVIOUS.
THEN I MUST JUST BE A DIM BULB TONIGHT. I NEED THE OBVIOUS INTERPRETED FOR ME.
I WANTED YOU TO GO TO THE DAMNED DANCE WITH ME--AS MY DATE.
SERIOUSLY? YOU WERE TOO SHY--OR AFRAID--TO ASK ME TO GO TO THE GALA WITH YOU, SO YOU PRETENDED IT WAS BUSINESS-RELATED?
YEAH, THAT'S ABOUT IT.
THAT'S PATHETIC.
REALLY? I WAS HOPING FOR SOMETHING MORE ALONG THE LINES OF, ODDLY, DISARMINGLY CHARMING.
WELL IT WASN'T. DON'T DO IT AGAIN. WE'RE COLLEAGUES, AND NOTHING MORE.
FINE.
SERIOUSLY. NEVER AGAIN. BACK OFF, BIGBY.
OKAY, LADY, I GOT THE MESSAGE. LOUD AND CLEAR.
The End—
FOR NOW.

Cover art by James Jean for the original trade paperback edition of FABLES: LEGENDS IN EXILE.

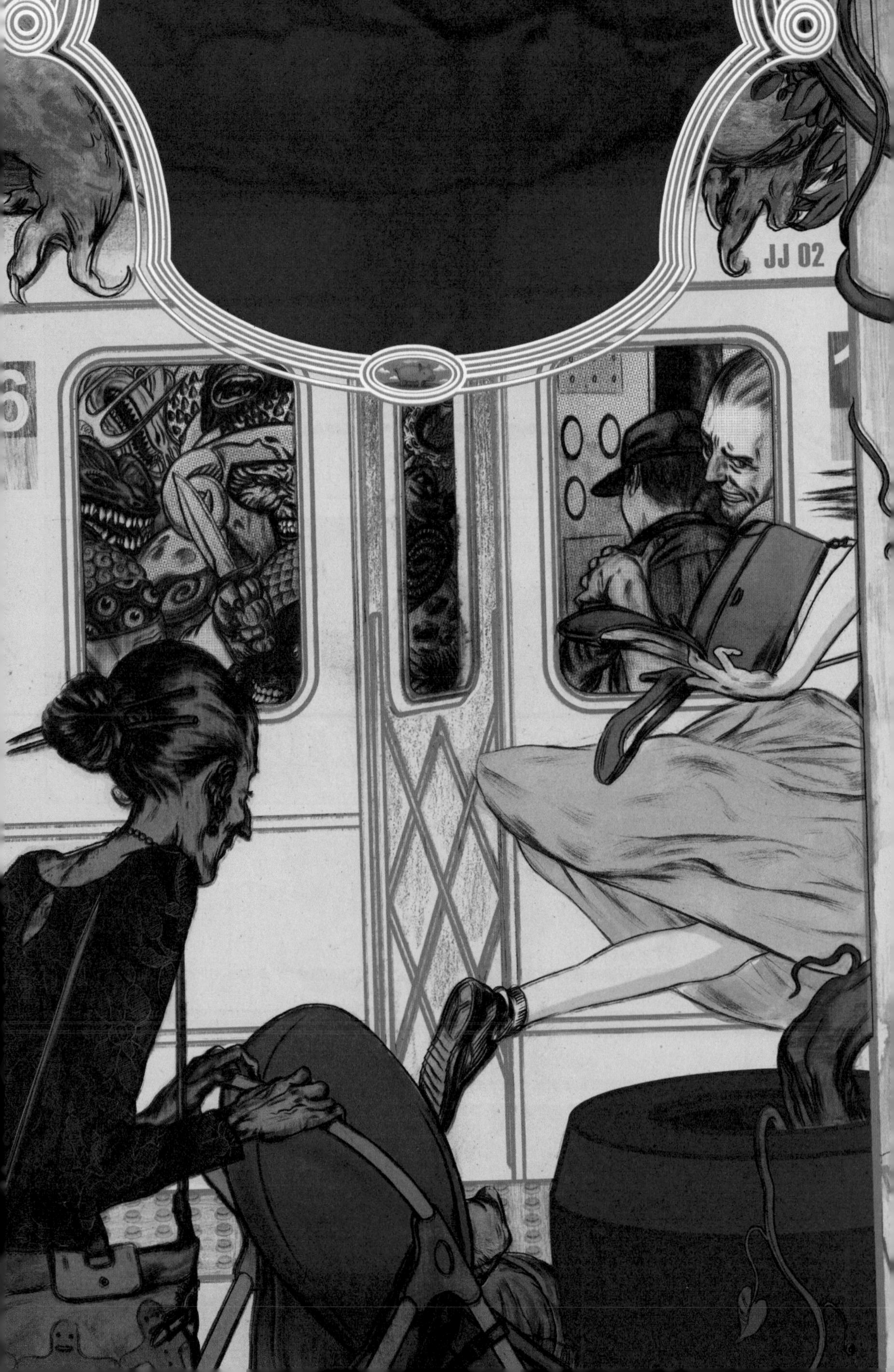
JJ 02

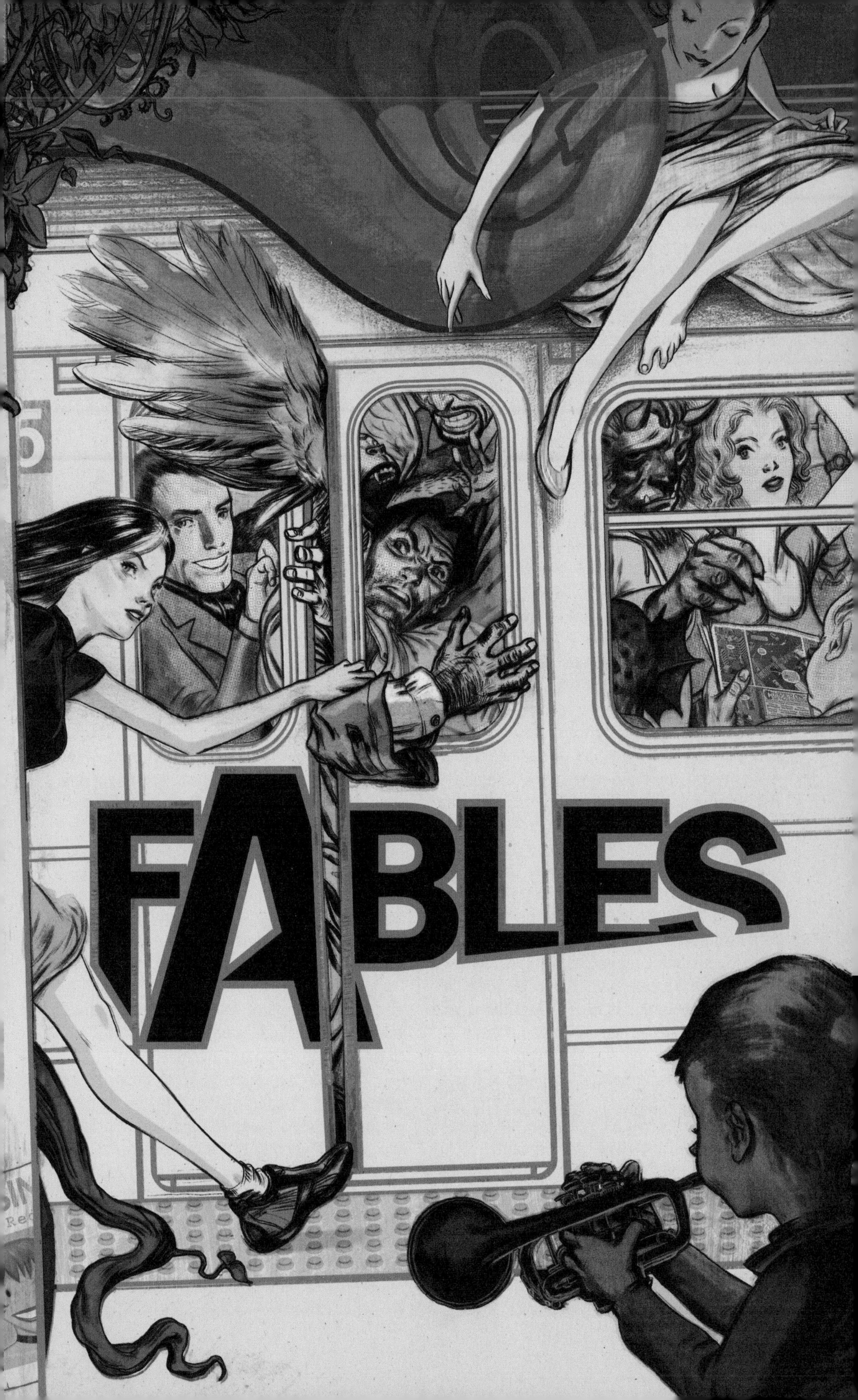
FABLES

When the invaders flooded into the valley, the old wolf came down from his warm den in the high hills to see what all the fuss was about. It didn't take him long to find the alien soldiers, for they tended to call attention to themselves. They wore suits of dark iron and marched in long, clattering ranks. They burned and pillaged wheresoever they went, enslaving those they could easily capture, while putting all others to the sword — those who resisted, to be sure, but also those who were too lame, too old, or too well educated to make able and subservient workers. The wolf took umbrage at these uncouth intruders, not only because they had the temerity to enter his territory uninvited, but also because they murdered wantonly, without craft or subtlety. In addition they killed or spirited away many of those living in the wooded valley that the wolf had marked in his mind to dine on one day, and such a breach of etiquette could not be endured.

In those days the wolf was still largely ruled by his belly, so he decided to sample a few of the invaders. They were easy enough to bring down, because, for all of his monstrous size, the wolf could strike with great stealth and cunning. In the deep woods between one isolated village and another, he picked off two stragglers as they marched behind a long column, biting easily through their shells of thick plate, and the ring-mail hauberks underneath, like a child crumbles autumn leaves. Once he'd stripped away the outer wrappings, he discovered misshapen, yellow-tusked gobliny things within. They screamed and pleaded and writhed well enough, as he savaged them, and their bones crunched satisfyingly, but their green and warty flesh was foul. Carrion three weeks rotting in the heart of summer tasted better than this!

That night, silent as a shadow, he crept into the army's sprawling encampment, thinking that their more human-looking captains might prove more suitable to his refined palate. He whispered past the watch-fires, ragged troop tents, and posted sentries — both sleeping and alert — until, quite undetected, he reached the camp's innermost ring, where the silken pavilions of the officers could be found. Choosing the biggest tent as the one most likely to house the sweetest confection, he leapt in, without so much as a breath of sound, and surprised a sleeper in his bed. He crunched the man's head first, like a red ripe apple, stifling any possibility of alarm, and then settled in for a long, leisurely repast. But after only a few bites, even this man's flesh proved unsuitable. It was tan and unblemished, but still carried a disturbing taint of corruption. The audacity of these people! Not only do they rob him of his preferred provender, but in turn they fail to provide anything approaching a suitable substitute?

The wolf's rage grew, and long into the night he pondered what to do about it.

In the days that followed, the wolf made himself a determined enemy of the invaders. He ranged far and wide, striking in this place and that, in the dead of night, or under the bright daytime sun. There seemed no pattern to his predations, which only increased the dread sown amongst his new adversaries. Relentlessly he hunted the soldiers and their masters, wherever he could find them — and he found them in abundance, infesting every land and kingdom, no matter how far afield he wandered from his own familiar territory. He slaughtered most of those he caught without hesitation or mercy, but spared a few long enough for questioning. From these he learned little of value. They were the advance forces of a remote and unnamed power — known only to the troops as their emperor — for he was by all accounts a creature bold with ambition and sorcerous might who'd decided to carve for himself a single, grand empire out of all the disparate kingdoms of fable.

"Why do you contend so against us?" one captive pleaded as he struggled helplessly under the wolf's massive forepaws. "For you are the very sort of monster we are commissioned to recruit into our ranks. You could rise high in the empire, commanding legions, or more!"

"Not interested," the wolf growled in return. "Even the highest office in service to another is too low a station for me." And with that the wolf sank his fangs into the captive's

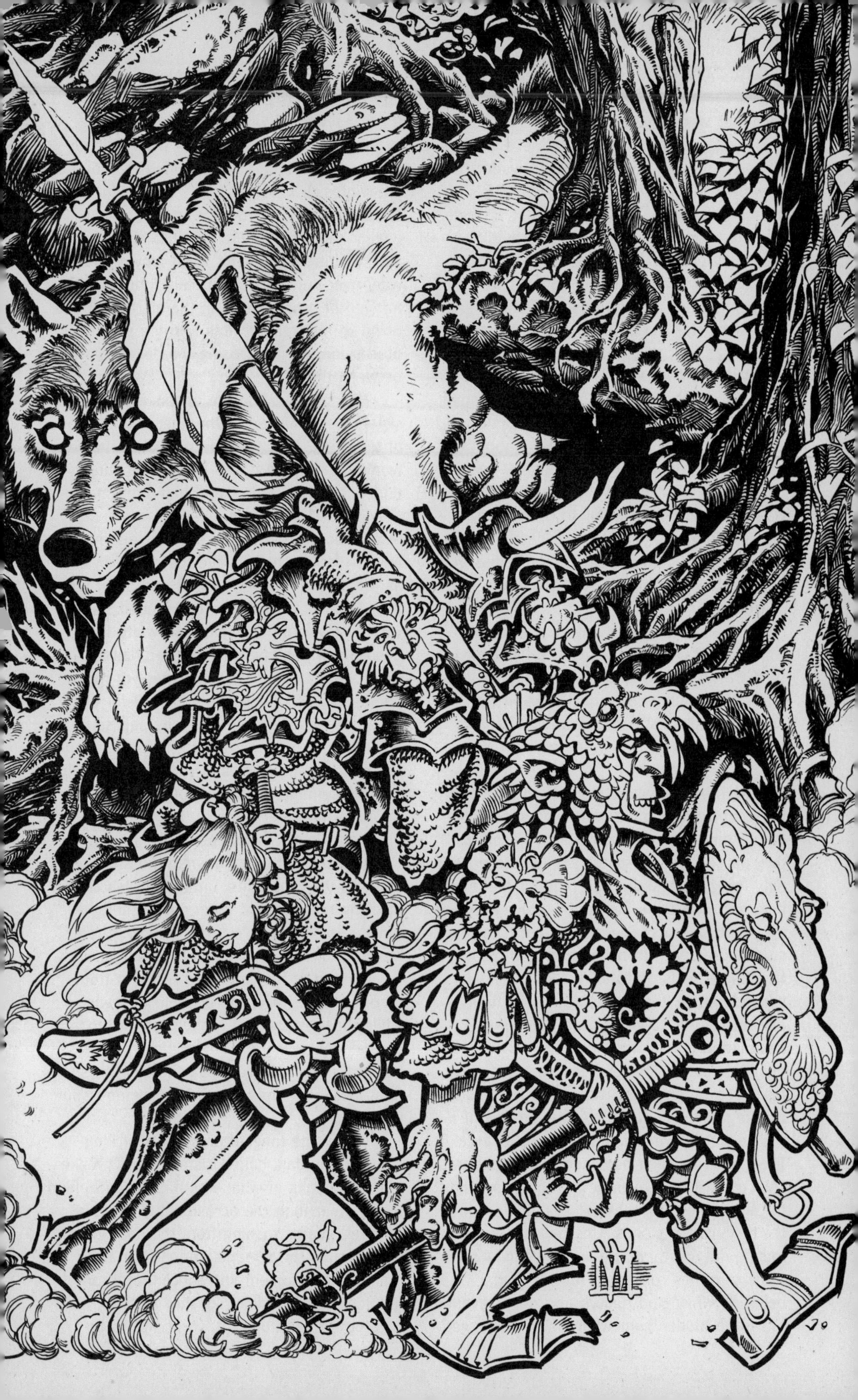

neck. A single, irresistible shake ended the soldier's tremors, instantly transforming living flesh into wet carcass.

Years passed in this fashion. The wolf hunted where he would, and the invaders trembled in their tents. But for all of his rapacious success, the wolf was but a single creature, where the Emperor could field seemingly endless battalions. Lands were methodically conquered and consolidated into the empire, despite his constant harassment. At best he was but an irritant in his unseen adversary's vast game of thrones.

Which isn't to say that his personal campaign went unnoticed in whatever distant country had spawned the invasion. Entire companies of the Emperor's most diabolical soldiers — trolls, giants and worse — were tasked with his capture or destruction. And when he eluded those, fell sorcerers and black-hearted warlocks were dispatched. He led them all a merry chase, and reflected from time to time that his life was good, all things considered.

One day, in the shadow of a range of tall white mountains that looked like the fangs of the Earth, bared to rend the heavens above, the wolf encountered a small force of the Emperor's soldiers escorting a much larger group of captives. They were led in heavy rattling chains, down out of the mountains' girdling foothills, where many tried to escape in recent years. From a concealed spot above the winding trail, the wolf watched them as they passed. The prisoners were wretched and dirty things, dressed in old rags for the most part, and new scars, no doubt received during the rough business of their capture. They stumbled along with bent backs and blank faces, sure signs that they knew, and finally surrendered to, the fate that awaited them — days of torture, to wring from them any information about other fugitives, followed by public execution. It seems the Emperor didn't believe in redemption. Those who resisted the all-too-generous initial welcome into his new regime were never offered a second chance. The guards for their part merely looked bored. They could hardly even be bothered to whip the slowpokes and those who stumbled on the trail's sharp stones. This had become routine duty to them, for many fugitives from many countries converged on this land, believing whispered rumors of a magic avenue of escape hidden somewhere in these rugged and forbidding hills. They arrived in droves and the soldiers captured them — most of them, anyway — with ease.

From his hiding place the wolf patiently watched and waited as he sniffed the cold pre-winter air for signs of a larger, hidden force. This wouldn't be the first time the enemy had tried to lure him into a trap with such inviting bait as this. He'd grown quite wary over the years. Eventually though, with no sign of other threats in the air, he padded down to the trail and followed the slow procession, silently closing the distance between them.

Nearly midway in the prisoner train, two sisters were chained to the line, one in front of the other. They were both lovely young women — though it was hard to be sure under the dirty clothes and half-dried mud that covered them from head to toe — and resembled each other, except that one had hair as dark as night while the other's was as red as the morning sun. In one other way they differed as well. The dark-haired sister wore a gown of rich velvet and white linen, bespeaking nobility, while the red-haired sister wore a simple peasant dress of rough homespun. Of course, the great leveler of extended hardship and adversity had so reduced each garment to egalitarian rags and tatters that only close and careful examination could determine their disparate origins.

Like the other captives, the sisters marched silently — except for the rattling chains manacled to each wrist and ankle — alone in their thoughts, until a sudden clamor of dying men startled them out of their private reveries. The commotion came from the back of the prisoner train, which abruptly compressed in the center, as those in front stopped to see what occurred in the rear, while those in the rear rushed forward to escape whatever it was back there that was killing the guards and filling the air with such feral, bestial sounds as to chill anyone's soul to the core.

Within the tangled press of panicking captives the dark-haired sister couldn't make out any details of what was happening behind them, other than the occasional glimpse of armored guards rushing from the head of the line towards the screams and clamor at its rear. For the moment she concentrated on holding onto her sister, as they worked together to keep upright, so as not to be trampled underfoot. Then the worst of the sounds died away, leaving only the whimpers of the chained prisoners, and while she was still being jerked and tugged, first one way and then the next, by the chains that attached her to everyone else, the mass of shuddering bodies opened up enough to finally reveal their new danger. A wolf had come amongst them, and such a wolf it was! On all fours it stood as tall as a yearling colt. Its fur was black, shading to brownish-gray on its flanks and belly, but at the moment most of its front end was painted red with the blood of the dozen guardsmen who'd so ruthlessly ruled their lives for many days past — right up until a moment ago. To a man they were all dead — savagely dismembered — their parts scattered up and down the trail, and the beast that destroyed them now stood no more than a pace or two from the center of the line, and the two sisters caught there. The women were held in place, stretched out to the limits of their shackles, as their chained companions on each end of the line tried to rush away from the middle, in an attempt to escape the terrible thing that stood amongst them. Some tried to run or crawl away, in both directions on the trail, while others tried to claw their way up the steep embankment on its hillward side. Still others simply surrendered to their certain doom and dropped where they were, trying to curl up or cover themselves as best they could. But the sisters didn't attempt to run or crawl or in any other way try to escape. Perhaps they knew that such attempts would be futile, or they found reserves of courage, or perhaps they simply knew something of what the cornered deer knows after the long chase, when it has finally resigned itself to becoming food for the lion. Whatever the reason, they stood where they were and stared into the yellow eyes that seemed to impale them in place. Entranced, they watched the steaming vapor of recent murder rise from each side of its red-wet muzzle. They listened to each ragged breath that issued from the bellows of its massive chest.

Then a sudden loss of tension in the chains seemed to break the dark one out of her spell — if only for a moment — but that was long enough for her to reach down by her feet where one of the guard's swords had landed during the carnage. She deftly snatched up the curved blade, slippery with its former owner's blood.

"Stay back, dire beast!" the dark sister cried. "My husband taught me well how to use this!" She held it in both hands, boldly brandishing it towards the wolf.

"I don't believe you," the wolf replied, and was that a tone of humor that colored its deep voice? It didn't attack her, but neither did it back away, or in any way seem concerned about the threatening blade held in a young woman's trembling hands.

"You will if you come closer and I chop you down."

"You misunderstand," the wolf replied, the grin of his long muzzle revealing rows of sharp fangs — the largest longer than a grown man's fingers. "I don't believe you've a husband. Though you're clearly no maiden, I can tell with a whiff and a sniff that it's been long years since you've visited anyone's marriage bed."

"My *former* husband!" the woman said. Under the caked grime, twin apples of ripening anger colored her alabaster cheeks.

"Put down your sword, woman. I doubt you could hurt me with it. But if you'll hold out your arms, I'll bite those shackles off you. Quit trembling so! I'm not going to eat you, or these other mewling creatures. It amuses me much more these days to frustrate the Emperor and his legions by spiriting his desired conquests safely out from his clutches. You two aren't from this land — your accents mark you as distant strangers — and yet here you are. I'll bet you've come hoping to find a certain witch's cave of legend. One with many twisting passages that lead to many distant worlds — at least one of which is far beyond the Emperor's reach and possibly even his knowledge."

"I'm amazed that you would know of such a place." This time it was the red-haired woman who spoke. Imitating her sister she had taken advantage of the moment to look for weapons within reach, but no other such device had fallen close enough.

The wolf ignored their efforts at self-defense, but suddenly dashed to nip at those on either end, still stretching out the chains in their efforts to escape. Eventually he herded them back into a loose and fearful cluster that for the most part left the long central chain hanging limp between each captive. Finally, when this was done, he returned to his former place, sat where he had been standing, and answered the red-haired sister.

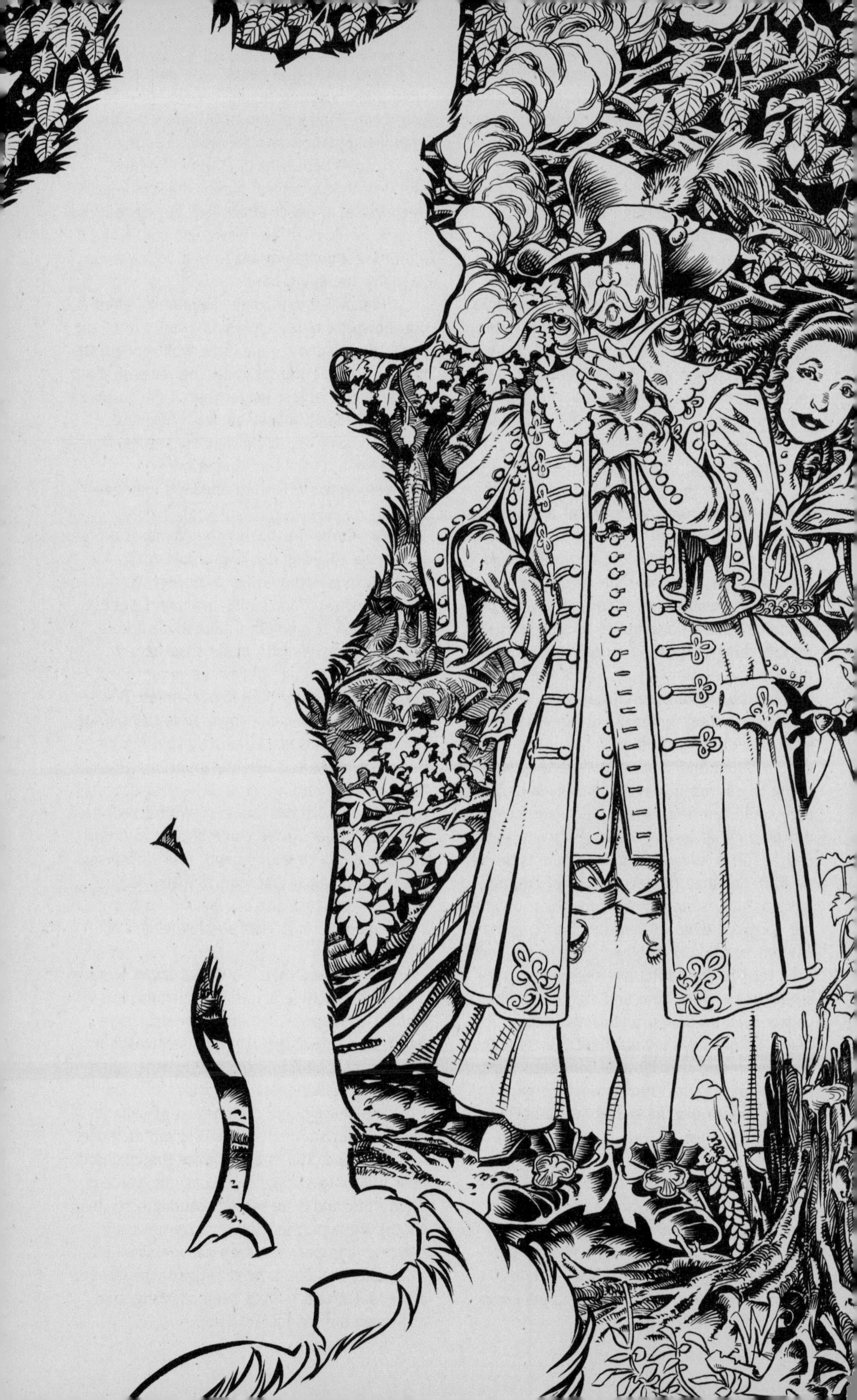

"I not only know of it, I'm the only one who can still find it, for the witch that made it is long gone, having passed through it to safety many years ago. And because she wanted none of the Emperor's minions following after, she left it cloaked in myriad spells and glamours that cause anyone seeking it to become misdirected and turned around so thoroughly as to be completely frustrated. But I can go there, straight and true, because I secretly followed the old hag that long lost day and marked the trail as only a wolf can."

"Then you are the one that we heard of — the great and terrible guardian of the way," the dark sister said. She hadn't lowered the point of her borrowed blade.

"You look like you expected someone else."

"We'd heard that you were a giant."

"I'm hardly tiny."

"And that you had at least three heads," the red-haired one said, "and by merely looking at you directly, we would be turned to stone."

"Stories do grow in the telling."

"And is the legend also false that you charge a dear price from those you allow to pass on to safety — to the unreachable world?" the dark one said.

"Not entirely, but it's not a matter of payment so much as precaution. The Emperor and his sorcerers have many devious ways to disguise his agents. He's often tried to slip one by me, and there's only one sure way to tell if you're genuine refugees, or more of his creatures in sheep's clothing."

"And what would that be?"

"I'll need a taste — just a little nip from each of you. No matter what shape they began in, or what form in which they present themselves, all of his minions have an unmistakable taint to their flesh. Since you two are so fair, under the accumulated dirt and grime of your recent trials, you'll want to pick a spot where the scar won't show."

"How are we to know that we can trust you, dread wolf?"

"I have no idea, but you'd better decide soon, or any number of bad things could happen. More soldiers could arrive, too numerous for me to overcome, I could grow bored and decide to leave all of you here, to your own devices — or I could grow hungry again and decide to stay."

For the first time since picking it up, the dark woman let the point of her blade drop, perhaps just an inch or two, as her look of fear and determination slowly, reluctantly gave way to something else.

———◆———

Two long centuries later the wolf was prowling the deep dark woods of his new home, in a wild land called Carpathia, when a quiet rustling of underbrush alerted him to the approach of two people. Even from downwind their scents reached him long before they did, identifying one as a stranger and one who seemed distantly familiar.

"You might as well finish coming forward," the wolf grumbled. "You've no chance of outrunning me now, should I decide to eat you, no matter what your starting distance."

The underbrush parted enough to admit two people into the small glade in which the wolf paused, under the spreading canopy of a great oak — a giant of lost ages that painted everything below in deep shadow. The first of the wolf's visitors was an achingly beautiful woman, with skin of whitest porcelain and silken hair darker than a raven's secret heart. She wore an expensive gown of charcoal gray, embroidered in dancing loops and swirls of burgundy thread. It was bowed out by any number of petticoats beneath — a ridiculous contrivance, the wolf thought, in which to go tramping through the woods. Over the dress she wore a long traveling cape, lined in white silk.

Her companion was dressed in similar opulence. He was a tall, slender, aristocratic fellow in matching breeches and waistcoat of powder blue, decorated with enough golden buttons, at the breast, waist and cuffs, to sate the avarice of ancient Midas himself. His vest was also of gold cloth and sported twin rows of even more gold buttons. He wore a broad-brimmed cap, set just so at a jaunty angle. It was of midnight blue, trimmed in more gold, and there was a long feather stuck through its band. He carried a long clay pipe and smoked it furiously, puffing an endless fog of white smoke into the air, almost obscuring his too-handsome features.

"Once long ago you promised not to eat me, Gaffer Wolf," the woman said, through a shy and tentative smile. In that instant the wolf recognized her.

"Only because sparing you then served a higher purpose," the wolf said. "But I no longer spend my days confounding the wishes of that hidden adversary in his far-off empire. I've returned to my former ways, and you're no longer guaranteed safe passage."

Leaving his pipe firmly clamped between his white and perfect teeth, the gentleman's hands drifted down to hover around two bulges distorting his waistcoat that the wolf hadn't noticed at first glance.

"Do you imagine you can retrieve whatever weapons you've concealed there before I can close my jaws around your throat?" the wolf said.

"I doubt you'll find my neck to your taste," the gentleman replied, showing not a hint of fear, "but try it if you must. It won't do me any permanent harm, and you'll be too close to avoid the twin shots of lead I've prepared for you."

"Stop such talk this instant," the woman said. "We didn't travel all this way for anyone to end up shot or eaten."

"Nature will win out," the wolf growled.

"Perhaps so, unless one has a way to change your nature," the woman said. "In any case I'm glad you finally decided to come over to this world."

"I had to. The Emperor's pet warlocks refined their methods of locating me over the years, until it finally became too dangerous even for me to remain there, prowling the numberless lands that had fallen under his heel. And since by that time there were rumors that other passageways to this world had been discovered, I decided my duty was done and it was time to see what sort of place I'd been sending folks to."

"And yet you chose to remain alone, in such a remote land as this?" the woman said. "We had the devil's own time finding you."

The wolf noted that the man moved each time he did, always shifting so as to keep positioned close enough to quickly interpose himself between wolf and woman. The fellow was a puzzle. For the first time in his memory he couldn't decipher a potential opponent's mood and intentions by the scent he gave off. There was a gentleman's cologne of course, but that couldn't mask his natural telltale musks — or at least it couldn't in any past encounter with such men. But beneath this man's sickly sweet perfume the wolf detected nothing — no fear at all, which was surprising

enough, but nothing else either. He turned to the woman again, whom he could still read easily.

"I purposely chose a home far away from those I'd sent here," he said, "so as not to let my hunger undo all of the work I'd done to save them. Here I'm free to hunt the mundane people of this land. They're a superstitious folk that blame everything I do on some fanciful local count who's rumored to be some fell spirit returned from the dead. It means I'm left alone for the most part, and he actually enjoys the notoriety. We visit from time to time. He's not a bad fellow and a good conversationalist, for when I want news of the wider world."

He faced the woman, but all of his attention was focused on her strange companion. He'd seen what these new things — these guns could do. He had no doubt they could do him great harm. If violence was required, he decided he'd first spring at the fellow's waist, rather than his neck. If he could crunch the pistols first, then he'd likely have the two of them in his power — no matter what his strange nature.

"You saved so many of us over the years — the centuries, in fact," the woman said. "I don't believe anyone who could do so much good can be such a monster as you present yourself to be. You belong among us, Gaffer Wolf, among those you saved and other refugees from the lost lands. That's why we've come here, to invite you to take your rightful place back among your own kind. We've started something in the far colonies — the New World. We've formed a community of Fables — two communities, actually — separated by distance, but as one in spirit and purpose. Those of us who can pass as normal humans live together in a remote town called New Amsterdam, far away from the hustle and bustle of this world. Those of us who can't pass as human live in a secret colony deep in the wilderness, in a place so remote that civilization will never overtake it."

"So you long for my company, woman, but plan to send me off to live amongst the animals, far away from you?"

"Not at all," she said and began to blush with embarrassment. "There have been dissenting opinions, threatening to destroy our community, before it begins. In point of fact the experiment is about to fall apart over the matter of what to do with you. On one hand you saved so many of us. On the other hand, your predations in the homelands were truly monstrous, and it's for those crimes that the wilderness colony won't have you. Of all the fell creatures who've escaped to this world, they fear you the most. But what we're attempting is predicated on the notions of equality for all, beginning with a universal pardon of all past crimes, debts and grievances. If one of us is singled out as not worthy of amnesty, then we're back where we started: picking and choosing and counting up past crimes. The community is still fragile and will surely crumble because of this division amongst us, perhaps not this year or the next, but inevitably. Since one colony won't have you, the other one must — but you'll have to be able to pass as human."

"And there's the rub," the wolf said.

"It can be done," the woman said. "You can live as a human, if you choose to." From under her cape she withdrew an ancient iron knife. Its blade was pitted and scarred and looked ready to crumble away in the next breeze. The wolf stiffened when he spied it, reflexively gathering himself to spring — either at her or at the man (or away as fast as he could run) he didn't know yet.

"What's the purpose of that?" he said.

"You found it necessary to bite me once long ago," she said, "so now it's my turn to bite back. This blade is tainted with an ancient magic — an enchantment that lets men walk as wolves."

"I've encountered those impostors, once or twice. They didn't impress me."

"The witch who sold this to me — at a very dear price I might add — said the curse... uhm, the enchantment should work as well in the other direction. A wolf can walk as a man."

"Why should I ever want to do that?"

"That's what we're here to discuss," she said. "And we're prepared to stay long enough to resolve it one way or another. Our hired coach is parked on the roadway down below. Can you direct us to nearby lodgings?"

"Perhaps his friend the count will volunteer shelter to a pair of noble cousins from distant lands," the gentleman said.

———◆———

The wolf was still getting used to all of the manifest irritations of his new shape when they made the sea crossing. He continuously tugged at and scratched under his woolen frock coat when he'd take his turns on deck. The woman — who turned out to be named after a type of weather in which hunting was typically bad — seldom left her cabin. She didn't like sea travel and claimed the constant pitching and rolling worked ills on her stomach. The wolf discovered he rather enjoyed it. He often encountered the strange gentleman on deck, who seemed not to be bothered by anything, as long as he could keep his ever-present pipe lit. He claimed to have too many names and titles to bother the wolf with and invited him to use Feathertop, which is how he was known amongst most of the Fables. The wolf never felt entirely at ease in the man's company, which Feathertop also noticed and remarked upon one day on the pitching deck.

"I was chosen to accompany the princess on this journey because, of all of the Fables living in this world, I'd be the one most safe from you, if you truly turned out to be monstrous again. I'm not really made of the sorts of things you like to eat." He wouldn't expand on those cryptic comments.

"But as long as we're trading personal secrets," he went on to say, "why don't you tell me why you really chose to come back with us? Though I fancy myself no mean rhetorician, I don't believe either her ladyship or myself argued you into doing anything you hadn't already set your mind to do. The truth now. Why are you here?"

The wolf didn't answer. Instead he turned his face into the gusting rain of a summer squall that had overtaken them, and he thought again about the tiny wisp of a girl, cloaked in equal parts caked grime and foolish bravado, on that long-ago mountain trail, prepared to fight off a ravening monster with but a thin sliver of borrowed steel. And he wondered why, of all the people he'd encountered in his long life, he couldn't quite get her scent out of his mind, no matter the passing of years. He stayed late on deck that night as the tiny wooden ship rode bravely over the rolling swells towards the New World.

"Funny, smart and full of old-fashioned thrills and spills, PETER & MAX: A FABLES NOVEL brings Bill Willingham's long-running comic series to the world of prose in a way that's sure to please old fans and make some new ones."
— io9

The following short story first appeared in 2009 in PETER & MAX: A FABLES NOVEL, written by Bill Willingham with black and white illustrations by Steve Leialoha. Newly colored by Lee Loughridge for this volume, "The Price of a Happy Ending" provides a glimpse into the future of Fabletown and its inhabitants — a destiny recorded in the ongoing series of FABLES collections available from VERTIGO.

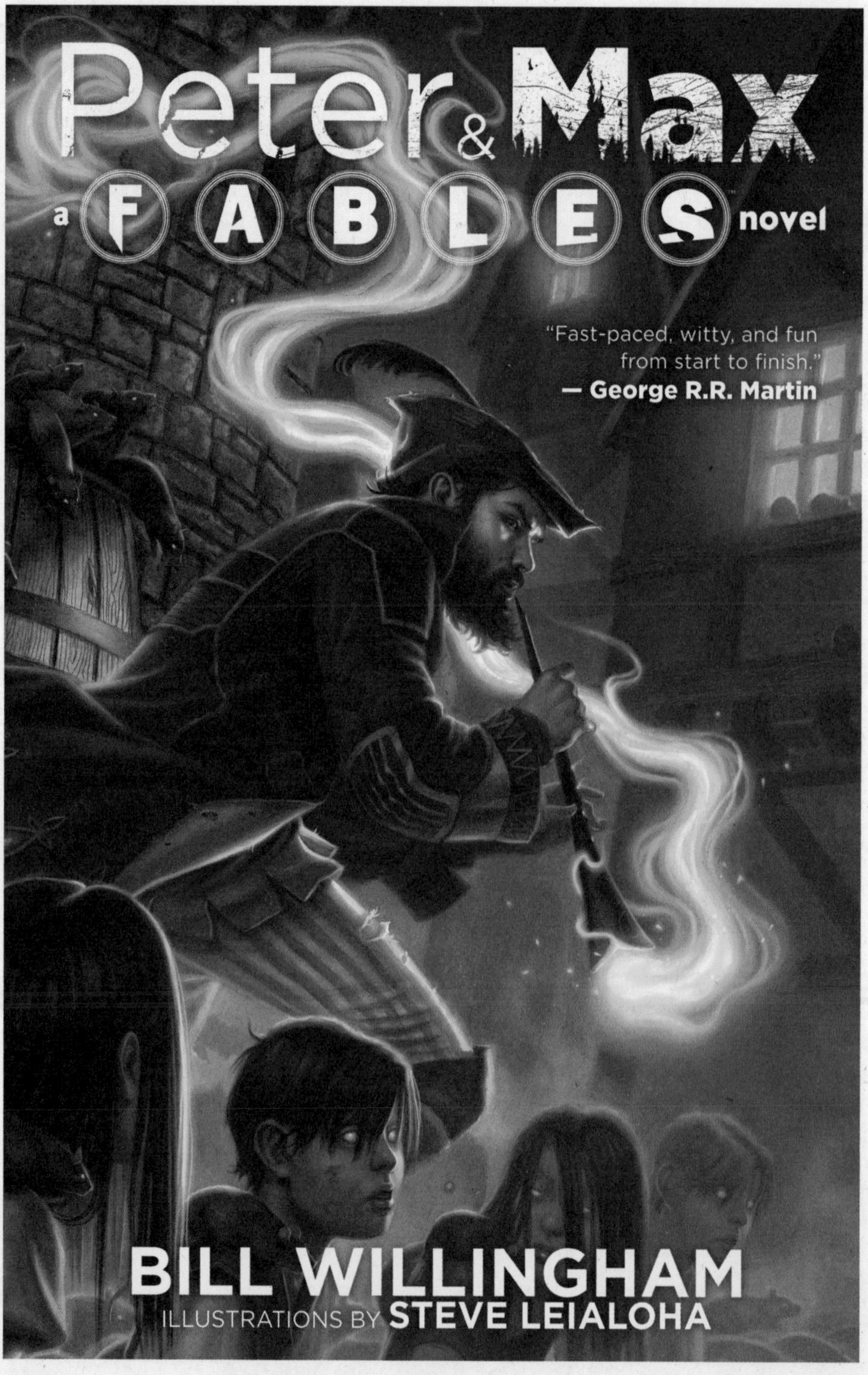
Peter & Max
a FABLES novel
"Fast-paced, witty, and fun from start to finish."
— George R.R. Martin
BILL WILLINGHAM
ILLUSTRATIONS BY STEVE LEIALOHA

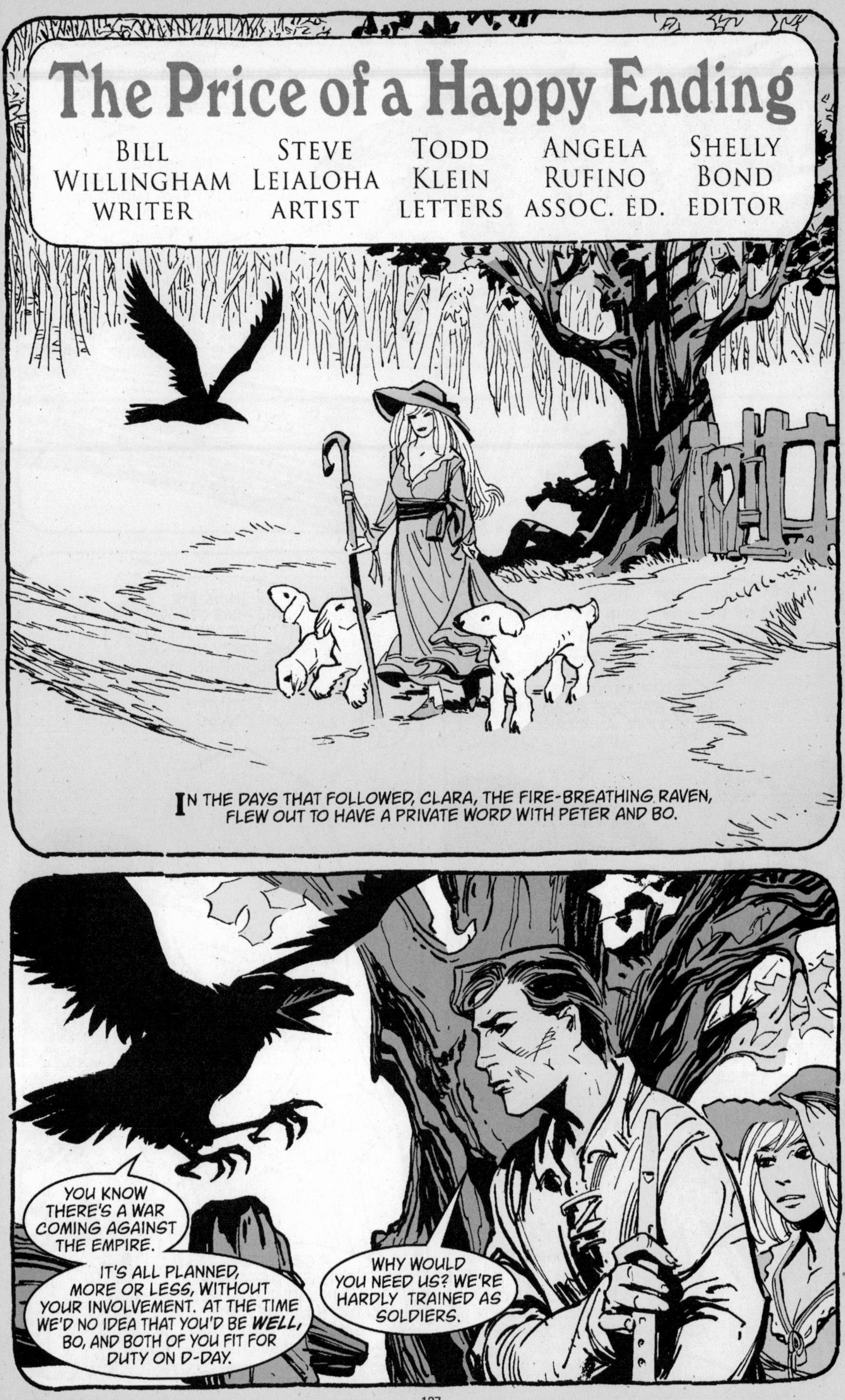
The Price of a Happy Ending
Bill Willingham Writer
Steve Leialoha Artist
Todd Klein Letters
Angela Rufino Assoc. Ed.
Shelly Bond Editor
IN THE DAYS THAT FOLLOWED, CLARA, THE FIRE-BREATHING RAVEN, FLEW OUT TO HAVE A PRIVATE WORD WITH PETER AND BO.
YOU KNOW THERE'S A WAR COMING AGAINST THE EMPIRE.
IT'S ALL PLANNED, MORE OR LESS, WITHOUT YOUR INVOLVEMENT. AT THE TIME WE'D NO IDEA THAT YOU'D BE WELL, BO, AND BOTH OF YOU FIT FOR DUTY ON D-DAY.
WHY WOULD YOU NEED US? WE'RE HARDLY TRAINED AS SOLDIERS.

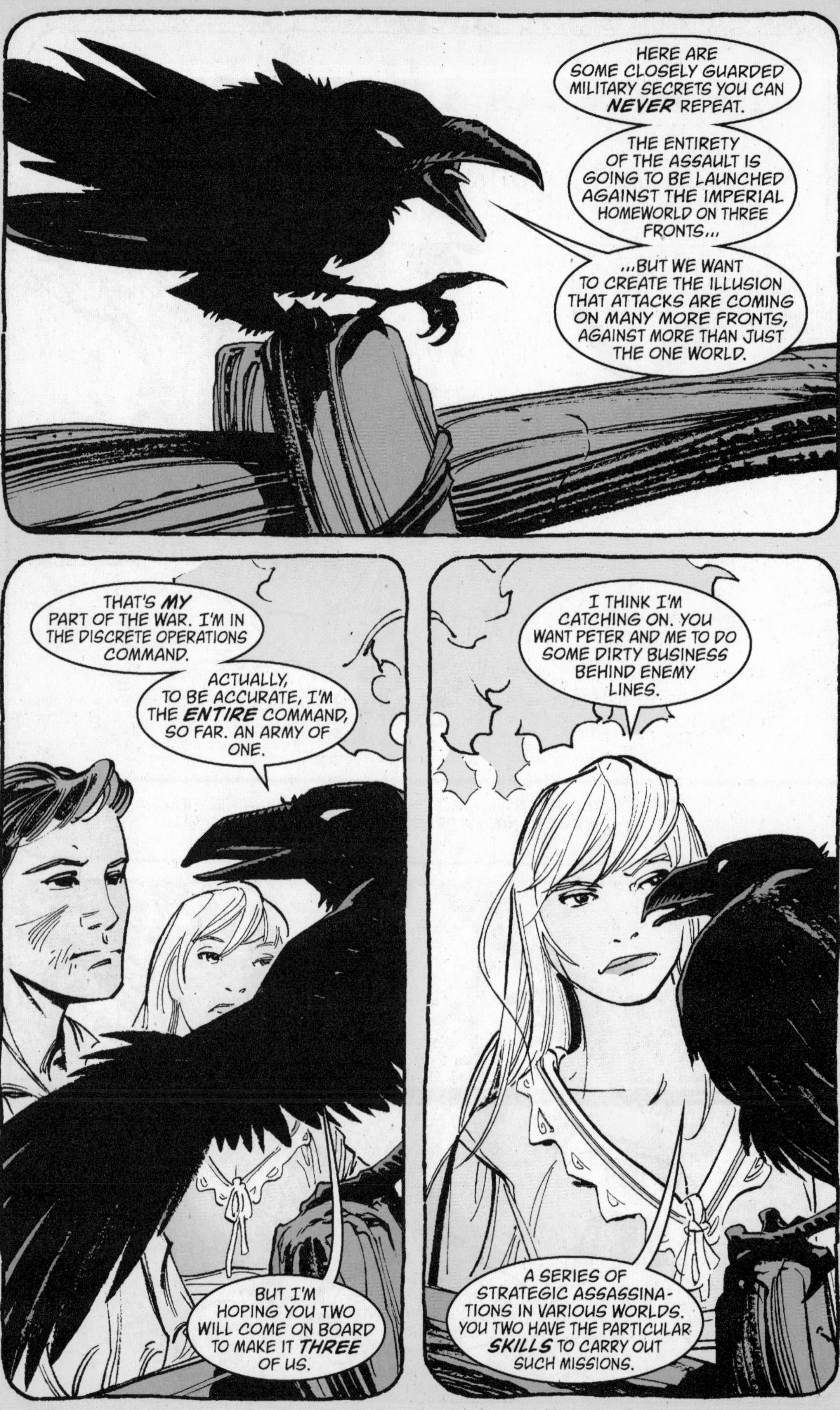
HERE ARE SOME CLOSELY GUARDED MILITARY SECRETS YOU CAN NEVER REPEAT.
THE ENTIRETY OF THE ASSAULT IS GOING TO BE LAUNCHED AGAINST THE IMPERIAL HOMEWORLD ON THREE FRONTS...
...BUT WE WANT TO CREATE THE ILLUSION THAT ATTACKS ARE COMING ON MANY MORE FRONTS, AGAINST MORE THAN JUST THE ONE WORLD.
THAT'S MY PART OF THE WAR. I'M IN THE DISCRETE OPERATIONS COMMAND.
ACTUALLY, TO BE ACCURATE, I'M THE ENTIRE COMMAND, SO FAR. AN ARMY OF ONE.
BUT I'M HOPING YOU TWO WILL COME ON BOARD TO MAKE IT THREE OF US.
I THINK I'M CATCHING ON. YOU WANT PETER AND ME TO DO SOME DIRTY BUSINESS BEHIND ENEMY LINES.
A SERIES OF STRATEGIC ASSASSINATIONS IN VARIOUS WORLDS. YOU TWO HAVE THE PARTICULAR SKILLS TO CARRY OUT SUCH MISSIONS.

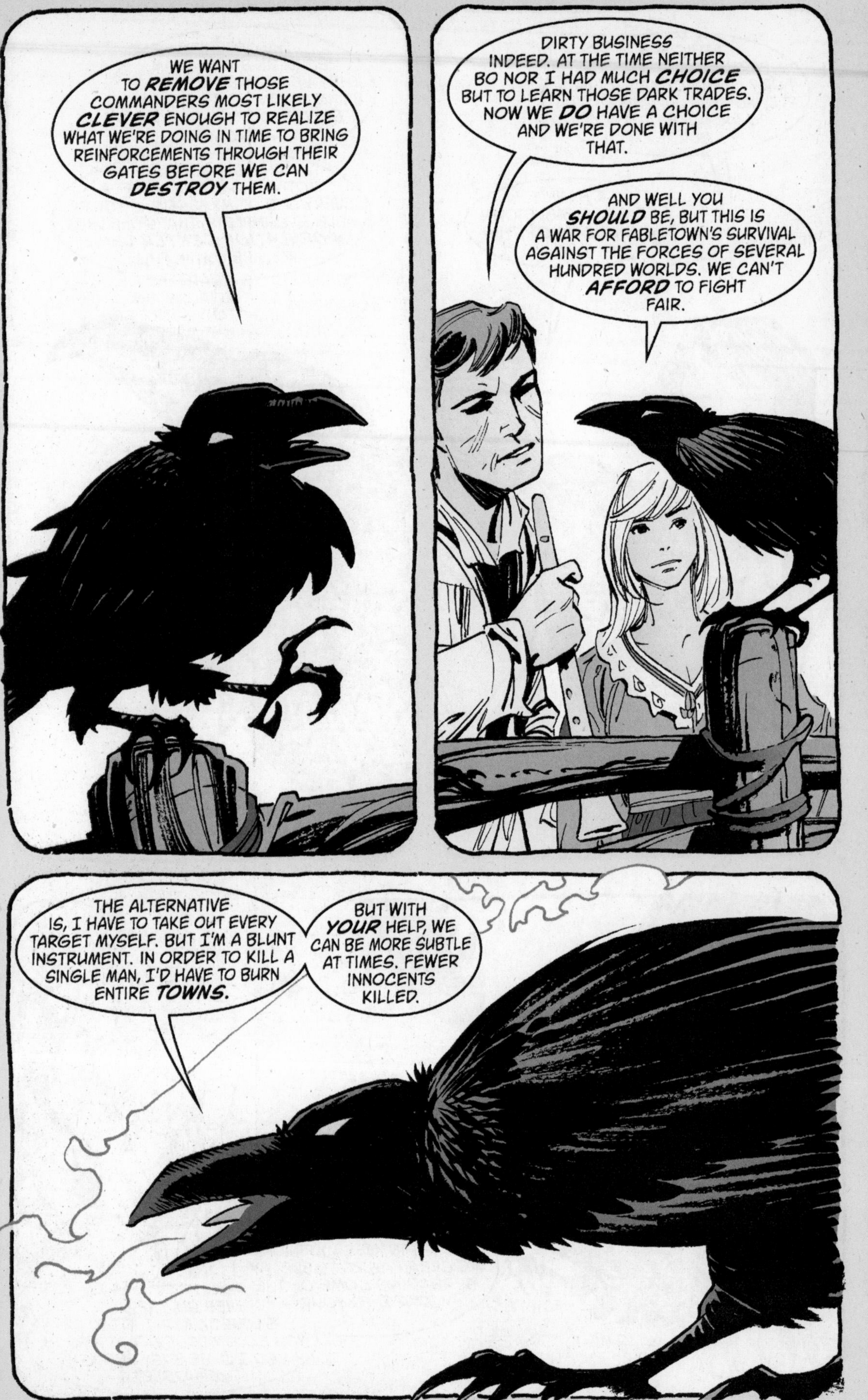
WE WANT TO REMOVE THOSE COMMANDERS MOST LIKELY CLEVER ENOUGH TO REALIZE WHAT WE'RE DOING IN TIME TO BRING REINFORCEMENTS THROUGH THEIR GATES BEFORE WE CAN DESTROY THEM.
DIRTY BUSINESS INDEED. AT THE TIME NEITHER BO NOR I HAD MUCH CHOICE BUT TO LEARN THOSE DARK TRADES. NOW WE DO HAVE A CHOICE AND WE'RE DONE WITH THAT.
AND WELL YOU SHOULD BE, BUT THIS IS A WAR FOR FABLETOWN'S SURVIVAL AGAINST THE FORCES OF SEVERAL HUNDRED WORLDS. WE CAN'T AFFORD TO FIGHT FAIR.
THE ALTERNATIVE IS, I HAVE TO TAKE OUT EVERY TARGET MYSELF. BUT I'M A BLUNT INSTRUMENT. IN ORDER TO KILL A SINGLE MAN, I'D HAVE TO BURN ENTIRE TOWNS.
BUT WITH YOUR HELP, WE CAN BE MORE SUBTLE AT TIMES. FEWER INNOCENTS KILLED.

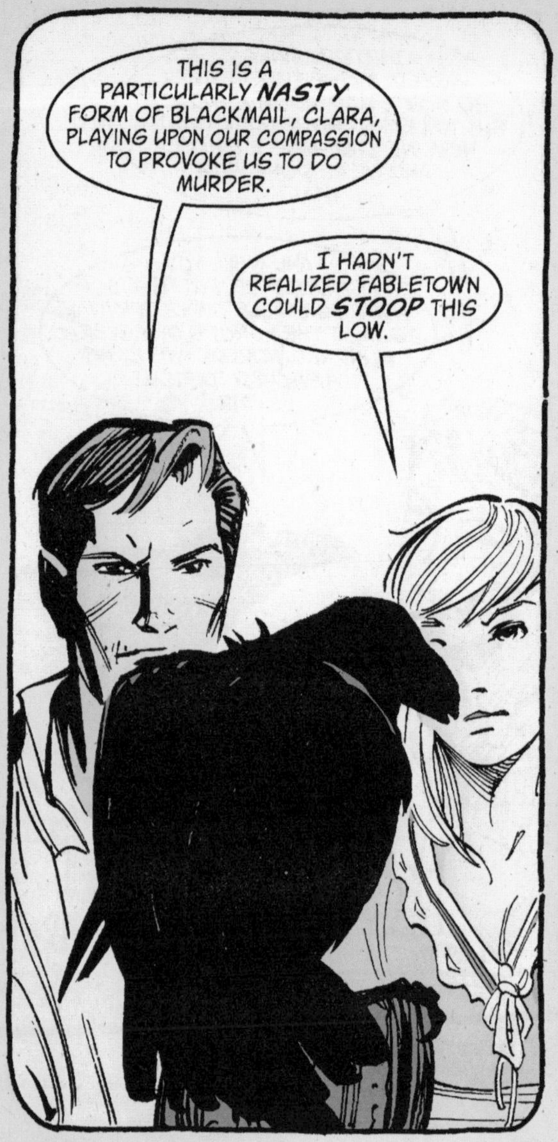
THIS IS A PARTICULARLY NASTY FORM OF BLACKMAIL, CLARA, PLAYING UPON OUR COMPASSION TO PROVOKE US TO DO MURDER.
I HADN'T REALIZED FABLETOWN COULD STOOP THIS LOW.

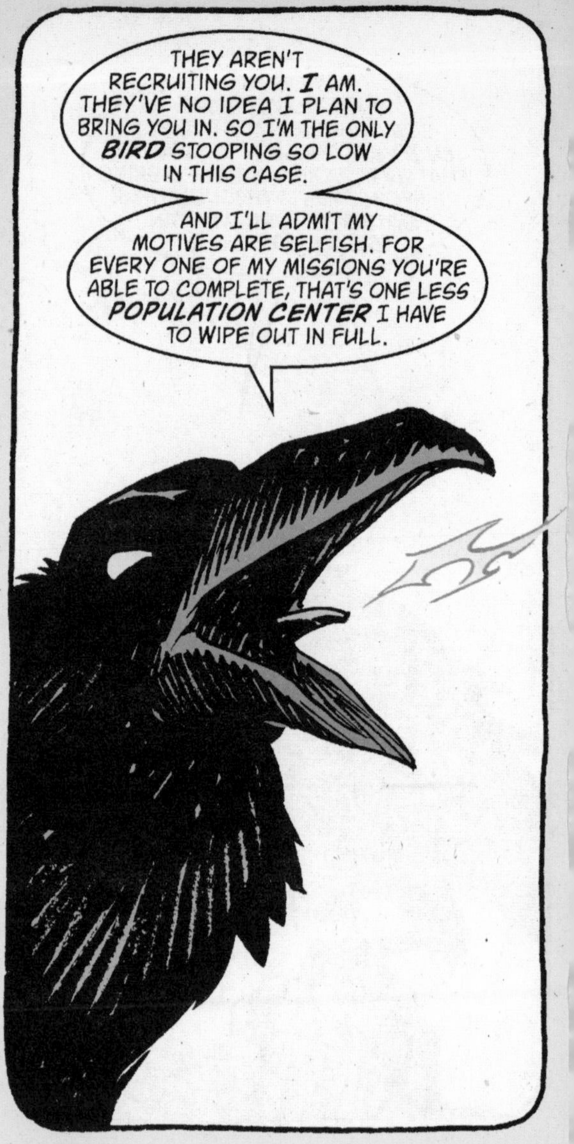
THEY AREN'T RECRUITING YOU. I AM. THEY'VE NO IDEA I PLAN TO BRING YOU IN. SO I'M THE ONLY BIRD STOOPING SO LOW IN THIS CASE.
AND I'LL ADMIT MY MOTIVES ARE SELFISH. FOR EVERY ONE OF MY MISSIONS YOU'RE ABLE TO COMPLETE, THAT'S ONE LESS POPULATION CENTER I HAVE TO WIPE OUT IN FULL.

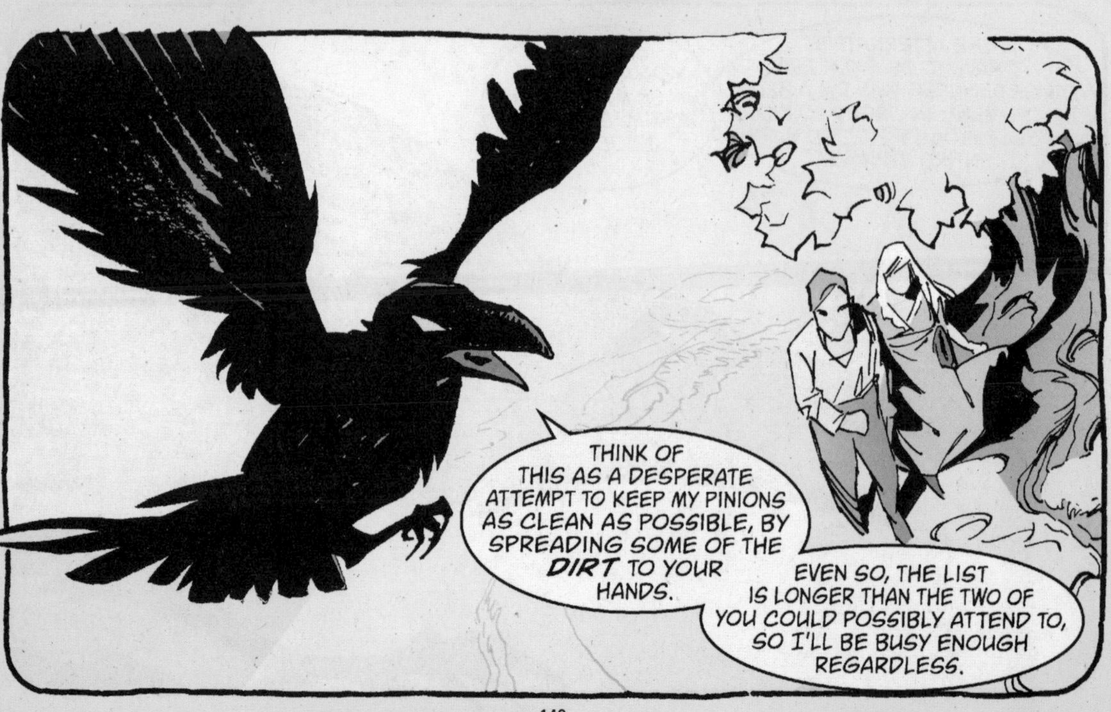
THINK OF THIS AS A DESPERATE ATTEMPT TO KEEP MY PINIONS AS CLEAN AS POSSIBLE, BY SPREADING SOME OF THE DIRT TO YOUR HANDS.
EVEN SO, THE LIST IS LONGER THAN THE TWO OF YOU COULD POSSIBLY ATTEND TO, SO I'LL BE BUSY ENOUGH REGARDLESS.

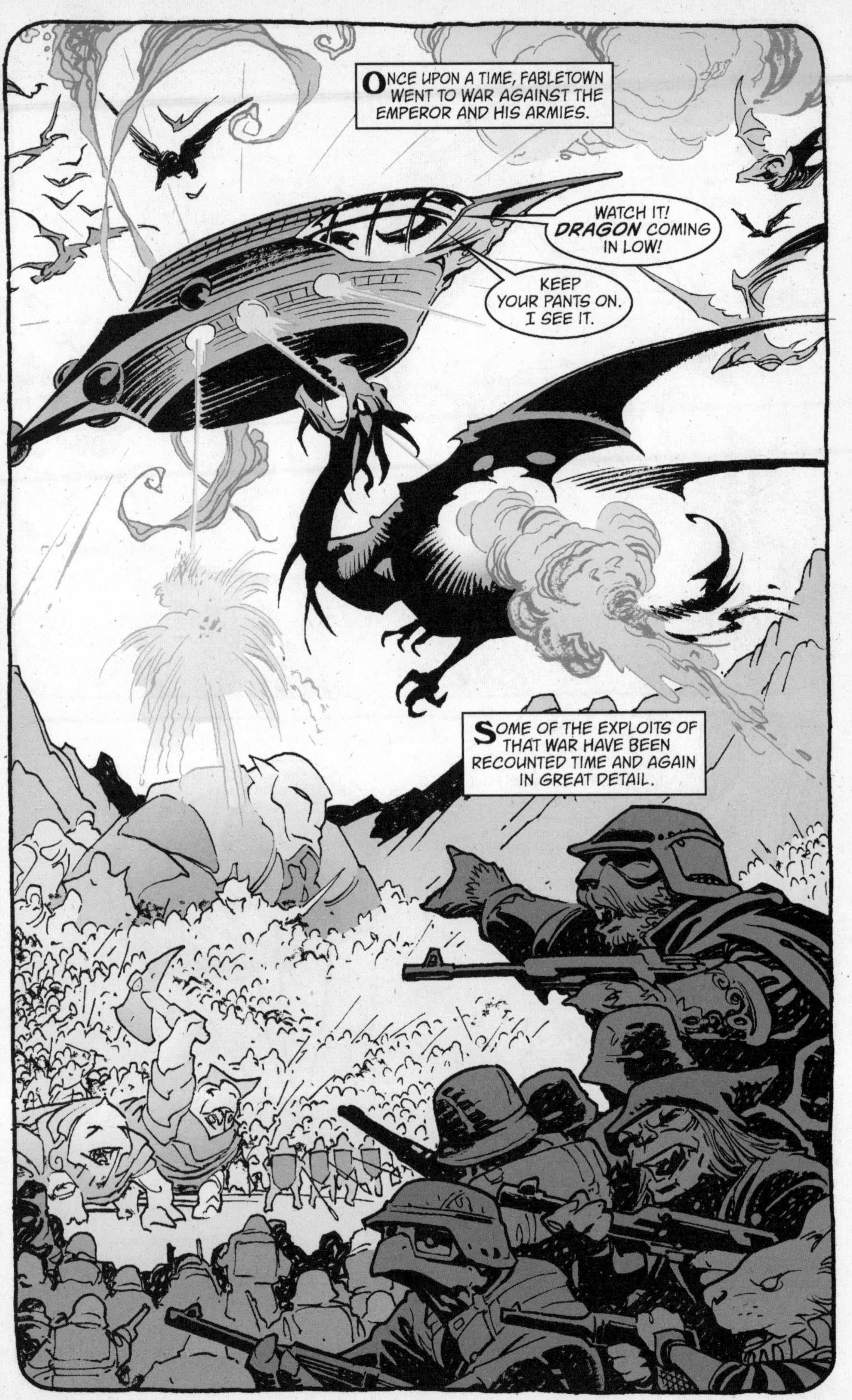
ONCE UPON A TIME, FABLETOWN WENT TO WAR AGAINST THE EMPEROR AND HIS ARMIES.
WATCH IT! DRAGON COMING IN LOW!
KEEP YOUR PANTS ON. I SEE IT.
SOME OF THE EXPLOITS OF THAT WAR HAVE BEEN RECOUNTED TIME AND AGAIN IN GREAT DETAIL.

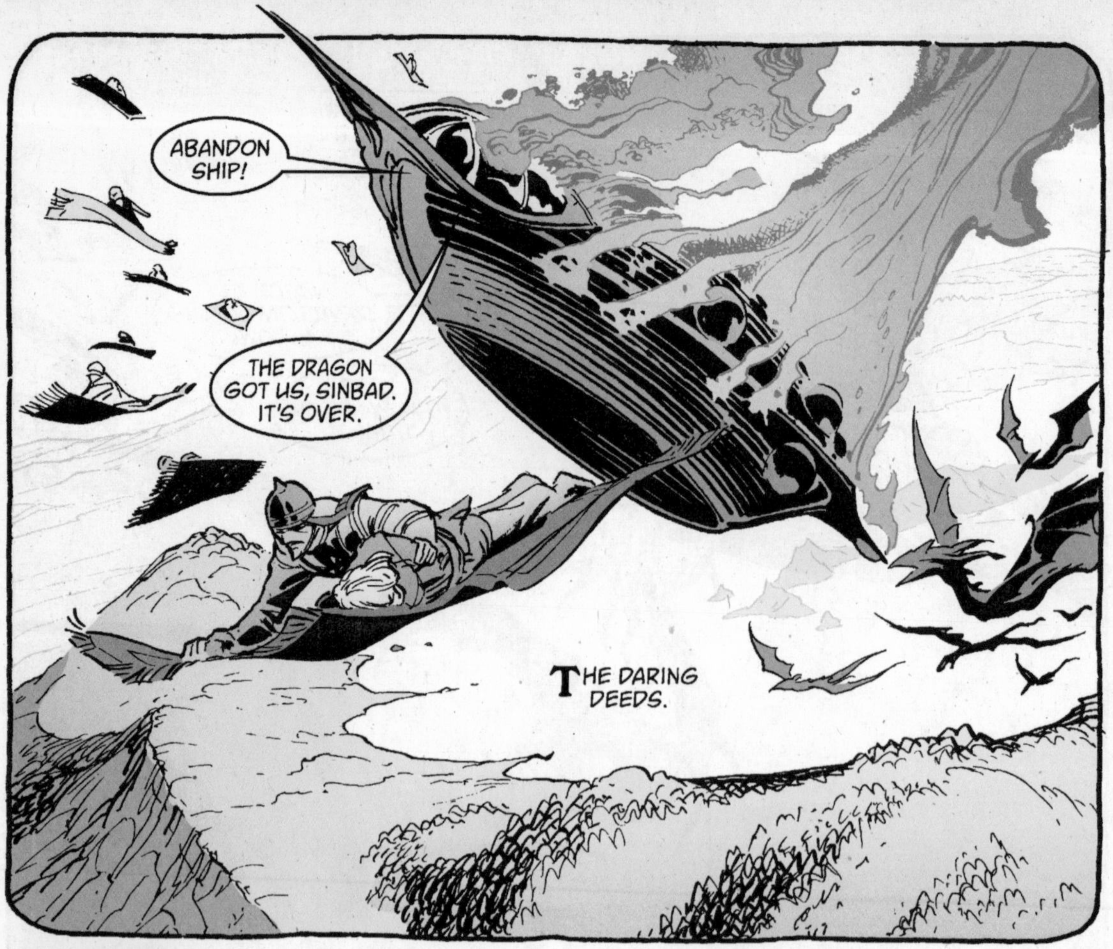
ABANDON SHIP!
THE DRAGON GOT US, SINBAD. IT'S OVER.
THE DARING DEEDS.

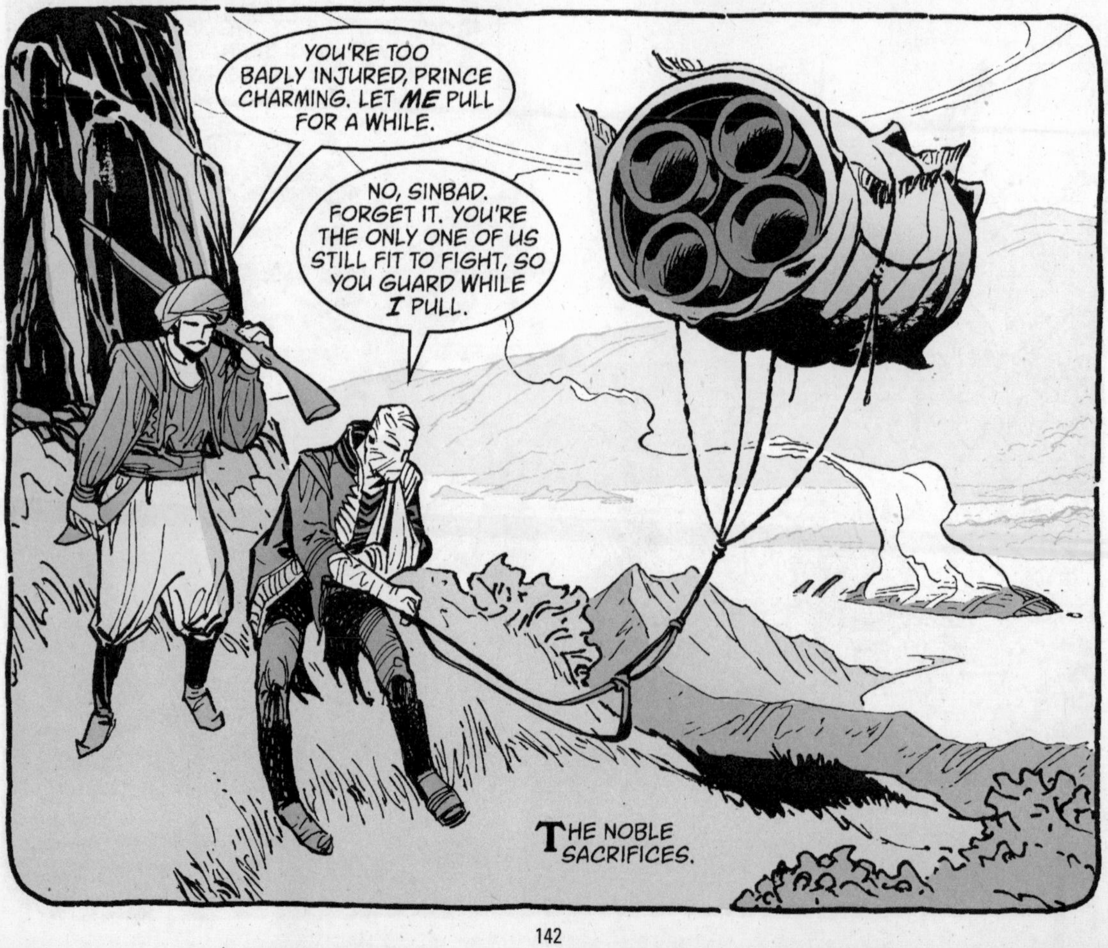
YOU'RE TOO BADLY INJURED, PRINCE CHARMING. LET *ME* PULL FOR A WHILE.
NO, SINBAD. FORGET IT. YOU'RE THE ONLY ONE OF US STILL FIT TO FIGHT, SO YOU GUARD WHILE *I* PULL.
THE NOBLE SACRIFICES.

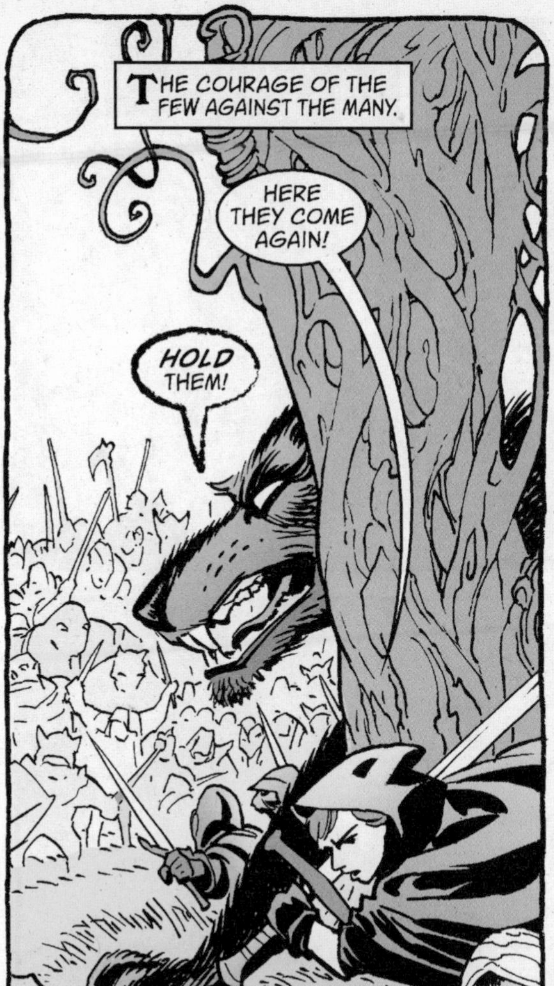
THE COURAGE OF THE FEW AGAINST THE MANY.
HERE THEY COME AGAIN!
HOLD THEM!

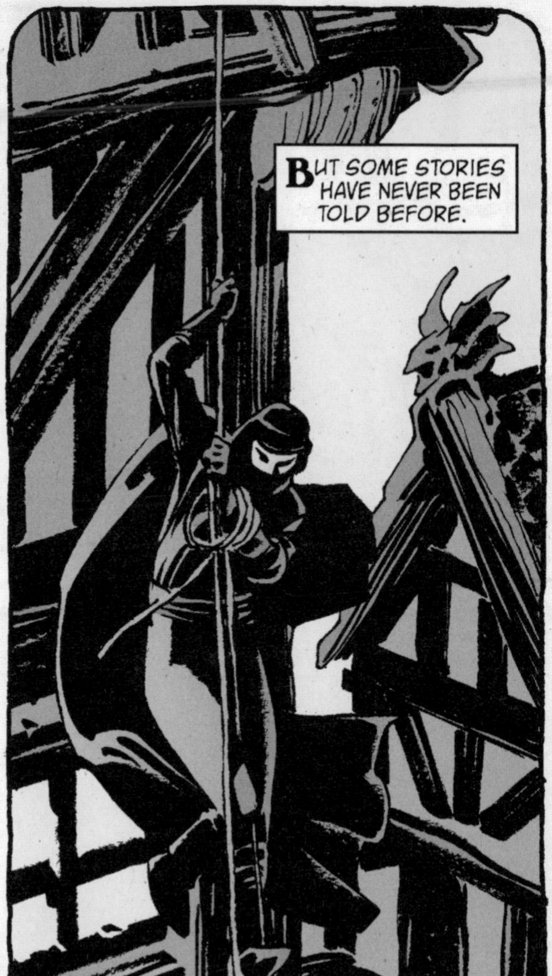
BUT SOME STORIES HAVE NEVER BEEN TOLD BEFORE.

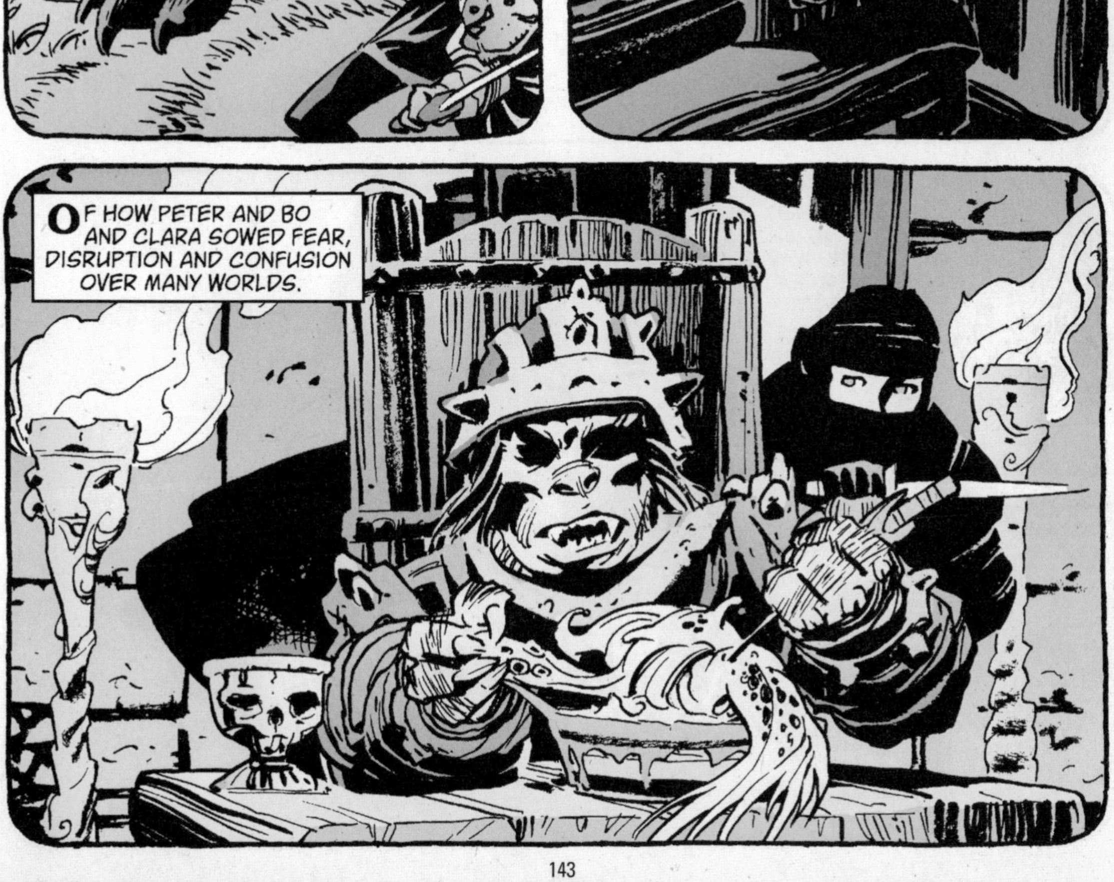
OF HOW PETER AND BO AND CLARA SOWED FEAR, DISRUPTION AND CONFUSION OVER MANY WORLDS.

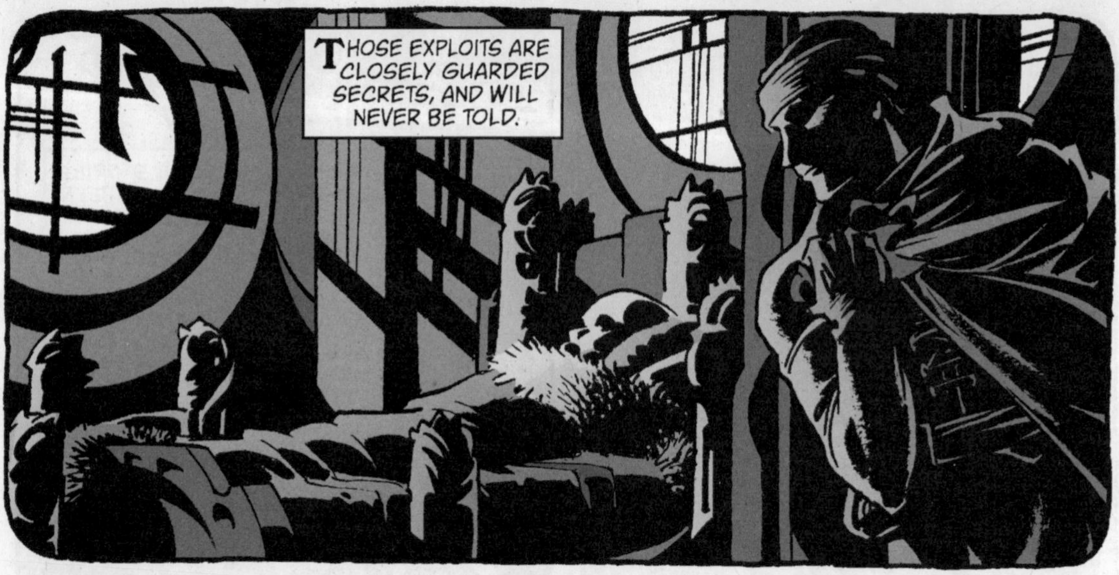
THOSE EXPLOITS ARE CLOSELY GUARDED SECRETS, AND WILL NEVER BE TOLD.

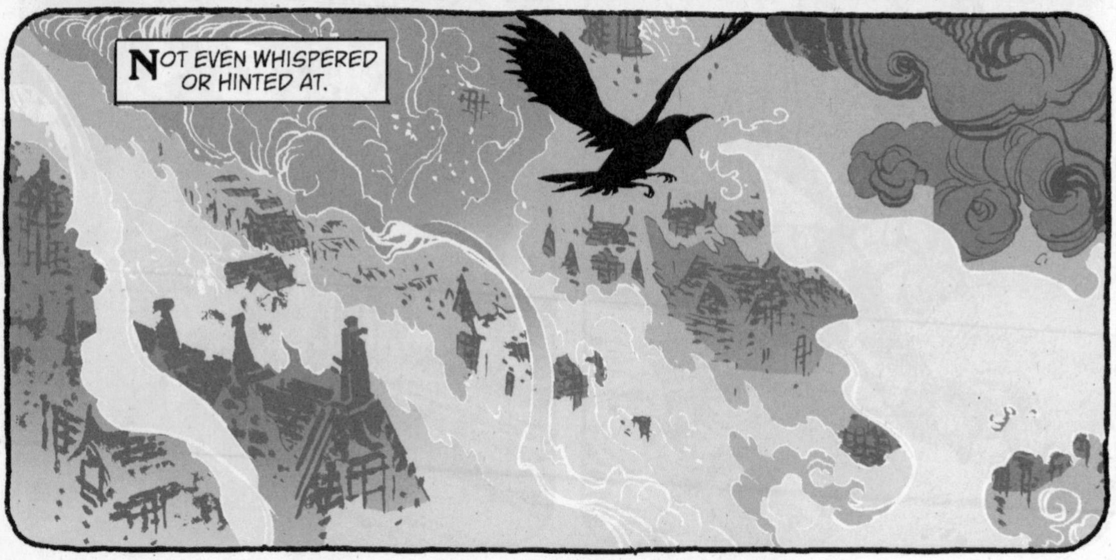
NOT EVEN WHISPERED OR HINTED AT.

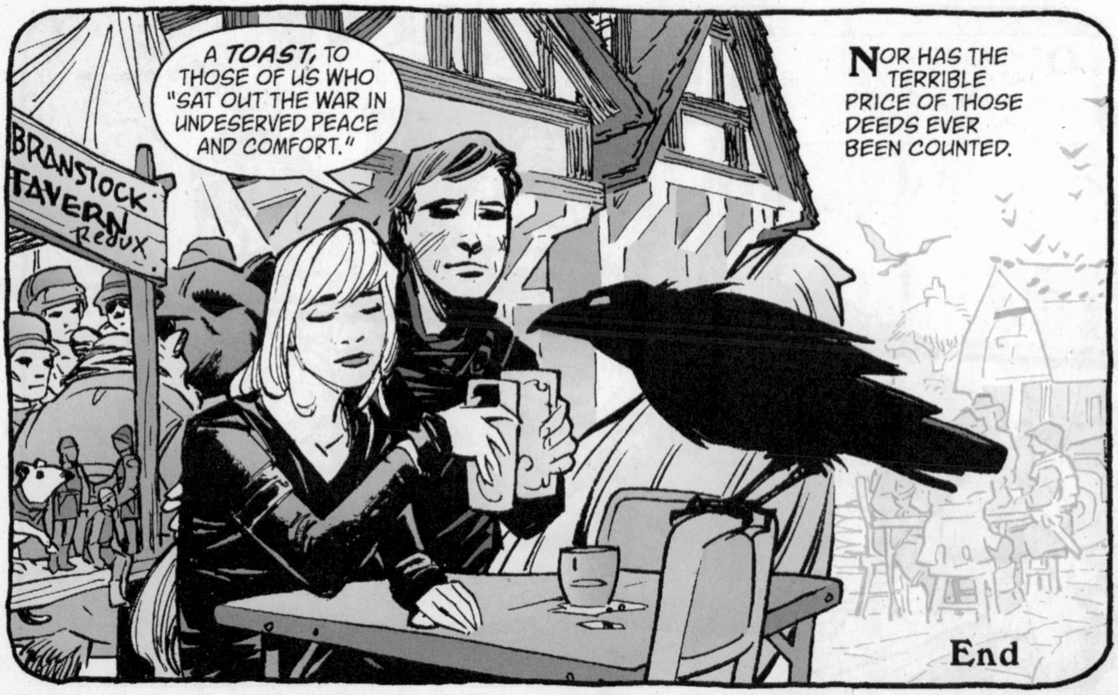
A TOAST, TO THOSE OF US WHO "SAT OUT THE WAR IN UNDESERVED PEACE AND COMFORT."
NOR HAS THE TERRIBLE PRICE OF THOSE DEEDS EVER BEEN COUNTED.
BRANSTOCK TAVERN REDUX
End

Over the years the FABLES saga has grown like Jack's magic beans into a towering edifice of adventure, with over two dozen volumes in print collecting the series and its related titles. The following excerpt from FABLES VOL. 2: ANIMAL FARM — featuring artwork by series mainstays Mark Buckingham and Steve Leialoha — finds Snow White and her sister Rose Red on an important assignment outside of Fabletown.

"There are shocks and thrills in ANIMAL FARM that I haven't seen in a comic book before."
— Comic World News

Ever since they were driven from their homes by the Adversary, the non-human Fables have been living on the Farm — a vast property in upstate New York that keeps them hidden from the prying eyes of the mundane world. But after hundreds of years of isolation, the Farm is seething with revolution, fanned by the inflammatory rhetoric of Goldilocks and the Three Little Pigs. And when Snow and Rose stumble upon their plan to liberate the homelands, the commissars of the Farm are ready to silence them — by any means necessary!

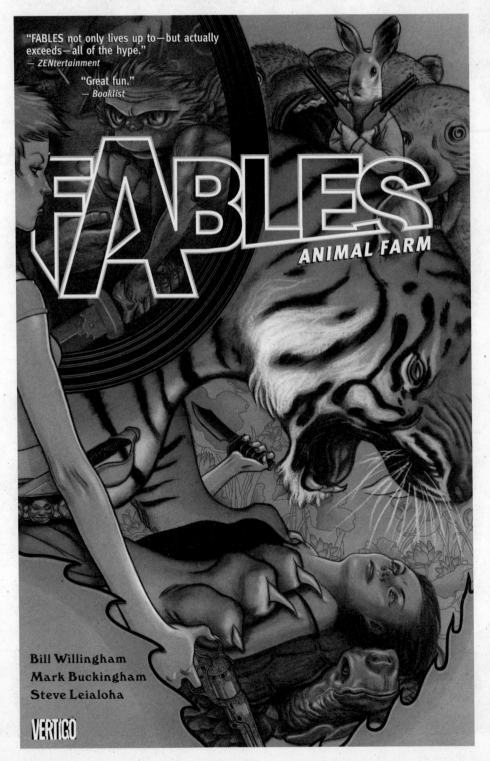

"FABLES not only lives up to—but actually exceeds—all of the hype."
— ZENtertainment

"Great fun."
— Booklist

FABLES

ANIMAL FARM

Bill Willingham
Mark Buckingham
Steve Leialoha

VERTIGO

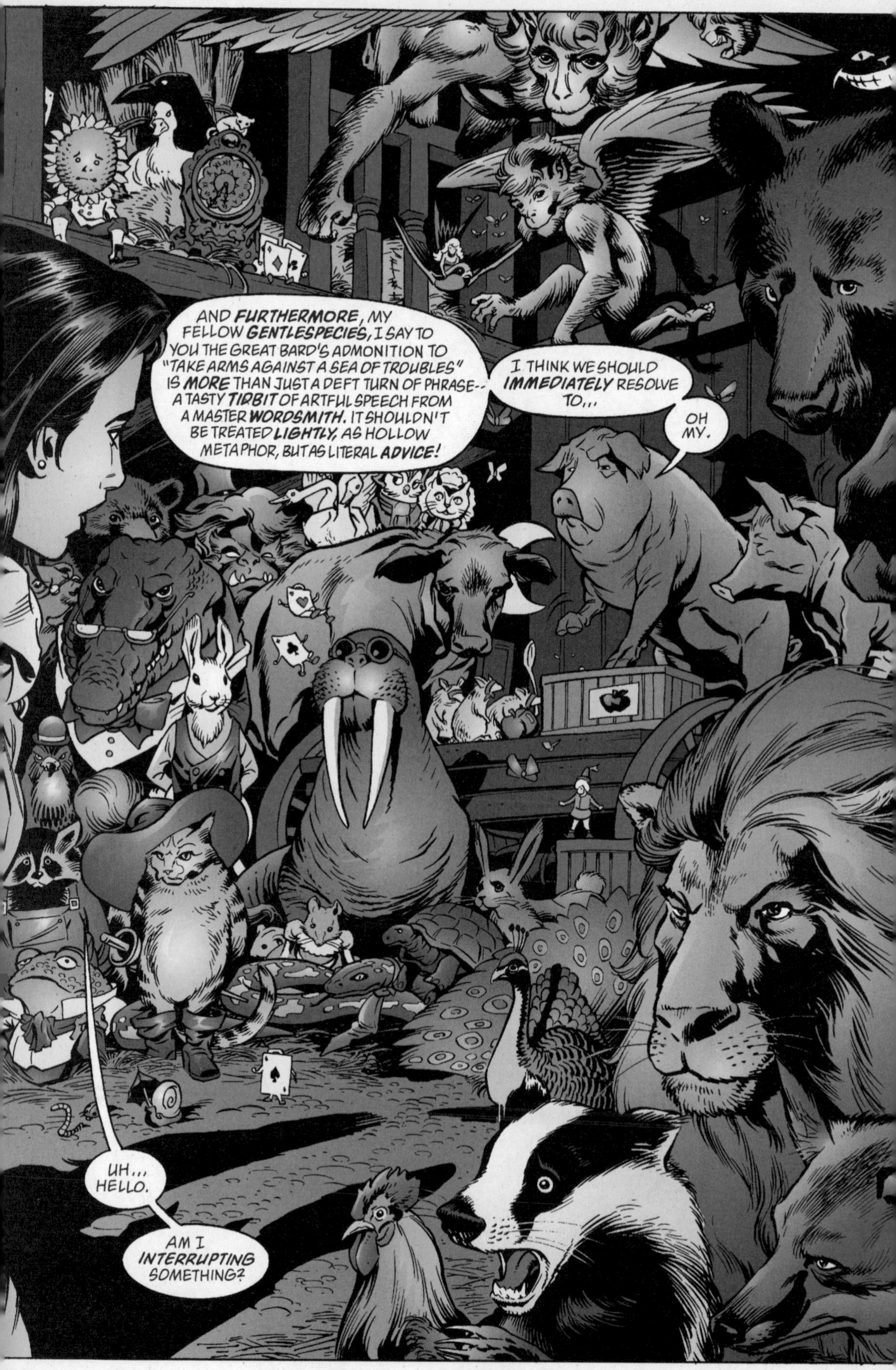
AND FURTHERMORE, MY FELLOW GENTLESPECIES, I SAY TO YOU THE GREAT BARD'S ADMONITION TO "TAKE ARMS AGAINST A SEA OF TROUBLES" IS MORE THAN JUST A DEFT TURN OF PHRASE-- A TASTY TIDBIT OF ARTFUL SPEECH FROM A MASTER WORDSMITH. IT SHOULDN'T BE TREATED LIGHTLY, AS HOLLOW METAPHOR, BUT AS LITERAL ADVICE!
I THINK WE SHOULD IMMEDIATELY RESOLVE TO...
OH MY.
UH... HELLO.
AM I INTERRUPTING SOMETHING?

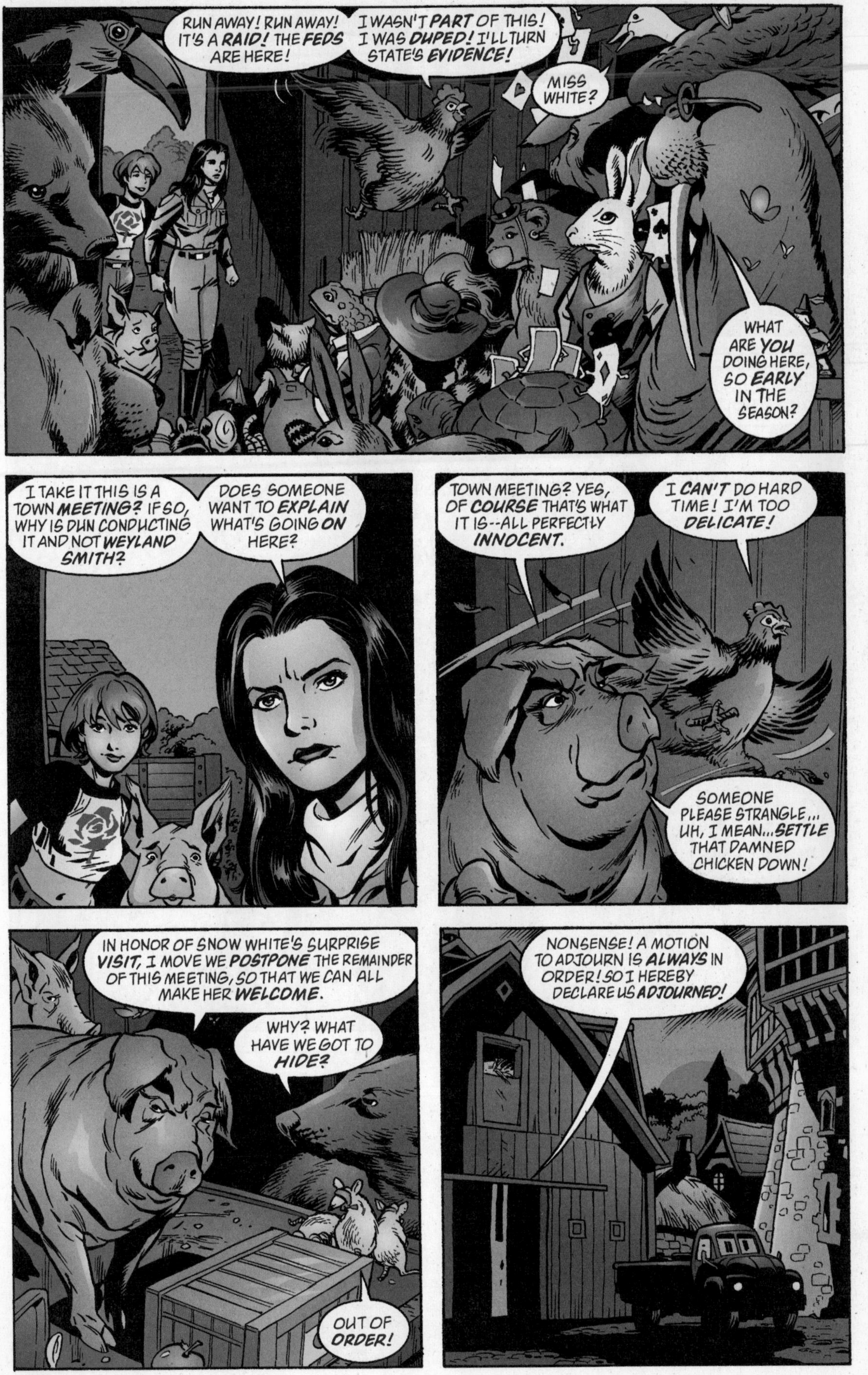
RUN AWAY! RUN AWAY! IT'S A RAID! THE FEDS ARE HERE!
I WASN'T PART OF THIS! I WAS DUPED! I'LL TURN STATE'S EVIDENCE!
MISS WHITE?
WHAT ARE YOU DOING HERE, SO EARLY IN THE SEASON?
I TAKE IT THIS IS A TOWN MEETING? IF SO, WHY IS DUN CONDUCTING IT AND NOT WEYLAND SMITH?
DOES SOMEONE WANT TO EXPLAIN WHAT'S GOING ON HERE?
TOWN MEETING? YES, OF COURSE THAT'S WHAT IT IS--ALL PERFECTLY INNOCENT.
I CAN'T DO HARD TIME! I'M TOO DELICATE!
SOMEONE PLEASE STRANGLE... UH, I MEAN... SETTLE THAT DAMNED CHICKEN DOWN!
IN HONOR OF SNOW WHITE'S SURPRISE VISIT, I MOVE WE POSTPONE THE REMAINDER OF THIS MEETING, SO THAT WE CAN ALL MAKE HER WELCOME.
WHY? WHAT HAVE WE GOT TO HIDE?
OUT OF ORDER!
NONSENSE! A MOTION TO ADJOURN IS ALWAYS IN ORDER! SO I HEREBY DECLARE US ADJOURNED!

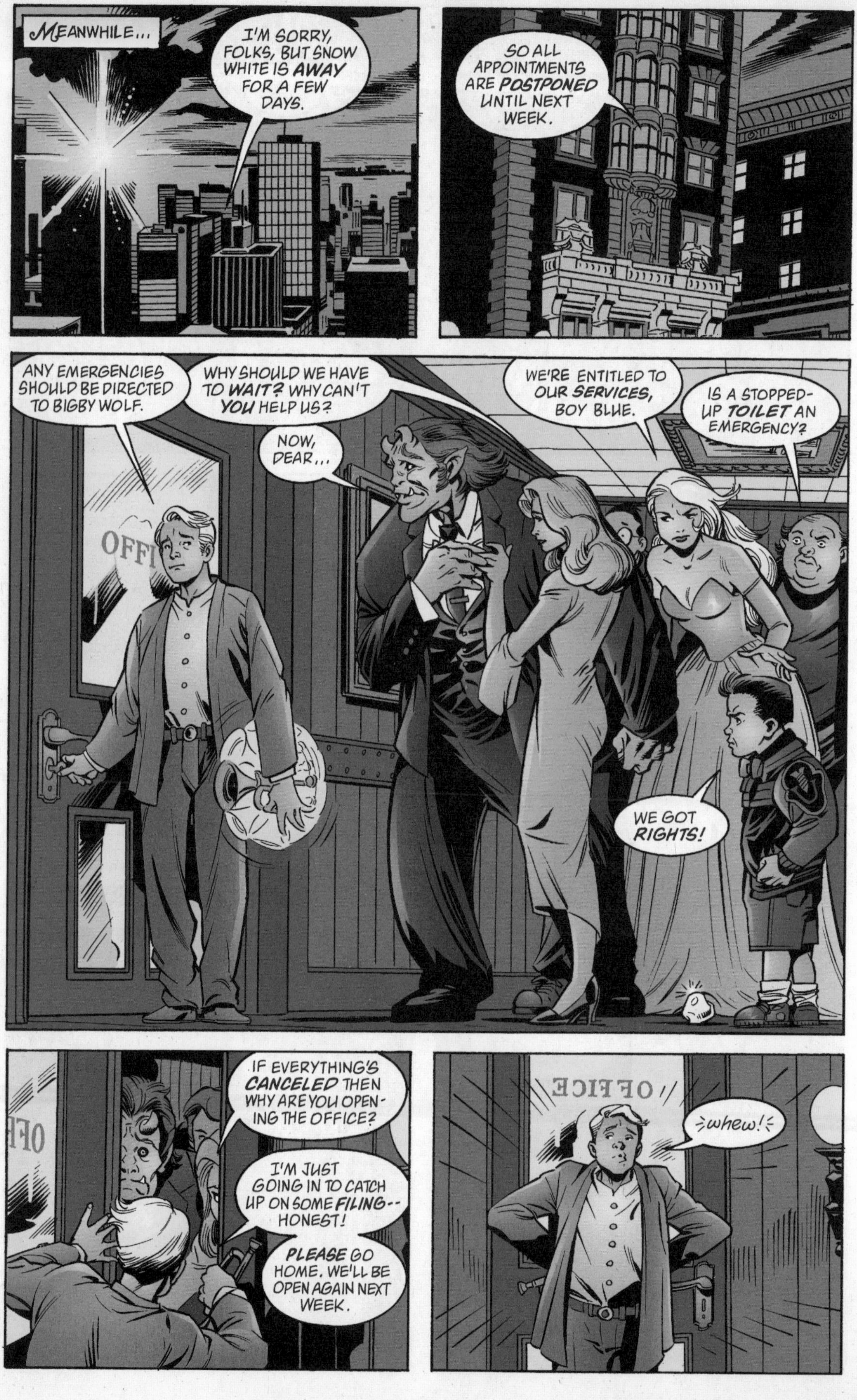
MEANWHILE...
I'M SORRY, FOLKS, BUT SNOW WHITE IS **AWAY** FOR A FEW DAYS.
SO ALL APPOINTMENTS ARE **POSTPONED** UNTIL NEXT WEEK.
ANY EMERGENCIES SHOULD BE DIRECTED TO BIGBY WOLF.
WHY SHOULD WE HAVE TO **WAIT?** WHY CAN'T **YOU** HELP US?
NOW, DEAR...
WE'RE ENTITLED TO OUR **SERVICES,** BOY BLUE.
IS A STOPPED-UP **TOILET** AN EMERGENCY?
WE GOT **RIGHTS!**
OFFI
IF EVERYTHING'S **CANCELED** THEN WHY ARE YOU OPENING THE OFFICE?
I'M JUST GOING IN TO CATCH UP ON SOME **FILING**-- HONEST!
PLEASE GO HOME. WE'LL BE OPEN AGAIN NEXT WEEK.
whew!

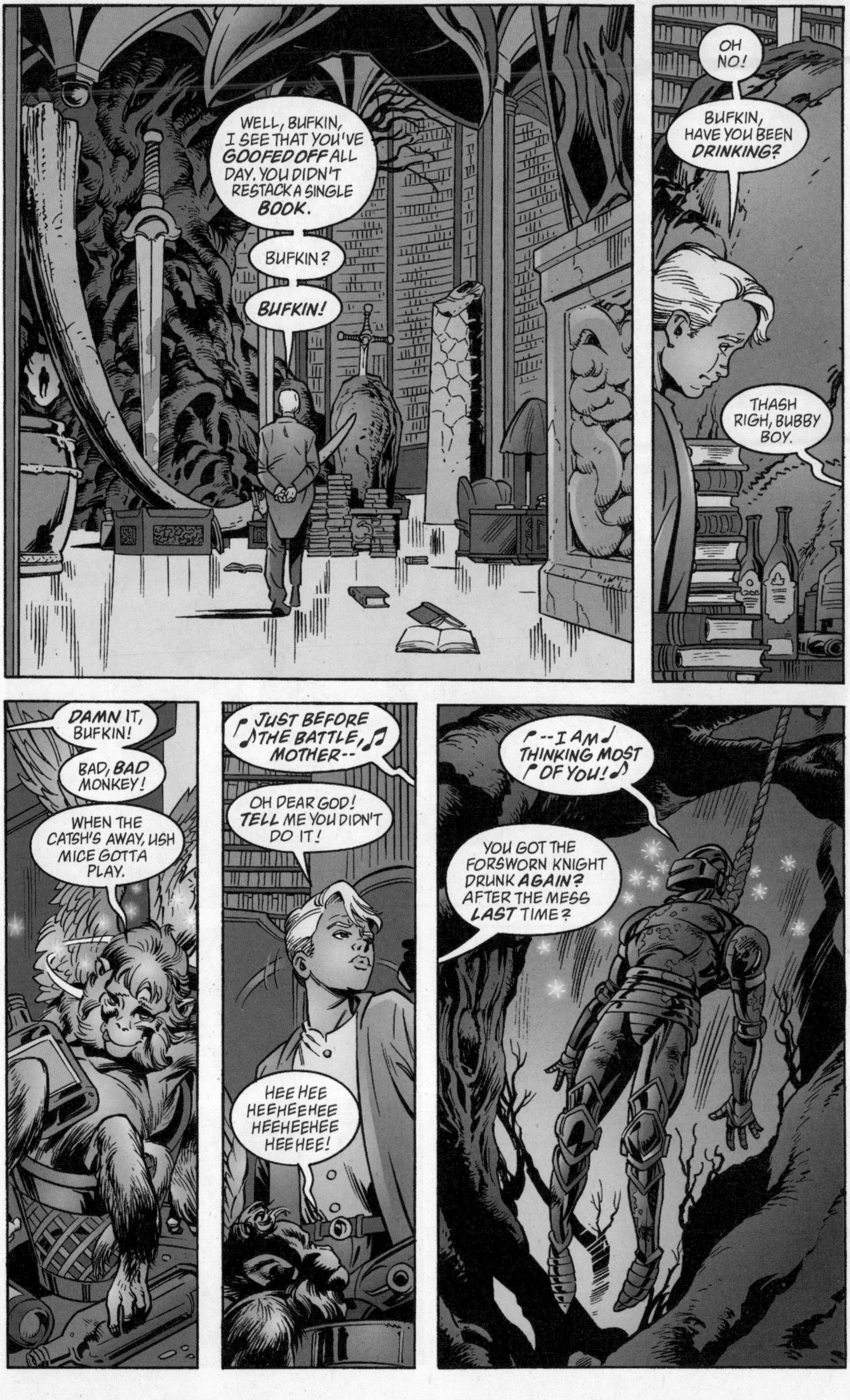
WELL, BUFKIN, I SEE THAT YOU'VE GOOFED OFF ALL DAY. YOU DIDN'T RESTACK A SINGLE BOOK.
BUFKIN?
BUFKIN!
OH NO!
BUFKIN, HAVE YOU BEEN DRINKING?
THASH RIGH, BUBBY BOY.
DAMN IT, BUFKIN!
BAD, BAD MONKEY!
WHEN THE CATSH'S AWAY, USH MICE GOTTA PLAY.
♪ JUST BEFORE THE BATTLE, ♫ MOTHER--
OH DEAR GOD! TELL ME YOU DIDN'T DO IT!
HEE HEE HEEHEEHEE HEEHEEHEE HEEHEE!
♪ --I AM ♩ THINKING MOST ♪ OF YOU! ♪
YOU GOT THE FORSWORN KNIGHT DRUNK AGAIN? AFTER THE MESS LAST TIME?

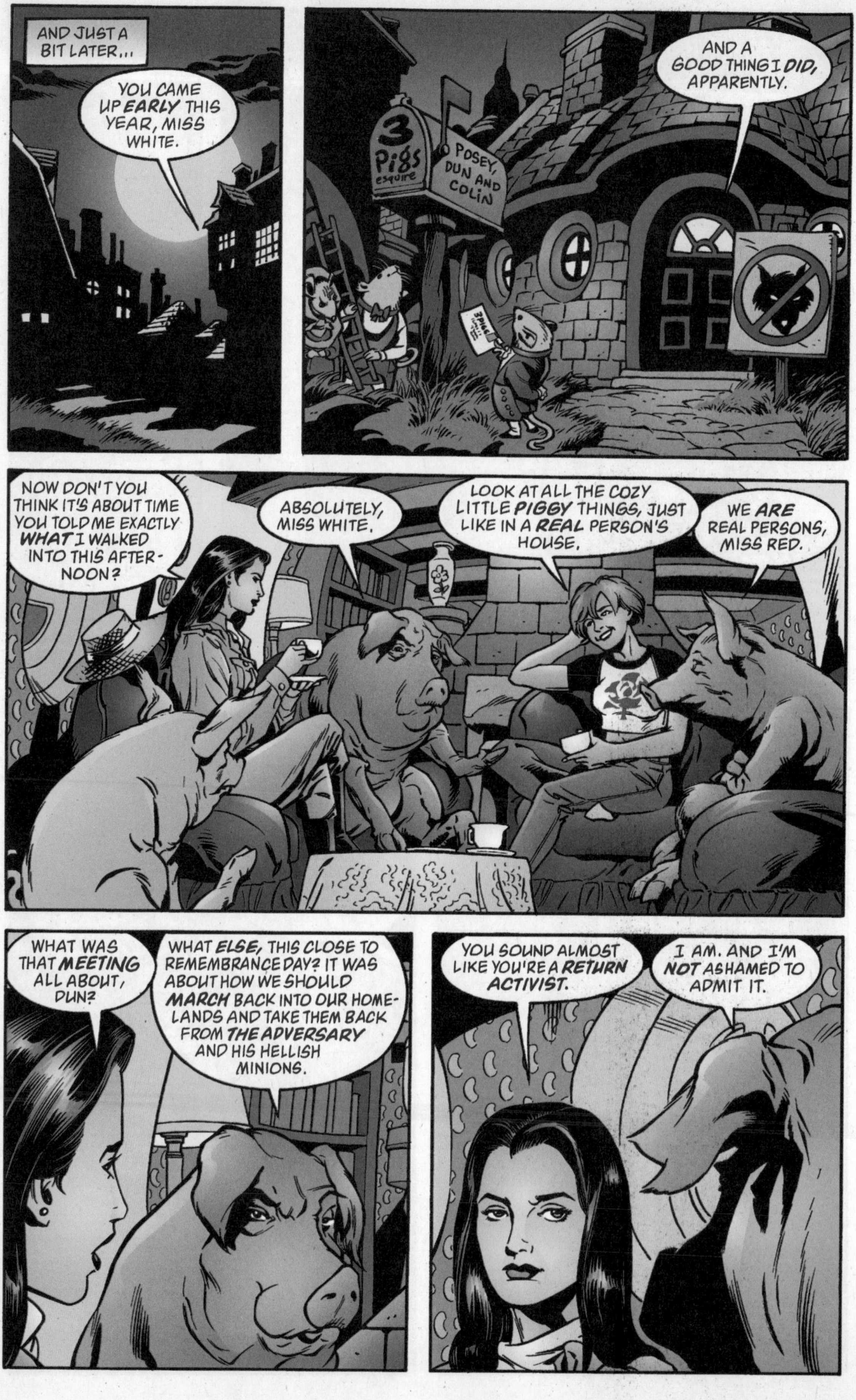
AND JUST A BIT LATER...
YOU CAME UP EARLY THIS YEAR, MISS WHITE.
3 Pigs esquire
POSEY, DUN AND COLIN
AND A GOOD THING I DID, APPARENTLY.
NOW DON'T YOU THINK IT'S ABOUT TIME YOU TOLD ME EXACTLY WHAT I WALKED INTO THIS AFTER-NOON?
ABSOLUTELY, MISS WHITE.
LOOK AT ALL THE COZY LITTLE PIGGY THINGS, JUST LIKE IN A REAL PERSON'S HOUSE.
WE ARE REAL PERSONS, MISS RED.
WHAT WAS THAT MEETING ALL ABOUT, DUN?
WHAT ELSE, THIS CLOSE TO REMEMBRANCE DAY? IT WAS ABOUT HOW WE SHOULD MARCH BACK INTO OUR HOME-LANDS AND TAKE THEM BACK FROM THE ADVERSARY AND HIS HELLISH MINIONS.
YOU SOUND ALMOST LIKE YOU'RE A RETURN ACTIVIST.
I AM. AND I'M NOT ASHAMED TO ADMIT IT.

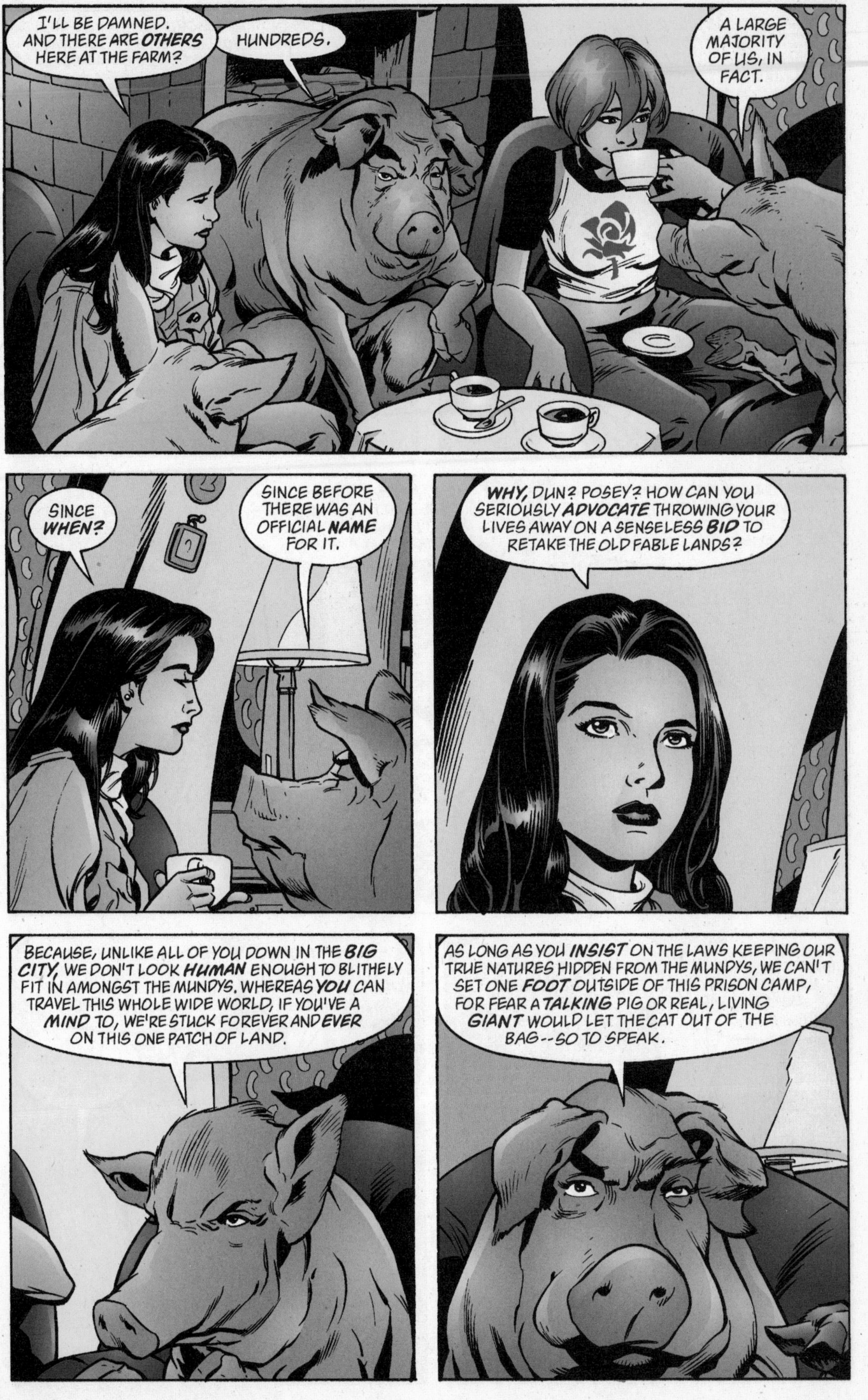
I'LL BE DAMNED. AND THERE ARE OTHERS HERE AT THE FARM?
HUNDREDS.
A LARGE MAJORITY OF US, IN FACT.
SINCE WHEN?
SINCE BEFORE THERE WAS AN OFFICIAL NAME FOR IT.
WHY, DUN? POSEY? HOW CAN YOU SERIOUSLY ADVOCATE THROWING YOUR LIVES AWAY ON A SENSELESS BID TO RETAKE THE OLD FABLE LANDS?
BECAUSE, UNLIKE ALL OF YOU DOWN IN THE BIG CITY, WE DON'T LOOK HUMAN ENOUGH TO BLITHELY FIT IN AMONGST THE MUNDYS. WHEREAS YOU CAN TRAVEL THIS WHOLE WIDE WORLD, IF YOU'VE A MIND TO, WE'RE STUCK FOREVER AND EVER ON THIS ONE PATCH OF LAND.
AS LONG AS YOU INSIST ON THE LAWS KEEPING OUR TRUE NATURES HIDDEN FROM THE MUNDYS, WE CAN'T SET ONE FOOT OUTSIDE OF THIS PRISON CAMP, FOR FEAR A TALKING PIG OR REAL, LIVING GIANT WOULD LET THE CAT OUT OF THE BAG--SO TO SPEAK.

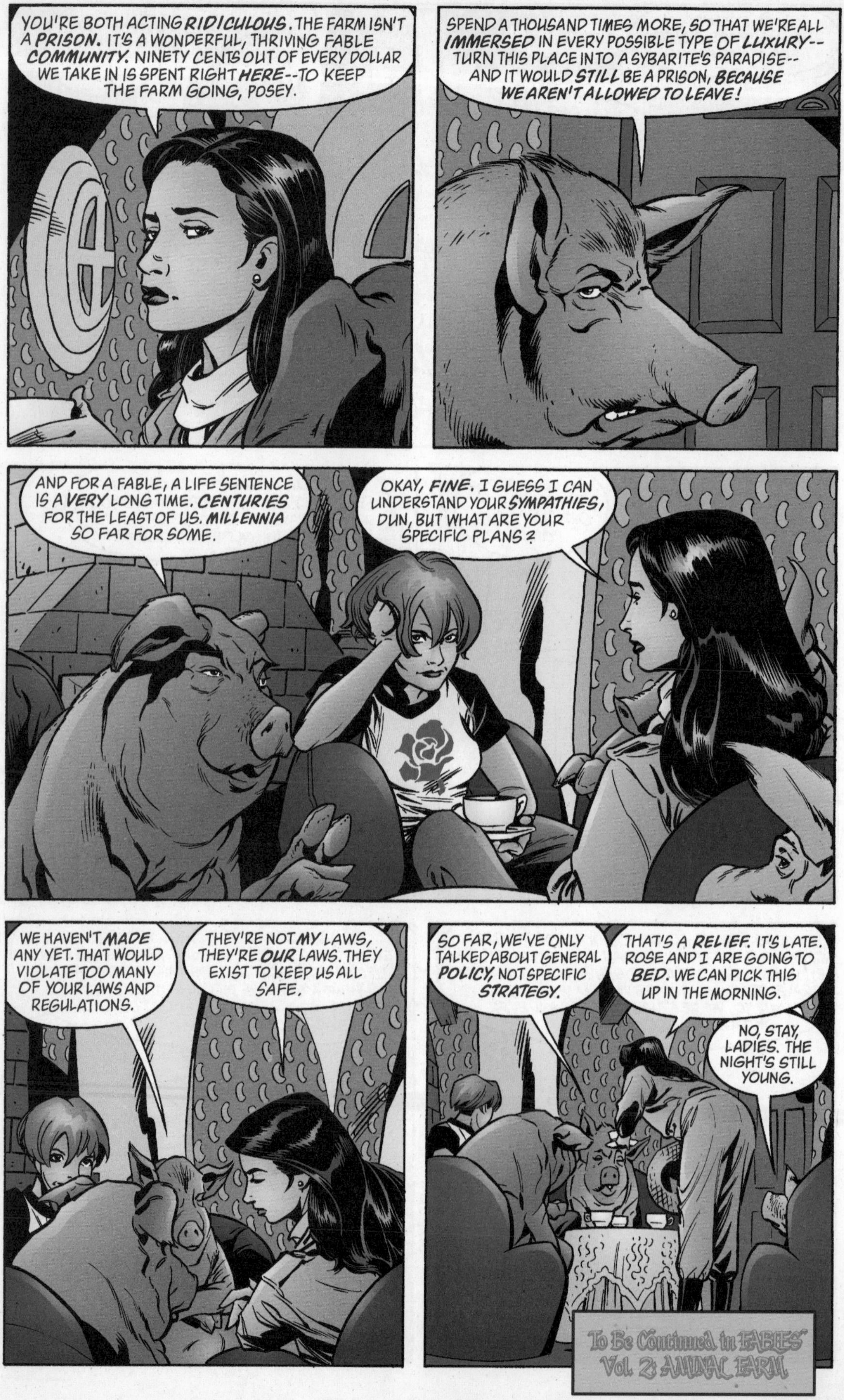
YOU'RE BOTH ACTING RIDICULOUS. THE FARM ISN'T A PRISON. IT'S A WONDERFUL, THRIVING FABLE COMMUNITY. NINETY CENTS OUT OF EVERY DOLLAR WE TAKE IN IS SPENT RIGHT HERE--TO KEEP THE FARM GOING, POSEY.
SPEND A THOUSAND TIMES MORE, SO THAT WE'RE ALL IMMERSED IN EVERY POSSIBLE TYPE OF LUXURY--TURN THIS PLACE IN TO A SYBARITE'S PARADISE--AND IT WOULD STILL BE A PRISON, BECAUSE WE AREN'T ALLOWED TO LEAVE!
AND FOR A FABLE, A LIFE SENTENCE IS A VERY LONG TIME. CENTURIES FOR THE LEAST OF US. MILLENNIA SO FAR FOR SOME.
OKAY, FINE. I GUESS I CAN UNDERSTAND YOUR SYMPATHIES, DUN, BUT WHAT ARE YOUR SPECIFIC PLANS?
WE HAVEN'T MADE ANY YET. THAT WOULD VIOLATE TOO MANY OF YOUR LAWS AND REGULATIONS.
THEY'RE NOT MY LAWS, THEY'RE OUR LAWS. THEY EXIST TO KEEP US ALL SAFE.
SO FAR, WE'VE ONLY TALKED ABOUT GENERAL POLICY, NOT SPECIFIC STRATEGY.
THAT'S A RELIEF. IT'S LATE. ROSE AND I ARE GOING TO BED. WE CAN PICK THIS UP IN THE MORNING.
NO, STAY, LADIES. THE NIGHT'S STILL YOUNG.
To Be Continued in FABLES™ Vol. 2: ANIMAL FARM

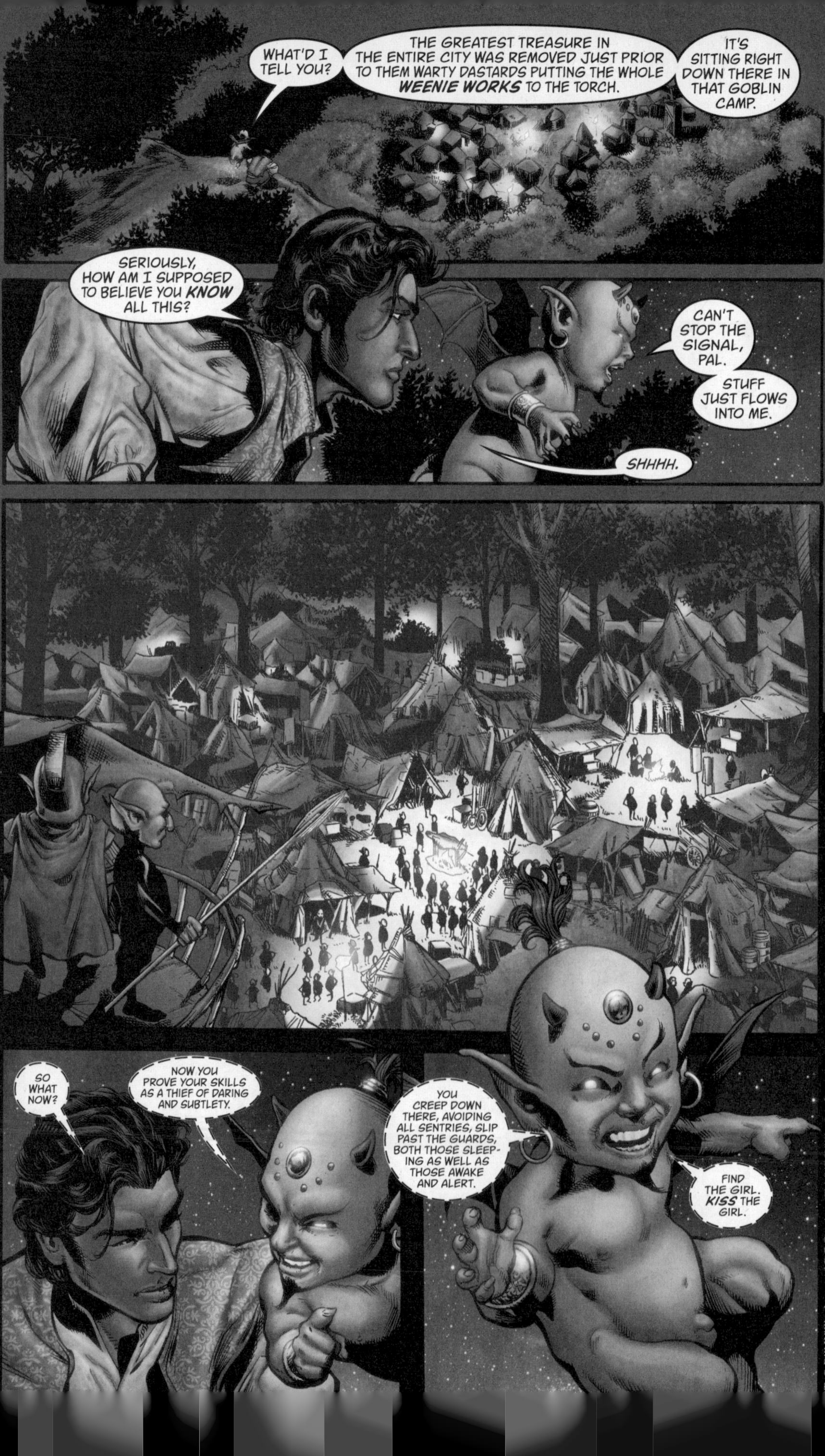

WHAT'D I TELL YOU?
THE GREATEST TREASURE IN THE ENTIRE CITY WAS REMOVED JUST PRIOR TO THEM WARTY DASTARDS PUTTING THE WHOLE WEENIE WORKS TO THE TORCH.
IT'S SITTING RIGHT DOWN THERE IN THAT GOBLIN CAMP.
SERIOUSLY, HOW AM I SUPPOSED TO BELIEVE YOU KNOW ALL THIS?
CAN'T STOP THE SIGNAL, PAL.
STUFF JUST FLOWS INTO ME.
SHHHH.
SO WHAT NOW?
NOW YOU PROVE YOUR SKILLS AS A THIEF OF DARING AND SUBTLETY.
YOU CREEP DOWN THERE, AVOIDING ALL SENTRIES, SLIP PAST THE GUARDS, BOTH THOSE SLEEPING AS WELL AS THOSE AWAKE AND ALERT.
FIND THE GIRL. KISS THE GIRL.

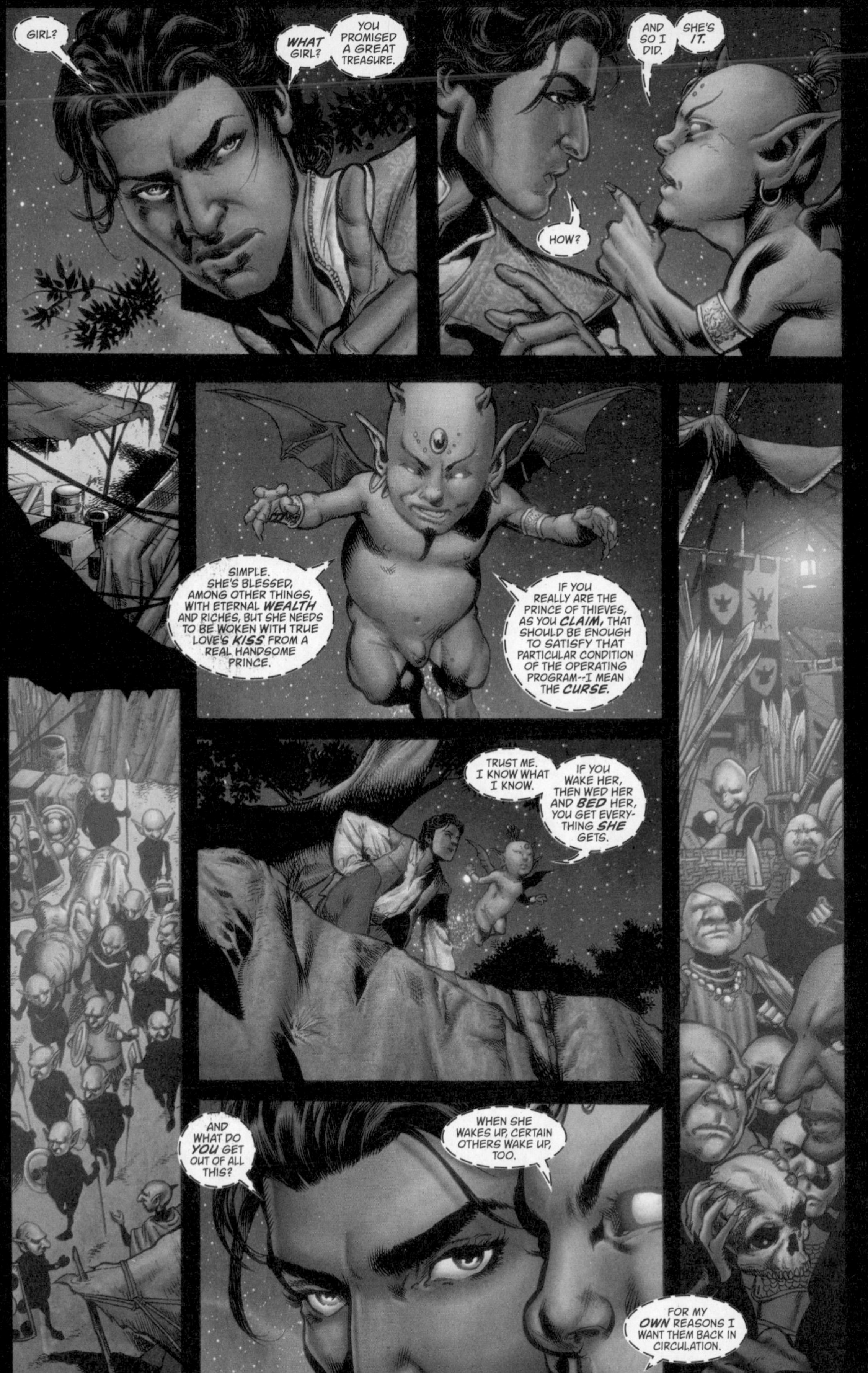
GIRL?
WHAT GIRL?
YOU PROMISED A GREAT TREASURE.
AND SO I DID.
SHE'S IT.
HOW?
SIMPLE. SHE'S BLESSED, AMONG OTHER THINGS, WITH ETERNAL WEALTH AND RICHES, BUT SHE NEEDS TO BE WOKEN WITH TRUE LOVE'S KISS FROM A REAL HANDSOME PRINCE.
IF YOU REALLY ARE THE PRINCE OF THIEVES, AS YOU CLAIM, THAT SHOULD BE ENOUGH TO SATISFY THAT PARTICULAR CONDITION OF THE OPERATING PROGRAM--I MEAN THE CURSE.
TRUST ME. I KNOW WHAT I KNOW.
IF YOU WAKE HER, THEN WED HER AND BED HER, YOU GET EVERY-THING SHE GETS.
AND WHAT DO YOU GET OUT OF ALL THIS?
WHEN SHE WAKES UP, CERTAIN OTHERS WAKE UP, TOO.
FOR MY OWN REASONS I WANT THEM BACK IN CIRCULATION.

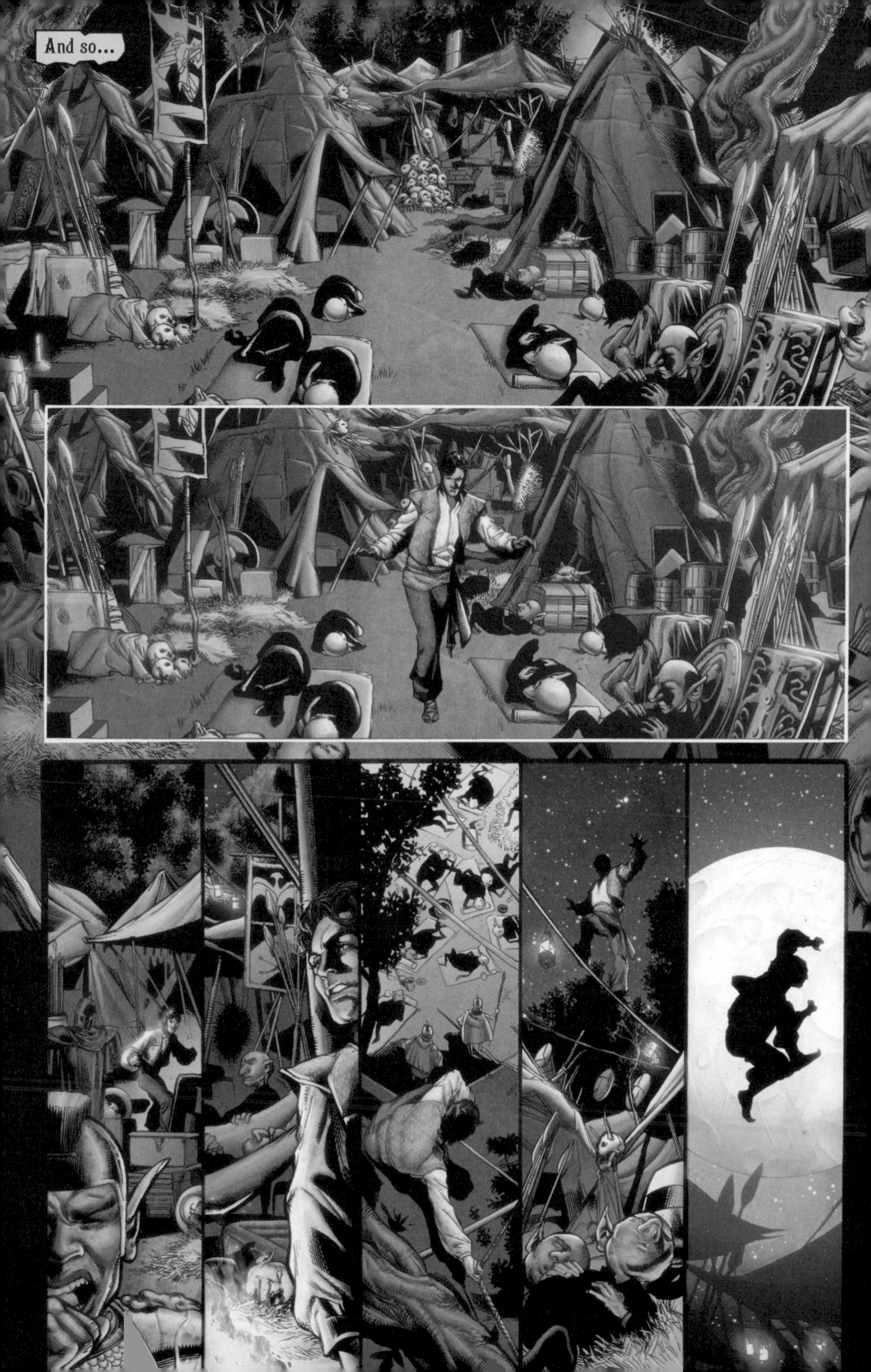
And so...

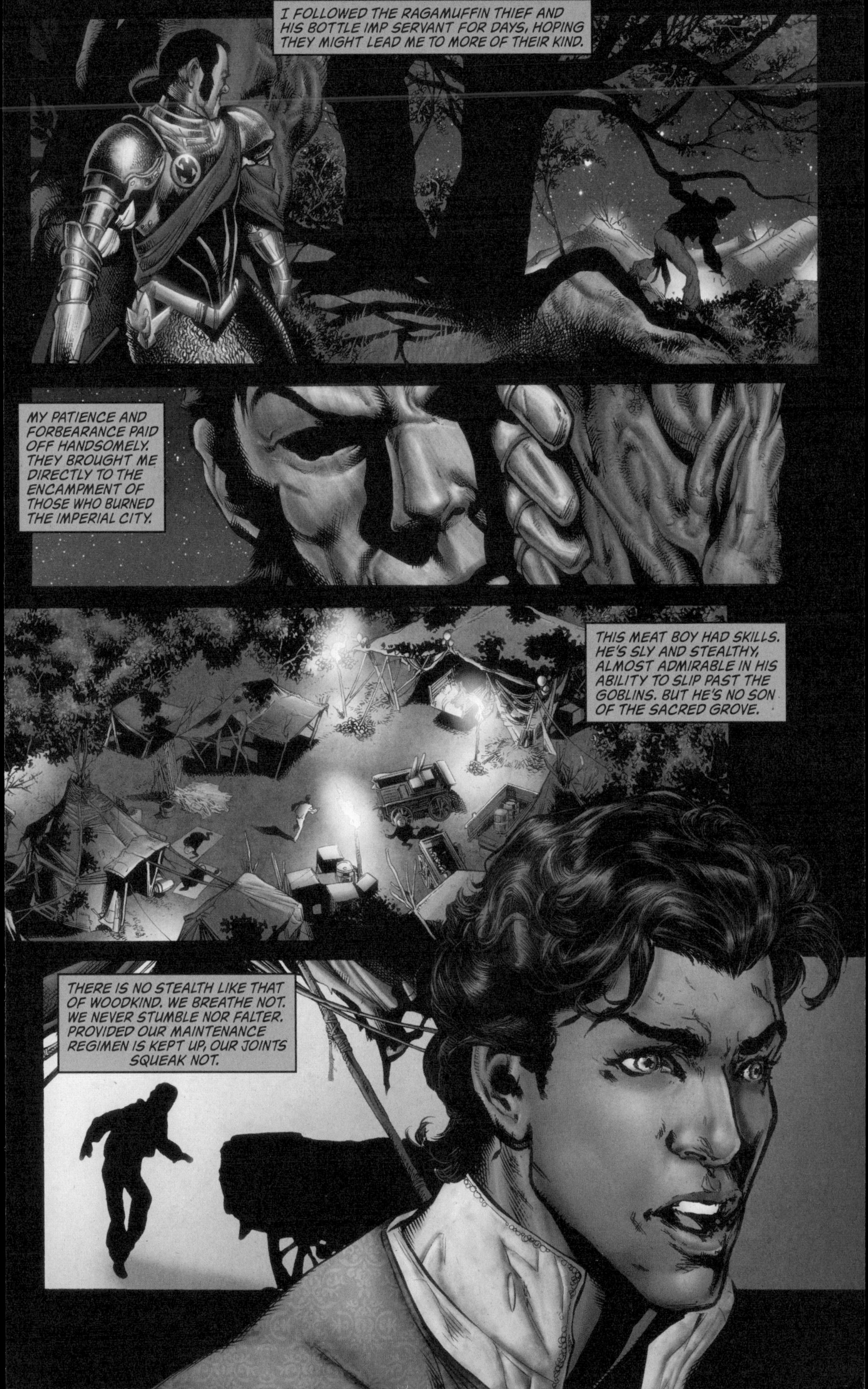
I FOLLOWED THE RAGAMUFFIN THIEF AND HIS BOTTLE IMP SERVANT FOR DAYS, HOPING THEY MIGHT LEAD ME TO MORE OF THEIR KIND.
MY PATIENCE AND FORBEARANCE PAID OFF HANDSOMELY. THEY BROUGHT ME DIRECTLY TO THE ENCAMPMENT OF THOSE WHO BURNED THE IMPERIAL CITY.
THIS MEAT BOY HAD SKILLS. HE'S SLY AND STEALTHY, ALMOST ADMIRABLE IN HIS ABILITY TO SLIP PAST THE GOBLINS. BUT HE'S NO SON OF THE SACRED GROVE.
THERE IS NO STEALTH LIKE THAT OF WOODKIND. WE BREATHE NOT. WE NEVER STUMBLE NOR FALTER. PROVIDED OUR MAINTENANCE REGIMEN IS KEPT UP, OUR JOINTS SQUEAK NOT.

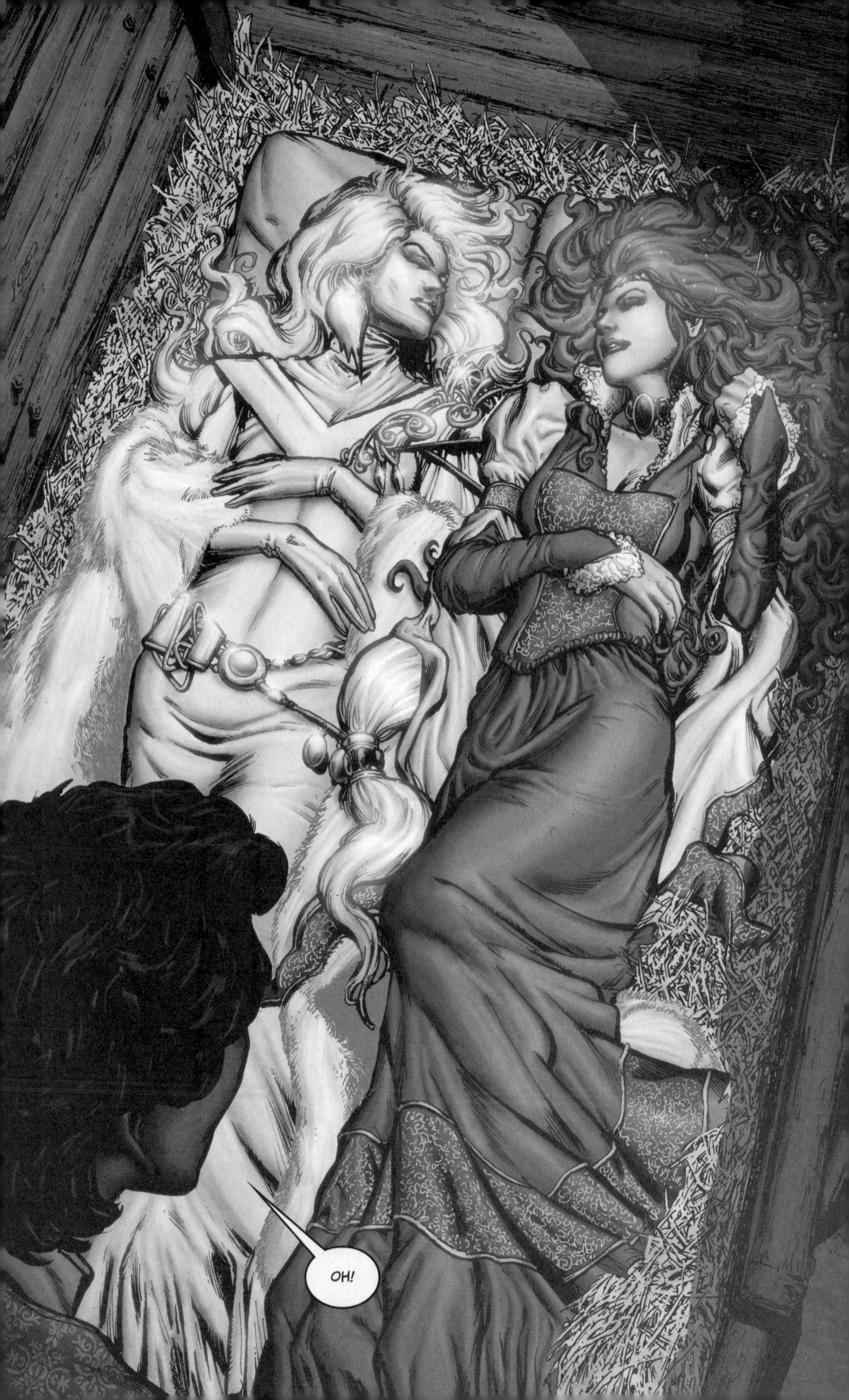
OH!

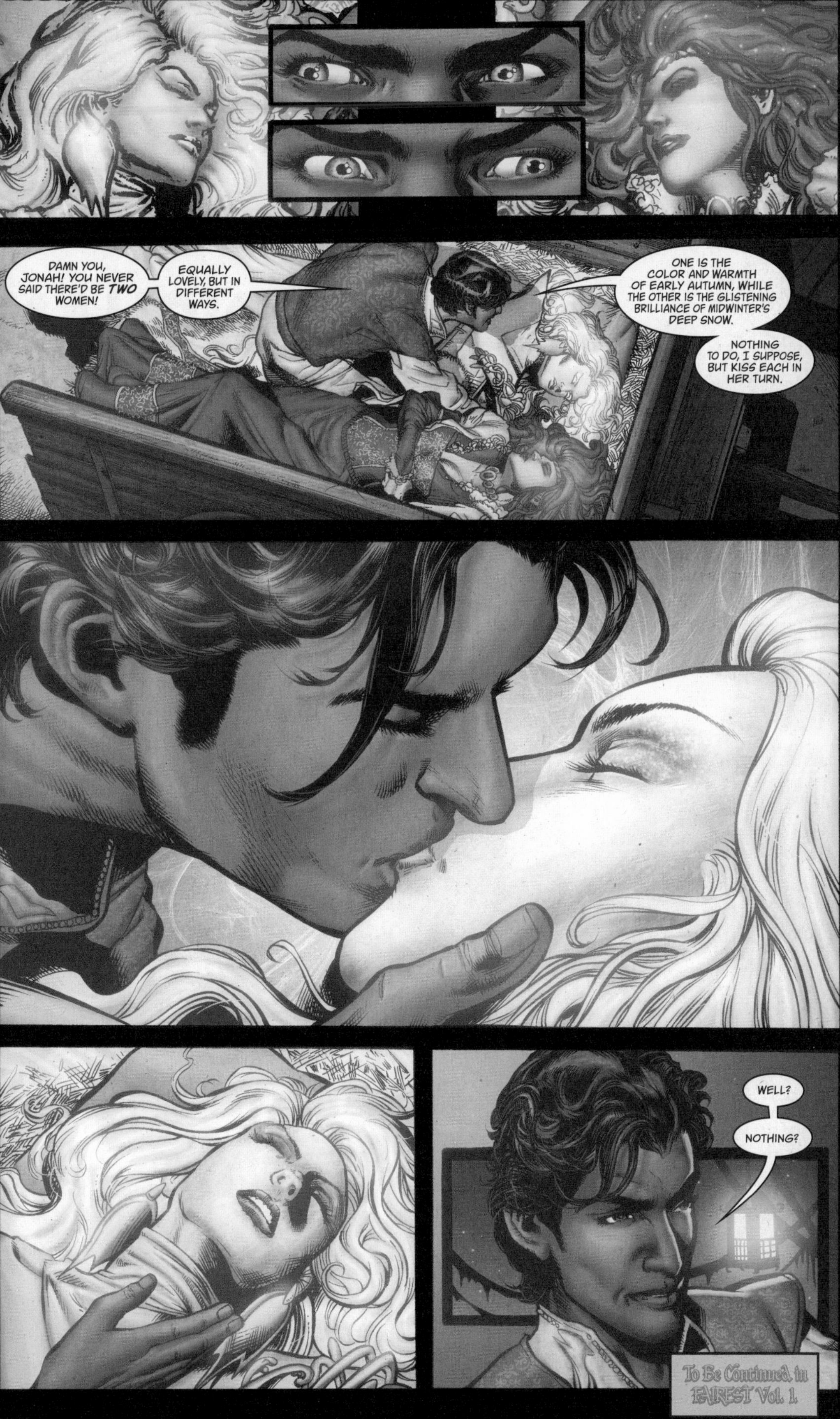
DAMN YOU, JONAH! YOU NEVER SAID THERE'D BE TWO WOMEN!
EQUALLY LOVELY, BUT IN DIFFERENT WAYS.
ONE IS THE COLOR AND WARMTH OF EARLY AUTUMN, WHILE THE OTHER IS THE GLISTENING BRILLIANCE OF MIDWINTER'S DEEP SNOW.
NOTHING TO DO, I SUPPOSE, BUT KISS EACH IN HER TURN.
WELL?
NOTHING?
To Be Continued in FAIREST Vol. 1.

"Fables is an excellent series in the tradition of Sandman, one that rewards careful attention and loyalty."
—PUBLISHERS WEEKLY

"[A] wonderfully twisted concept…" *"features fairy tale characters banished to the noirish world of present-day New York."* —
WASHINGTON POST

"Great fun." **—BOOKLIST**

BILL WILLINGHAM
FABLES VOL. 1: LEGENDS IN EXILE

THE #1 NEW YORK TIMES BEST-SELLING SERIES

FABLES
Legends in Exile

"A top-notch fantasy comic that is on a par with SANDMAN." — *Variety*

DIRECTOR

BULLFINCH STREET

Bill Willingham
Lan Medina
Steve Leialoha
Craig Hamilton

VERTIGO